ENTERTAINING WITH ELEGANCE

Geneviève Antoine Dariaux

ENTERTAINING
WITH
ELEGANCE

DRAWINGS BY SHEILA GREENWALD

Doubleday & Company, Inc., Garden City,
New York, 1965

Library of Congress Catalog Card Number 65–19881
Copyright © 1965 by Geneviève Dariaux Antoine
All Rights Reserved
Printed in the United States of America

Table of Contents

INTRODUCTION

Entertaining is generally composed of two elements: the friendly offering of hospitality, and the sharing of some form of meal or refreshments. On some occasions lodging may be added to these, and in certain ancient civilizations, including parts of the Orient today, even clothing may be furnished. In short, entertaining a guest means taking charge of all of his needs and trying to satisfy them better than he could himself.

Hospitality is a very elementary quality, since it is manifested even by domestic animals—often with considerably greater spirit and conviction than by the most accomplished society hostess! However, in spite of my unbounded admiration for the canine species, I must admit that when it comes to sharing a meal, my dog considers that everything I have is his, but that his bone belongs to him alone. And so in this domain, we must recognize the undeniable superiority of the human race, which is happy to share its food and even its shelter not only with the young but also with other adults.

It is possible that countless centuries of various religious doctrines and practices are responsible for modern man's almost instinctive hospitality. In any case, it is a fact that the more civilized a society becomes, the more its members feel the need for social intercourse. The sacrifices and gifts to the pagan gods of ancient times were not, after all, very different from our modern business luncheons. In both cases the principal purpose is to obtain a favor.

Chamfort, a witty moralist who wrote a famous collection of *Maximes* during the French Revolution, claimed that society can be divided into two great classes: those who have more dinner invitations than appetite, and those who have more appetite than dinner invitations.

At our present degree of civilization, when at least half of the world is normally provided with sufficient nourishment for survival, hospitality is no longer very often an act of charity. It is an art, and like all arts it has its rules, refinements, and elegance. Entertaining one's friends has, in fact, become one of the principal activities of contemporary community living.

Our modern code of social behavior, like our modern Occidental conception of cuisine, is derived from Renaissance Italy, whence both were imported and refined at the eighteenth-century French Court at Versailles. While the demands of modern life have greatly simplified both the manners and the recipes, European traditions maintain their domination in this field. Without forgetting for a moment the many marvelous American specialties, I think it safe to say that where the preparation and service of food are concerned, the French tradition reigns supreme, especially in international and diplomatic entertaining, and whenever there is any pretention to elegance. And so, if you detect a Continental flavor in the ideas and attitudes expressed throughout these pages, particularly where formal entertaining is concerned, please do not accuse me of chauvinism! You only need to glance at the menu of any fashionable American restaurant, or read the newspaper report of a smart dinner party in San Francisco, New York, or Washington, to be convinced that this is simply the way things are.

Fascinated by the elegance of personal attire to the point of making fashion my career, I suppose it is only natural that I have also always loved to entertain guests and to be entertained in return. The art of dressing well and the art of gracious entertaining have many points in common, but in my opinion the most important is this: organization, imagination, and personality can very satisfactorily replace an abundant bank account.

ENTERTAINING WITH ELEGANCE

ACQUAINTANCES

❦ No longer a stranger and not yet a friend, an acquaintance will usually either regress to the first stage or advance to the second, for acquaintance is more often a transitory phase than a permanent status.

Entertaining acquaintances presents a slightly different problem than entertaining friends who are already aware of your virtues and indulgent with your faults. Moreover, since you are not perfectly familiar with the taste and interests of people you have met only recently, it is usually better to limit your first invitations to the most neutral, traditional type of entertaining, such as an informal small cocktail or dinner party, rather than an evening at the opera or a beach picnic, which may be the very thing they most abhor. It is, by the way, always elegant (some would say obligatory) to include in your first invitation the friends who introduced these new acquaintances to you.

Of course you will want to put your best foot forward, but you should at the same time remain your natural self. It is much too great a strain to play indefinitely the role of an idealized version of yourself, even though you may succeed in getting away with it for one evening, as many women do in the hope of making a good impression. But you want your new acquaintances to know and like you as you really are, and this is possible only if you behave as you normally do.

If you get along beautifully, you will soon become friends. But what of the awkward and not infrequent eventuality when one side of the acquaintance desires to advance to a closer relationship, while the other is more or less obviously reticent? If it is you who wish to discourage new acquaintances who are less congenial than you at first supposed, try not to be too brutal about it. Above all, do not accept any of their invitations, so that you will not be under obligation to return them. It seems to me that after three consecutive "regrets," the situation is fairly clear and everybody concerned should realize that there is no point in insisting further.

AFTER DINNER

⟨[It is no longer unusual for a hostess to plan a dinner party for ten to twelve guests, and to invite as many additional guests to come after dinner. It is a modern formula for entertaining that has its advantages and its weak points.

Pro:

—You can entertain many more guests than could be accommodated in your dining room, or with limited household help.

—The arrival of a fresh group of faces right after dinner (which is all too often the lowest point of the evening) will give the party an immediate lift.

—You can double the number of friends you may wish to present to a particularly interesting or distinguished guest of honor, or to share an entertainment of some kind, or cards, or dancing.

Con:

—The friends you invite to come after dinner may feel like "second class" guests, so you must be very careful about whom you choose. I would say that all of them should be intimate friends whom you know well enough to be able to explain when you telephone your invitations that, although you would love to, it is impossible to have them for dinner for some tactfully invented reason beyond your control, but that the evening would not be complete without their presence, etc., etc.

—The timing of the dinner must be well coordinated with the arrival of the new contingent. The diners should already have left the table, and the hostess should be free to greet her afterdinner guests and to make the necessary introductions. As a matter of fact, she should greet her afterdinner guests with special warmth in order to dissipate any possible feelings of inferiority, offer them something to drink at once, and integrate them as quickly and smoothly as possible into the company already present.

AFTERNOON

❲ The afternoon no longer exists as far as entertaining is concerned. The male population is absorbed by business and careers, while the women of leisure who used to be "At Home" one afternoon each week are now either toiling at a business or career of their own, working at a volunteer job, or desperately rushing from a committee meeting to pick up the children at school to chauffeur them to a music or riding lesson, while trying to fit in a bit of essential shopping, a hairdresser's appointment, and a hundred miscellaneous errands. The only social afternoon activity that finds a place in a modern woman's busy program is connected with career or charity, such as a benefit tea or a charity bazaar. There is, of course, Sunday afternoon, but Sunday is traditionally a "family day."

And so, except for a few rare holiday occasions and summer weekends when tennis or swimming bring people together, it has become almost more of an imposition than a pleasure to plan a party in the afternoon—unless the guests you wish to invite consist entirely of elderly maiden aunts. And even then, most of the maiden aunts I know would far prefer to be invited at five-thirty to drink a Dry Martini in mixed company.

ANNIVERSARIES

❲ There are any number of anniversaries encircled in red on the calendar of a sentimental woman—to commemorate, for example, the date on which she first met her husband or became engaged, or the date on which she moved into a new house, or when her husband was promoted to an important job. For a brand-new bride, even the date that marks one month of married life seems to be a milestone! However, all of these occasions are so intimate and personal in character, that they should be feted in private. It is perhaps a great temptation for a happily married, romantic young couple to invite the friends who first introduced them to each other to celebrate the anniversary of that fateful date, but unless you can refrain from reminiscence and entertain in a perfectly normal way, it is best to celebrate the occasion *à deux*, because a dinner doused in sentimentality is highly indigestible to many people.

As a matter of fact, aside from birthdays and important professional or public milestones, there are only two anniversaries that it is elegant to celebrate in large company: a silver (twenty-fifth) and a golden (fiftieth) wedding anniversary. Since the guests are practically obliged to bring with them a gift of silver or gold, these should be essentially family affairs, with perhaps a few very old, very close friends. It is, moreover, customary for one's children or relatives to organize the party, in order to avoid giving the impression of personally soliciting a shower of expensive gifts.

If you should ever be called upon to organize a silver or golden anniversary fete for your parents, grandparents, or more distant relatives, your first duty as a hostess is to gather together as many members of the family as possible. Then you must plan a rather fabulous table decoration of white and silver or gold, as the case may be, a sumptuous menu built around dishes that are sure to please the guests of honor, and order a marvelous specially decorated cake. Champagne should be served throughout the meal, and one or more members of the different generations should be appointed beforehand to prepare toasts. All of you should try to set a note of cheerfulness and gaiety, without becoming overly sentimental. Your guests of honor are certain to be so touched by this demonstration of affection that they will discreetly have to wipe away a tear or two, but you do not want them to be dissolved in tears throughout the evening.

You must decide in advance with the other members of the family whether you will each offer an appropriate gift, or pool your resources in one splendid present, suitably engraved to commemorate the occasion (which, it must be admitted, is becoming an exceedingly rare one). If you have decided to give one important gift, it might be presented after the feast and toasts, when the guests have returned to the living room for coffee. Afterward, you can quickly clear a space for dancing, and put on the record player the anniversary couple's favorite tune for a very short period of dancing, led of course by the guests of honor.

Everyone should have agreed beforehand on a rather early curfew, for the evening will be all the more successful if it is not too long and drawn out. Emotional experiences, even very heartwarming ones, are exhausting, especially to elderly people, and besides, the honored couple should be permitted to terminate their happy day between just the two of them, in the perfect harmony they have built up together during the past twenty-five or fifty years.

(See Birthdays, Dinners, Menus, Tables)

ASHTRAYS

❡ *In the living room* they should be
> big but shallow
> stable
> plentiful (especially at cocktail parties)

and emptied when they are full. (It only takes a second more to clean them at the same time by wiping them with a piece of tissue.)

Standing ashtrays are not at all chic, no matter how practical they may be, perhaps because they are so characteristic of public waiting rooms and hotel lobbies. On the other hand, it is elegant to use as ashtrays all kinds of original and artistic receptacles, such as large sea shells, small Oriental dishes, odd antique plates and saucers, but you should avoid forms that are too deep and materials that are too fragile.

On the dining table they should be
> small
> pretty (preferably of crystal or silver)

and there should be one for every place setting, or one for every two guests at the most.

On a terrace they should be
> slightly deeper and
> windproof.

On a coffee table two medium-sized ashtrays are more attractive than one giant one, which only attracts greater attention to the unaesthetic sight of smokers' debris.

In a den, a bar, or playroom souvenir ashtrays from famous restaurants and hotels in foreign lands are perhaps colorful and amusing, but they are out of place in the living room, not to mention the dining table—even if they were stolen from the Ritz.

On the bridge table you should place an ashtray at each corner, or two larger ones at diagonal corners, since many bridge players are also inveterate smokers.

In the guest room there should be at least one ashtray (but not necessarily on the bed table, for etiquette does not require a hostess to encourage bad habits!).

All of which represents quite a collection—to which you should add, if you often give large cocktail parties or buffet dinners, an extra set of ten or twelve plain, matching ashtrays to be scattered in strategic spots on these occasions when an astonishing number of otherwise well-bred people will not hesitate to drop a cigarette stub on the floor, into a precious porcelain vase or even a flower pot, if there is no ashtray right at hand.

(See Smoking)

ASSETS (AND LIABILITIES)

❲ Just as a woman who wishes to be well dressed must begin by establishing a balance sheet of her physical assets and liabilities in order to make the most of the former and to attempt to conceal the latter, a woman who wishes to entertain with elegance should be rigorously objective in recognizing her positive and negative qualities as a hostess.

I realize that this is easier said than done, for it is certainly simpler to face the readily visible fact of a heavy bosom or twenty pounds of overweight than to evaluate what may be entirely intangible resources as a hostess. Consequently, many a woman who wouldn't dream of squeezing herself into a slinky black satin sheath if she had heavy hips will blithely attempt to give a pretentious formal dinner party in an apartment that is too small, with inadequate help, and on a scale that is beyond her means. The reaction she inspires is likely to be the same as to the heavy-hipped woman in the satin sheath: "What a pity, when she is really most attractive and looks so lovely in her blue silk trapeze dress" becomes "What a pity, when she's really such fun at one of her informal buffet dinners!"

Once you are aware of your entertaining assets, it is a simple matter to exploit them. Some of those that I consider particularly enviable are:

— a charming, sociable, witty husband who enjoys entertaining.
— a host of friends, and the personality to attract new ones.
— a lawn, a swimming pool, a tennis court, a large garden, a boat, or a terrace equipped with an outdoor barbecue.
— an excellent cook.
— a special talent, hobby, or interest.
— personal beauty, wit, or charm.
— plenty of free time.

If you are blessed with one or more of these advantages, you can capitalize on them by, for example, inviting your friends to a cocktail-cruise, an old-fashioned garden party in the summer, a swimming-pool picnic, or by giving a series of exquisitely composed gastronomic dinners, as the case may be.

On the other side of the ledger, however, there may be liabilities, such as:

— several very young children and no nursemaid.
— a tiny apartment, perhaps no more than a studio.
— a shy, reserved husband.
— an elderly invalid sharing your home.
— a houseful of boisterous teen-agers, etc., etc.

As with fashion liabilities, it is sometimes possible to turn them into assets. In your tiny studio apartment, you can make a specialty of intimate cocktail parties, which are essentially one-room entertaining. You can show off the intelligence and charm of your shy husband by entertaining one other couple or two at the most at intimate dinners where the emphasis is on unusual food and stimulating conversation. You can pack your children in the car along with a hamper of delicious picnic fare and invite another entire family to join you in Sunday expeditions to a secluded beach, a nearby national park, or a lovely wood you have discovered.

By exercising your originality and ingenuity, you can devise other means of limiting your liabilities. But whatever you do, don't permit yourself to develop a complex over real or imaginary handicaps. The elegant woman accepts them with good grace and tries to make the most of what she has—without, however, expecting miracles. In short, the most valuable assets of all in entertaining are intelligence and a sense of humor.

ATMOSPHERE

❲ It has been increasingly the fashion for charity balls to re-create the atmosphere of some spectacular spot in order to lend glamor and originality to the occasion. Thanks to the creative talents of dozens of resourceful socialites, the technical skill of a crew of professional decorators, planeloads of imported flowers and delicacies, and acres of satin and velvet, the results are often fantastically alluring—and the cost stupendous. Of course, no private hostess could attempt to reproduce "A Summer Night on the Côte d'Azur" in New York City, as did the organizers of the famous "April in Paris" ball one recent year. As a matter of fact, the socialites who run the European equivalent of this highly publicized event, the *"Bal des Petits Lits Blancs,"* have come to the conclusion that it is simpler to hire a couple of jet planes and to transport all of the guests to Lebanon or Dublin, rather than to try to reconstruct these colorful atmospheres in the heart of Paris for just one night.

On a smaller and less lavish scale, it can be very amusing to plan a really atmospheric party, setting a somewhat more modest scene evocative, for example, of a gold-rush tavern in the West, a flamenco fiesta in Granada, a Venetian palazzo (ideal for a masked ball), a Munich beer hall at carnival time, or what have you. But these ambitious enterprises involve a good deal of expense and work, and few hostesses possess the means or courage to undertake such a delightful but exhausting project more than once in a lifetime. Which is not to say that atmosphere is of no importance in everyday entertaining. On the contrary, it is an element that can determine the success or failure of a party.

Atmosphere, or as we say in French, *ambiance,* is to a room, a home, a restaurant, etc., what personality is to an individual. Its variety is infinite; only its total absence is undesirable.

Usually the atmosphere of a home is the reflection of the personalities of those who inhabit it, and most of all of the "mistress of the house."

Generally speaking, a home possesses one or two different sorts of atmosphere: young, informal, friendly, and gay; or more traditional, formal, refined, and elegant. I know very few women who are capable of creating both of these moods with equal success. Besides, few homes are equally adaptable to both of them because of the character of the architecture and decor—unless there is both a formal salon and an informal living room.

Just as a woman should stick to her type if she wishes to be elegantly dressed, it is useful to be aware of one's personality type as a hostess. Very often a rather shy, retiring, and insecure person feels more at ease in a conventional atmosphere, perhaps because there is a certain comfort in tradition and etiquette. On the other hand, the personality of a woman who is self-confident, original, enthusiastic, and adventurous is enhanced by a casual, friendly atmosphere. The first type of woman would certainly have more success as a hostess at refined dinner parties where careful thought is given to the perfection of every detail; whereas the second would probably excel in giving parties where spontaneity, gaiety, and informality set the keynote. Both of them should, however, beware of exaggeration. It would be disastrous if the atmosphere of informality degenerated into disorder, the gaiety into rowdiness, or the refinement into stiffness and pretention.

The atmosphere of a private home cannot be fabricated in an evening, as at the charity balls, for it results from the gradual crystallization of the personalities of its inhabitants. Thus, a snobbish woman will gradually build up in her home a stuffy atmosphere, and a blasé woman, one of boredom. Furthermore, a hostess often attracts guests who resemble her, and the persons one receives contribute to the atmosphere as well. The conclusion is obvious: if you dream of receiving your friends in an atmosphere that is warm, friendly, refined, and gracious, you should realize that this will be possible only if you express warmth, friendliness, refinement, and graciousness in your daily life, week after week, year after year.

ACHELORS

❡ The two most important species of bachelors in an entertaining woman's life are the confirmed kind, and those whose status she would like to change.

Confirmed bachelors are very useful to a hostess, but unfortunately they know it. Sometimes they become so spoiled that they develop into Spongers, Snobs, and Bores, which are discussed in other sections of this book. While they will send you flowers from time to time, you should not expect them to return your invitations, because they are seldom well organized for entertaining. Neither are they usually very well organized for providing their own meals, and so when a bachelor's hunger coincides with a hostess's necessity to find a last-minute substitute for an ailing guest or a dinner partner for an elderly spinster, they can render each other invaluable services. As a matter of fact, when a bachelor who has been attached for years to a particular hostess decides to get married, he risks finding his name struck from her invitation lists, and it may dawn upon him at last that his principal social virtue was not his wit and charm but simply the fact that he was an available extra man.

The bachelor whose status you wish to change is quite a different case, for he becomes (although you will do your best to keep him unaware of the fact) the guest of honor at all of your receptions. I am told that it is preferable to invite him to a home-cooked dinner in your own apartment, where you remain incontestably in control of the proceedings, rather than to let yourself be inveigled into preparing a cozy meal in his own bachelor flat. Naturally, you will want to impress him with your superior qualities as a hostess and a cook—but take my advice and do not feed him *too* well, or he will be so satisfied with the arrangement that he will never again want to take you out to dinner in a restaurant.

(See One Room, Romance)

BALLS

⟨ A ball is the most ostentatious form of entertaining, as well as the least frequent and the most extravagant.

It is the official consecration of a debutante daughter, and an absolute must in a certain fast-diminishing sector of society. I know quite a lot of people who would consider it outrageously extravagant to buy a first-class airplane ticket, but who unhesitatingly spend a minimum of two thousand dollars to celebrate their eighteen-year-old daughter's "coming-out."

Of course, a ball can be given at any age, and I personally know of no other kind of reception that is as exciting. But if you decide to give one, you should realize that in order to be successful, a ball cannot be mediocre in any way, and that you need to have a luxurious setting, hundreds of friends, an excellent orchestra, a buffet table groaning with rare and refined dishes, tons of flowers, a fabulous evening gown and comfortable shoes, a dozen waiters—in other words, a sturdy bank account.

Since every single detail must be perfect, this is not an occasion for either amateurism or economy. You must hire the finest available caterer, the best ballroom orchestra, and professional specialists to install the dance floor and the floral decorations. There is consequently no point in going into these subjects in detail, because if you cannot afford the services of experts in these various fields (and who can afford it nowadays, aside from a few millionaires?) you should not attempt to give a ball at all, but instead select a more modest type of party that is well within your means. A sumptuous barbecue or informal buffet dinner will always be elegant, but a "budget ball" is inconceivable!

BARBECUES

❨ Only a few years ago, the most ordinary steak sprinkled with herbs and grilled out of doors over an open fire would elicit raves from all the guests. But now that barbecue entertaining has become so widespread, the quality of the food, the equipment, and the hospitality must be of a very high order if a barbecue party is to be successful. I must admit that when I see the trouble that is taken to procure a special cut of meat, to steep it in some secret marinade for hours or days, to prepare a perfect fire hours ahead of time, and to invest in all sorts of expensive barbecue gear and accessories, I wonder if it isn't finally less bother (and less expensive, too) to entertain at a conventional sit-down dinner.

It is, however, undeniable that simple dishes prepared and consumed in the open air are particularly delicious. And the fact that the host, or in some cases the guests themselves, prepares the meal, sets a mood of informal fun that can never be reproduced in an indoor dining room. Personally, I have adored barbecues ever since my Girl Guide days, when we used to roast sausages over a campfire.

The only thing that can dampen the spirits (and perhaps put out the fire) is an unexpected rainstorm. For this reason it is risky to schedule a barbecue party too far in advance in uncertain climates, unless your grill is installed on a covered patio, or you are perfectly prepared to transfer everything indoors should the need arise. But perhaps this warning is quite unnecessary nowadays, for most of the American houses I have visited seem to have two barbecues: one in the backyard and the other on a protected terrace.

A barbecue dinner is more spectacular than a barbecue luncheon because of the glowing fire. But you will need supplementary lighting out of doors at night, and it seems to me that hurricane candles and old-fashioned gasoline lanterns are far more atmospheric than electricity. By gaslight or sunshine, the great delight of barbecues is that they are carefree and fun. However, it takes considerable planning ahead of time in order to be free of cares and not obliged to run back and forth to the kitchen. There is one unavoidable awkward moment when it is time to clear the main course dishes before serving the dessert. The ideal solution for a large party would be to have one or more servants who are continually clearing away used plates and glasses and distributing clean ones. Otherwise the hostess and the host, aided perhaps by a teen-age son or daughter, should be prepared to take care of this vital chore as swiftly and unobtrusively as possible at the proper moment.

The simplest menu plan in my opinion is to reserve the barbecue grill for cooking the main course (which can just as well be fish or lobster as meat), and to serve as an *entrée* (which, for me, means the first course of a meal, though restaurants sometimes use it to refer to the main dish) either a cold dish that has been prepared in advance, such as a *salade Niçoise* or an assortment of pâtés, or a hot soup, such as a shrimp or lobster bisque with chunks of seafood in it, a black bean soup garnished with bits of smoked ham and seasoned with sherry and thinly sliced lemon, etc. These hot dishes can be prepared in the kitchen and served outdoors from a steaming tureen that is kept warm on a hot plate or over a chafing-dish flame.

As for the barbecued main dish, it is highly recommended that you rehearse your recipes in private until they are absolutely foolproof. If you are fortunate enough to have an excellent butcher, nothing could be more delectable than a superior piece of well-marbled beef grilled over a hickory or charcoal fire, or a marvelous leg or saddle of lamb, or an entire suckling pig roasted on a spit. In order to be suitable for spit roasting, you need a rather large piece of meat, at least three or four pounds, and you must carefully estimate the cooking time, which will be rather long. With smaller pieces, such as chops and small fish, it is safer to clamp them between two grills equipped with a long handle. If you live near the seashore where very fresh fish is available, you can grill the most ordinary kinds of fish or the most superb lobster, and if they are freshly caught they will all be delicious. But when your raw materials are not of excellent quality, it is better to select more original recipes and to take greater pains with the preparation, accompaniments, and seasonings. In this regard, it is useful to know that a well-seasoned, red-wine marinade will tenderize the toughest steak, and that lemon juice is a great tenderizer for fowl.

Thick cubes of meat strung lengthwise on skewers with or without alternating chunks of onion, tomato, mushrooms, bacon, pineapple, peppers, etc., lend themselves to all kinds of subtle variations, from the classic shish kebab (squares of seasoned beef, lamb, or pork alternated with onion quarters, tomatoes, green pepper, and a bay leaf) to more exotic combinations of flavors, such as scallops, Canadian bacon, and tomatoes; or lamb, eggplant, onion, and tomato. The ideal accompaniment to all of these is rice.

Among the best fish for grilling over charcoal are rainbow trout, halibut, turbot, salmon, sea bass, fresh tuna fish steaks, and fresh sardines (delicious boned and stuffed with chopped spinach and herbs and brushed with olive oil before cooking).

Game birds, in my opinion, are best roasted in the oven. But chicken is marvelous when barbecued, especially when it has been marinated in olive oil and lemon juice seasoned with tarragon, parsley, salt, and pepper, and basted with the marinade as it grills. You may also wrap it in bacon, and in this case basting is unnecessary, but you should blanch the bacon first in boiling water or its sharp flavor will permeate the fowl. Duckling is also an excellent barbecue fowl and requires very little basting.

If you wish to dazzle your barbecue specialist friends, you might serve them an adaptation of a foreign barbecue dish, such as the *méchoui* (whole roast lamb on a spit) of the Arabs, accompanied by couscous (available in groceries that carry foreign foods as well as in cans) and a salad. You can prepare a pretty good imitation of the typical sweet North African desserts by filling a baking dish with shredded wheat biscuits; drench with honey, sprinkle with pine nuts, and bake. In France the Camargue region, home of our Gallic cowboys, is famous for its outdoor grilled steaks, which are flavored with all sorts of herbs, especially fresh rosemary, oregano, and thyme, and served with an assortment of highly spiced sauces.

To accompany your barbecued main dish, all you need is a huge mixed salad in a wooden bowl, and a rather rustic dessert such as a blueberry or a deep-dish apple pie. If there are many guests, a barrel of draft beer would be spectacular, or a large peasant jug of ordinary red or rosé wine. Instead of a mixed salad, you might set out a series of bowls filled with various ingredients, such as quartered hard-boiled eggs, anchovies, tomatoes, olives, tuna fish, green peppers, grated carrots and celery, chives, cottage cheese, etc., an assortment of greens, and two or three different salad dressings (Roquefort, French, and tarragon, for example), and let each guest mix his own.

Depending on the number of guests, you will have one large table or several small ones attractively set in a rustic style and placed where they are not too far from the house or from the barbecue, but still

sheltered from the wind and smoke and, in the daytime, from the blazing sun.

The service at a barbecue party is a mixture of classic buffet style
and Army chow line, and therefore presents no particular problem (except for clearing away the main course). As a matter of fact, the principal preoccupation of the hostess is to see that everybody has plenty
to eat. Open-air appetites are notoriously hearty, and it is therefore best
to be unusually generous in your estimates of quantity.

The quality of your fire is as important as the quality of the food you
cook. If you use a wood fire, it is useful to know that maple, ash, beech,
and hazel blaze the most, while glowing embers are best produced by
oak, hickory, and elm. If you use charcoal, it should be spread out in
a single layer to provide the slow heat necessary for roasting a whole
leg of lamb or an entire duckling or chicken. But for grilling kebabs,
small whole fish, or thin steaks, the charcoal should be piled up several
inches high in order to provide a fire that will sear the meat surface
quickly and thus seal in the juices. To avoid smoking, you should push
new charcoal into the center rather than piling it on top of the burning
embers. You must have the patience to wait until the charcoal is just
at the right stage before attempting to cook over it: it should be glowing
red at night and ash-gray in the daytime. The meat or fish should always be at room temperature and not fresh from the refrigerator, which
means that you must remove large pieces several hours ahead of time.
And don't forget to brush the grids of the grill with oil in order to
prevent sticking.

Fragrant herbs, such as rosemary, sage, and thyme, will flavor delicate meats more subtly when they are sprinkled in the fire as well as
over the meat or in the marinade. You might also try tossing a cut
clove of garlic on the hot embers or, when you are cooking pork, a
little lemon or orange rind.

The art of giving a successful barbecue party is not as simple as it
may seem, nor is it within the means of every hostess. So if you are
not perfectly equipped for this kind of entertaining, and if you do not
possess the necessary outdoor space, enthusiasm, and skill (and a very
cooperative husband), it is preferable to limit yourself to more conventional patio dinners and luncheons when you wish to entertain in
the open air.

(See Insects, Lighting)

BATHROOMS

❲ Far be it for me to advise American women on the installation of their bathrooms. Theirs are the most luxurious, the most practical, and the most beautiful in the world, and my sole regret is that most of them lack a bidet, which is an essential article of daily hygiene in other countries. (In Portugal, they even have them in restaurant washrooms.)

European bathrooms, with few exceptions, are antediluvian by comparison, and it is not easy for us to modernize them attractively because we do not yet have at our disposal your immense choice of lovely coordinated bathroom equipment and accessories. Perhaps one of the reasons for our backwardness in this regard is that strangers seldom see the inside of our bathrooms. In America, it seems to be quite normal for at least half of the guests at a dinner party to excuse themselves at one point or another during the evening in order to "wash their hands," but such a thing never occurs in France. Do you suppose it has something to do with the fact that the French drink wine with their meals, and Americans weak coffee?

At any rate, there is hardly any point in my suggesting that the bathroom be prepared for company whenever you entertain just as the dining room and living room are, because those that I have visited in America have always been impeccable. Preparing a bathroom for company simply means putting away all of your personal toilet articles, medicines, and clothing, arranging fresh towels on the racks, seeing that there is a clean bar of soap and an ample supply of toilet necessities. It also means removing the toothpaste spatters from the mirror.

The ideal arrangement for entertaining is to have a separate guest bathroom on the ground floor near the coat closet and the front hall. In this case it is a very simple matter to maintain it in perfect condition and supply it with scented guest-sized soaps, a flacon of toilet water, face tissues, etc., and a stack of pretty, individual guest towels. The linen kind are, of course, much more elegant than paper, but the paper ones are very practical when you are entertaining children.

When you receive a large number of guests, for example, more than ten or twelve, it is best to provide separate facilities for the men and women whenever possible. Usually it is most practical to let the men use the downstairs or front-hall cloakroom and bath, and to place your own bedroom and bath at the disposal of the women, after having put away all of your personal clothing and articles. Needless to say, no well-bred person would read someone else's mail, even an opened letter lying in plain sight. But still, it is not a good idea to offer such temptations to feminine curiosity—unless, of course, the letter is signed by some famous name and you want everyone to know it!

When you entertain a houseguest, there is no problem at all if you have a separate guest bathroom, which is fully equipped. But if you must all share the same one, the situation is very awkward indeed, and I would therefore not recommend this arrangement for more than a single night and only in an emergency. In this case, it is best simply to set aside a special towel rack, a separate clothes hook, and a separate drinking glass and soap dish for your guest, and hope that he will be tactful enough to keep the rest of his personal toilet articles in a plastic bag in his bedroom.

(See Guest Rooms, Houseguests)

BEACH

❰ The beach party, one of the greatest joys of childhood summer holidays, seems to be dying out nowadays, no doubt a victim of the craze for backyard barbecues and swimming pools. Or perhaps it is because the prettiest beaches in many shore areas are either municipally owned and therefore crowded and noisy, or else they are surrounded by intimidating barbed wire and "No Trespassing" signs. In the case of public beaches, there may be permanent picnic installations (which are seldom very isolated or inviting), or maybe picnicking is strictly prohibited. And so the first requirement of a beach party is to find a suitable beach that is safe for bathing, free from crowds, set in attractive, natural surroundings, and where picnickers are welcome. Otherwise, I must confess that a picnic on your own patio would undoubtedly be more pleasant. The dream, of course, would be to own or borrow a private beach, or to discover a deserted, secluded cove from which there is no danger of being chased away by an irascible property owner. In these conditions, nothing could be more agreeable on a hot August day than to plan a picnic lunch or dinner at the beach.

Since absolutely everything has to be brought with you in the car, it is impractical to plan a beach party for more than ten or twelve persons at the most. The best formula probably consists of two or three entire families, since the delight of the children contributes much to the pleasure of the occasion. Because the planning and preparation of the meal must be perfectly organized down to the last detail, it is more practical for one person to take complete charge of the provisions, rather than trying to divide the responsibilities, in which case some indispensable item, such as the salt, the can or bottle opener, or the sugar for the coffee, is inevitably left behind.

For a picnic lunch at the beach, the best plan is to prepare a rather simple, light, cold meal, based on sandwiches and food that is easy to serve and handle, such as the classic cold fried chicken, cold cuts, tomatoes, carrot sticks, stuffed hard-boiled eggs, etc., and for dessert fruit and cookies, or ice cream on a stick (kept frozen in a special bag with dry ice). In addition to the lunch itself, you should think of including an extra snack for the children later on in the afternoon, such as brownies and milk, or fruit juice and cookies. Iced tea or coffee or canned beer are probably the most suitable beverages for the adults, and for the children cold milk, lemonade, or an assortment of soft bottled drinks, all of them well chilled in the refrigerator at home and kept cold in thermos coolers. It is not a bad idea to include a large bottle of cold drinking water, too.

Most elderly persons are more comfortable picnicking on a folding table complete with tablecloth and folding chairs, but I am inclined to agree with children that half of the fun of a picnic is eating on the ground. And so I prefer to open the picnic hamper on a plastic tablecloth spread out on the sand and to let everybody sprawl comfortably on cushions, towels, and beach mats.

The principal difference between a picnic luncheon at the beach and a picnic luncheon in the country is the problem of keeping the food from spoiling in the heat of the blazing sun, and of keeping sand out of the sandwiches and insects away from the dessert. You should therefore store the hamper in the coolest part of the car under a damp towel, place everything that risks spoilage in thermos containers, and eliminate the use of sand-collecting shallow plates (even paper ones) by wrapping everything in individual portions in aluminum foil or waxed paper, and by inviting your guests to eat with their fingers. It is more important than ever to avoid such foods as cream puffs and salads mixed with mayonnaise, which develop dangerous bacteria when they have been submitted to excessive heat. It is also a good idea to avoid food that is long or difficult to digest, such as pork, turkey, and duck, because it will be difficult enough to prevent the children from going into the water within the hour or hour and a half that it is advisable to wait before swimming again after having eaten even a rather light meal.

It is advisable to include in your equipment a beach umbrella and plenty of beach rolls and towels for after-lunch siestas, as well as a beach ball and a few simple games. An excellent plan for passing pleasantly the hour following the picnic lunch is to organize a sand-castle contest, or a competition in which each child attempts to collect the greatest number of seashells, or the widest variety of colored pebbles within a certain time limit.

Finally, when it is time to go home, you should not leave behind the slightest trace of your beach picnic. If there is no provision for litter disposal in sight, you must take every greasy paper, empty bottle, and paper napkin back home with you and dump them all in your own garbage can.

An evening beach party is quite different. You will, of course, want to build a fire, and once you have built the fire, why not cook your meal on it? Many public beaches possess permanent barbecue installations, but you may prefer to bring from home your own portable barbecue to which you are accustomed. In any case, it is important to make sure beforehand that evening barbecues are permitted on the beach you have in mind.

Unless you hire a team of specialists to do your barbecuing for you on a big scale, you should again limit your guest list to ten or twelve persons at the most. A larger group would probably require two fires, which would seriously complicate the question of materials and would double the work of the chef.

Again, you must make a complete list of everything you will need down to the smallest detail, so that you do not forget a single thing—not even the drinking water, can opener, matches, extra ice, seasonings, flashlight, first aid kit for cuts and burns, a bucket for dousing the fire before you leave, blankets and beach mats, towels, and extra sweaters to slip on as the night air grows cool.

Again, you should attempt to foil the beach bugs by placing all the food in covered jars or wrapped in waxed paper or aluminum foil, and by taking it out only just before it is needed. A large bottle or tube of insect repellent may come in handy, too.

The host family should arrive well ahead of the others in order to install the equipment and to start the fire. In summer the days are fortunately long, and it is best to schedule your party rather early in order to prepare the meal before nightfall if possible. When there is a bright full moon you may not need any supplementary lighting at all. Otherwise, it would be a good idea to provide more atmospheric lighting than automobile headlights. Perhaps a butane gas lamp is the most modern solution.

Everything possible should be prepared at home ahead of time: the bread or rolls already buttered, the steaks or chops or fish ready for grilling, and everything wrapped in individual portions and labeled if the contents are not readily identifiable. It is, incidentally, very simple to cook certain foods directly over the coals if they have been wrapped in foil: for example, baked potatoes, carrots, squash slices, and corn on the cob. As always, you should serve hot foods really hot and cold foods really cold, and this is no longer very difficult thanks to modern portable iceboxes and vacuum containers.

As with a daytime beach picnic, food that can be eaten in the fingers is more convenient than food requiring plates and cutting, and you should therefore ask your butcher to cut your steaks thinner than for a home barbecue in order to serve them in toasted sandwich buns. Hamburgers and frankfurters are, of course, the simplest of all to prepare and to eat, and you can palliate their banality by providing a wide assortment of unusual relishes.

Before inviting guests to an evening beach picnic, it is a good idea to make a family experiment first, for the quality of your equipment, organization, and technical skill is what will finally determine the success or failure of the party. You must be prepared to furnish a good deal of time and effort beforehand, and a lot of work during the party, but the cleaning up will be quite simple since you can simply burn the paper plates and cups and take the empty receptacles home with you. While there may be more work than for an ordinary party, you will also have a lot more fun.

A *clambake* is certainly the most spectacular and epicurean form of beach party. It requires even more work and even longer preparation, but the results are unforgettable.

The type of beach at your disposal is of particular importance, for you will need both sand and stones. First you must dig a pit about one foot deep and three feet wide. At least four hours before you plan to serve the feast, you line the pit with a layer of smooth round rocks, and cover with a layer of firewood or charcoal. (Wood is preferable, especially oak, orange, apple, and hickory.) You light the fire and proceed to fill the pit with alternate layers of stones and wood until there is a pile about two or three feet above the ground. As it burns down during the next two or three hours, everything will settle in the pit and the stones will be extremely hot. At this point, you rake away the embers and cover the rock surface with a thick layer of clean seaweed that has been well rinsed in sea water. Over the seaweed you spread the clams—about ten soft-shelled clams per person, or a bushel of clams for fourteen or fifteen guests. Cover with another layer of seaweed on which you place a live lobster for each guest, then an ear of corn on the cob for each guest (only partially husked, but with the silk removed), potatoes and onions, and a final layer of seaweed. Some people like to add another baking layer consisting of quartered broiling chickens (wrapped in cheesecloth or foil) and frankfurters. Always terminate with a layer of seaweed or corn husks. Sprinkle a bucket of sea water over everything and quickly cover tightly with a large tarpaulin that has been soaked in sea water and which generously overlaps the rim of the pit. The edges of the tarpaulin must be weighed down with a ring of rocks, for the steaming process will make it puff up and it is vital to keep the steam well sealed inside. The baking process will take at least an hour, and you can test for doneness by carefully pulling out a lobster. When the lobster is done, everything else will be ready for eating too.

To complete this succulent feast, all you need is salt, pepper, lots of melted butter, plenty of cold beer and soft drinks, a simple dessert such as iced watermelon or ice cream in individual cups, and finally a steaming thermos of hot coffee. It is also a good idea to bring along a supply of damp and dry towels for cleaning buttery faces and sticky fingers.

If all of these preparations intimidate you, it may interest you to know that in many beach areas there are enterprising young men, experienced in organizing clambakes, who offer their services for the evening at a reasonable fee. In any case, it would certainly be advisable to observe the clambake preparations of an expert before attempting to take everything into your own hands, and to experiment on a small scale with a family clambake before inviting guests. If you are gifted at this sort of thing, you will find that a clambake is a marvelous way to entertain twenty or thirty hungry friends on a clear, hot August night. (But to make absolutely sure that the night will be hot and clear, you should check with the almanac as well as the weather bureau before issuing your invitations!)

BEDS

⟨[The only way to verify the comfort of your guest room bed is to spend at least one night in it yourself, and every conscientious hostess manages to do this in order to be completely confident of the quality of the hospitality which she offers to her guests.

Twin beds are the rule for guest rooms, whenever this is possible, because it can be very difficult for a married couple that is used to separate beds to become accustomed to a double one. Besides, statistics show that after a certain number of years of marriage, most couples prefer twin beds. Moreover, you can perfectly well accommodate two teen-age girls or boys in a guest room with twin beds, whereas this would sometimes be less feasible if there were just one large one.

In any case, you should never economize on the quality of the guest bed mattress. A houseguest will much more quickly forgive and forget a bad meal than a sleepless night. Personally, I have found synthetic or rubber foam-type mattresses highly satisfactory for the twin beds in a guest room because they seem to suit most people and they will never develop lumps or hollows. But they are, in my experience, less comfortable on a large double bed, for which I prefer an innerspring mattress.

Each guest bed should be provided with two pillows (one of which may be stored in a closet or cupboard), one or two lightweight blankets, and one winter blanket or quilt, if you live in a normal, four-season climate. Nothing is more luxurious than a mohair blanket, but I would rule out electric blankets for the guest room since there are still some people who are terrified by them.

Unless you are in the habit of receiving a steady stream of houseguests, or of indulging yourself in the supreme luxury of changing the sheets every day, you do not need more than two sets of sheets and pillow cases for each guest room bed, so why not splurge on some really beautiful ones? Such pretty patterns are available today, and such lovely shades, that you can surely find an attractive patterned border, for example, neither too feminine nor too severe, that harmonizes with the decoration of the room.

If the extra bedding is stored in the guest room closet, your guests can add or subtract according to their particular needs. Only during a really bitter cold spell need you inquire to make sure they have enough blankets.

In a servantless household, most guests will make their own beds every morning as a matter of course (except for the day on which they leave, when they should on the contrary unmake it). But if they don't—which is more often the case with adolescents than with adults— it would be more elegant to take the necessary ten minutes and make it yourself, rather than to bring the lapse to their attention.

(See Guest Rooms)

BIRTHDAYS

❡ A birthday is one of the best pretexts in the world for giving a party. It seems to me that everybody has the right to be feted and spoiled at least one day of the year. Besides, celebrating birthdays with a feast is one of the most ancient traditions of entertaining. A birthday party may be as simple or as grand as you wish, although sixteen, eighteen, twenty-one, and fifty are the ages that most naturally call for the most elaborate celebration.

Birthdays have an extraordinary importance to children, and it is customary for a child to be the host at his own birthday party, whereas adults can only hope that somebody will give a birthday party in their honor. Unless a child has the bad luck to be born on the twenty-fourth or the thirty-first of December, this is an ideal occasion not only to offer him the treat of being a star for a day but also of training him to be a gracious host to all his little friends.

A birthday party is probably the simplest kind of children's party to carry off successfully because of the delightful rituals of presents and birthday cakes and candles which all children adore. A charming custom in some European countries, and which has been adopted to some extent in America, is for the birthday child who receives a gift from each of his guests to offer each of them a small gift in return. Any small toy or trinket will do, since the purpose is simply for everyone to have a surprise package to open.

It is best to serve the refreshments at one large table, covered with a gay paper or plastic cloth, so that all the children can admire the birthday cake, which should be as spectacular as possible. When there are only a very few candles, try to buy rather thick ones so that the lights can be turned off or dimmed as the candlelit cake is brought into the room to the strains of "Happy Birthday." Perhaps it is considered hazardous by modern pediatricians, but I have always loved the old custom of scattering fortune-telling favors (including the coveted dime for the future millionaire) throughout the birthday cake, so that there is one in every portion. If all of them are wrapped in squares of waxed paper or aluminum foil, there is really very little chance of their being inadvertently swallowed. You might even simply insert the wrapped favors in a store-bought angel food or sponge cake, which you afterward frost and decorate yourself.

Because of the distraction of the gifts, it is often better to feature some form of entertainment rather than games. A magician would be perfect, or thirty or forty minutes of movies—although the latter are no longer the special treat they used to be before the advent of television. In any case, it is a very simple formula and specialized rental firms will supply all of the necessary equipment and a vast selection of appropriate films. If you start the party with the exchange of gifts, then proceed to the prepared entertainment, and terminate with refreshments (either a light, simple dish and ice cream and cake; sandwiches and milk and ice cream and cake; or merely the indispensable ice cream and cake), your tiny guests will have spent a delightful, well-occupied afternoon, so there is no point in prolonging the festivities.

Adult birthday parties are quite different. In the first place, if you decide to give a birthday party for yourself, and you announce the fact that it is your birthday at the time you invite your guests, all of them will feel obliged to bring a gift, which you will seem to have solicited. If, on the other hand, you merely mention the fact casually during the course of the evening, they will feel guilty about having arrived empty-handed. It is therefore more elegant to let another member of your family or a close friend give a birthday party in your honor, since the hostess can then discuss the question of birthday gifts without embarrassment. And if you are simply longing to organize a birthday party, give it for your husband or your best friend. Personally, I adore both offering and receiving gifts, and I have found it a good method to suggest that each guest bring a small present costing no more than, say, two or three dollars—which means that it should be witty rather than beautiful. In this way the guest of honor has the surprise and fun of opening a pile of packages, and nobody runs the risk of appearing either extravagant or niggardly.

A birthday party dinner for adults is just like any other dinner party, except that it is thoughtful to cater to any particular gastronomic preferences of the guest of honor. And, of course, the only possible dessert is ice cream and a birthday cake, accompanied by champagne.

While you would not consider placing on a child's birthday cake anything but the number of candles representing his exact age, the question is more delicate with guests of honor who may not be very anxious to reveal how old they are. This is the system I have adopted:

For children: one candle for every year.

For myself: the exact number of years. (On my fiftieth birthday the candles required such an enormous cake that I was obliged to climb up on a stool in order to blow them out—so from now on I suppose I will have to use a few larger candles to represent each decade!)

For my husband: the same as for myself.

For adults in general: twenty-one candles, if you wish to be very tactful.

For a pretty woman: the most flattering number I can think of.

For somebody over eighty: it all depends. Beyond a certain age, coquetry consists of proudly claiming the maximum years of age—so that it is all the more marvelous, I suppose, to appear so young!

(See Children, Dinners, etc.)

BOOKS

❡ The library of a perfect hostess should include a few indispensable volumes:

(1.) A complete, up-to-date book of etiquette, such as the very modern and sensible one by Amy Vanderbilt.

(2.) A complete, up-to-date, basic cook book—plus an unlimited number of specialized ones if you are very interested in cooking or (like me) simply enjoy reading delectable recipes.

(3.) A set of telephone directories—of adjacent towns as well as your own, if necessary. The classified directory of the nearest big city is also extremely useful.

(4.) Your personal address book, carefully kept up to date.

(5.) A separate household address book with the telephone numbers and addresses of shops and tradesmen. I have found, incidentally, that it is more convenient to list these names by categories such as Plumber, Television, Caterer, etc., rather than to enter the names alphabetically. It is usually the name and not the service that I forget!

(6.) The official bridge rules—to settle card-party arguments.

(7.) Guide books and a map of your city or state. (These are always of great interest to foreign visitors and out-of-town guests.)

(8.) A collection of current best sellers and detective stories for the guest room.

(9.) A party book, in which you keep a record of all of your receptions, large and small, indicating the date, the occasion, the guest list, the seating arrangement, the menu, the entertainment, if any, and the table decoration. This is the only sure means of avoiding repeating the very same kind of party twice in succession for the very same guests.

The traditional guest book or *Livre d'Or* has practically disappeared from current use except in the case of a few stately homes, official residences, large yachts, and certain fashionable restaurants, where guests may still be asked to sign their names along with a brief and witty commentary in a beautiful gilt-edged leather-bound album. I suppose that the abuse of autograph collecting is responsible for the abandonment of this ancient entertaining tradition, and perhaps also the fact that we entertain more often and much more casually than did our grandparents. Today it would seem rather pretentious to have one's guests sign their names in a book after an ordinary dinner party, but it might be amusing to revive the custom on special occasions. Besides, if any of your friends should become very famous, what a delightful souvenir to leave to your heirs!

BORES

❪ I was too strictly brought up ever to forget the manners I was taught as a child, so that today I am unfortunately incapable of turning my back on all the bores one inevitably encounters if one circulates a bit.

Nevertheless, there is no excuse for establishing a continuous relationship with this tiresome breed, unless of course the bore in question happens to be your husband's boss. But in all the other cases, the only thing to do is never to accept their invitations so that you will never have to return them. And if you are really absolutely obliged to invite them just once, it is preferable to try to drown them in a crowd.

The most prolific type of bore is the person who is madly infatuated with himself, who talks only about himself, interrupting you to tell his own story, which is always, in his eyes at least, much more interesting than what happened to you. There is no point in attempting to amuse or impress him with an account of the evening you spent at the White House, of the three holes-in-one you shot the other day at golf, or even of the grand slam you made when doubled by Charles Goren himself. This kind of bore will always have a story to top yours, and he will drag it out for hours.

But there are also other deadly varieties: the lecherous elderly men who insist upon dancing with all of the prettiest young women; the indiscreet ladies who bombard you with intimate questions; the men who detect a spicy double-entendre behind each innocent phrase; the talkers who clutch your arm or grab your husband by the lapels to make sure that he won't get away; those who might have enjoyed a magnificent career as an undertaker, so solemn and gloomy is their expression and so nonexistent their smile; people who drink too much; those who talk about nothing but politics or the price of beefsteak, or the children's diarrhea, or various repulsive physical ailments, or the performance of their new car, or their exploits at hunting or fishing . . . in short, (because this enumeration is by no means complete), all those to whom you have absolutely nothing to say and who reduce your entire personality to the size of an eardrum. There is only one effective strategy in the presence of all these bores: flight.

BREAKFAST

❲ Early morning habits are highly individual, and everybody has his favorite rites for waking up and preparing to face the world another day. Consequently, breakfast is not a very appropriate meal to share with guests, and when you do, it is generally in the form of a brunch party, which is halfway between a late breakfast and an early lunch.

Sometimes a very busy woman is obliged to receive an early-morning visitor at breakfast simply because there is no other free time in her crowded schedule. As in the case of all visits, you should be prepared to offer refreshments that are appropriate to the time of day. Most often the caller will already have breakfasted at home, and it is quite sufficient to offer an extra cup of tea or coffee, accompanied by a coffee cake or Danish pastry that you have warmed in the oven, or merely a fresh batch of hot buttered toast. So casual is the hospitality in these circumstances that it can hardly be considered "entertaining," and it seems to me that it should be reserved for your most intimate women friends.

Whenever you entertain houseguests, you should ask them what is the hour and the menu they prefer for breakfast, since most persons have established once and for all a formula which they repeat every morning of their lives. If they take no more than orange juice, toast, and coffee or tea, it is really far simpler to serve it to them in their rooms on a tray, which can be laid out the night before and prepared in no time at all in the morning. Every woman I know adores having breakfast in bed, but men do not usually share our appreciation of this simple luxury. I cannot imagine why, either, because it must be much more comforting to drink one's coffee before shaving, and this is possible only when the coffee is served in the privacy of one's bedroom. (Needless to say, the sight of a stubbly growth of beard should never be imposed on one's hostess at the dining room table.)

If, on the other hand, your guests possess hearty appetites and are accustomed to start the day well fortified with fruit, cereal, ham, and eggs, you have no choice in the matter but must offer them their habitual fare. In this case, it is of course most practical to serve the

meal in the dining room, family style, and you should suggest to your
guests that they come in their dressing gowns.

Even if you have already taken your own breakfast earlier, it is
courteous to join your guests at table for an extra cup of coffee. If you
have a thousand important things to do, you can perfectly well abandon
them temporarily after this hospitable gesture. But be sure to leave
them the morning newspapers—in their entirety, and not a tattered
copy with the crossword puzzle already solved and all of the most
interesting department store advertisements torn out!

(See Brunch)

BRIDGE

❲ A bridge party for a group of guests who are fanatics about the game
is perhaps the ideal form of entertaining, because for once you can be
certain that everybody is going to have a good time.

Depending on the size of your home and the number of guests,
there are various ways of organizing a bridge party:

—For a couple of close friends with whom you have established the
tradition of playing bridge once a week after dining each in his own
home, it will be sufficient to serve cake or ice cream in the middle of the
evening—it can be eaten even during a game—and to install a refreshment bar in a convenient nearby spot. Remember to provide coasters
under every glass. In addition to light snacks, you should set out a
supply of whisky, fruit juice, Coca-Cola, etc., in other words, whatever
your friends, whose habits you know well, usually prefer to drink.

—With guests whom you have invited to dinner first, you should
be sure to specify that you intend to play bridge afterward. You might
as well begin the game right after the coffee has been served if you
wish to go to bed at a fairly reasonable hour. In this case, you would
simply serve the usual long drinks and fruit juice during the latter part
of the evening, just as you do at an ordinary dinner party.

—For the real bridge party with several different tables of card-
players, there are two possible plans: to dine beforehand, or to serve
supper afterward.

The solution I prefer is the Sunday evening bridge that starts at five o'clock, with a buffet of snacks and drinks where the dummies and the guests who are waiting for their turn to play can serve themselves as they wish. It is, by the way, preferable not to have too many leftover guests waiting to play, for some rubbers seem endless and the real bridge enthusiast greatly prefers playing to watching. However, it is a good idea for the host and hostess to be the odd player at two different tables, not only as a safety measure in case one of the guests drops out at the last minute, but also because it will leave them free from time to time to supervise everything. At around nine o'clock, all of the games are brought to a close, the bridge tables are covered with tablecloths, and set with glasses and a bottle of wine (champagne or red wine); each guest goes to the buffet, takes a plate and silverware, and serves himself what he likes. It is necessary for the hostess to arrange to clear the tables after the main course is finished, when the guests return to the buffet for the dessert.

During the week, you can also invite guests at about six-thirty or seven o'clock to dine at two tables of eight or ten persons, and to play bridge afterward. Unfortunately, with this larger number of guests, it usually turns into a very late party. It also requires more personnel to serve the meal and especially to clear the tables in order to transform the dinner room into a cardroom as quickly as possible.

It is always the responsibility of the hostess to set the stakes of the bridge game, and she should choose a tariff that is too low rather than too high, unless all of her guests are millionaires.

Finally, you might organize a bridge tournament by pairs. This is a very amusing system but the party lasts a long time. It requires quite a lot of room, so that one table does not hear what is being bid at another, and it also requires a great deal of organization. You must provide special card cases in which the different deals must be arranged as they have been played at one table, and then passed on to the other, with the score of the first table marked but well concealed. You will also need the services of a bridge expert in tallying up the final scores. Finally, you must present a pretty prize to the winners, and an inexpensive but witty consolation prize to the losers.

Of course, a hostess cannot entertain exclusively at bridge parties, for she would deprive herself of the friendship of many charming people who do not like to play cards. But if you have many friends who enjoy this particularly fascinating game, a bridge party is probably the best way of entertaining them.

(See Cards, Gambling)

BRUNCH

(Like so many other typically American inventions, a brunch is practical, ingenious, and fun. Neither a breakfast nor a luncheon but a little of both, it takes place later than the former and earlier than the latter—ten or eleven o'clock are the most customary hours, after a lazy morning in bed. Sunday is therefore the likeliest day for a brunch party.

Since it is an informal, even extremely casual form of entertaining, ten or twelve guests is, it seems to me, a maximum in most cases— including your weekend guests. As a matter of fact, a Sunday-morning brunch party is an ideal occasion for presenting a houseguest to your friends in a delightfully informal atmosphere. You might even invite one or two entire families whose children are the same ages as yours (but, to be on the safe side, over eight or nine years old).

It is a very simple matter to receive either a greater or smaller number of guests, since the mood and service of a brunch are highly informal. The usual method is to lay out all of the menu on the dining room sideboard, with the hot dishes kept warm in covered chafing dishes or on electric hot plates, and to let the guests serve themselves buffet style. You may either set places at the dining room table, or allow your guests to take their plates into the living room, on the patio, or wherever they please. On a warm summer morning you might even transfer the buffet itself to the patio. With a large number, a combination of seated and wandering guests may be the most successful system. In other words, at a brunch party, your guests should be given complete freedom to come when they like (more or less as at a cocktail party), dressed as they like (in their go-to-church clothes, or in a woodchopper's outfit, depending on the activities they have planned for the day), and to eat and drink whatever appeals to them most.

Upon arrival, every guest should be given a drink, and it is generally best to serve this in the living room or den. The most classical before-noon cocktails are probably a Bloody Mary (two jiggers of tomato juice, one jigger of vodka, the juice of half a lemon, and a dash of Worcestershire sauce), Whisky Sour (one jigger of bourbon or rye, one-half jigger of lemon juice and a teaspoonful of sugar), an Orange Blossom (one-half orange juice, one-half dry gin), and a Screwdriver (one-half orange juice, one-half vodka). But the most delicious morning cocktail of all in my opinion is a Champagne Orange, which is merely one-third fresh orange juice and two-thirds chilled champagne. A pitcher of tomato juice and one of orange juice should also be on hand for morning teetotalers.

Brunch menus are supposed to be a combination of breakfast, which they reinforce, and luncheon, which they usually replace entirely, and it seems to me a mistake to turn the meal into an early light luncheon by serving a series of refined or spicy dishes that are too subtle or complicated for appetites that have just got out of bed. And so I prefer by far the straightforward, old-fashioned specialties of the hearty, traditional English breakfast, such as:

Smoked kippers
Finnan haddie
Creamed kidneys, chicken livers, mushrooms, or sweetbreads on toast
A very fine chicken hash
Grilled shad roe and bacon
Kedgeree (rice combined with lobster, cod, salmon, or other seafood, and minced hard-boiled eggs in a cream sauce)
A modified mixed grill with kidneys, lamb chops, sausages, bacon, tomatoes, and mushroom caps.

The larger the party, the greater the choice of dishes should be. As a general rule, I would suggest one "main dish," to be supplemented by one egg dish: creamed, scrambled, or in an omelette, or perhaps combined with bacon, ham, or even lobster or crabmeat in the form of a quiche.

If there is somebody to help in the kitchen, popovers or cornbread hot from the oven are always highly appreciated. In any case, you should offer as wide an assortment as you can muster of hot breads and rolls: coffee cake, Danish pastry, English muffins or scones, blueberry muffins, French brioche, and croissants, etc. (And by the way, breakfast or brunch is the only appropriate time to serve brioche and croissants, even though some fashionable American hostesses mistakenly serve them for luncheon and dinner, too.) In addition to these, you can set an electric toaster on the table or buffet and let each guest toast his own choice from a selection of white, whole wheat and wheat-germ bread, and Ry-Krisp.

A very simple do-it-yourself formula for a small group is to place a bowl of batter for waffles, pancakes, or the makings of French toast on the table or buffet along with the appropriate appliance, and let each guest be his own chef. He can then select the accompaniments from a platter of bacon, sausage, or ham, and an array of toppings, such as honey, maple syrup, cinnamon and sugar, brown sugar, apple butter, marmalade, and other fruit preserves. Three or four different kinds of jam, such as strawberry, raspberry, grape, and apricot, are not too many.

You will need to provide of course, a generous amount of fresh butter, a pitcher of coffee cream, a bowl of sugar, and a continually renewed supply of freshly made, steaming coffee and tea in unlimited quantity. It is also thoughtful to have a pitcher of iced water on the buffet and, if there are children present, a pitcher of cold milk or, in the winter, a pot of hot chocolate.

The principal difference between a British breakfast and a brunch is that the latter includes some kind of a dessert. It might be merely a fresh fruit cup, if the other dishes have been rather substantial, or it can be some kind of an unfrosted cake, such as an applesauce cake, gingerbread or an upside-down cake studded with fruit, all of them served with a bowl of freshly whipped cream; it might be an apple pie, a date-nut loaf, or—again for the special benefit of the children— a plate of homemade brownies.

Remember that it is better to prepare generous quantities of a few dishes than a wide assortment of dishes that quickly disappear except for that one last helping, which nobody dares to take. Latecomers should never have the feeling that they are eating leftovers or drinking dregs, and so you should try to keep the serving dishes filled as far as possible, and to brew fresh coffee and tea whenever necessary.

There is no need to plan any activity or entertainment for your guests at a Sunday-morning brunch party, for, replete with these delectable dishes that they seldom have the opportunity to taste on any other occasion, they will return to their usual Sunday occupations thoroughly satisfied.

But if you wish to retain them longer, and if you live in the country, for example, and possess a swimming pool, a badminton or tennis court, or the equipment for some simple and amusing outdoor game, you might suggest when you invite your guests that they bring their bathing suits, tennis racquets and sneakers, as the case may be. On a bracingly beautiful autumn day, you might suggest a walk in the country, or, if you live in the heart of the city, a stroll through the park and a visit to the zoo. If the weather outside is bleak but your living room is extremely comfortable and your guests consist of a few intimate friends, I can think of nothing cozier than to buy several copies of every available Sunday newspaper and invite your guests to settle down in front of a blazing fireplace with their favorite sections.

BUFFETS

〖 Few things exert so magnetic an attraction on a crowd as a well-garnished buffet table, and nowhere can one observe a more devastating caricature of ruthless rapacity than around a buffet laden with free food at a large official reception. In private homes, a certain sense of politeness restrains the guests from unbridled gluttony, but in official receptions they behave like a swarm of grasshoppers, making a rushing attack on the buffet, pushing and elbowing their way to the table, and then holding onto it firmly with one hand while the other is used to grasp everything edible within reach, until a new wave of starvelings manages to dislodge them and to take their place. It is a race against time with no holds barred, in which well-mannered people are beaten before they start, and the disdainful expression on the faces of the waiters at the other side of the table is always my secret delight.

My parents were very good friends of one of the former French presidents, Gaston Doumergue, and before the end of his term it was decided that, although I was only fifteen years old at the time, I would be given my first long dress and taken to the Elysée Palace for the annual diplomatic reception because it was something "everyone should experience at least once in a lifetime."

It was a very chic party and the guests included, it seems, many distinguished personages. Nevertheless, despite the presence of the papal nuncio, the British ambassador and a roster of excellencies, it was on that occasion that I first saw a group of supposedly well-bred people behaving like animals in a zoo at feeding time.

While I haven't the slightest recollection of the decor of the salons, I will remember as long as I live a certain petit four with shiny lavender icing that was given to me by an athletic young diplomatic attaché, who bravely captured it from the buffet after a dramatic struggle. He must have been touched by my youthful helplessness as I vainly attempted to make a breach in the barrier of coattails and bare backs that crowded around the refreshment table, leaving the center of the salons practically empty. That lavender petit four was, moreover, the only food I tasted all evening, and my parents, rather amused by my disappointing impression of society, had to take me to supper in a restaurant afterward.

It requires a budget as ample as that of the State Department or the chamber of commerce to provide a buffet with sufficient refreshments for three or four thousand guests. But if you should ever be called upon to organize this kind of a reception, take my advice and order twice as much food as you would for a party of your own, and above all, instruct the waiters to lay out the refreshments little by little and not all at once.

In other sections we will consider appropriate buffet menus for various kinds of parties, but the point to remember is this: never underestimate the irresistible attraction of free food.

(See Dinners)

BUSINESS

❡ The most confirmed misogynist recognizes that a wife can exert an enormous influence on her husband's career even in fields other than politics and diplomacy. Quite often in the business world a woman may be called upon to entertain her husband's employer, his customers, his competitors, and his colleagues, and there are certain nuances that should mark the manner in which she receives these different categories of business guests in her home.

Nothing could be simpler than entertaining your husband's boss intelligently. While your menu should be perfection and your welcome of the red-carpet variety, spiritually if not literally, you must never attempt to dazzle him with the sumptuousness of your hospitality, for his immediate reaction will be to wonder if your husband isn't highly overpaid! The food should be simple but of excellent quality and beautifully prepared. You should seek your husband's advice as to the exact composition of the menu, for he has probably attended business luncheons with his boss often enough to know the sorts of dishes he prefers. In any case, it is always preferable to serve a prime quality steak rather than imitation caviar, and a first-class beer rather than cheap champagne.

You can invite at the same time either relatives or friends whose social standing is equal or superior to that of your husband's boss. Your purpose is to point out subtly that your husband's present subordinate role in business is due solely to his youth, but that his excellent education and social position equip him to handle a much more important job on a moment's notice. This is one situation where I advise you to be rather snobbish in the choice of guests. It is essential to the success of the party that your guest of honor be the shining star, but he should shine for people he considers worth impressing. A dinner for eight people seems to me to be the ideal number in order for the conversation to remain general.

The boss's wife should be the object of your greatest personal attention, because it is likely that she exerts considerable influence on her husband. You should try to impress her with your efficiency as a homemaker. Remember that it is she and not her husband who will spot the spider web or the chipped china, and you can count on her eagle eye to detect the slightest imperfection—so be prepared. The best technique is to flatter her by asking her for her advice. Even if you have never been invited to her house, tell her you have heard that her home is simply beautiful, her cooking marvelous, her children brilliant, etc., etc. I do not know of a single instance where a well-phrased compliment of this kind has not accomplished miracles. You should at the same time scrupulously avoid making the slightest request of any kind on behalf of your husband, for this would immediately demote him to the role of a little boy under the protection of a solicitous mother. I realize that no normal woman thinks her husband is adequately appreciated until he has been elected president of the United States, but it is inadvisable to express your opinion in front of his employer. It is, on the other hand, very good politics to tell the boss's wife that you know how much her husband has done for yours and how grateful you feel toward him—even if there isn't a word of truth in it.

If it is a customer whom you have to entertain, you should try to arrange everything so that he leaves at the end of the evening in an utterly blissful mood. You must therefore take great pains over the menu and the drinks and devote yourself entirely to his comfort and pleasure. It is better not to invite anybody else—unless you have a very beautiful sister-in-law and your guest is noted for his appreciation of pretty women. I would even recommend that you concentrate on the customer while your husband turns his charm on the customer's wife. The most effective plan for entertaining an important client is to offer him two or three excellent cocktails, a succulent meal (prepared by a caterer or a hired cook if you are not absolutely confident of your own culinary talents) accompanied by a good wine, and afterward a relaxed interlude of digestion in the most comfortable armchair while you cleverly persuade him to tell you the story of his life, to which you listen with rapt attention. It is essential for him to feel intelligent and fascinating, and eventually perhaps to be inspired by the desire to please you—for example, by signing that order your husband has been trying to land!

If it is a competitor whom your husband wishes to entertain at home, it is quite appropriate to try to impress him a little, and you can very well include him in an elegant dinner party for twelve. You should, of course, be absolutely charming, but there is no point in pampering him as if he were a customer.

As for your husband's colleagues—simplicity is the rule. Anyway, you will have to resign yourself to making conversation with the wives because, like college fraternity brothers, business and professional colleagues have their secret language and their private jokes, and it is hopeless for you to try to understand them. You can be certain of one thing: the more successful the party has been in your husband's opinion, the more you will have found it boring.

(See Dinners)

CANAPES

❡ It would seem to be an easy matter to invent literally thousands of different kinds of original canapés, and yet it is almost always the same old familiar friends that greet you on the buffet tables of most cocktail parties.

Of course, the foundation of most canapés is the same: a small square of white, brown, or rye bread, plain or toasted, a pastry shell, or a salted cracker. Fillings and spreads that are based on mayonnaise, salad mixtures, mushrooms, sweet red pimentos, asparagus, and cucumbers are more presentable and above all easier to handle when they are served in the form of tiny sandwiches. Sandwiches are also simpler to prepare than the open-faced canapé, for all you have to do is to spread a spoonful of filling over one bread square, top it with another, and arrange the sandwiches attractively on a platter, garnished perhaps with watercress or parsley. Canapés take longer to spread and garnish, and they must be buttered first so that the garnish will adhere. The bread should have lost enough of its freshness so that it does not disintegrate into soft crumbs, and the butter must be removed from the refrigerator at least two hours ahead of time in order to be soft enough to spread.

There are countless ways of garnishing open canapés: with tomato slices and slices of hard-boiled eggs, hard-boiled eggs and ketchup, hard-boiled eggs and anchovies, chopped hard-boiled eggs with capers, tomato, and pickles. The color of a canapé is as important as its taste, but I am resolutely opposed to mayonnaise tinted pink, green, or mauve.

I also prefer slices of sausage, from which the skin has been removed, served as it is, rather than on rounds of bread. On the other hand, beef tongue is best on rye bread, and one of the most popular sandwiches in the world is, and I suppose always will be, lean ham on well-buttered white bread.

There is also an entire range of fish and seafood to explore, from caviar to creamed herring. I do not particularly care for the various imitations of caviar, which have only the color in common with the real thing. But red salmon caviar is delicious, especially when it is garnished with a thin slice of peeled lemon, or served on squares of black bread with a dab of sour cream. Smoked cod liver is very inexpensive and also very delicate in flavor, as are shad roe and smoked eel. Smoked salmon is exquisite, but of course much more costly. All of these garnishes are best on buttered toast, and because of their strong aroma they should be given a platter of their own and not be mixed together with other kinds of canapés.

All sorts of tricks can be played with cheese: from simple cubes of cheddar to a mixture of cream cheese and seasonings, such as shallots or onions, garlic, chives, and parsley, spread on toast squares or crackers. There are an infinite number of ways of presenting cheese snacks, including such hot preparations as baked cheese pastries and tarts, and miniature fried or grilled cheese sandwiches. Some particularly tasty combinations are walnuts with Roquefort cheese; cream cheese with paprika and curry powder; cream cheese with chopped black radish, topped with a tiny whole red radish; and there is also my personal favorite: pieces of celery an inch or two long, stuffed with a mixture of Roquefort or cream cheese, chives, garlic, and parsley.

You can also stuff tiny individual soft rolls with *crème de foie gras* (goose-liver paste), or with ham or Swiss cheese. These rolls will break the monotony of flat canapés because they can be arranged on platters in pyramids. But if you intend to spread out all of your refreshments on a buffet table, you should plan to have two trays of rolls, because symmetry is indispensable to the elegance of a buffet.

If you order all of your canapés for a large party from a caterer, be sure to ask him not to glaze everything with a film of aspic, for this is not at all chic. Among the best professional specialties, which are too complicated to make at home, are the tiny filled baked pastries we call *pains surprise,* and the variety I prefer is made of whole-wheat raisin bread and filled with a paste of walnuts and butter.

The best formula for a very large cocktail party is to order part of the canapés from a caterer and to make at home those that require the least time and effort to prepare, but the most originality to invent.

CANDLES

❨ Is anything more symbolic of gracious living than candles on a dining table? In addition to shedding the most flattering light in the world, they immediately create an elegant party mood. The simplest menu tastes more refined when served by candlelight, just as the plainest woman seems more beautiful. And so I cannot recommend too strongly to include candles in all of your dinner party decors (but never, of course, on a luncheon table).

The ultimate elegance would be to light the entrance hall and even the living room with real candles in lovely period wall appliqués, and thanks to the invention of dripless candles, this is no longer impractical and dangerous, although they still require a certain amount of supervision. While you will undoubtedly need to supplement their flickering flames with soft electric lighting as well, the effect is always magical.

The candles on the dining table will perhaps need to be supplemented by a minimum of electric lighting too, for your guests should always be able to see quite clearly what they are eating, not to mention each other—a principle that certain restaurants seem to ignore! With additional lighting, as few as two candlesticks on the table, one at each end, are sufficient to create a mood, while a single candlestick in the center of a small round table, such as the small tables set for a buffet dinner, makes a graceful centerpiece when it is adorned with a wreath of ivy and flowers.

A sense of harmony and proportion are the only sure guides as to the number and size of your dining table candlesticks, for there are no definite rules. However, the candles should never be so dense nor the candelabra so imposing that they form an impenetrable barrier down the center of the table and prevent the guests from looking across at the diners on the other side.

High candlesticks are undeniably the most elegant to the eye, but low candles are more modern in effect, and candles whose flame is at chin level shed a soft, shadowless light that is the most flattering to a woman's face. A hostess therefore has to choose, I suppose, between two different kinds of vanity.

Beautiful table candelabra are made in every imaginable material, but the most elegant are undoubtedly of antique silver, while the only kind that are quite horrible (and, thank heavens, seldom seen any more) are those that have been fitted with electricity and flame-shaped bulbs—even worse when each bulb is fitted with a tiny lampshade.

Candelabra of silver, bronze, porcelain, and crystal (which, in my opinion, are more suitable for a sideboard than a table when they are ornamented with crystal pendants) are of course more refined and elegant than those of wrought iron, glass, or pottery, but the latter kinds are very chic on a rustic country table, where the more formal style would be out of place.

Whatever their style, all of the candlesticks on a table should match. It is quite possible to place a different kind on the sideboard; for example, silver candlesticks on the table and a pair of crystal candelabra on the sideboard. But the candles themselves should all be of the same form and color.

Remember that a cheap, simple candlestick from Woolworth's can be almost completely concealed, and at any rate completely transformed, by arranging a wreath of flowers around the base and by twining ivy around the stems. Such an improvisation is much prettier and practically as cheap as sticking a candle in an empty jug or bottle and letting the wax run down, which was the fad among the Bohemians of the twenties but has been so overdone by Italian restaurants and arty nightclubs that today the idea is more banal than amusing, and in any case not at all elegant.

The height of your candles depends on the proportions of the candlesticks, and only an artistic eye can judge. Their color too depends upon the general table composition you have in mind, and today the range is amazingly wide, from plain white and cream (which are elegant in all circumstances) through the most subtle pastels and the brightest shades, to brown, navy blue, and black. These dark colors are particularly chic at the moment, and are much favored by antique dealers and decorators in displaying their eighteenth- and nineteenth-century treasures. It is unattractive to mix different shades of candles in the same room, except perhaps for some special Christmas decor. Certain Scandinavian table decorations are designed around a spray of multicolored candles, rather like a fireworks display, but while they are gay and modern they are also less practical and far less elegant than the classic styles. As a matter of fact, most fantasy candles lack chic, and these include the painted, sculpted, twisted kinds as well as those that have been treated with an exaggeratedly brilliant coating. The only occasion when gold candles are permissible is at a golden wedding anniversary party.

Personally, I prefer deep-colored candles, especially brown ones surrounding a centerpiece of autumn leaves and flowers, or black with a very formal table setting of silver, crystal, and lace. For informal dinners, I like to match the color of the candles to the border of the dishes, the embroidery of the tablecloth, or the color of the place mats. And since only brand-new candles should be used for a company dinner, I have a special drawer in the kitchen which I can easily reach even if I have to grope in the dark, and there I store all the bits of burned-down candles along with a box of matches in preparation for the stormy nights when the electricity invariably breaks down.

Another very good idea is to place on the coffee table or a convenient side table after dinner a single lighted candle from which smokers can light their cigarettes. A lighted candle is also supposed to absorb much of the smokiness in a room.

Before we leave the subject of candles, I must confess that I have never understood the vogue for candles tinted to imitate jade or quartz and molded in the shape of Buddhas, birds, and exotic dancing girls, which were a fashionable gift item of a few years ago. They may be amusing, but they are not chic, and they are not at all practical either. Do you know anybody who has ever had the courage actually to set a match to one of them and watch it melt? I cannot imagine what we are supposed to do with them, but of this I am sure: nothing is more ridiculous than to display them as if they were objets d'art.

(See Lighting)

CARDS

❡ Among the many popular card games that have been invented over the centuries, the most intelligent is undoubtedly bridge and the most exciting poker. These also seem to be the most widespread and enduring, and I suppose that they will still be played long after the world has forgotten such entertaining pastimes as gin rummy and canasta, not to mention the numerous variations that are invented almost as regularly as new ballroom dances.

Bridge and poker are such absorbing diversions to their devotees that they can provide the entertainment for an entire evening. In fact, many a dinner party has been merely a pretext for an afterdinner card game. For hard-bitten enthusiasts, the fun begins only when they are settled in their places around the card table, and the criterion of the success of a party is whether or not the cards ran well.

But not everybody shares the same passion. And so, when you intend to entertain bridge or canasta fanatics and you suspect that the evening is likely to end up around the card table, you should consider this likelihood when filling in the rest of your guest list. In general, the party will be more successful if everybody present plays, with the possible exception of the hostess. In any case, it is best to have no less than three leftover guests, since it would be difficult for a smaller number of nonplayers to sustain an animated and interesting conversation off in a corner by themselves.

Card playing annihilates conversation—or at least it should, if the rules of the game and of common courtesy are respected. It would therefore be thoughtless as well as a tactical error to herd your guests to a card table when the conversation is enthralling, or when your guest of honor is bursting to describe his point of view on the last elections or his recent trip to Moscow. Much as I love both bridge and good conversation, whenever I am faced with a situation where I must choose between the two, I unhesitatingly prefer the latter.

On the other hand, if you are entertaining a group of very close friends who see each other all the time and are so well informed as to each other's opinions and activities that they haven't very much to discuss (and what they usually end up discussing in these conditions are the peccadilloes of absent friends), a card game is a useful means of filling the interval between the time that dinner is over and the moment when they can decently go home. I suppose it is for this reason that card parties always played such an important part in the leisure hours of society in the Colonies, and still do at Army and Navy outposts, among foreign residents abroad, as well as in the restricted social circles found in provincial towns and on college campuses—in fact, in any very closed society that is somewhat isolated from the rest of the world by language, geography, tradition, or by choice.

Like all games, cards require a certain amount of equipment, and it should be in perfect condition: a stable, well-lit table (floor lamps are best), covered with a felt or plastic (less chic) cloth in order to prevent the cards from slipping about; scoring pads and pencils, plenty of ashtrays, and an ample supply of standard playing cards. Plastic-coated cards are by far the most practical. Beware of the beautiful imported kind, for the symbols and letters for the face cards may be entirely different and this can lead to needless, sometimes costly, errors. Be sure to put each deck away in its case every time the cards are used, checking them to make sure that none are missing. Old sets should be discarded as soon as they begin to look or feel the slightest bit soiled, for nothing is more disagreeable than to play with grimy cards. If you often have the occasion to organize impromptu bridge tournaments, you might also keep on hand in the game cupboard a few amusing, inexpensive gift items to be given away as prizes.

Needless to say, before attempting to organize a card game or to teach a new game to somebody else, you should be sure you know the rules. A game encyclopedia is a useful addition to the family reference library, and if you often play bridge at your home, a copy of the latest official contract bridge regulations is indispensable in order to avoid futile arguments.

Some of the simpler card games, such as rummy, hearts, and that old-fashioned favorite Russian bank, can be diverting pastimes on a rainy Sunday afternoon or after a quiet family dinner, if there is nothing interesting to watch on television. Then there are card tricks and fortune-telling with cards, both of which are infallible party entertainment, provided that they are performed with wit and skill and never twice for the same audience.

I recently attended a dismal dinner party, which was dying a slow and painful death until it was saved in extremis by one of the guests, who asked for a pack of cards after dinner and expertly performed a series of simple and amusing tricks. In this particular case, our hostess had made the mistake of inviting at the same time such a disparate group of guests, including several very shy and taciturn individuals, that it was impossible to spark an interesting conversation. Which brings us back to where we started: card games are mortal enemies to conversation, but when the conversation is already faltering or nonexistent, an exciting game of cards can fill the breach and save what might have been an unsuccessful evening.

(See Bridge, Conversation, Gambling)

CATERERS

⟪ Since the principal purpose of the catering profession is to take the work and worry out of entertaining, the process of hiring a caterer for a party, large or small, couldn't be simpler. All of the arrangements can be made over the telephone if you wish, and the only precautions the hostess must take are:

(1.) to select the very best caterer in town; and

(2.) to make her preparations sufficiently far in advance, which usually means at least one month ahead of time for a date during the height of the social season or the Christmas holidays.

In selecting the very best caterer, you will of course have to pay more than for the second best, but you will have the unwritten guarantee of a finer cuisine, more elegant equipment, and more stylish personnel—and you can even proudly leave the little stickers on the petit fours. (To tell the truth, when I order a single dish for a dinner party from a caterer, such as a *jambon en croute* or a *chaud-froid de vollaille,* I always prefer to transfer it to one of my own serving dishes whenever possible, no matter how great the prestige of the caterer's trade-mark on the platter.)

Once you have established a relationship with a good caterer, it is in your interest to remain faithful to him, and even to request the same waiters or waitresses who have already given you satisfaction. And incidentally, the personnel is always grateful for a small tip in addition to their wages, which are normally included in the caterer's bill.

Hiring a catering service for a party offers a considerable saving in time and headaches for a hostess, but it is very extravagant financially. While it is indispensable to have a professional caterer organize a very large reception, the best formula for smaller parties, in my experience, is to combine your efforts with his—that is, to order from a caterer a certain number of dishes (and perhaps the necessary help), and to prepare the rest in your own kitchen.

You should prepare the simple dishes yourself and have the caterer's chef make the more complicated recipes and the difficult sauces. For example, a typical half-and-half menu might be

Seafood Newburg in a Large Pastry Shell
(from the caterer)

A Baked Ham, Roast Beef, Roast Turkey, or Cornish Hens
(baked in your own oven)

Salad (homemade)

Cheese Tray

A fancy Ice Cream Dessert
(from the caterer)

As you see, there is only one dish you have to cook yourself: the roast.

This half-and-half method is much less than half as expensive as a one-hundred percent catered party, and it is also much more personal. When you do not require a full range of catering services, you can even order one or two dishes from a restaurant whose chef prepares a particularly delicious specialty, or from a "little woman" who has perfected a limited list of excellent homemade dishes.

In short, there is no way of getting around the fact that a good caterer is expensive. However, it is almost always possible to alleviate the banality of catered cuisine by taking the time to discuss your requirements in detail and to compose a menu that is a little bit out of the ordinary.

(See Cocktail Parties, Dinners, Help, Luncheons, Menus)

CELEBRITIES

❆ A more common, less enduring species than VIPs, celebrities owe their fame to practically anything, and not necessarily to personal accomplishment. Their glory is apt to be of the ephemeral kind, sometimes lasting no more than a single season. They blossom rapidly in the warmth of publicity (more often solicited than spontaneous), but they may fade just as quickly when the spotlight sweeps on to illuminate newer faces and more newsworthy names. Thus there are fashions in celebrities. A celebrity who is the rage one day may be almost forgotten the next.

Earl Blackwell, the founder of an organization called "Celebrity Service," which keeps track of the comings and goings of these highly migratory creatures, defines a celebrity as a person whose name is so well known that he needs no further identification. If this is so, it is clear that celebrity is limited in time as well as in geography. For example, the name "Liz" in a newspaper headline not so many years ago referred to the future Queen of England, but today nobody would fail to recognize Elizabeth Taylor. "Wilson" at the moment is the British prime minister, but only a few months ago any loyal British subject would have said he was England's leading tennis player, while in the United States everyone knows that Wilson was a peace-loving former president, except for a brief recent period when a Wilson was president of General Motors and then secretary of defense. Yves, on the Paris boulevards naturally means Yves Montand, but on the Faubourg St. Honoré it is Yves St. Laurent. And what about Nelson (Rockefeller or Eddy?), Margaret (Truman or Princess?), Hubert (Humphrey or Givenchy?), Elsa (the African lioness or the social lion huntress?), Grace (Vanderbilt, Moore or Kelly—it all depends on the generation to which you belong!).

It has always been considered a coup for a hostess to snag a fashionable celebrity for a party, and perhaps more so today than ever before. There is no doubt that most people are delighted to find themselves face to face with a person whose photograph they have seen in every magazine and whose name they have read in the newspapers, although they may have absolutely nothing in common and very little to say. Even the very serious governor of the Bank of France enjoyed himself immensely when he was the dinner partner of Brigitte Bardot. But usually, it seems to me, it is better to invite celebrities to a large cocktail party, a buffet dinner, or a dance, where they will be able to satisfy the curiosity of a maximum number of guests without being expected to be interesting, intelligent, and congenial as well.

There is a definite technique for wangling acceptances to your invitations from celebrities, and some hostesses, among whom the late Elsa Maxwell was the undisputed queen, are virtuosos in the art. The strategy consists of using one celebrity as bait to hook another, and the art is in knowing the psychology of your celebrities so well that you select a bait they find it impossible to resist. For example, a hostess might tell Audrey Hepburn that Van Cliburn is coming to dinner and that his dream is to meet the celebrated film star in the flesh. Then she would tell Van Cliburn that Audrey Hepburn is coming to dinner, and that the dream of her life is to meet him in person. I suppose this kind of subterfuge fails more often than it succeeds, and this is not at all intended as a recommendation, but merely as a recognition that such methods do exist—and are, in fact, rather widely practiced in certain circles.

Celebrities do not necessarily call for any special protocol, as with the VIPs. In fact, this would in some cases be slightly ridiculous. But remember that their kind of fame is often a fleeting thing, and it is thoughtful to accord them a certain amount of deference, attention, and flattery, for this is sometimes the only compensation they receive in exchange for the sacrifice of their private lives.

(See VIPs)

CEREMONIES

(Much of the appeal of ceremonial occasions is due to the traditions that are observed and perpetuated, and that is why it is always desirable for tradition to be rigorously respected at such ceremonies as christenings, weddings, funerals, etc. At the same time, however, our contemporary attitudes are more informal as well as more discreet than in former days when expressions of joy and grief were unrestrained. And so, if you ever have to organize or play a leading role in a ceremonial occasion and wish to carry it off with elegance, the first thing to do is to inform yourself as to the exact conventions to be respected, either by consulting an excellent book of etiquette or by seeking the advice of an experienced and authoritative person. Then, when you are perfectly briefed for the event, appropriately clad, confident and relaxed, you should try to play your part with a maximum of dignity, but with a minimum of stiffness and solemnity.

(See Christenings, Funerals, Weddings)

CHAIRS

(A cocktail party is the only form of entertaining for which it is unnecessary (and usually impossible) to provide as many chairs as there are guests. On many occasions, a hostess even has to provide two places for each of her guests to sit down: one at the dining table, and another in the living room. During a large dinner party, it is quite possible to serve the before-dinner cocktails in the living room or den in stand-up, cocktail-party style, but after the meal is over the necessary number of seating places should be available in the salon, even if it means transporting extra chairs from the dining room.

Supplementary chairs can always be rented for an evening when you are receiving a large number of guests. But if you entertain a great deal, it is more practical to invest in a set of four, six, or eight folding chairs. There are many attractive models to choose from nowadays, with comfortable upholstered seats and styling details that harmonize with every kind of interior decoration. When you are making a permanent acquisition, it is wise to measure the height of your dining room table to make sure that the chairs are suitable, to select a sturdy model with a seat large and broad enough for solidly built masculine guests, and to choose for upholstery a classic color and material, such as red or black leather, which can be attractively integrated into any room in the house. If, when you buy a bridge-table set, you select a model with a certain luxury and style, the matching chairs can do double duty in the dining room in an emergency.

If you haven't enough dining room chairs of the same kind for all of your guests and must mix two or more different styles, it is better to alternate them rather than bunching each type at different ends of the table. And do not worry too much about the mixture. Most of your guests will never notice.

Very few folding chairs are equally suitable for indoor and outdoor use, and if you do a great deal of patio entertaining, it would be advisable also to invest in a set of folding canvas deck chairs, Hollywood-director style, which take up very little storage room. A clever friend of mine has adapted this folding X-model for indoor use in her English-style interior by staining the wooden frames a dark mahogany shade and covering the seat and back with black leatherette, affixed by rows of gilt-headed upholsterer's nails. The effect is refined and charming, and the idea might be worth copying if you are handy with a hammer.

The modern penchant for comfort and the current fashion for short skirts are seldom compatible. And so, if your easy chairs and sofa are ultrasoft and extra-deep, it is considerate to provide plenty of small, firm cushions in order to preserve the modesty and posture of your women guests.

(See Dining Rooms, Seating)

CHARITY

(Never before within my memory has there been so much entertaining for charity, perhaps because humanity has never before been so aware of the sufferings and needs of others, and because there have never before been so many worthy causes to which to contribute time and money. Modern charity is organized and practiced on such a large scale, more often than not extending even beyond national boundaries, that a private hostess would no longer be expected to organize and produce a charity function all by herself. These worthwhile projects have been expanded beyond the possibilities of a single organization in many cases, and they are conceived and realized by a federation of different associations with long lists of committees that fill entire columns in the society pages of the newspaper. By pooling the ideas of amateur and professional volunteers, American women are forever inventing more ingenious and appealing ways of raising charity funds through entertaining, far more original than the time-honored (and still effective) charity bazaar and bridge party. How irresistible is the idea of your kitchen and garden tours! And how profitable, it seems, the one-hundred-dollar-a-ticket ball, the theater or film preview, art exhibits, hobby shows, barbecues and sporting events that are organized for charitable purposes.

Since a woman is practically never called upon to shoulder the responsibility of entertaining for charity as an individual hostess, my only word of advice is this: Whenever you invite friends to a philanthropic social occasion, you should specify very clearly in your invitations that it is a charity event, so that should there be a collection of money during the course of the evening, your guests will be prepared for it.

CHEESE

◀[Cheese is one of the most varied, most nourishing, most healthful, and most useful foods there is, equally appetizing in a sandwich, on a cocktail canapé, on a cheese tray, and in a thousand cooking recipes. It can be served at almost any time of day from early morning (as in Holland, where it is traditional to place a generous slice of Gouda or Edam on the morning breakfast tray), until after midnight (as in America, where cheese and crackers are one of the most popular midnight snacks).

Most of the American cheeses are reproductions or adaptations of European types, but there are many strictly original inventions as well, often based on the addition of supplementary ingredients, such as pimento, chopped ham, olives, bacon, hickory-smoked flavoring, etc., in order to create new and appetizing spreads. American cheeses are sold in every supermarket, but it is also possible to buy imported cheese in foreign or fancy grocery stores in many parts of the country. So-called "processed cheeses" cannot be considered a satisfactory substitute for the real thing, although they are useful as sandwich fillings and spreads.

All natural cheeses fall into one of several different categories:

Fresh, unfermented cheese, such as cream cheese, cottage cheese, and yogurt. These are the least rich in fat, the most easily digested— and the most insipid, unless they have been flavored with herbs or sweetened with sugar or honey.

Fermented cheese, which may be *soft* like Brie, Camembert, Pont l'Evêque, or the pungent Münster (which is traditionally served enrobed in caraway seeds). These are the most delicate cheeses to store, for they attain a point of perfect ripeness after which they begin to acquire an unpleasant sharp tang. They also become runny and spoil quickly once they have been cut open.

— or it may be *pressed,* like Cantal, Reblochon, Edam, Gouda, Stilton, Cheshire, and Cheddar—all solid, flavorful cheeses that keep very well.

—or it may be *cooked*, like such Swiss cheeses as Gruyère, Emmentaler, Comté, etc., and also Parmesan.

Roquefort cheese is in a class by itself, since it is made from ewe's milk, whereas blue cheese and Gorgonzola, which are also streaked with a mold called "penicillium," are made from a blend of milks. All of them are slightly sharp and extremely tasty, but Roquefort is the richest. In fact, it is perhaps the most aristocratic if not the most expensive of all cheeses, and it is therefore highly impressive to serve an entire twelve-inch cylinder of Roquefort cheese at a buffet dinner.

Goat cheese may be soft or hard, depending upon the variety and the season. It keeps for a very long time, becoming as hard as a rock as it dries out and this is how some gourmets prefer it. Chabichou and Chavignol are two of the best-known French varieties, but goat cheese is also produced in considerable quantities in the Scandinavian countries, and these usually possess a rich, nutty flavor.

Considering that France alone produces over a hundred different kinds of cheese, and that the Dutch, Danes, and Italians are prolific and imaginative masters in this field, a hostess should have no difficulty in composing an appetizing assorted cheese tray for a party. In order to offer a fair choice, it is best to select a type of cheese from three or four different general categories, rather than to present at the same time, for example, Cheddar and Edam, or Brie and Camembert, which are similar in type. (There is, incidentally, a special point of etiquette concerning cheese such as Brie, which is served in pie-shaped wedges: you should always serve yourself by cutting along the long edge, and you must never take the entire point. To do so would be considered very ill-mannered in France, at least, for this is the choicest part.) All cheeses should be taken out of the refrigerator half an hour before serving, and all of them—with the exception of Roquefort and blue cheese—should be removed from their boxes or wrappings.

A separate cheese course is a simple means of adding a company touch to an ordinary dinner, when you have to entertain unexpected guests. It is also the ideal moment to serve a fine rich red wine. Aside from the gastronomic pleasure of wine and cheese, the tannin in the wine combined with the albuminous elements in the cheese is said to produce an excellent digestive effect.

When there is a cheese course, you really do not need an elaborate dessert as well, and you can simply pass a bowl of fresh fruit or a bowl of berries. If you have opened a choice bottle of wine for the occasion, you might add some fresh nuts to the fruit bowl, for, like cheese, nuts are highly appreciated by connoisseurs as an accompaniment to fine wine. The supreme refinement would be to serve a wine from the same region as the cheese, for example a rich Rhône wine to accompany Roquefort. Other classic wines to serve with a cheese course are Nuits-Saint-George (a Burgundy), Pomerol or Saint-Emilion (from Bordeaux), Côte Rôtie and Châteauneuf-du-Pape (Côtes du Rhône) and Chinon (from the Loire Valley). However, with Stilton cheese, no British hostess would dream of serving anything other than a glass of old port.

Cheese is a precious ally in entertaining from the beginning of the evening when cocktails are served until after the guests have gone home and the hostess can at last relax with her husband over a snack of cheese and crackers and discuss the events of the evening.

For example, cheese can make an appearance with

Cocktails

Cheese spreads and dips and stuffings (for pieces of celery, cucumber, tiny tomatoes, etc.) are popular cocktail accompaniments and they can be endlessly varied by the addition of herbs and flavorings. The Danes make a spread out of their delicious blue cheese by mashing it to the desired consistency with butter and rum.

Soup

A bowl of grated Swiss cheese and a plate of croutons are an essential accompaniment to French onion soup, as well as to Mediterranean fish soup and bouillabaisse. But grated Swiss or Parmesan cheese also add flavor and consistency to many other kinds of soup, including tomato, chicken, vegetable and Italian minestrone.

Entrées

A cheese soufflé is always a marvelous dinner entrée, although it is risky to serve it at a dinner party since it will fall if it has to wait for latecomers. It is also a very refined main dish for a light luncheon.

The same is true of quiche Lorraine, a delicious cheese custard pie with bits of bacon or ham. (As a luncheon main dish, however, I prefer it when the bacon or ham is replaced by lobster or crab.)

An authentic Welsh rarebit (Cheddar or Cheshire cheese melted with beer, without a pinch of flour but with a good dash of Worcestershire sauce), although most often served as a supper dish, is also an original entrée for dinner or luncheon. Then there are cheese puffs (unsweetened cream puffs filled with Béchamel sauce and heated in the oven), *crêpes au fromage* (thin pancakes filled with Béchamel and gratinéed with cheese) and a very simple French favorite called *croûte au fromage,* for which you simply spread half a slice of bread with a very thick cheese sauce and deep fry it. Both quick and simple to prepare is the dependable standby, cheese omelette, made with Gruyère, Parmesan or Cheddar, or a combination.

Main Courses

Cheese combines perfectly with eggs, fish, and shellfish, and with many meats aside from hamburger, in particular with ham and veal. A good way to stretch a roast of veal when there is unexpected company is to remove the meat from the oven fifteen or twenty minutes before it is done and to slice it evenly, but without cutting the slices all the way through. Between each slice you then place a thin slice of Gruyère cheese, a thin slice of ham, and a spoonful of thick cream or cream sauce. The roast is then tied together in its original shape with string (which will be removed later) and returned to the oven to complete its cooking.

It is even possible to compose a main dish entirely of cheese by serving a Swiss fondue. This is a dish of melted Gruyère cheese and dry white wine, which is amusing for an informal party and is much in vogue in Paris at the moment. The fondue is prepared and served in a copper chafing dish that is placed in the center of the table and in which all of the guests dip cubes of toast or bread speared on a fork. There are many excellent recipes for fondue, since each Swiss province has its own special version. But one of the best I ever tasted was served at a Paris restaurant called Androuet, where the entire menu is composed of nothing but cheese dishes. (I hasten to add that in normal practice, two appearances of cheese during a meal are ample: once in a cooked dish, and once in its natural state.)

Vegetables

Potatoes, pasta, and most vegetables, such as string beans, cauliflower, asparagus, celery, broccoli, spinach, tomatoes, etc., are considerably dressed up when they are served au gratin, by stirring into them a cheese-flavored white sauce and topping it off with grated cheese, bread crumbs, and dots of butter; the dish is then placed in the oven until the cheese has melted and browned. These au gratin recipes have an added advantage: they can be prepared in advance, even in the morning, for the dish can be placed in a hot oven to warm and *gratiner* about twenty minutes before it is to be served. In all of these preparations, as well as in a cheese soufflé for that matter, a combination of one-third grated Parmesan cheese to two-thirds grated Swiss Gruyère produces the most delectable results.

Salads

Roquefort, blue, and Swiss cheese combine the most successfully with salads: the first two mixed in a salad dressing or crumbled over a tossed green salad, and the last cut into slivers to be mixed with slivered chicken, tongue, ham and celery in a chef's salad; with sliced Belgian endive and sliced radishes in a crisp and refreshing spring salad, etc. In France, a cheese tray is never passed at the same time as the salad, which normally accompanies the meat course. However, the combination of salad and cheese is apparently popular in America, and I have nothing against it. But you should know that the only kinds of cheese suitable for serving at the same time and on the same plate as a salad are Roquefort and blue cheese—never, never, Camembert or Brie.

Cheese Course

When cheese is served as a separate course, as is always the case during a French dinner party, it should follow the main course and salad and precede the dessert.

A separate cheese course may consist either of (1.) a single perfect cheese, such as a choice Camembert at the point of ripeness, its white coating gently scraped with a knife, then covered all over with fine breadcrumbs and surrounded by curls of butter; Münster cheese can also stand alone, accompanied by a dish of caraway seeds or red-currant jelly (the latter combination is not at all French either, but I find it very tasty). A single cheese, unless it is a very large one, is of course suitable only for an intimate party or—(2.) you can compose an attractive assortment of cheeses, preferably presented on a wooden tray along with a slab of butter or decorated with butter curls. French bread is a fine accompaniment to cheese, but if this is unobtainable, crusty dinner rolls will do, along with an assortment of crackers and biscuits. (You can attenuate the rather stale taste by heating them in the oven for a few minutes.) Crisp celery sticks and leaves of endive presented in a goblet are also appetizing and original accompaniments to cheese.

Some good combinations on a cheese tray are Camembert, Roquefort, and a baby Gouda; six or seven different kinds of goat cheese (this is a specialty of Burgundy restaurants); a cream cheese in a thick coating of paprika, a slab of Emmentaler, and one of Gorgonzola. With only two cheeses, one should be soft and the other dry, for example: Camembert and Gruyère; Pont l'Evêque and Cheddar; Port Salut and Brie. The possibilities are endless (and for more ideas, *see* Dinners).

Dessert

Some delicious sweet pastries are made with cream or cottage cheese. Many of these recipes originated in Hungary and Austria, and the best, in my opinion, is cheesecake. Another very simple dessert whose tastiness depends upon the perfect quality of the different elements is simply toasted crackers, cream cheese, and guava or currant jelly. I do not think that our Fontainebleau cheese is exported to the United States, but you might be able to create an imitation of this rich but light delicacy by mixing together cream cheese and whipped fresh or sour cream. Then you can serve it as we do, in one large mold or several individual ones, surrounded by fresh strawberries or with hot chocolate sauce.

My mother used to make a very simple cream cheese dessert that she called *crème Suisse*. It was made by mixing into a smooth thick paste the necessary amount of cream cheese, some very heavy whipping cream, and an egg yolk. Then the egg white, whipped very stiff, was stirred into the cheese mixture, and sugar was added to taste along with a small liqueur glass of Kirsch. This delicate dessert must be chilled in dessert goblets in the refrigerator until serving time.

After Dinner

It is a British tradition to serve a "savory" course at the end of a dinner, and this is often a Welsh rarebit, a highly seasoned cheese tart, or simply cheese and crackers. Need I add that this custom is rather disputable, gastronomically speaking—at any rate, it has not to my knowledge been adapted by any other country.

Bits and pieces of leftover cheese can be incorporated in your cooking recipes in countless different ways. But it would not be elegant to serve a piece of cheese that has already been cut into to your dinner guests. You can, however, perfectly well finish the remains at a family meal, if you have taken the precaution of wrapping each piece of cheese in waxed paper or replacing it in the original box, and storing it in a cool place. Swiss-type cheeses will keep for as long as a month if they are wrapped first in waxed paper, then in a damp towel and placed in the vegetable compartment of the refrigerator. Grated cheese will also keep for a month or more in a covered jar in the refrigerator—but I hesitate to mention this because freshly grated cheese has twice as much flavor as the prepared kind, and it is well worthwhile to take the trouble of grating it at the very last minute.

(See Dinners, Menus)

CHILDREN

❡ In Margaret Mitchell's Civil War novel, *Gone with the Wind*, Scarlett O'Hara flew into a rage when she learned that she was going to have a baby, because it meant that she could not go to any parties during the next nine months—and there was, of course, no question of her giving a party herself. How times have changed! Nowadays, fashions for expectant mothers are so cleverly designed that in many cases their condition does not become visible until a few weeks before the baby is born. Moreover, modern prenatal medical care has eliminated much of the malaise experienced during this period. As a result, it is quite usual for pregnant women to go to parties as long as they feel like it, and as long as their appearance does not inspire alarm. Neither is there any reason why they should not entertain in return, if they wish. However, most often their personal inclinations coincide with their obstetrician's advice in this regard, and they restrict their receptions during the last few months to quiet informal dinners with a very few close friends, planning a simple menu that is easy to prepare, an entertainment confined to bridge or conversation, and an early bedtime.

The first two or three months after the birth of a baby is not the ideal moment for elaborate entertaining either, and the new mother's social program is preferably limited to receiving afternoon visitors until her recuperation is complete. There is also the problem of reorganizing her household in view of the enlargement of her family, and until the adjustment has been made, it is best to avoid entertaining at home on a large scale. If your husband is obliged to invite an important customer to dinner, for example, it is advisable to take him out to dine in a restaurant and perhaps to the theater afterward, if you have a nurse for the baby or have managed to find a baby-sitter who is willing to stay until midnight.

Everybody will ask to see the new baby, but the proud mother should realize that this is seldom more than a rite of etiquette, as are the inevitable gushing compliments. Her role in these tribal ceremonies is simply to present her baby, well scrubbed and preferably half asleep, to her visitors and to take him back to his crib as soon as possible.

As a matter of fact, the social life of a child during his first few years should be restricted to brief, ceremonial appearances of this kind. You may permit him to visit a little longer with members of the family and very close friends, but even then it is best to avoid putting too much of a strain on the patience of either the adults or the child.

The advisability of formal entertaining during this period is an individual matter, depending mostly on the size of your home and on the servant situation. If you possess a large house or apartment, with the nursery beyond earshot of the reception rooms, and if you have a baby nurse in whom you have complete confidence, there is no reason why you should not entertain as you always have. But if you have neither help nor space, it is advisable to be patient a little longer and to receive only close friends and members of the family at informal small dinners, until you can put your child to bed before the guests arrive without the slightest risk of his awakening during the evening and clamoring for attention. Nothing is less compatible with the atmosphere of an elegant dinner party than a sudden outburst of cries or hiccups from the other end of the apartment, and the anguished expression of the hostess who frantically struggles with her impossible dilemma: Would it be better to rush to the side of her child and risk spoiling the dinner, or to complete her sauce or finish serving the soup while the screams echoing down the hallway completely ruin the elegant mood she has tried so hard to create? This particular period may very well be especially happy and carefree for lucky women with plenty of help and space and money. But it is rather awkward for the young bride on a budget, living in a tiny apartment, whose only assistance is the voluntary baby-sitting of her mother-in-law, and whose child tends to be turbulent, like his father. The only thing to do under these conditions is to be patient for a little longer, to retain your good humor, and above all to avoid undertaking ambitious entertaining projects.

Modern children make their social debuts in the role of host or hostess *at the age of three or four,* and the ideal occasion for a child's first party is his birthday. You should send out the invitation two weeks in advance, inviting up to twelve little boys and girls from three o'clock until five, for example, in the afternoon. The entertainment will present no problem, for every child will bring a gift, and all of them will soon be completely absorbed in playing with the windfall of new toys. You might also organize a few very simple games, such as musical chairs. But generally children of this age amuse themselves simply by playing together, and the principal role of the hostess and the other mothers present is to separate squabblers, to calm criers, to escort the infants to the bathroom when necessary, and to distribute the refreshments. Incidentally, if none of the other mothers can stay throughout the party, be sure to enlist the aid of a sister, brother, friend, or your baby's nurse; in no case should you attempt to supervise the party all alone.

The best menu is also the simplest: sandwiches, ice cream, and a birthday cake; and the ideal way to serve it is at a table gaily decorated with a paper or plastic tablecloth, paper plates, cups, napkins, and a small favor for every child. After "Happy Birthday" has been sung, the candles blown out, and the cake devoured, it should be time for the children to go home. This is a perfect opportunity for the mothers present to give their children their first lesson in the etiquette of hosts and guests, by guiding the farewells just as they guided the greetings at the beginning of the party. It may amaze you to see how natural to most children is hospitality on the part of the host and courtesy on the part of guests. But do not forget to compliment your child on his good behavior.

With children who are a little older, for example, *six or seven years old,* you can plan a longer party of about three hours, with more guests (between twelve and thirty is the best number), and many more organized games. These should still be rather simple, such as "Pin the Tail on the Donkey," and that sort of thing. Some of them may also be more highly competitive, such as a potato race or an egg and spoon race, and there should be a great number of prizes so that every guest wins something, even if you have to invent some special awards. The mother of the host child will still need to be aided by a few of the other mothers. It would seem to me that there should be at least one adult for every six or eight children in order to keep everything under perfect control.

The menu should remain simple, but it may be more copious: sandwiches (or perhaps hot dogs and hamburgers), ice cream (with the makings of all kinds of sundaes, which each child concocts himself), cookies and cake, and plenty of orangeade and soft drinks. Children of this age adore to do things for themselves—for example, to scoop their own ice cream into a cone, as they have watched it done for them at the corner drugstore.

It would be an excellent idea to supplement the organized games with a rather brief prepared entertainment. All children love magicians, puppet shows, clowns, trained animals, an organ grinder with a monkey, etc., and the services of these performers are readily available in many large cities. There are even professional children's party organizers in many areas, and you might consider availing yourself of their experience and skill when you wish to give a very large children's party, or if you are not particularly successful in dealing with children yourself. Before the advent of television, the classic children's party entertainment was Laurel and Hardy or Walt Disney films, but these have become the daily fare in so many modern nurseries that movies are no longer considered a special treat by the increasingly sophisticated younger generation.

In general, it is easier and more fun to entertain a large group of children of this age out of doors on a warm summer afternoon than in a crowded living room, which furthermore is not always adaptable to the small scale and the destructive tendencies of little boys and girls. If you do not have a rather large playroom in your home, I would therefore recommend warm weather outdoor entertaining whenever there is a sizable group, until the children are older. Besides, there is a practically unlimited choice of outdoor entertainment and games. One that requires a great deal of preparation but is always highly appreciated is a treasure hunt. Another irresistible attraction is a rented pony for pony rides. Or perhaps you can hire the services for the afternoon of a real cowboy who will fascinate the little boys if he teaches them a few simple rope tricks.

As a matter of fact, as children reach *the ages of seven or eight*, a definite divergence of interests between the boys and girls begins to appear. The boys are passionately interested in cowboys and Indians, cops and robbers, guns, cars, trucks, and airplanes—and they consider little girls terribly boring. The girls, on the other hand, are engrossed in all of the feminine pursuits: dolls, housekeeping, cooking, playing house, clothes, and dressing up. It is therefore a good idea to separate the sexes for small parties, and to let your eight-year-old daughter, for example, invite four or five friends to a fudge-making party, while for your eight-year-old son and his playmates you would prepare more masculine diversions, such as the cowboy demonstration, or a series of playground-type team games with lots of prizes.

If, however, you invite a large number of guests, it is preferable to mix the boys with the girls. You should even attempt to get them to make new friends by introducing every child to every other if possible, and by forming groups and teams that you change for each new game. For this reason, games are perhaps better than audience entertainment at this stage, with the exception of certain children's entertainment performed by professionals who understand the importance of encouraging audience participation. A costume party, or a party with a theme, such as Washington's Birthday, or Columbus Day, is also an excellent idea, for children of this age adore to dress up and the costumes alone will lend an air of fete to the occasion and add novelty to the most familiar games.

In the event of bad weather, you should always be prepared to move an outdoor party inside the house, and to subsitute for the outdoor games a less athletic kind. Card games employing illustrated cards of authors, animals, flowers, etc., which must be matched or collected in sets, are very popular with this age group, perhaps because the children feel very grown-up to be playing with cards just like their parents.

Do not try to be original, particularly where the refreshments are concerned. Incidentally, with these slightly older children, when you plan energetic outdoor games, you should prepare a considerably greater quantity of food and soft drinks. Perhaps the best plan is to offer each child a snack the moment he arrives, and to serve the sit-down refreshments after the play period, during which they are sure to develop ravenous appetites.

Children *between the ages of ten and twelve* will enjoy more intellectual competitive games, including written ones, such as the memory game, in which you prepare in advance a tray of objects that they are permitted to examine for one minute and then try to list as many as possible in a written inventory, or the smelling game, in which they sniff the contents of fifteen or twenty tiny bottles and try to identify the aroma as cinnamon, onion, ammonia, banana, carnation, etc. Educational toy shops are full of amusing games for children of all ages, and it is an excellent idea to keep a special cupboard filled with games and the prizes to go with them, even if you have no children of your own. You will be surprised how often it will come in handy.

There are a few general rules that apply to all kinds of children's parties:

—Always keep the family pets shut up in their pens or in a separate room during a children's party—as much in the interest of the pets as for the safety of the children!

—Always prepare more entertainment than you think is necessary, so that you can change to another game if the one you first select does not enchant them.

—Always give lots of prizes on the slightest pretext.

—Keep the refreshments simple to serve and to eat, but copious in quantity; use disposable paper equipment and decorations, and give the children a choice of foods. Do not try to plan a refined or highly original buffet. Most children want their parties to be just like all the other children's parties, and if there are any local fads or customs in your region, you should try to respect them.

—Always remove everything fragile and dangerous from the room in which the party is to be held, and particularly matches and cigarette lighters—or, if possible, make it an outdoor lawn party.

— Do not overtire young children by allowing the party to last too long. And do not exhaust them with a program that is overorganized. Remember, the purpose of all parties is to provide an opportunity for social intercourse, and if you keep the guests too busy solving riddles and running races, they will never have a chance to make new friends.

— Do not feel that it is your duty to plan a brilliant social life for your young children, no matter how sociable they seem to be. Organizing a successful children's party involves an enormous amount of work, and no mother is expected to give more than one per child a year.

— Remember that while a party should first of all be fun, it is also an opportunity to teach your children the good manners and rites of hospitality that will be important to them throughout their lives. The better the foundation you establish, the greater their poise and self-assurance will be when they reach the age of twelve or thirteen and are no longer considered children, but teen-agers—and present you with a whole new set of problems!

Finally, until they have reached the stage where their good behavior is dependable and their conversation fairly interesting, you should not impose your children on your adult guests except on special occasions and with very close friends. At the same time, it is a charming custom to present your children to your guests at the beginning of an informal evening, on condition that the children are dismissed after ten minutes or when they start to forget their manners— whichever comes first!

(See Birthdays, Teen-agers)

CHRISTENINGS

❮ A christening luncheon is a rather intimate kind of luncheon party, because it is usually limited to members of the immediate family of the christened child, the godparents, a few very close friends, perhaps the godparents of the other children in the family, and possibly the officiating minister, if he is also a friend of the family.

Despite the relative solemnity of the religious ceremony, a christening is a joyful, rather tender occasion. It is therefore nice to prepare a particularly attractive and delicate table decoration all in white, or in white with pale blue or pink, and to plan a menu that is refined without being unduly pretentious. For example:

Lobster Mayonnaise
(one small cold lobster per person)

Roast Turkey with Chestnut Dressing
(in the winter)

OR

Roast Leg of Lamb
Surrounded by an Assortment of Fresh Vegetables
(spring and summer)

Salad

Cheese

The Christening Cake

Champagne—and a carafe of red wine for the cheese

The traditional dessert is always a white cake with white frosting on which the baby's name is written in pastel icing. The British custom used to be for a bride to save the top layer of her wedding cake to serve at the christening luncheon of her first child. But while this appealing idea may be acceptable in a land where Christmas cakes are baked on the first of October, I am afraid it would have less success in countries, such as France and the United States, where we are fanatic about freshness in our food.

Unless a member of the clergy is present, the guests of honor on this occasion are the godparents, whose number varies. It is nowadays most usual to have one godmother and one godfather, but quite often there are two, and some royal babies, such as Prince Charles of England, have no less than four of each!

If the christening takes place in the early afternoon instead of at the end of the morning, the parents should give a tea party instead of a luncheon, with sandwiches, petit fours, and the same white christening cake. In addition to tea, there should be champagne for drinking a toast to the newly christened infant—who by this time, I hope, is soundly asleep in his crib.

(See Ceremonies, Luncheons, Tea)

CLOSETS

⟨ Modern architects seem to have recognized at last the importance of closets in a home, and the majority of recently constructed houses and apartments are provided with built-in closets in every bedroom and one for coats adjoining the front hall. But even the cleverest architect cannot perform miracles, and often, due to the restricted dimensions of modern buildings (or, to pin down the cause at its source, due to the high cost of city real estate), a hall closet is no more than a cubbyhole.

The minimum depth required for a coat closet is twenty-two or twenty-four inches, and a few additional inches are very useful since they permit you to install on the inside of the door a hat rack, umbrella rack, a mirror, and perhaps even a narrow shelf with a raised rim for holding gloves, a clothes brush, and Fido's Sunday leash. Of course, the dream would be to have a real walk-in closet in which you can build the clothes rack along one side and still have room for a washstand or dressing table. In this case, it is really a powder room as well as a closet, and it would be very chic to decorate it in an original or precious style.

If, on the other hand, there is no room in which to build a closet of normal depth, or if there is more width than depth available, you should be able to construct a long shallow closet equipped with extension rods on which the coats are hung parallel to the wall.

One young apartment-dwelling woman I know who has no front closet at all, solved the problem by fixing a row of pretty brass clothes pegs all along the narrow corridor connecting the front hall with the kitchen. There must be at least a dozen of them, with double hooks, and the procedure of leaving and retrieving one's coat at her frequent cocktail parties always takes place without the slightest confusion.

In other words, a hostess should exercise her ingenuity in order to devise some kind of permanent system for hanging up her visitors' coats. It is disorderly and not very hospitable besides to invite them simply to drape their vicuña or mink over the chairs and beds.

In country houses it is practical to install an additional closet or coatrack near the back entrance, for hanging up wet or muddy outdoor clothing.

The second essential closet for entertaining, is, of course, in the guest room. No matter how limited the space, there are countless possibilities. In a very large room, even that massive old-fashioned piece of furniture we call an "armoire" can have a great deal of chic when it is well designed and placed in a rustic decor. Armoires are also made in modern styles and these are far less cumbersome but also far less attractive. I would personally prefer to have built-in closets, perhaps with louvered doors resembling window blinds, which seem to me particularly elegant.

Americans have taught the rest of the world how to design fabulous built-in closets complete with special shelves, racks, and drawers for shoes, hats, shirts, ties, suitcases, etc., and they need no advice from anyone concerning this specialty, which they have perfected to the ultimate degree. Coordinated closet accessories are also extremely elegant in America, and some of your most irresistible department store merchandise is to be found in the closet and bath departments. So I have nothing to express but envy where furnishing a closet is concerned.

I might mention, however, an ingenious space-saving idea I admired in the tiny bedroom of a modest Swiss hotel. Closets had been built along one entire wall of the room, with a niche in the center for the head of the bed. As a matter of fact, there were closets and drawers on just one side, for when you opened the double doors on the other side you found a built-in washstand and mirror and even a bidet that swung out from underneath. The closets were painted and decorated with the same moldings that decorated the other walls, except for the niche, which was papered with a blue and white Toile de Jouy pattern to match the bedspread. The effect was charming, and the room required hardly any additional furniture in order to be livable. The same idea might very well be adapted to a guest room in a private home. If it is impossible to install the necessary plumbing for a washstand, it could be replaced by a built-in dressing table or writing desk.

(See Coats, Guest Rooms)

CLOTHES

❰ I recently wrote a three-hundred-page book describing in detail the clothing it is elegant to wear on every different kind of occasion, and it is therefore difficult for me to resume this complex and fascinating subject in just a few lines. However, I must insist upon two basic principles:

(1.) A hostess should never try to be more elegantly and expensively attired than her guests.

(2.) Whenever you entertain, you should inform your guests very precisely as to the kind of dress you yourself intend to wear, especially if it is a long one and if your husband will be wearing a dinner jacket. I know of nothing more irritating than the hostess who says, "Wear whatever you feel like——" which always makes me want to reply, "All right, I'll come in my nightgown!"

Do not forget either that if you ask your guests to dress in evening gowns and dinner jackets, they have the right to expect a rather refined menu, lots of people, candles, and champagne. The clearer you are in explaining to your guests the type of party you have planned for them, the less is their risk of being disappointed. An elegant décolleté formal evening gown is hardly the most comfortable and appropriate attire for a spaghetti dinner, although this kind of a party can be great fun if you have warned your guests ahead of time of the simplicity and informality of the occasion.

If you entertain a great deal, you will quickly amortize a very simple long dress or a long skirt made out of tweed in the winter and of cotton in the summer. You can wear one of these ensembles at your informal cocktail parties as well as for dinner, when your husband wears a dark suit. At least it will be a welcome change from your "little black dress," which you will always have plenty of occasions to slip into when you are entertained by friends. A woman should wear gloves in her own home only when she is giving a grand ball, but never a hat, not even for a wedding reception.

Finally, even if your only dinner guest is your own mother, you should leave your apron in the kitchen and your bedroom slippers in the bedroom.

If you possess a marvelous (and decent) long hostess gown or housecoat, you can pretend every once in a while that you have a sore throat and receive one couple (not more) in this attire. If you are divinely slender, you can make the same use of Chanel-style hostess pajamas. In these cases your husband might dress in a very elegant lounging jacket of broadcloth with silk revers, worn with pumps and a foulard in the open collar of his shirt. This ensemble is an excellent Christmas present, which will give him pleasure throughout the year, because the first thing most men like to do when they come home from work is to change into something comfortable.

CLUBS

❲ A membership in an exclusive club with an excellent dining room is undeniably an invaluable asset in entertaining. Club reception rooms are usually much more attractive and homelike than the salons of a hotel or restaurant, and the cuisine is often more personal and frequently less expensive. Since you already feel at home in the atmosphere of your club, and since you know the waiters and the rest of the personnel, it is almost the same as if you were receiving guests in your own home. Of course, to receive a guest in one's own home is undoubtedly the most complimentary kind of hospitality. But on the other hand, some guests would get a greater thrill from being admitted for an evening to a sanctum that they would not otherwise have an opportunity to penetrate, for example, a famous exclusive club such as the Jockey Club, or one whose membership is limited to certain professions or colleges, such as the Explorers Club, the Harvard Club, and the Lambs.

Entertaining in a club may be the ideal formula for bachelors and single women. It is also very useful for single persons living with their parents in a small house or apartment, when they wish to receive friends without turning the occasion into a family party—and without having to send the rest of the family to an all-night movie.

Finally, one of the greatest advantages of club entertaining is that everything will be billed to you automatically without the embarrassment of paying a check in front of your guests, which is the one really awkward moment of entertaining elsewhere than in your own home.

Just as the smart dining club is a valuable resource in the city, a country club can be exploited in entertaining in an infinite number of ways. If there are guest rooms in the clubhouse, you can even put up your weekend guests there. Sunday luncheon at your country club is an ideal way of entertaining weekend guests because you can precede it with a game of golf or tennis or a swim, and follow the meal with a pleasant stroll through the grounds, which are often landscaped with a view to providing attractive walks.

Needless to say, the more elegant the club, the more elegant your entertaining will be. Without wishing to appear snobbish, it seems to me that most municipal country clubs (which are seldom renowned for the excellence of the cuisine) are fine for a game of golf or a set of tennis, but that it is preferable afterward to return to your own home for luncheon or dinner, or to take your guests to a more picturesque or gastronomic dining place.

COATS

⟨ Perhaps because of professional chauvinism as a member of the fashion industry, I have great respect for these garments, which happen to be my favorite item of clothing, and it dismays me to see them piled on a bed in an untidy heap or placed several on the same hanger (which is probably too short or too straight), as is often the case during a large dinner party.

Modern apartments are seldom equipped with ideal hanging space for a dozen extra winter coats. But with a little thought a hostess can devise a practical system for accommodating these bulky garments without torturing them all out of shape.

The best solution of all is to hang up coats properly on a coat hanger in a closet, the men's coats on large, wooden, shaped hangers, and the women's on smaller, shaped ones, preferably padded. If you have a front hall closet, this is the logical place for guests' coats, and if necessary you should remove your own garments in order to make room for them before a party. When the number of coats exceeds the capacity of the front closet, it is best to reserve the closet for the men's coats and to let the women use the guest room or your own bedroom. Furs suffer the least from being laid out on a bed, as long as there is not a heavy heap of them and they are perfectly dry. But it is considerate to provide hangers for cloth coats and a place to hang them— the emptied guest room closet, a temporary standing coatrack, or merely an American gadget I discovered that fits over the top of a door, extending far enough to allow for at least five or six winter coats.

When you entertain a very large number of guests, let's say more than fifty, a more organized coatroom system is indispensable, with large schoolroom-type racks (which can be rented), coat checks, and an attendant. If your front hall is too small for this enterprise, as is usually the case, the checkroom may be installed in one of the bedrooms. In a city apartment, it is usually possible to set it up outside of the apartment either in the floor corridor or even in the downstairs lobby, if the superintendent gives permission. The caterer who prepares and serves the refreshments can also arrange a cloakroom for you.

There are two kinds of coats that require special accommodations: (1.) Dripping wet or snow-covered storm clothing, which is best hung in the entrance hall or in the back entry, where the flooring has been chosen for its resistance to mud and rainwater; if there is not room for a coatrack and hangers, ordinary pegs or an old-fashioned coat-tree will do. And (2.) Fur stoles. Unchic and impractical, they slide off hangers and coat pegs alike. If you cannot provide foam-rubber covered hangers that prevent slipping, the only thing to do is to toss them on a bed.

(See Closets)

COCKTAIL PARTIES

❡ For business organizations as well as for the private hostess, the cocktail party is the invention of the century. This form of mass entertaining has even become so overdone and banal that very chic people make a point of claiming that they never go to one, and if they invite you to their home at 6 P.M., they always say, "Come for a drink," carefully avoiding the fateful word, "cocktail" (which is, furthermore, very seldom served any more).

Nevertheless, I give cocktail parties, you give cocktail parties, we give cocktail parties—and we may as well do it with elegance.

There are, generally speaking, just two different kinds of cocktail parties: small ones and big ones, the first being infinitely more elegant than the second, which should be reserved exclusively for publicity and business purposes.

Small Cocktail Parties—or—"Come for a Drink!"

Composed of ten to thirty guests, the intimate cocktail party may be as simple or as elaborate as you wish. The smaller one's living room, the greater the chances of success of this type of gathering, and if you happen to live in a very spacious dwelling, it is preferable to hold your party in one of the coziest rooms. This is an excellent way to entertain visitors from out of town, newcomers to a community, or an interesting person you would like your friends to meet. You may even invite to this kind of a reception an attractive couple you recently met at a dinner party, whereas it would seem somewhat aggressive to have them to dinner on the strength of so slight and recent an acquaintance. In this way the small cocktail party is one of the most useful entertaining methods of sociable people who wish to enlarge their circle of friends, as well as of popular people who have a great many friends with whom they wish to maintain social relations.

When there are very few guests, you must at all cost avoid dispersing the centers of interest. Since a cocktail party is essentially a stand-up reception, your guests will move around more easily if there is not too much furniture or too many chairs in the middle of the room. You can arrange a few conversation corners for weary or elderly persons, but each should be able to accommodate at least five or six people in order to avoid trapping your prettiest, wittiest guest on an isolated love seat with the weariest, oldest one.

The atmosphere will be more informal if you do not set up a buffet table, but instead place platters of appetizers all around the room on the tables, side tables, piano, etc., and from time to time pass around a tray of hot hors d'oeuvres. Generally speaking, the smaller the number of guests, the more they will eat. You will need to provide at least six or eight canapés apiece when there are only twelve of you, whereas with forty or fifty guests the quantity can be reduced to five or six per person, but there should be a wider variety. Before the war, when sweet aperitifs were in fashion, the rule used to be to prepare one tray of sweet tidbits (petit fours, candied fruit, tiny cake squares, etc.) for every two or three trays of salted snacks and sandwiches. But tastes have changed, and nowadays one to four would be a more realistic proportion, and at a small party the sweets are often eliminated entirely.

The bar can be set up on a rolling tea cart or an equivalent piece of furniture (even the top of a commode), with all of the glasses and bottles needed for drinks, which the host or hostess serves to each arriving guest. With less than twenty-five guests, you should be able to manage without a waiter. At the moment, in Europe at least, it is quite sufficient to offer no more than a choice of Scotch, with soda or plain water and ice, or Vodka, tomato or orange juice; in the United States you would add bourbon, and an assortment of soft drinks as well as the favorite drink of your particular community, along with the hallowed Dry Martini—and if you wish to give me a special treat, the ingredients of a Whisky Sour! Dry sherry, slightly chilled, is simple to serve, as are Dubonnet and even champagne if you are feeling festive and rich. Remember that the general trend today is toward drier, more straightforward drinks such as sherry and Scotch on the rocks, rather than the sirupy aperitifs and complicated mixed cocktails of a few years ago. This has so simplified bar inventories that today, if you are provided with bitters, a few lemons and limes, tiny cocktail onions (which transform a Dry Martini into a Gibson), a little sugar, a jar of olives and one of cherries, in addition to a few bottles of liquor (scotch, bourbon, rye, gin, French vermouth, vodka), you are prepared to fill any normal cocktail order.

At a small cocktail party it is very chic to offer in addition one personal specialty, such as a hot buttered rum or mulled wine in the winter, or in the summertime a mint julep, Pimm's Cup, planter's punch, etc., attractively garnished and served in special glasses or mugs, a frosty pitcher, or a fragrant steaming bowl, as the case may be.

It is difficult to estimate how much your guests will drink, for capacities and habits vary enormously. The average consumption is probably two or three drinks per person, and you can expect to get twelve to sixteen glasses from an aperitif bottle, six glasses from a bottle of champagne, and about twenty drinks from a bottle of whisky. Often your liquor dealer will agree to accept for refund afterward any unopened bottles, and it is always better to have leftover liquor than suddenly to run short, which can either cause your guests to leave earlier than you'd hoped, or oblige them to mix their liquor with possibly disastrous results! In any case, be sure to have on hand plenty of ice cubes and soda water, plus a pitcher of plain water and one of fruit juice for nondrinkers.

When there is no host to serve as bartender and no professional help, you can ask a good friend to fill this role. If he is at all experienced in cocktail parties, you will not need to remind him that the time-honored barman's technique is to make the first drink on the stiff side, with the following rounds somewhat milder. Should your volunteer desert his post, it is usually better to call on another or to take over yourself, rather than expect your guests to help themselves.

Don't forget to have plenty of ashtrays scattered around at strategic spots, along with several cigarette boxes filled with an assortment of cigarettes, and matches or a couple of table lighters that really work. You will probably be too busy introducing new arrivals, keeping your guests circulating (but without ever breaking up a genuinely absorbing conversation) and seeing that nobody is stranded or stuck to have time to empty overflowing ashtrays, so use large ones. (But take the time to empty them into a covered receptacle if they ever become offensive to the eye or nose.) A lighted candle is supposed to be an effective antidote to smoke-filled rooms, while the perfumed kind masks the stale odor at the same time.

The essence of the art of being a perfect cocktail-party hostess can be expressed in a few brief phrases: the ones the hostess pronounces when she greets each guest, and her introductions as she presents them to each other. The first should immediately put each arrival in a relaxed and friendly mood, and the second should contain a clue to a mutually interesting subject of conversation. In other words, the principal duty of a cocktail hostess is to provide her guests with amusing or rewarding social intercourse in addition to the refreshments. With more than ten or twelve guests, this mission can be quite preoccupying, especially when many of them are strangers; and if there are more than twenty, it is unlikely that she will find time to enjoy her own party—particularly if she has the misfortune to be harassed by one of the following problems:

She has invited thirty guests and wonders how many of them will actually turn up.

Usually you can expect about three out of four at an average party, and about two out of three at a large one. But the only elegant thing to do is to prepare sufficient food and drink for all of them, even if you have to eat party leftovers for the rest of the week.

One of the guests has had too much to drink and is becoming aggressive (or loud, or amorous, etc., etc.).

Immediate first aid for mild cases is to ply him with food. But there is just one permanent remedy: ask a good friend to take the person home.

The Wallflower.

Take her by the hand and introduce her to a good, kindhearted friend. But don't attempt to integrate her into a large group, for this will only intimidate her more.

The guest who arrives too early.

Fifteen minutes early: "How marvelous! We can have a nice chat before the others arrive!"

One hour early—when you are not even dressed yet: send excuses and a drink via the maid or your husband. (But this will not happen often.)

The guests who never want to go home.

If they are not important to you: kick off your shoes and yawn.

If they are very important: make the most of it. Be witty, vivacious and so delighted by their company that perhaps your husband will get an offer of a better job. And be sure to protest when at last they make a move to go, "Oh, must you *really* leave so *soon?*"

The invitations said "From 6 to 8," but it is already 6:45 and there are only four disappointed-looking arrivals.

Perhaps you haven't invited enough people, or perhaps another, more popular hostess is entertaining on the same evening. Next time you should check the social calendar to make sure that yours is the only party scheduled for that particular day—or at least the most enticing.

But wait until seven before becoming discouraged, because the great majority of cocktail-party guests arrive in a bunch during the middle.

Personally, I have always disliked the formula "5 to 7" or "6 to 8," for it seems to me ungracious to place a time limit on your hospitality. It is of course unavoidable when you have rented a salon, which must often be cleared by a certain hour to make way for the next party, and this is one of the major disadvantages of entertaining in a hotel or club. Furthermore, if you do not mention a closing time, some guests may have the impression that they are being invited for the entire evening, including a buffet dinner. Nevertheless, I prefer to word my cocktail party invitations: "Cocktails from six o'clock on," and if a guest interprets it as meaning ". . . on until midnight"—see above.

Large Cocktail Parties

If you have to entertain a large number of guests at one time, and if you consider it a tiresome obligation, the best way to get it over with gracefully is to invite at least two hundred people for cocktails in the salons of a smart hotel or a private club. All you will have to do is to sign the check.

You will station yourself near the entrance of the reception room to greet the arriving guests and to bid good-by to those who are leaving. But you will hardly have a chance to exchange any real conversation with them (which may not always be a bad thing). In Europe, a few hostesses still employ an *aboyeur* (literally, a "barker"), a sort of major-domo in livery who announces each arriving guest in stentorian tones, and in this case the hostess does not even have to remember their names.

At a large party of one hundred guests or more, it is impossible for the hostess to abandon her post in order to mingle with her guests, who must more or less fend for themselves. She can, however, make a point of getting any complete strangers off to a promising start.

A large party is usually more mobile and animated when it is not confined to a single set or age group. You should also invite all of the prettiest women you know, and as many extra men as possible. For some reason, the appearance of a social gathering is always more elegant when the men outnumber the women. A few celebrities or persons of importance are also a precious element, for these minor and major stars will always attract a circle of satellites and thus help to keep things moving. Judging from my personal experience, I would say that it is possible really to enjoy oneself at a cocktail party only when there are no more than fifty guests. Beyond that number, all that you can expect is to see and to be seen—which is why I consider these huge receptions strictly for publicity!

In order to insure the elegance of this kind of a party, you merely have to exercise discrimination in selecting the best hotel or the most attractive club in town, and leave everything up to their experienced staff. Needless to add, anybody who is willing to pay the same price can give the same party with the same sandwiches and the same bouquets in the same salon. But you might as well face the fact that it is impossible to give an out-of-the-ordinary party if you are unwilling to do any of the work yourself.

If your home is very large, you can invite a throng of guests to your own house, and this alone will make your party more refined and personal than if you held it in a club or hotel. It is not practical to have canapé trays passed around in such a mob, and the best solution is to set up two or three buffet tables (the rule of thumb is one buffet table for each thirty or forty guests), which will insure at the same time that your guests will not get stuck in firmly rooted clusters. Be sure to locate the buffets in the far corners of the rooms and not right near the entrance, where they would be sure to cause an inextricable traffic jam.

You will also need to provide a well-organized and well-staffed cloakroom system, complete with coat checks and rented hangers and racks. And I strongly advise you to take out a special insurance policy for the occasion, if possible, to protect you in case a valuable mink coat should disappear. Remember, too, that a large crowd literally warms the atmosphere to an amazing degree. In wintertime you should turn the heat down lower than usual, and in the summer open all the windows or turn the air conditioner on High.

All of the refreshments should be ordered from a caterer, whose business it is to estimate exactly how much food and drink and how many waiters will be needed. Try to persuade him to emerge from his usual routine and to prepare a few original hors d'oeuvres, in addition to the eternal stuffed eggs and cocktail sausages. And do not hesitate to supplement his inevitably more ordinary efforts with a few of your own specialties if you have any; for example, a marvelous pizza or a chocolate cake cut into tiny squares. You might add a colorful platter of raw vegetables cut in bite-size pieces: carrots, celery, radishes, cucumber, cauliflower, etc., accompanied by a bowl of highly seasoned mayonnaise or cheese sauce into which each morsel is dipped. The point to remember is that if you wish to entertain with elegance, it is absolutely indispensable to add a personal note to the decorative and gastronomic composition of the buffet table, even when you are receiving several hundred guests.

COFFEE

❡ It is always more elegant to serve afterdinner coffee from a tray in the living room rather than at the dining table. It is also simpler to serve coffee in the living room when you have no help, because you can abandon the dessert remains on the dining room table, and the coffee tray can be prepared in advance. Coffee-making, like wine-pouring, is one of the noble rituals of gastronomy and can perfectly well be performed in front of one's guests in an electric or alcohol percolator. I suppose that some coffee makers are not really aesthetic enough to leave the kitchen, but the only one I personally would condemn is the individual filter. This diabolical method is unreliable, interminable, and, thank heavens, is at last being routed from our Paris cafés by Italian espresso machines. Many Paris hostesses employ two coffee-making methods: a filter, drip, or percolator type for breakfast coffee, and an espresso type for the more concentrated afterdinner brew.

There is an enormous difference between freshly roasted, freshly ground coffee and the canned kind, although Americans have become so accustomed to the taste of slightly stale coffee that they have perhaps forgotten what they are missing. Oxygen is, of course, the great destroyer of flavor in coffee, and while modern packaging does limit the damage as far as possible, as soon as a coffee can has been opened and air has entered, the deterioration is very rapid. It does not help much simply to buy unground coffee beans, because flavor is also lost a few hours after the beans have been roasted, so you must insist on its being freshly roasted as well as freshly ground. Unfortunately, very few modern shops are equipped to furnish this epicurean service, but if you are lucky enough to find a specialist in your neighborhood, it would be well worth the trouble to buy your afterdinner coffee as fresh as possible in small quantities once or twice a week. Otherwise, you can only shop around among the different prepared brands until you settle on the one that satisfies you best.

Afterdinner coffee should be rather strong and free from bitterness, which is a sign of staleness (or perhaps of an imperfectly washed coffeepot). It is served in demitasse cups, preferably from a silver or porcelain coffeepot, because these materials retain the heat the best. The pot should be warmed before it is filled with coffee by rinsing it out with boiling water. It is very refined to warm the coffee cups in the same way. This strong, digestive, afterdinner brew is best served only with sugar. But some people like to add a spoonful of brandy, and the Viennese tradition is to top each cup with a spoonful of slightly sweetened whipped cream. In India, coffee may even be served with sliced lemon, just like tea—although I tried this once and do not particularly recommend it! On the other hand, I simply adore Irish coffee, made by pouring an inch of Irish whisky into a thick glass, filling it with coffee and sugar, and floating a layer of rich cream on top by pouring it gently over the back of a spoon. Whenever coffee is served after a meal, it is thoughtful to offer a decaffeinated brew as well. If a number of guests have requested it, you might make a coffeepotful. But if it is just one or two persons, you can perfectly well serve them a decaffeinated coffee powder, and a pot of boiling water.

Breakfast coffee should be more lightly brewed, for it is consumed in far greater quantity, most often with sugar and cream or, best of all, with sugar and hot whole milk. In France we often add a small dose of chicory to the breakfast coffee blend because of its tonic effect, although this imparts a slightly astringent flavor.

The custom of serving coffee throughout a meal may appeal to American palates, but it should be abandoned whenever you entertain. Not only is it an antigastronomic habit, but also terribly unsophisticated.

It is always more elegant to serve lump sugar than the plain granulated kind with coffee, but the most chic of all is the unbleached, unrefined Gaylord Hauser type sugar that is sold in organic food shops and comes in uneven, sand-colored chunks. American women may not be aware of their good fortune in being able to buy cane sugar in every corner store, because European hostesses go to great pains to procure it for serving with coffee in place of the beet-root sugar with which we are ordinarily supplied. If there are dieters in your entourage, it would be thoughtful to provide on the breakfast table and coffee tray an artificial low-calorie sweetener as well.

Iced coffee is a marvelously stimulating beverage to serve on a hot summer afternoon. I am, needless to add, less enthusiastic about it as a luncheon beverage, but I haven't the courage to go to war against this firmly entrenched Anglo-Saxon custom. I must insist, however, that even when it is served cold, coffee should be fresh in order to be delicious, and the best method is to pour hot, strong, freshly brewed coffee over ice cubes in a tall glass containing a silver spoon (in order to help absorb the heat and to prevent the glass from cracking), and then to add more ice cubes. If you simply chill a pitcher of weak coffee in the refrigerator, most of the flavor will be lost within a few hours and only the bitterness and color will remain.

While true coffee lovers are willing to go to an immense amount of trouble to brew a special blend of coffee from freshly roasted, freshly ground beans, they are certainly the exceptions to the rule. And even for fanatics, there are a few emergency occasions when the most practical coffee-making method is simply to dissolve a spoonful of frozen or powdered coffee in a cup of water. This is not, however, a very elegant procedure to indulge in before your guests, and besides, there is a chance that they will not detect the subterfuge if you mix your powdered coffee in the kitchen out of sight. As a matter of fact, it is possible to create a fairly good illusion of fresh coffee if you use a superior powered brand, measure out an extragenerous dose for each cup in a heated coffeepot, and use only the purest water that has just come to a boil. If the tap water in your region is highly chlorinated, try using a pure bottled water, and you will be amazed by the difference!

(See Drinks)

COMMITTEE MEETINGS

❰[Since some kind of refreshment is an integral part of almost every form of entertaining, and since you are entertaining every time you receive friends in your home, you should always be prepared to provide some kind of a snack even if the purpose of the gathering is to review the annual budget of the music or garden club.

When you are hostess at a committee meeting, it is best to greet your guests in a friendly but rather businesslike manner, avoiding above all personal chitchat, so that you can settle down to business without delay. Of course, you should have cleared the room of personal clutter and arranged the proper number of chairs—around the dining room table is often the most suitable spot—and you can set the scene like a General Motors' board of directors meeting with ashtrays, pads and pencils, glasses and a carafe of water. You should also try to insure that you will not be interrupted by children, tradesmen, or telephone calls.

The refreshments may be served after the meeting has been adjourned, when the table is cleared of papers and the atmosphere is more relaxed. Just as your hospitality is only a pleasant supplement to the business on the agenda, your refreshments may be symbolic rather than sumptuous: for example, coffee and doughnuts, coffee cake, sweet rolls, or Danish pastry at the end of a morning meeting; tea and sherry with tiny sandwiches and perhaps a plate of petit fours in the afternoon; cookies with iced tea or coffee in the summer and hot tea or coffee in the winter. It is the gesture that counts, not the quantity or the extravagance of the food. Nevertheless, when men are present—or if the meeting has been a stormy one—it might be a good idea to offer whisky too.

CONVERSATION

❡ Although every detail of a party may have been carefully prepared, the occasion can still be spoiled if the conversation takes an unpleasant turn, and it is the duty of the hostess to keep her ears as well as her eyes open. As soon as her guests begin to launch into a heated discussion of politics or religion, she should tactfully but firmly change the subject, if necessary by interrupting them. It is preferable to cut off a guest in the middle of a sentence rather than to permit the atmosphere to become strained because of a pointless argument between two people who do not share the same views.

Certain subjects are almost always perfectly safe: the weather, the day's headlines, current movies, plays, books, past or future voyages, and vacation plans. A comment or question on one of these topics is an infallible conversation opener. However, when your guests are very interesting or very intelligent, it would be a pity to waste the evening in small talk, and you should try to steer the conversation around toward more stimulating subjects as soon as a friendly mood has been established.

While a clever hostess subtly directs the conversation, she should never monopolize it. You should never forget that you are entertaining in order to give pleasure to your guests, and you are under an obligation to furnish that pleasure in addition to the refreshments. A detailed account of how you lost your only appendix or your last molar, the scholastic problems of your youngest-born, or the stupidity of your cleaning woman are hardly likely to be passionately interesting subjects to your guests, unless you are a fantastically gifted raconteur.

There are a few people who earn their dinners by furnishing in return so brilliant a conversation that all are spellbound by their wit and charm. Society hostesses vie among themselves to snag them for their parties in order to guarantee the conversational quality of the evening, and caterers really ought to supply them along with the waiters. They are our modern troubadours. But while the medieval troubadour talked only of love, his modern counterparts all too often apply their talents to tearing apart their absent friends. Some sensitive souls do not particularly care for this kind of verbal massacre, and others may feel slighted because they cannot get a word in edgewise. And so it is best not to overdo the presence of these conversation specialists at your parties, and in any case, never mix them with very shy people.

The ideal guest is one who has truly extraordinary personal experiences to relate, but who also knows how to listen to other people's stories. The accomplished hostess might be compared to an orchestra conductor, and like him she must know when to signal for the entrance of the flute or the violin and when to cut off the bass drum.

If the conversation lags and the evening begins to seem long, she can always adopt the proven technique of asking questions in order to get her guests to talk about themselves. This is certainly the topic that is dearest to them, and it doesn't matter a bit if she is secretly suppressing a yawn. She can always act as if she were deeply interested in what they have to say by listening with rapt attention. They will thus find her exceptionally intelligent, and even more so if she approves of their actions and agrees with their opinions (for there is no point in going to the bother of disagreeing or disapproving when she couldn't care less). Her guests will be delighted with their evening, which was her goal—even if she silently vows as she bids them good night that it is the last one they will ever be invited to spend at her house!

Never forget that vanity is a much more widespread sin than gourmandise, and that the guest whom you have permitted to shine at one of your parties will be infinitely more grateful to you for this moment of glory than for the most delicious dinner.

(See Dinners)

COOPERATIVE PARTIES

❡ Progressive parties, in which each course of a dinner is prepared and served in her own home by a different hostess, have practically disappeared, due I suppose to insoluble traffic and parking problems. They have been replaced in certain sets by cooperative parties, in which each course is supplied by a different hostess but the entire meal is eaten in a single home.

This is a novelty form of entertaining that is generally more appealing in theory than in practice. It may be amusing to teen-agers, especially those who are going through the stage where they adore to cook, but it is not very suitable for adults. I would consider it possible only for a spur-of-the-moment evening among a few very intimate friends when, because of lack of time, or because all of the shops are closed, or for some such reason, it is impossible for a single hostess to prepare the meal all by herself. However, I imagine that these circumstances must be extremely rare today, when almost every kitchen is equipped with a spacious Deep-freeze, and every hostess keeps a well-stocked emergency shelf for just such impromptu occasions.

A cooperative party may seem to be the ideal solution for a young couple on a tiny budget, particularly if the cooperating guests offer to supply the liquor, which is often a major expense. But before committing yourself, I wish you would consider the many other ways of entertaining economically with infinitely greater elegance.

In the traditional cooperative dinner party, which is planned in advance, there is naturally a certain amount of feminine rivalry. Each cook wishes her dish to be the most extraordinary and delicious, and the result is often a disastrous mixture, with indigestion the ultimate consequence. Furthermore, in her desire to outshine all the others, a woman is tempted to spend as much money on her single dish as it would have cost her to prepare an entire normal company meal.

With the exception of teen-age dancing parties, where the boys supply the beverage and the girls the food, cooperative entertaining is unheard of on the Continent.

Perhaps that is why my opinion of cooperative parties is this: Fine for teen-agers, but not a very good substitute for normal entertaining, however modest.

(See Economy, Marketing)

DEBUTANTES

❦ It is very much to the credit of the younger generation that even before doting fathers began to balk at the fantastic expense of a traditional debutante ball, the debutantes themselves decided that it was folly to spend a small fortune on a coming-out party, ostensibly in order to introduce them to a society in which they had already been circulating with the greatest of ease for several years. And so, within the past decade, the lavish individual coming-out party has practically disappeared, to be replaced by the collective debutante ball, during which fifty or a hundred debs or more are presented all together, with proceeds going to some worthy charity.

While each official debutante also gives a party of her own, it is on a much smaller scale than during the era of Brenda Frazier, who was undoubtedly the most publicized debutante of all time (and who, incidentally, refused to let her own daughter go through the same debutante routine). Moreover, it may even be a tea dance instead of a ball; or perhaps a luncheon followed by dancing, a dinner dance, or a late supper dance. In the provinces of France and England, it is customary to give one party in London or Paris and another in the country, just as a New York society woman might give one party for her debutante daughter in Manhattan, and a more informal one in Palm Beach. An outdoor dance in the summer under tents is, it seems to me, the most spectacular and elegant kind of a coming-out party, but it is also one of the most expensive to organize. It is also increasingly frequent for the private parties to be collective to a certain degree, with two and some-times three debutantes combining their private balls in one large gala evening.

Originally a coming-out party really did represent the first introduc-tion of a young girl to society, and the round of social events that oc-cupied her debutante season was designed to provide her with an op-portunity to hook a husband from among all the eligible dancing partners. But since this method of husband-hunting has become passé, as most young women meet their husbands in college, at work, or on vacation, the purpose of present-day debutante balls is simply to have fun. The atmosphere is consequently gayer than it used to be, and there is far less ceremony and solemnity—some parents would add, less de-corum, too. Nevertheless, they are essentially conventional affairs, and should be organized in the traditional way if they are to be elegant. This is not the time for novelties in dress or entertainment.

It is the parents or grandparents who are the official hosts of a debu-tante's coming-out party, and they greet the guests at her side in the receiving line near the entrance to the ballroom.

A successful debutante dance requires a lovely setting, either at home or in a smart hotel, a lavish floral decor, an excellent dance or-chestra, a well-stocked buffet, ample liquid refreshments, including champagne and plenty of soft drinks and fruit punch as well as whisky, and last but not least, a long stag line so that every girl will feel like the belle of the ball. In addition to the buffet supper, a breakfast should be served at about two or three o'clock in the morning, or even later.

The honored debutante wears a white dress with long white gloves. During a tea dance or daytime party, she may dress as she pleases, but preferably in rather unsophisticated clothes and never in black.

Engraved formal invitations should be sent out at least three weeks in advance, and as much as two months in advance in cities where the deb season is very active. It is necessary to check the date with the other debutantes in order to avoid conflict. In large cities there are specialized social secretaries who make up the invitation lists from a file of approved names. Mothers who take this sort of thing seriously go to a great deal of trouble and expense and play a great deal of social politics in order to insure their debutante daughters of a brilliant "sea-son." It is indispensable to be on good terms with all the other mothers and to plan your social strategy in close collaboration with them. There-fore, unless your social position and connections are impeccable, it would be advisable to enlist the aid of a more powerful society leader or of a specialist in this particular field if you wish to launch your darling daughter in a blaze of glory.

DECORATIONS

❬ Every woman wants her home to be more beautiful than ever when she entertains, but her guests should have the impression that this is the way it always looks.

When you are giving a luncheon, cocktail, or dinner party, you can arrange a fresh bouquet of flowers in the usual place in the living room, but that is all. (Besides, there is always a chance that one of your guests will send you flowers and you should leave room for them, since gift flowers should always be displayed in a most prominent place.) It is better to devote your time and energy to seeing that the living room is spotlessly clean, the furniture and silver polished, the ashtrays empty, the lampshades and light bulbs dusted, and the desk and tables tidied. You do not want to leave the coffee table and side tables completely bare, of course, as if they were part of a furniture display. But the only objects, magazines, and books that remain on them should be those that you have left on purpose. Usually this means hiding the detective novels and movie magazines, and leaving Teilhard de Chardin and the *Atlantic Monthly*. But a book dealing with a subject of particular interest to one of your guests may also be an excellent conversation opener.

No special decoration is necessary in the hall, and in the dining room a pretty table setting with candles and flowers is quite sufficient. It is best to limit the decoration of the sideboard to a pair of candelabra, for it should be kept free to fulfill its basic function, which is to hold the dishes and platters for the meal.

While it is not chic to decorate your home for normal entertaining, there are a few special occasions when you can release all of your pent-up decorative urges:

At Christmastime, you can indulge in an orgy of decoration, with wreaths on the doors, candles in the windows, sleigh bells hanging from the doorknob and mistletoe from the ceiling, holly stuck around the picture frames, an array of Christmas cards on the mantelpiece, a manger, and a Christmas tree, as sophisticated or old fashioned, as dainty or gigantic as you like. Your front hall, living room and dining room—in fact, the entire house—can cry out "Merry Christmas!" to everyone who enters.

At children's parties, you can also let your imagination run riot, decorating the party room either according to a particular juvenile theme, or merely with a gay display of balloons and paper garlands. Remember that children adore anything that appeals to their sense of fantasy.

At a masquerade ball or a costume party, the decor may be as extraordinary and fabulous as you wish. You can completely transform the aspect of your home for the occasion, just as you and your guests attempt to disguise your own appearances beyond recognition.

At a dinner party with a foreign theme, it is amusing to accentuate the exotic cuisine with a few decorative elements typical of the land from which you have borrowed your recipes. Although most of your efforts will be concentrated on the decoration of the table, you can carry a few touches over into the living room as well, with paper Japanese lanterns for an Oriental meal, for example, or a Spanish mantilla draped over the piano and a lace fan on the mantelpiece for a Spanish evening. This kind of decoration should be more restrained than the others, for its purpose is merely to suggest an atmosphere and not to create a stage setting.

Finally, there is the case of the young married couple just getting settled in their first home, which they are attempting to furnish little by little. There is no reason for hesitating to give a party in a half-furnished room as long as the welcome is warm and the food delicious. But it is also fun (and in this case quite chic) to camouflage the bareness of the setting with gay and imaginative party decorations, until the room has acquired its permanent decor.

In short, if you have a lovely home it is almost always best to refrain from adding special decorations, for they are usually rather juvenile, and at best more amusing than elegant.

(See Tables)

DESSERT

❪ Even the most delicious dessert in the world cannot figure in all of your party menus, and you should have a variety of them in your repertoire. It is worthwhile taking special pains over the selection, preparation, and particularly the presentation of a dessert. Since this is the last course of your meal, it should also be its crowning point, so that your guests will leave the table with a feeling of pampered satisfaction.

The choice of a dessert is limited by a few gastronomic and conventional restrictions. Some are not considered sufficiently refined for company, even though they are quite delicious and favorites at family meals. These would include most gelatine desserts, simple puddings and custards (except for Floating Island), such as rice, tapioca, and bread pudding. Baked apples and stewed fruit are also in the family category, whereas fresh fruit cup is an excellent dessert for a dinner party whose main course is rather rich, especially when it is presented in a hollowed pineapple shell or melon and decorated with sprigs of fresh mint. Some particularly delicious combinations are pineapple and strawberries in a pineapple shell; cantaloupe and peach slices in the melon shell; and a few canned or fresh litchis added to a mixed fresh fruit cup.

But the most classical company desserts are found among the mousses, soufflés, charlottes, and Bavarian creams (in which the only flavoring considered to be not very elegant is vanilla), not to forget the infinite variety of pies and tarts that are a particularly appropriate climax to a rather light meal, where the main course has been, for example, a fish dish.

In this category is one of my favorite desserts, which my mother used to make, a chocolate-chestnut gateau. If you cannot find imported French, Italian, or Spanish chestnuts in order to make a fresh purée, you can buy a can of chestnut purée that is already sweetened (but it will not be as good). Chill the purée well the night before. Butter and line with waxed paper a dessert mold in which you plaster the purée, leaving a good-sized hollow in the center. Chill again. A few hours before the party, fill the hollow with whipped cream that has been slightly sweetened and flavored with vanilla, and unmold on a serving dish.

Melt three bars of chocolate with a tablespoon of butter in a double boiler, cool slightly, and spread the chocolate over the chestnut mold. Return to the refrigerator until serving time.

I have often made another of my mother's chocolate recipes, which she called "Secret Chocolate Cream," for it is ridiculously simple and quick to prepare and perfectly delicious to eat. It must, however, be made in advance. You simply take one egg and one bar of chocolate per person. Soften the chocolate in the oven to spreading consistency. Place it immediately in a bowl with the egg yolks and mix well until it is a very smooth cream. Whip the egg whites very stiff and add them spoonful by spoonful to the yolk mixture, stirring constantly. Finally, cut a tablespoon of very fresh unsalted butter into tiny pieces and add them bit by bit to the mixture. Serve very well chilled.

Then there is the safest dessert of all because it goes with everything and pleases everybody: ice cream and cake. You can add a touch of originality by selecting an unusual combination of flavors: pistachio ice cream with chocolate cake, coffee ice cream with caramel-pecan cake, chocolate ice cream with coconut or orange cake. A huge meringue shell ordered from the bakery may be filled with ice cream and garnished with whipped cream and berries to make an impressive dish we call a *vacherin*. For a change, you can serve as a sauce a rich liqueur such as crème de cassis with vanilla ice cream, or green crème de menthe with lemon sherbet. The possibilities are endless!

If you are a clever cook and are giving a small, informal dinner, there are a number of lovely flambée desserts that you can prepare in a chafing dish right at the table: flambéed peaches or bananas, or flambéed bing cherries to be spooned over vanilla ice cream, and, of course, crêpes suzette, which are really quite simple to make if you prepare the crêpes ahead of time and warm them on a covered plate placed over a pan of boiling water while the first part of the dinner is being served.

Aside from the rather loose distinction between "family" and "company" desserts, your choice should be governed by the composition of the menu. A light meal may be followed by a rather rich dessert, but a rich meal should be followed by a light one, and you should avoid repetitions of any kind, for example, a pizza pie to start with and an apple pie to finish, or a creamy pudding when there has been a creamed main dish.

Choosing a dessert is the most delightful part of menu planning, and so it is with some reluctance that I deprive myself of this pleasure on certain occasions when time-honored tradition cannot be ignored. Would

Christmas dinner be complete without a plum pudding served aflame with brandy? Or Thanksgiving without a pumpkin or mince pie? Or a birthday party without a cake and candles and ice cream? Tradition and popularity concord in the case of children's parties, for ice cream and cake is far and away their favorite dessert.

* * *

In certain special circumstances, the entire party fare may be confined to dessert and coffee. I would not recommend this formula when men are to be present because they hate interrupted meals. Nevertheless, a hostess can add a touch of personal hospitality to an otherwise routine gathering, such as a committee meeting or an afternoon bridge or French lesson, by saying, "Come at two o'clock for dessert and coffee."

In this case, the dessert should be rather special, and if there are many women present you might even offer them a choice of desserts, such as a chocolate mousse and a coconut cake, or a homemade pie and ice cream with a variety of hot and cold sauces. It is simplest to serve this type of refreshment buffet-style, with everything laid out on the dining room table (which means that you will probably have to eat lunch in the kitchen), unless there are very few guests, in which case you will probably be more comfortable seated at the table as if it were a normal, full-course meal. When you serve buffet-style, you should provide an adequate number of little tables in the living room so that every guest will have a place to sit and a place to lay her plate.

It is not such a good idea to invite a group of friends for dessert and coffee after dinner, mainly because men do not like it, and because the timing is difficult. It would be much more agreeable to ask your friends to arrive a half-hour or an hour after dinner and to serve them a drink right away and some choice refreshments (a cake, sandwiches, homemade brownies and date bars, etc.) later on in the evening.

(See Menus)

DIETS

❡ With fashion decreeing slimmer and slimmer silhouettes and the medical world insisting on the dangers of overweight, more people than ever before are watching their waistlines. To tell the truth, they watch it expand as often as they watch it shrink, especially if they are often invited to dinner parties, which provide the best excuse in the world for going off one's diet.

Out of consideration for these hapless people who, as fate would have it, are usually obliged to deprive themselves of the very foods they most enjoy, a thoughtful hostess includes in her party menus no more than one really fattening dish. Besides, a perfectly balanced menu should never be so rich that it leaves the diners with a feeling of satiety—and possibly of guilt. If the main dish is to be rather heavy, there should be a very light first course and a huge green salad so that dieters can fill up on these harmless foods and not be forced by hunger to overindulge in calories. Unfortunately, some of the most appreciated party foods are in the fattening category, such as avocado, duck, goose, tuna fish, salmon, mincemeat, creamed soups, creamed casserole dishes, and pastries, and it is more difficult to banish these delicacies from your gala menus than it is to eliminate lentils, baked beans, macaroni, pork, spaghetti, and fried foods, which are also guaranteed to put on weight.

When a party meal consists almost entirely of one hearty dish, such as spareribs and sauerkraut, or spaghetti and meatballs, it is advisable to mention this to your guests at the time you invite them in order to make sure that they like it and are permitted to eat it. Another helpful aid for dieters is a written menu placed at each end of the dinner table, which enables them to plan their caloric consumption during the course of the meal. In a servantless household, it is better for everyone concerned to pass the serving dishes around the table and let each guest serve himself, rather than to have the host fill the plates in old-fashioned, head-of-the-family style (which is, moreover, not at all elegant when guests are present).

There are many diets aside from the reducing kind, and no hostess can be expected to be familiar with all of them. However, everyone should be aware of the fact that certain religious sects observe strict dietary laws and that it would be most tactless to serve meat on Friday to a Roman Catholic (especially during Lent), pork or shellfish to an Orthodox Jew, that most Hindus are vegetarians, and that Moslems are not supposed to drink alcoholic beverages. If you are ever obliged to entertain foreign visitors from an exotic country whose culture and religion are quite different from your own, it would be wise before you plan the menu to inform yourself of any special dietary restrictions that ought to be observed.

It may not be considered a sin to break a medical diet, but the immediate consequences can be far more serious. Here again, no hostess can possibly be expected to know the diets prescribed for every kind of physical condition, and she cannot even know that a guest is following a special diet unless she is advised beforehand. In that case she can, when planning her menu, try to avoid the particular forbidden dishes. But if the diet in question bans everything that is essential to an appetizing meal, such as salt or fat, it is preferable to prepare a delectable normal dinner for the rest of the party and something special for the convalescent. The important point is to serve it discreetly so as to attract as little attention as possible to your guest's misfortune.

Then there is the mystery of allergies, which are more often caused by food than by any other substance. The most active villains are mussels, clams, oysters, fish, and shellfish, chocolate, eggs, milk, game, cabbage, spinach, melon, strawberries, and rich old wines. But unless you are certain that a guest is allergic to a particular food, the only ones that are rigorously banned from dinner-party menus, in France at least, are clams and oysters. Aside from the allergies they inspire, oysters seem to divide humanity into two camps composed of the people who love them and those who hate them. There is no middle ground. Neither is there any way of pretending to eat an oyster by politely pushing it around with a fork. And this is why an experienced hostess never serves them at a large party, when she cannot be well informed as to the gastronomic prejudices of all of her guests.

Finally, there is the case of the dieting hostess. It should be unnecessary to say that reducing diets ought to be followed in private, and that a woman who is limiting herself to a grated carrot and a lettuce leaf twice a day has no business inviting friends to watch her eat her frugal repast. If you simply must entertain despite these conditions, ask your friends to come for a drink or take them to the theater. But do not have them to dinner until you are a size twelve, or whatever is your goal, and can share with them an epicurean meal and hang the calories!

There are, however, exceptions to this rule in the case of persons who, as a result of an illness such as jaundice or a gallbladder problem, are obliged to follow a diet for the rest of their lives. Needless to say, it would be highly unfair to deprive them of the pleasure of entertaining as well.

DINING ROOMS

❡ It is perfectly possible to give very elegant dinner and luncheon parties even if you do not have a separate dining room in your home. This is, in fact, increasingly the modern formula in city apartments, where the dining room is often suppressed in favor of a big living room with a dining corner or alcove. But if your family is large, and there are always many of you at the table, or if you wish to entertain frequently at large sit-down dinners, a separate dining room is practically indispensable.

Dining room decor depends upon the architecture of the room, your personal taste, and the furniture you already own. But there are a few special decorative points that it is wise to keep in mind:

—Solid-colored *carpeting and rugs* show stains more noticeably than any other kind of floor covering, and it is therefore better to choose a patterned rug or a solid-colored carpet (if you insist) with a patterned texture. Marble floors are extremely elegant but awfully cold, and the table area should be carpeted—unless you are able to provide for every guest, in the eighteenth-century fashion, a velvet foot cushion underneath the table! Vinyl squares are a good substitute for marble (and also very chic in the entrance hall), especially rather large white squares with tiny black ones set at every corner in a cabochon pattern. But never use vinyl flooring in kitchen-type patterns or colors in your dining room.

—When selecting the *color scheme* for a dining room, you should keep in mind its psychological effect and choose the most "appetizing" shades, such as blue, green, and yellow. Because your guests must remain seated at the table and are thus unable to move away from a clashing color or an unflattering background, it is considerate to select rather neutral shades that harmonize with a maximum of colors and complexions. On the other hand, because you spend a relatively short time in the dining room, it is possible to indulge in greater fantasy than in a living room. For example, a somewhat theatrical decor can be most effective in a dining room, whereas it would soon become tiresome in a living room or bedroom. One of the most cheerful and striking dining rooms I know has its walls entirely covered with warm golden-yellow velvet, on which is hung a marvelous collection of blue and white porcelain plates. In New York I discovered some stunning American wallpapers that imitate malachite, marble, and period boiseries, and any of these would be beautiful in a dining room, particularly since one of the most fashionable trends in modern interior decoration is *trompe l'oeil*.

—The scale of your *dining room furniture* should naturally suit the dimensions of the room, but this is not always within your control if you have, for example, inherited your grandmother's heavy oak dining room set. Usually the old-fashioned sideboard is the most cumbersome piece, and sometimes this can be cut in half and remodeled into two different pieces of furniture (this is a favorite trick of antique furniture dealers); or perhaps only the doors can be utilized to decorate built-in cupboards, which take up no room at all. In any case, plenty of cupboard space is indispensable in a dining room. If the room is really tiny and there is no possibility of lining one wall with built-in cupboards, you may still be able to build in two or more corner cupboards, with the bottom part closed and the top part fitted with shelves and concealed built-in lighting in order to display your prettiest china and silver.

—*Dining room tables* are made in all shapes, sizes, and styles, and since this is the element that sets the tone of your entire room, it should be selected with care (if you have any choice in the matter). A round table that can be expanded by inserting extra leaves is by far the most graceful, in my opinion, as well as the most practical—except perhaps in an extremely long and narrow room, where an oval table would be ideal. Both oval and round tables seem to favor good conversation. Sturdy legs that are placed at the center are more practical than those placed around the edges, for they permit any kind of a seating arrangement without having to take into account the awkward places in front of the legs where it is impossible to seat a guest comfortably. In a home without a separate dining room, an excellent idea is to buy two square lamp tables, rather long-legged and of bridge-table size, which can be used as lamp tables on either side of the sofa and joined together at mealtimes to form a comfortable dining table.

—Next to the dining room table, *chairs* are the most important furniture in the room. Modern copies are sometimes preferable to original antiques, for they are scaled to modern dimensions and they may also be sturdier. In aristocratic Paris dining rooms there is often one pair of rare original antique chairs, while all the others are modern reproductions of the identical design. Leather upholstery is chic, and so is plastic leather, even though it sticks to trousers and skirts during hot weather. It is a mystery to me why men are always harder on chairs than women, but this is so. Consequently, if you have any antiques covered with a precious old silk, it is safer to assign them to women guests.

— Careful thought should be given to the dining room *lighting*, which should be soft but sufficient. Too little light is even more unpleasant and unappetizing than too much. First of all, you will need to provide a general soft lighting by means of daylight streaming through the windows in the daytime, and at night by wall appliques, concealed indirect lighting or perhaps by well-lit display cabinets or pictures evenly spaced around the room. In addition, the table itself should be highlighted either by candles for a company dinner or a fixture suspended from the ceiling for family meals. Very elaborate chandeliers are no longer in fashion, but many charming and less imposing models are designed nowadays to harmonize with every period and style of decoration. It is necessary to check up on the dining room lighting from time to time because worn out electric bulbs can cast a dismal light to which you may have become accustomed. Even at intimate family meals, two kinds of lighting are taboo: a floor lamp standing beside the table, and an electric lamp or electrified candelabra in the center of the table.

— While it is not often possible in a small room, it is always a good idea to hide *the kitchen door* behind a pretty folding screen. A swinging kitchen door is practical, even if you have nobody to wait on table.

— Porcelain and pewter plates are an attractive and appropriate *decoration for dining room walls,* and they can very well substitute for pictures. Green plants are also attractive in this part of the house, as are wide plate glass mirrors to reflect candlelight and silver. A real woodburning fireplace (gently flaming in the wintertime and filled with plants or flowers in the summer) would be heavenly!

— The modern trend in decoration is to display very little *china and silver* on the dining room table and on the sideboard, just a few well-selected pieces. All of them should be well polished and perhaps protected by one of the tarnish-preventing products. In the case of metal candlesticks, vases, etc., the base should be lined with felt in order to avoid scratching the table or sideboard surface. Doilies or runners would offer the same protection, of course, but these are no longer in fashion and they seem rather fussy and quaint today. While it is always elegant to compose a display of silver and china all of the same period and in the same style, it is even more chic nowadays to form a rather eclectic arrangement of a few decorative objects that reflect your personal taste. As a matter of fact, it is elegant to display an impressive amount of china, pewter, silver, etc., only when you possess a really admirable collection of museum quality, or if you present the objects in a very original way, as, for example, does a friend of mine who has on her sideboard a collection of five or six English silver coffeepots set all in a row in decreasing size.

— If your dining room is actually part of the living room, it should take its cue from the living room decor. Unless there is some form of architectural separation, if only a low room divider, the decor should preferably be the same. If the dining room section is more or less separate but still plainly visible from the living room, the decor may be entirely different, but the color schemes should harmonize.

— Finally, if you have no dining room and you find it difficult to arrange a dining corner in the living room, it may be possible to furnish a wide entrance hall so that it can be transformed into a dining room; or perhaps one side of the kitchen can be arranged for family dining. Remember, too, that in warm climates a covered outdoor terrace can serve as a dining room during much of the year.

(See Chairs, Tables)

DINNERS

❮ A dinner party is practically synonymous with entertaining, for it is the most traditional means of honoring one's guests.

According to Gabriel-Louis Pringué, a prominent figure in Paris society before the war, who entitled his memoirs *Thirty Years of Dining in Town*, to be invited to tea, to a dance or a ball by a leading society hostess used to be thought of as elegant, but of little social significance; whereas to be invited to dinner proved that you were an intimate friend, a member of the same exclusive circle, and securely perched on the same rung of the social ladder. Times have changed, but there is still a certain amount of truth in his quaintly snobbish observation.

The number of guests at a dinner party can, of course, vary widely—from one or two to infinity (a theoretically unattainable point that is very rapidly reached in our compact modern apartments!). But it is a curious fact that while these one or two guests should really be highly complimented, considering that everything has been arranged for them alone, they actually only begin to feel flattered when there are at least six at the table. As a result, the problem of planning the menu for a dinner party is child's play compared to the problem of planning the guest list, with the exception, of course, of family dinners. At a family dinner, since everybody already knows everybody else and everyone has the same right to be present, the only thing that really matters is the menu.

Before examining in detail all the different kinds of dinners and their settings, it is wise to keep in mind one general principle: There is no doubt that in this day and age, and with the exception of official and diplomatic functions, it is more elegant to exclude all forms of rigid solemnity from your dinner parties and instead to concentrate your efforts on the refinement and originality of details, as well as the warmth and friendliness of the atmosphere.

Dinners for Two

After all, why shouldn't a woman feel as if she were giving a dinner party for her husband every evening? I realize that to accomplish this requires a great deal of energy, much time, and a six-foot shelf of cookbooks, but it seems to me very worthwhile going to a bit of trouble in order to give your husband the impression that every time he comes home in the evening he is going to a party.

First of all, you must give a little thought to the decor, especially if you dine in the kitchen. It is a very good idea, whenever possible, to divide the kitchen in two by means of a rather high counter like a bar, equipped with shelves and cupboards on the side that opens onto the part of the kitchen where the sink and stove are located. Your room divider thus provides an ideal storage place for all the cooking equipment you need to have near at hand, but which is not especially aesthetic to the eye. In the other half of the room, which has now become two rooms, you can arrange a cheerful dining corner. The simplest decor, composed for example of a wrought-iron garden table underneath a real striped awning, which is lit from above by several concealed electric light bulbs to create an impression of sunshine, will form a gay and charming dining corner that has only the name in common with the rather depressing, workmanlike kitchens of our grand-mothers.

American women are the luckiest in the world where furnishing a home is concerned. It is in the housewares department that I lose my head when visiting your department stores. Every article seems to have been conceived in order to avoid tiresome chores, and at the same time everything is much more attractively designed and far less expensive than in Europe. You should therefore have no trouble at all in provid-ing yourself with a number of gay table mats with matching napkins, pretty plates, and large, stable glasses. Then when your little stage setting is ready, you should give a thought to your own appearance and arrange to greet your dinner guest (even though he is in this case your own husband) smiling and fresh, with your hair neatly arranged, wear-ing a pretty fresh house dress. Most important of all, you should ar-range to serve the dinner on time.

Try to put aside until later your worries and problems. Don't over-whelm him the moment he arrives. He usually spares you the detailed account of whatever disagreeable moments he may have experienced during the day's work, so at least give him time to forget them.

Try also to vary your menus as much as possible. If you attempt to please your husband by preparing his favorite dish night after night, he will eventually come to loathe it. Taste in food, as in many other things, can be educated, and he will become as fine a gourmet as you wish if only you give him the opportunity to acquire a gastronomic edu-cation. But in attempting to broaden his taste, you should naturally keep in mind his personal likes and dislikes. To say that the way to a man's heart is through his stomach may be a hackneyed adage, but there is a great deal of truth in it. The succulent home-cooked dishes that inspire a man's devotion are no more of a myth than the new hat that gives a lift to a woman's morale.

By putting into practice these simple ideas, both of you will enjoy one pleasant dinner after another, and toward the end of your life you will be amazed to discover what perfect serenity you have achieved to-gether, simply because you have always treated your husband as your most important dinner guest.

Dinners for Four

It is never considered a gala occasion to invite just one other couple to dinner. Generally the reason for giving this kind of a dinner is because "It's been ages since we've seen each other," or because there is a particular project you wish to discuss. In short, your guests are intimate friends, and there is no reason to make a big production out of the occasion.

On the other hand, since you are perfectly familiar with their tastes and even their diets, it would be inexcusable to serve them a dish that they either dislike or are not allowed to eat. If there is one gastronomic specialty that you prepare especially well, even if it is only an omelette, by all means make it—but not every time. In any case, never attempt to prepare a series of complicated or pretentious dishes for this kind of a dinner. One unusual recipe is quite enough. You might, however, splurge on some extravagance such as smoked salmon, lobster, or foie gras as an entrée, or wild rice and game, if you are sure that your friends like it. It is always much more fun to share a luxurious food in a very small group, not to mention the fact that it is a lot easier on the budget to buy extravagant delicacies for four than for twelve!

In spite of the intimacy of the occasion, the decor is still an important factor to be considered. Even if you eat in the kitchen, a touch of fantasy and imagination will help to create a party atmosphere. However, before considering the choice of color of the tablecloth or candles, it is a good idea to pay closer than usual attention to the impeccable condition of your dishes, silverware, table linen, and serving plates. Personally, I far prefer a perfectly spotless plastic tablecloth to an embroidered linen heirloom that is wrinkled and carelessly laundered, and simple but sparkling clean dishes to the most precious chipped porcelain. Don't forget to check the silverware for tarnish, especially the tines of forks. Everything should be inspected, just as you scrutinze yourself from tip to toe in your mirror before going out. Even your very best friend may be unable to resist the temptation of pointing out to her husband your imperfections as a housewife, if only to increase her own prestige in his eyes.

All of the dishes, silverware, and serving plates that are to be used should be laid out ahead of time either on a sideboard or on a rolling tea table, the latter being more practical, since it enables you to whisk everything out of sight as soon as the meal is over. The less often the hostess has to leave the table, the more smoothly her dinner will proceed. (But during one of her absences, she should take time to remove the remains of the before-dinner cocktails from the living room, to change the ashtrays, and to set the coffee tray on a low table.) Here, for example, are three types of simple menus that are guaranteed to put four people in a good mood, even though each includes only one dish requiring last-minute preparation:

I

Smoked Salmon with thin toast, butter, and lemon halves; or, if it is the end of the month, thin toast canapés garnished with smoked cod liver, capers, and lemon; or red caviar, Baltic herring, etc.

Omelette (with ham, truffles, chicken livers, asparagus tips, mushrooms, etc.)

Salad with French dressing (oil and vinegar), dressed up with fresh herbs, tomatoes, cucumber, cold string beans, or almost any kind of vegetable.

Fruit Tart, that is, an open-faced fruit or berry pie; or perhaps an old-fashioned apple pie.

Everything can be prepared in advance except for the omelette, which can be whipped ahead of time and cooked in ten minutes or less while your guests are finishing the first course.

2

Smoked Ham (Italian prosciutto is best), cut in very thin slices and rolled around a fresh fig or a canned peach half, held in place by toothpicks. During the summer melon season, the same smoked ham may be served with cantaloupe slices, as in Italy.

Veal Scallops in Cream. Although the effect is very gastronomic, nothing is simpler to prepare if you take the pains to brown the scallops well and to add to the frying pan a good pinch of thyme, rosemary, or, lacking these fragrant herbs, a finely minced onion. When the scallops are browned on both sides, you cover the pan and cook for ten minutes more, and if there is not enough juice in the pan you can add a tablespoonful of water. Then turn off the burner, or set it as low as possible, and add a tablespoonful of Cognac (or of whisky, if your husband screams as you reach for his precious brandy bottle), plus two tablespoonfuls of heavy whipping cream, which you blend together into a sauce, scraping into it everything that has stuck to the bottom of the pan. To accompany this dish, which should be served on a heated platter (warmed in a slow oven or by running hot water over it for a few minutes), you can choose either boiled new potatoes, buttered noodles, or rice, which can all be kept hot in the oven until it is time to serve them.

Fruit Cup. In the winter, when it is made with canned or frozen fruit, I always add at least a few fresh ones: oranges, bananas, apples, or even a few raisins and candied fruit. If you arrange the mixture in a hollowed pineapple shell, sugar it well, and sprinkle with rum, you will have prepared in no time at all a perfectly beautiful dessert. The extra fruit salad should be placed in a glass bowl to be passed around for second helpings. And a few crisp cookies should always be served with this kind of a light dessert.

3

It is quite possible to eliminate the first course entirely, if you serve a very hearty main dish that is brought steaming to the table as soon as the guests are seated. For example: Beef or lamb stew, New England boiled dinner, chicken in the pot, French *pot au feu* or Indian curry. With all of these dishes, it is a good idea to prepare in advance a set of relish bowls filled with various condiments, such as cole slaw, cottage cheese, spiced peaches, olives, radishes, horseradish sauce, pickled watermelon rind, sweet gherkins, slices of dill pickle, etc. To follow this main dish, which should be copious, either a salad or preferably a perfect French or Italian cheese selected in a fancy grocery, and a light dessert, such as a mousse, a creamy pudding, or ice cream, and you will have served a charming dinner without having to leave the table for a minute until time for dessert.

These three types of menus, all of them extremely simple and within the means of the least experienced homemaker, can be accompanied by one kind of wine, according to your budget and to your taste. A simple red wine would go with everything, except for the smoked

salmon (with which a tiny glass of Vodka would be perfect, to be followed by the red wine). It would be preferable to serve only water
rather than coffee during the meal, if only because it is a gastronomic
heresy to drink something sweetened while eating something salted.

There is also a delicious Spanish specialty called *sangria,* which is a
wine punch and is always a great success at this kind of an informal
dinner party. It is prepared by pouring into a large pitcher a bottle of
ordinary red wine (rather strong, at least thirteen percent alcohol), a
sliced lemon and a sliced orange, including the rinds; two tablespoons
of granulated sugar, a liqueur glass (or two) of Cognac, and six ice
cubes. Chill it in the refrigerator at least two hours before serving.

Dinners for Six or Eight

If the six or eight guests are all close friends, the problem is exactly
the same as for four, except that the quantities are increased. But if
your guests are merely acquaintances, it would not really be considered
elegant to receive them with the same degree of casual informality.

Much more difficult to carry off successfully than the planning of
your menu is your responsibility as hostess to lead the conversation,
and that is why it is wise to select with infinite care and tact the two
or three couples whom you wish to introduce to one another. Furthermore, the fewer the guests, the greater their affinities should be.

Naturally, it is not always possible to predict the reactions of people
whom you yourself may not know very well, but as a general rule it is
better never to invite together two lawyers, two doctors, two architects
—in other words, two representatives of the same liberal profession—
for they will very seldom hit it off well together, especially if they
live and practice in the same town. On the other hand, two businessmen
or two industrialists will usually find a thousand absorbing topics to
discuss. But never invite at the same time an important executive and
a subordinate employee of the same company. For that matter, you
may unwittingly be committing a dreadful gaffe by inviting together
any two employees of the same firm, so it is safer to avoid it.

An infallible way to spend a boring evening is to invite together
three couples to whom you owe a dinner, but who have absolutely
nothing in common aside from the fact that they all know you. If,
despite your efforts, you perceive that not the slightest current of sym-
pathy springs up among your guests, you should at least be well enough

informed about them to be able to turn the conversational spotlight on each one in turn.

When you first introduce each guest, try to describe in a few words what each one does, and do not hesitate to increase his prestige by exaggerating if necessary. For example: "George is the most brilliant junior executive at Coca Cola [Du Pont, or Ford, as the case may be], which would have folded up long ago if he wasn't there." Of course, such outrageous flattery won't fool anyone, but it will please the person concerned and the others will be able to label him in their minds right away. However, if you are inviting the president of one of these famous companies, or even of a much smaller firm, you should mention the fact to the other guests ahead of time when you telephone them, because, like movie stars, these distinguished personages think that everybody knows who they are and they expect everyone they meet to be imbued with respect.

As for unassuming Mary Smith, she may be either a champion golfer (or at least the champion cook of whatever special dish she may have served you at her dinner), or she may grow the most gorgeous roses in Connecticut, or own the most beautiful cocker spaniel in the world, or have raised the most extraordinarily well-brought-up children —and on this subject your praise will never be as lofty as the opinion of the parents, so superlatives are imperative! With a little thought, you can surely find something about her worthy of praise, and if not, why on earth did you ever bother to accept her invitation, not to mention inviting her yourself!

At this kind of a dinner party, it is very difficult to get along without somebody to wait on table. But if it is really impossible for you to hire a waiter or waitress for the evening, try to begin with a hot entrée and to continue with cold dishes that can be prepared in advance and laid out on the sideboard. For example: a roast beef or veal, broiled filet mignons, or a leg of lamb with vegetables; then a cold pâté or cheese or salad; and finally a dessert.

However, a more elegant and classical menu for a small dinner would be composed of an entrée (either hot or cold fish, creamed chicken or seafood in a pastry shell, a soufflé or a quiche, or an egg dish very attractively presented); meat or chicken (simply roasted if the entrée included a sauce), accompanied by vegetables, and a salad served at the same time but on a separate salad plate; a cheese tray, and a dessert. In our house in the South of France, where I have nobody to help me serve meals, I often pass around with the before-dinner cocktails (which today very often consist simply of whisky or vodka), well-laden trays of rather hearty hors d'oeuvres, which replace the entrée and at the same time leave me free to put the last-minute finishing touches on the main dish.

You should remember that your talents as a hostess and housewife are going to be judged by these guests, who neither know you very well nor see you very often, and that every detail in the arrangement of your home should be an honor to you. The evening before the dinner party, you should have undertaken a thorough housecleaning, whisking out of sight every object that is soiled or broken; you should have checked the tableware that is not regularly used and which becomes dusty very quickly, especially in a city apartment; you should have pressed the tablecloth (over its table pad, right on the table) and polished the silver. A dessert that can be prepared the night before is also one less thing to worry about the next day, as is all of the marketing that can be done in advance.

On the day of the party, you should never forget to reserve in your busy program at least one full hour for yourself, in order to take a luxurious bath, to get dressed and made up and to do your hair. You should already have decided in the morning what you are going to wear, and checked to make sure that your dress needs no ironing or mending. Before the party, all you have to do is to lay your things out on the bed—and it is a good idea to lay out your husband's clothes too.

Without this hour of your own, you run the risk of hearing your guests ring the doorbell when you are dressed only in your slip, with your hair in disorder, panting from the last-minute rush and irritable from nervous tension. Besides, one of the secrets of successful entertaining is always to give the impression to your guests that you have spent a most leisurely and agreeable day and are just as relaxed as they are. Entertaining is a marvelous pleasure for everyone concerned, and should never appear to be a chore.

Formal Dinners

Slightly more pretentious is the large dinner party consisting of ten to twelve people (this number being the maximum possible for the average-sized dining room table and for the usual supply of dishes, table settings, and glasses a hostess possesses); but you may invite even more if there is sufficient room and equipment.

In preparing your guest list, it is somewhat less important to select people who share common tastes and interests because there will never be a moment when all of them are talking together in one large group. Your most important preoccupation is the seating arrangement at the table, and having made your plan in advance, you should make a point of seeing that each guest has been introduced to his neighbors and given a clue as to their interests and occupations. How many times have I found myself seated between two gentlemen whose names I hadn't quite caught (because in France no one ever dares ask a person to repeat his name), not knowing whether they were university professors or icebox salesmen, talking in riddles until the meat course!

Unfortunately, aside from the question of compatability, the hostess must consider etiquette in placing her guests at the table, and in this regard there are a thousand amusing anecdotes, dating mostly from the turn of the century when society apparently was more preoccupied with the question of protocol than with the problem of earning a living. One of my favorite concerns Count Aimery de la Rochefoucauld, a very gallant man and a perfect gentleman, who seems to have been particularly sensitive about the protocol of the dining table. Tradition required the host and hostess to be seated opposite each other in the middle of the table, with the most honored guests at their right and left and then in descending order of importance toward each end. When the Count learned of a recent marriage in which the social standing of the bridegroom was distinctly inferior to that of the bride, he sadly exclaimed, "For one night of love—forty years at the end of the table!"

To be seated at the right of the host must be a meager compensation for the years of loveless marriage that such an honor might imply, and I am not sure that I would not prefer, like Peter Pan, to enjoy eternal youth and to find myself much more often at the end of the table. Not only is the conversation apt to be livelier, but I would also be spared forever the sometimes perilous exercise of being the first to cut into an elaborately mounted dessert! In actual practice, the most successful system and the most usual nowadays is to place the host and hostess at each end of the table, with the least honored guests thus being seated in the middle.

You must count on at least an hour between the time the party is supposed to begin and the moment dinner is served, in order to give your guests time to become acquainted and to relax over a few cocktails. But be careful not to prolong the cocktail interlude unduly, because they might become either too noisy or prematurely drowsy.

You should take special pains with the decoration of the dining table, and I assume that you have left nothing to last-minute inspiration and have borrowed any equipment you may lack a day or two ahead of time. You will need a pretty tablecloth, preferably embroidered or of lace, two or three glasses per person (the large one filled in advance with ice water, the others for wine), a centerpiece of flowers or fruit, candelabra with colored candlesticks, sparkling silverware and, at each end of the table, a menu card written by hand. It is up to you whether or not to set handwritten place cards in front of each plate. Personally, I only do this when there are a great many guests, since I prefer to draw a little plan of the table and to seat the guests myself by indicating to each his chair. Even if you have to spend two full hours of hard work in setting a lovely table—and one hour is generally the minimum time required to set a table for ten— you will be largely rewarded by the admiring exclamations your efforts are certain to elicit from your guests. It is supposed to be bad manners to mention food at the table, but in my opinion it is even more impolite to refrain from complimenting one's hostess, who has probably gone to a great deal of trouble in your honor.

For this kind of a dinner party, it is indispensable to have one or two persons to wait on table. One waiter or waitress for every six guests is the standard rule, and it will be more elegant if at least one of them is a waiter. A very experienced waiter may be able to serve a simple meal to as many as ten guests. But when there are more than twelve, it is best to have two waiters and even two identical platters of each course on the menu. You will also need a person to help in the kitchen, because on this occasion it is out of the question for you to leave your place at table. If you are not fortunate enough to have an excellent cook, it is highly recommended to have two out of three courses on the menu prepared by a caterer. They should be ordered at least three days in advance, and you should make a point of requesting not too fancy a presentation, because everything should give the illusion of having been prepared in your own kitchen, and such professional caterers' fancies as bits of decorative pastry or pimento cut in curious shapes would immediately betray the secret that the dish in question came straight from the local restaurant or pastry shop. Nothing is less chic than an overly elaborate platter. The appetizing appearance of a dish is, of course, a very important element in gastronomy, but the fact remains that a Japanese garden sculpted in aspic, or a lobster artfully arranged to resemble a still-life masterpiece are rather vulgar.

You should also beware of the menu that starts out with caviar and lobster, for this easily gives an impression of *nouveau riche*. According to Pierre Daninos, a Parisian authority on snobs, an exaggerated predilection for caviar and lobster is the first symptom of very recently acquired riches, because people who are accustomed to prosperity are already so stuffed with these expensive delicacies that they can no longer bear the sight of them. I do not mean to imply that caviar and lobster should automatically be banished from your dinner table, but neither should they automatically figure in every one of your formal dinner party menus. Besides, as I have said, it is much more fun to enjoy such luxurious treats when you are dining with just a few close friends. On the other hand, it is perfectly elegant to serve caviar canapés with the cocktails, (and you need to buy far less than if it were to be the appetizer course). But there are a thousand excellent and more original first courses for a formal dinner party: creamed seafood in a huge pastry shell, fresh cold salmon, fish soufflé, turbot with Hollandaise sauce, trout with almonds, cold jellied trout, and even foie gras if you simply insist on spending a lot of money.

For the main course, nothing is more appropriate nor more elegant during the hunting season than roast game, such as pheasant, squab, partridge, or venison, accompanied by wild rice or a purée of chestnuts, currant jelly or Cumberland sauce, and tiny pastry shells filled with a prune purée, to add a note of originality. During other seasons, the most classical choices for a formal dinner would include such dishes as roast chicken garnished in an unusual way (with prawns, for example, or pork sausages); *Tournedos Rossini* (filet steaks topped with a slice of foie gras and truffle and served with a Madeira wine sauce); a whole baked ham in a pastry case with Madeira sauce, or garnished with pineapple, peaches, and prunes; a roast suckling pig; a roast beef; not to forget the traditional turkey, duckling, and goose. You can serve at the same time a green salad with a simple dressing on a special salad plate. The crescent-shaped plates, incidentally, are the most fashionable.

The main course can be followed by a cheese tray and an assortment of biscuits, and for this the guests might very well use their bread and butter plates, which are at the left of each place setting with a pat of butter and a dinner roll or two or three half-slices of bread. In Europe the cheese course is a very important part of a formal dinner party, and all of the leading shops will arrange an attractive assortment on a straw or wooden tray with tiny flags identifying the different varieties. The standard minimum of four includes one mild, solid type (Edam, Swiss Gruyère), one aged (Roquefort, Gorgonzola, etc.), one soft fermented type (Camembert, Pont l'Evêque, etc.), and one fresh creamy cheese, which can assume any number of disguises. In the United States, where cheese is more often eaten in sandwiches than as a separate dinner course, an authentic Continental cheese tray is perhaps more difficult to prepare in all but the most cosmopolitan cities. But you can at least try to have a minimum of three different kinds. Two large cream cheeses from the local supermarket can be given a new flavor and appearance if one of them is generously coated with paprika, and the other with caraway seeds. Another delicious trick is to split a creamy Swiss-type cheese in half like a sandwich bun, and put it back together again around a thick layer of walnuts.

Your dessert should be superb but not too heavy, which means that you should avoid such rich dishes as cream cakes and butter-cream pastries. A molded ice cream served with chocolate or hot caramel sauce, with a fresh fruit sauce, with macaroons—a sort of sundae, in other words—would perhaps be the most agreeable ending to a meal like this, which is more copious and richer than the usual daily fare. After the dessert it is always elegant to pass a basket of fruit and a plate of cookies or petit fours. When fruit is to be served, you should always provide your guests with finger bowls, placed on a doily on the dessert plate and set by each guest in front and to the left of his place. As a matter of fact, at a formal dinner finger bowls are considered to be a part of the table service no matter what the dessert is to be.

As for the beverage, wine is virtually obligatory, and there are two schools of thought on the subject: the old-fashioned style, which consists of serving a dry white wine with the fish, a red Bordeaux type with the roast, a red Burgundy type with the cheese, and champagne or a Sauterne with the dessert. Aside from the fact that this requires four different wine glasses for each guest, it is almost certain to make most of them sick, and so this tradition has been practically abandoned even in Europe in favor of the second, modern method: to serve champagne throughout the entire meal, with the exception of the cheese course, during which a simple red wine is passed. Nevertheless, it is always a good idea to have a carafe of red wine on the table throughout the meal, because many people prefer it to champagne.

When there are more than eight of you, you will need one wine bottle or carafe at each end of the table.

Each course, except for the cheese and fruit, should be passed around twice, and the hostess should always automatically take a second helping in order to encourage guests who might be too shy to do so if they did not have her example to follow. It is therefore a wise precaution, if you are not very hungry or are on a diet, to take a rather small helping the first time. At a formal dinner like this one, all of the women guests are served first, starting with the one seated to the right of the host and ending with the hostess, before serving the men by starting with the guest on the right of the hostess and finishing with the host. Out of respect for the cuisine, it is the custom in many foreign countries, including France, for each person to start eating a hot dish as soon as he has been served. While this may not be considered absolutely proper etiquette in America, I would personally give three cheers for the hostess who urges her guests to adopt this custom, and especially when the menu includes lamb or pork, which loses much of its flavor if it has been allowed to get cold. The hostess should never, however, overly insist that a guest take a second helping, and certainly not disregard his protestations by placing a generous serving on his plate herself!

When everybody has finished, the hostess rises from the table and moves to the living room, or to the other side of the room if there is only one, to take her place at a coffee table (from which the cocktail remains have in the meantime been removed), where the coffee is on a tray ready to be served. Nowadays the thoughtful hostess prepares one pot of normal coffee and another of a decaffeinated brew, out of consideration for incurable insomniacs. The brandy and liqueurs that are served immediately after the coffee can be laid out on the same tray.

In the meanwhile, the waiter clears the table as swiftly and quietly as possible, so that the room immediately recovers its normal aspect. And now, in my opinion at least, the hostess's real problem begins.

At nine out of ten dinner parties, the conversation has usually been gay and animated at table, but as soon as the guests are asked to move to the other room there is an interruption. Those who were neighbors at the table are separated and usually regroup themselves with the guests they already know well, except in the rare cases when they have become involved in a really absorbing discussion. Nothing is more distressing than to see all of your men guests gathered together in one corner exchanging views on politics or business, while all of the women are left to themselves to compare notes on household hints and child-rearing. Your best strategy is to try to form two different mixed groups, one centered around yourself, and the other around your husband. A single general conversation is practically impossible to organize with a group this size, unless you happen to have as guest of honor an outstanding celebrity who will monopolize the attention of all present.

If some of your guests are impassioned bridge players, there are at least four or five people happily taken care of. If they are dancing enthusiasts, hurrah for the latest dance fad (there is a new one every six months). Let's hope that you have had the foresight to buy the latest records and to learn the new steps—unless it is your husband or one of your guests who shines in this particular field. An impromptu dancing lesson of this kind always amuses everybody, and perhaps most of all those who are content merely to watch. In short, try anything your ingenuity suggests, but by all means avoid letting your guests all sit around in a circle like patients in a dentist's waiting room. In general, the older they are, the more difficult this will be.

About an hour after dinner, or even sooner, you can animate the atmosphere somewhat by serving a tray of long drinks and fruit juice.

To tell the truth, I have practically eliminated this kind of a dinner party from my entertaining program, simply because I have so often found the two hours that follow the meal interminably long when they are spent attempting to digest more or less successfully a rather heavy meal, and to dispel one's sneaking suspicion that everybody is secretly longing to go home and go to bed.

Buffet Dinners

The buffet dinner party has become more and more fashionable, and it is also the formula I prefer. Perhaps it is not the ideal way to entertain very elderly people—but are there any left? I have not met a woman who looks elderly for years.

A buffet dinner permits a greater number of guests, and extra ones may even be invited at the last minute. For this reason it is always much gayer and more relaxed than a formal sit-down dinner; it requires less personnel and allows everyone to chat and visit with whomever they wish without any problem of a prepared seating arrangement. It is, in short, perfectly adapted to modern life, in which informality has become synonymous with elegance. Basically, a buffet dinner is no more than a cocktail party with more substantial refreshments; it lasts longer and has a more restricted guest list.

The ideal number of guests for a successful buffet dinner varies between twenty and forty, depending on the size of one's home; but the same formula can be adapted for as few as eight, ten, or twelve.

Since it is impossible for the hostess to look after every one of her guests at the same time if it is a large party, it is preferable for the majority of them already to be acquainted and to come from more or less the same social set, for this assures that several different groups will automatically be formed. If some guests are comparative strangers, or do not know a single soul, you can ask a close friend to look after them and see that they are included in a group. In this case, too, introductions are most important, the idea being to give every single person present the impression that he is the guest of honor.

I cannot resist injecting at this point a fashion tip. Here is the ideal occasion for the hostess to wear what is aptly described by the fashion press as "a hostess ensemble": a long simple sheath dress of tweed in the winter and of linen in the summer, with one or two pieces of jewelry at the most.

A buffet dinner party can be just as successful when you manage on a very modest budget as when you go all out in a sumptuous splurge. The only pitfall to be avoided is banality. As a matter of fact, the most unpretentious formula of all—spaghetti and meatballs and red wine—is particularly fashionable among the snobs.

The buffet table itself will be the center of attraction. A long table (which might be no more than a sturdy plank supported on trestles) should be set up in the corner of the room that is most accessible to the guests as well as to the kitchen, and placed just far enough away from the corner for a waiter or waitress to work comfortably behind it. At an informal buffet without waiters, however, it is usually more practical to set the table in the center of the room so that the guests can circulate all around it.

The entire meal should be spread out from the very beginning (except perhaps for very strongly perfumed cheese and melting ice cream desserts), for it should give the impression that it is absolutely laden with mountains of delicious food.

I keep on hand for just such occasions a magnificent bright red tablecloth, which is simply a white damask cloth of my grandmother, which I dyed myself. I cover the table so that the cloth hangs to the floor in front, and then pin up the corners so that it does not trail on the carpet, and I decorate the façade with ribbons and bows. With an array of gleaming silver or pewter serving dishes, the effect is extremely pretty and warm to the eye. As a centerpiece, I build a pyramid of decorative fruits, flowers and vegetables, or whatever I happen to lay my hands on. (Hmmm—to tell the truth, I start planning the table decoration at least three days beforehand!) As a final touch, candles and large paper napkins in the same bright red as the tablecloth, and the decor is complete.

At one end of the buffet table you should place the piles of plates and the necessary silverware, always counting a few pieces more than you should actually need. Remember that you can always borrow from your family or friends if your own household resources are insufficient. It is best to have the drinks and glasses laid out somewhere other than on the buffet table, because you will also be serving cocktails before dinner. And so you must set up a bar on a tea cart or simply on a chest of drawers, equipping it with all the glasses and liquor you will need and the largest thermos ice bucket you own. Before your guests arrive, you can distribute plates of tiny sandwiches, salted almonds, and cocktail crackers at strategic points around the room on side tables and other furniture, and later on pass hot hors d'oeuvres, such as cocktail frankfurters, miniature pizzas, and tiny cream puff or éclair shells filled with a thick cheese sauce, just as if it were a cocktail party. Remember that many people cannot (or should not) drink liquor on an empty stomach.

When the desired mood has been achieved, usually about an hour or an hour and a half after the arrival of the first guest, when the atmosphere has had time to become warm and animated but your guests are not yet tired from standing up, you must perform an exploit of prestidigitation. Like a magician, you will suddenly produce a number of tables around the edges of the room—round ones, if possible, or failing that, bridge tables, all of them covered with matching tablecloths. Charming plastic ones cost only a dollar or so. Individual tables that can be nested together are not really suitable for this kind of an occasion, as they have always seemed to me to be awfully antisocial. However, any kind of a table at all is better than asking your guests to balance a plate on their knees.

You ask your guests to serve themselves at the buffet, where you station yourself in order to help them. If you do not possess enough chairs for all of your guests, you will have to rent the folding kind. But if you entertain fairly often at large buffet dinners, it would probably be an economy to buy a set of folding chairs once and for all, because renting them can become quite expensive.

As far as the menu is concerned, it is of course easiest if everything is cold and can be prepared in advance. If you have a well-organized kitchen and at least one person to watch the stove, you can serve a single hot dish, which should be rather hearty and extremely copious, such as a Spanish paella, barbecued lamb with couscous (an unusual and tasty North African specialty), baked whole ham, beef stroganoff with rice or noodles, or sauerkraut in the Alsatian style, garnished with an assortment of smoked and boiled ham, pork sausage, frankfurters, etc. If you are an excellent cook, you might prepare it yourself in the morning so that it only needs to be warmed up half an hour or so before serving (the larger the casserole, the longer it will take); or you can order this type of a main dish from a caterer or a restaurant. In either case, it should be kept piping hot on the buffet table over an electric or candlepowered hot plate so that the last guests to serve themselves will not be faced with a stone-cold casserole.

For a change, you can build your entire menu around an international theme featuring the national specialties of Italy, or Spain, or Mexico, Scandinavia, Russia, China, Japan—the possibilities are endless. In this event, your decorative scheme might also be in the colors of the country you have chosen to honor, with an attractive arrangement of native objects on the buffet table and even typical background music. I am the first to admit that these ideas can hardly be described as ingenious or original, but they are very simple to realize and are certain to give your party an atmosphere of novelty and gaiety, and yourself an aura of a seasoned globe-trotter.

Remember, if you are tempted to serve both a fish and a meat course, that you will need twice as many dishes and twice as much silverware, so this is only practical when there are not very many guests. But the only dish you should peremptorily ban from such a dinner is that sad old standby, chicken à la king. On the other hand, all varieties of cold meats, ham and delicatessen specialties or, to introduce a Continental note, cold jellied *boeuf à la mode* (with onions and carrots), rabbit in aspic, or cold duck with orange would be most appetizing. You should not, however, cut them or slice them until the very last minute in order to prevent the slices from drying out. To accompany these main dishes, let your imagination run riot in selecting an assortment of unusual and exotic condiments presented in an array of little Chinese rice bowls, and in preparing at least two different salad bowls that are rather out of the ordinary. Two salads that I often serve at my buffets and which go together perfectly are:

(1.) Cold rice that has been well drained and then dried out in a low oven, seasoned with mayonnaise to which mustard has been added to taste (the mustard flavor should be quite pronounced), a half a jar of Chutney, a can of sweet red peppers (pimentos) cut in small dice, green pistachio nuts, and seedless black raisins. It is a lovely dish to look at and very flavorsome.

(2.) A green salad, composed of mixed greens (the curly varieties are the most appetizing), raw sliced mushrooms, fresh herbs such as chervil, tarragon, or chives, seasoned with a French dressing (oil, vinegar, mustard, freshly ground pepper).

To complete your buffet, try to buy a whole cheese—a wheel of Roquefort, Blue, Stilton, etc.—to be served after the meat course has been cleared. Its entrance is certain to create a stir, and you will have no trouble at all thinking up ways in which to use the leftovers.

Now we are ready for dessert, and here again ice cream and cake or petit fours is probably the most widely appreciated as well as the simplest to serve. But if you are particularly renowned for your coconut cake or coffee mousse, these would be even better. For that matter, anything that is at the same time out of the ordinary and really delicious would be better.

The best seating plan is for you to install yourself at one little table and your husband at another. But in actual practice, you will be absent from your place much of the time, helping to clear away the first part of the meal in order to make way for the dessert, because this is the critical moment when there is the greatest risk of confusion.

Where beverage is concerned, the simplest solution is to place a bottle of wine on each table. Champagne is best of all, but it is becoming increasingly fashionable to serve a simple red wine of the Chianti, Bordeaux, or Beaujolais type. A *sangria* is always very much appreciated and is also certain to create an atmosphere of conviviality.

Since the buffet has been served rather late and has lasted quite a long time, there is no what-to-do-afterward problem as with a sit-down dinner. It will probably already be eleven-thirty or even midnight by the time the meal is finished. You should have arranged to have the buffet table cleared of its empty platters and set with a selection of long drinks and a tall icy pitcher of fruit juice. Your last catering duty as a hostess is thus discharged, and I would be very surprised if your party has not been a perfect success.

Dinner Dances

Since it is practically impossible to provide an impeccable service around one large table if the guests are continually getting up to waltz or twist, a successful dinner dance requires a large number of guests and a sufficient number of small round tables each seating six, eight, or ten persons, arranged around the edges of the dance floor if the room is very large, or in a room adjoining the one in which the orchestra plays. If you do not possess this much space, as well as a perfectly trained household staff, I would not advise you to give a dinner dance at home. Instead, put everything into the hands of the staff of a club or hotel, which is experienced and equipped to organize this kind of a reception. All that you will be required to do is to take out your checkbook.

One of the most recent dinner dances I attended was also one of the most successful, and I am sure that Madame Pierre Gabard, the charming wife of the French consul in Philadelphia, will not mind if I describe in some detail the ideal evening she arranged in honor of the Comédie Française, which was on a tour of the United States at the time.

The party followed the opening-night performance of the troupe, and in a case like this when the hostess arrives at the same time as her guests, it is absolutely necessary for part of the serving staff to be already familiar with the house in order to supervise the extra help during her absence. It is also especially important for everything to be prepared well in advance.

Upon our arrival after the theater, the hostess ushered the women guests to her bedroom to leave their wraps and fix their hair, while the consul directed the men to his room. Cocktails were served by two waiters in a charming library on the same floor, during which time the host and hostess attempted to introduce as many of the guests as possible. (No mean task, since there were seventy-five of us!) This interlude immediately created a friendly and vivacious atmosphere. Then, very soon afterward, the hostess gave the signal to go downstairs for supper. On a side table in the hall were laid out tiny white and gold envelopes, each bearing the name of a guest, with a card inside indicating the number of the table where each would find his place either in the living room or the dining room. The entrance hall was very large, with the living room on one side and the dining room on the other. The hall had been cleared for dancing, and the music could thus be heard in either room.

Each table was covered with a matching tablecloth and lit by matching candelabra decorated with fresh flowers. When everyone had found his place at table, we all introduced ourselves to the others if this had not already been done. It is always helpful to add a phrase more or less explaining why you happen to be there, since this is the best means of entering into conversation and preventing an embarrassed silence from setting in as soon as the presentations have been completed.

It is customary to place husbands and wives at separate tables, except during the first year of marriage and throughout the engagement period. It is, needless to say, considered very bad manners indeed to leave one's place at a table before the end of the meal in order to join another one that may appear to be more amusing.

On this particular occasion, our hosts managed to spend a few minutes at each different table, taking the place of guests who were constantly getting up to dance. There was a great deal of movement. The delicious meal, consisting entirely of cold dishes, was served by a large staff of waiters, who also served champagne throughout the meal. As the guests began to leave (at two o'clock in the morning) the personnel cleared the empty tables and whisked them away, so that little by little the rooms recovered their normal aspect and never once resembled an abandoned battlefield, as is so often the case toward the end of a party.

This occasion, since it followed a theater première, was, strictly speaking, a supper dance. But a dinner dance is exactly the same except that it starts earlier and the little tables remain in place until late refreshments have been served about forty-five minutes or an hour after dinner.

*　　*　　*

For all their countless variations, successful dinner parties have much in common. They may differ as to quantities and trimmings, but the basic ingredients are the same:

— An attractively decorated table.

— An excellent meal.

— A group of guests who get along well together.

— A hostess who, like a masterful film director, makes admirable preparations down to the last detail and then remains in the background, imperceptibly guiding the course of events and bringing out the best in her guests so that each of them feels that he is the star of the evening.

DIPLOMACY

❨ Entertaining has been an essential element of diplomatic life ever since the beginnings of history, and today it is just as important as ever although perhaps somewhat less personal than it used to be. Still, every diplomatic post is generally provided with an official hostess, and an ambassador who is unmarried or a widower usually asks a sister or a grown-up daughter to fill this indispensable role.

Diplomatic entertaining is more often an official duty than a question of personal pleasure. In major embassies and in times of crisis, a hostess hasn't even the right to make out her own guest list. The protocol experts on her husband's staff will take charge of every detail concerning invitations, menus, and refreshments, and they may also brief her in making introductions and in leading the conversation at table. Being the wife of a foreign diplomat is thus a laborious full-time job, and not merely a glorious honorary social position. I have known several diplomats who certainly owe a great deal of their success in international affairs to the charm and cleverness of their wives. On the other hand, there are some whose careers have been seriously hampered because of the inability or unwillingness of their wives to fill their complementary role correctly.

Needless to say, a woman who has spent her entire life in international society possesses an incalculable advantage over the person who has never stirred beyond the borders of her own hometown. However, if the latter is endowed with charm, tact, intelligence, adaptability, good taste, discretion, and above all conscientiousness, it is perfectly possible for her to make a brilliant success and even to enjoy herself immensely in the process, as has been proven by any number of American ambassadors' wives who have been catapulted overnight from a quiet suburban home into the complex, sophisticated realm of foreign affairs. Some of the best hostesses in the world can be found among the women who reign over a foreign embassy thousands of miles away from home.

Everything is much more difficult for the woman who lacks not only the training but also the talent and inclination for such a life. Surrounded by strangers, in a foreign land where she is not familiar with the local customs, language, and politics, it is very easy to make a blunder. But the situation is never hopeless. Every diplomatic staff includes professional experts who are perfectly versed in the subtle techniques of diplomatic entertaining. All the inexperienced newcomer needs to do is to follow their advice. I would even suggest that she start by seeking experienced counsel on the very smallest, apparently insignificant details of her duties as a diplomatic hostess until she herself has gained experience, and eventually self-confidence.

There are techniques of social behavior—particularly in the abnormally artificial world of diplomacy—just as there is a technique for playing the piano or hitting a tennis ball, and all of them can be mastered by means of expert coaching and concentrated practice. Rather than feeling resentful or intimidated by the responsibilities of a diplomat's wife, a woman should be honored and challenged by them. If she starts out her diplomatic career with this attitude, half of her battle is already won.

DISHES

⟪ There are so many different styles and forms of dishes manufactured today and so many of them are elegant, that it is difficult to form any sweeping statements about them. As with all elegance, it is the questions of harmony and appropriateness that count the most: harmony with the rest of your table and with your dining room decor; and appropriateness to the meal that is to be served and to the occasion. However, if I had to recommend one style of dishes that is always chic and goes with everything, I suppose my choice would be the all-white Capo di Monte Italian ware, with a decorated border in relief, and I would always use with it a colored tablecloth. The only style of dishes that I personally dislike is the ornate blue-and-gold Sèvres porcelain. Although it is extremely valuable, I find it far too ceremonial for anything but state occasions in a stiff and formal setting.

Most women possess two sets of dishes: a simple, relatively inexpensive one for informal and family meals; and another more precious service for formal entertaining. This is certainly the most practical policy, especially when there are children in the family. It is advisable, moreover, to select both sets in an open-stock pattern so that individual pieces can be readily replaced as they are chipped or broken. Alas, a certain amount of breakage is inevitable. One of the principal disadvantages of purchasing beautiful tableware during a trip abroad is that ordering replacements can be very complicated and sometimes impossible, unless of course you deal with a large and famous firm—whose wares are probably widely distributed in America anyway.

Porcelain is much more expensive than earthenware, but it is well worth the difference in price, not only because of its inherent value and beauty but also because most earthenware is porous and absorbs grease, leaving dark stains that are impossible to remove. I therefore prefer porcelain in an appropriate design and color and in a simple form, even for houses in the country.

Unbreakable glass dishes are practical in very simple circumstances—at a seashore bungalow, for example, or on a boat. But on an elegant table, glass or even crystal is suitable only for accessories such as salad plates (preferably the crescent-shaped kind), ice cream dishes, finger bowls, etc. The prettiest dessert service I have ever seen consisted of a set of glass fruit dishes placed on golden dessert plates.

Dish sets usually include a wide range of matching serving dishes, and among these the most useful are one large and one small round platter, one large and one small oval platter, a gravy boat, a soup tureen, and a salad bowl. A crystal bowl would be prettier for serving fruit, and a wooden salad bowl is very chic for informal meals, but less suitable than the matching porcelain one for a really formal dinner.

In addition, there exist all sorts of special services for grapefruit, artichokes, oysters, asparagus, caviar, etc. Almost all of them are amusing, practical, or chic. But none of them is really indispensable.

Baked casseroles can be served at the table in the dishes in which they were cooked (except at a formal dinner), and it is therefore worthwhile buying attractive, presentable ones. The Porcelaine de Paris is only one of numerous different firms that design really lovely ovenware.

Soufflés and baked custards must, of course, be served in their cooking receptacles, and for these, classic white porcelain, plain or patterned, is more elegant than ovenproof glass.

DIVORCE

⟨ Divorce has become such a common occurrence in modern society that even the Queen of England has had to relax the restrictions banning divorcées from the royal enclosure at Ascot, and the only social events I know of from which divorced persons are still rigorously barred are the receptions of Madame de Gaulle.

Nevertheless, divorce can sometimes pose a delicate problem for a hostess—for example, when friends whom you have often entertained as a couple decide to dissolve their marriage. If you continue to invite only one of them, you will appear to be taking sides. And if you continue to see each of them separately, you risk becoming involved in their differences and maybe even being exploited as a source of information. Still, it seems to me that this is the best course if you like them both. In any case, to strike both of your friends from your invitation lists would seem to me unnecessarily severe.

Of course, it is extremely tactless to invite a husband and wife who are in the throes of a divorce to the same party without warning each of the other's possible presence, although, in view of the many friendly modern divorces, you may very well be surprised by the cordiality of their relations. But it is generally best to limit your invitations to them during this period to large receptions such as cocktail parties. The same holds true later on, when your friends have remarried. With my Gallic mind, I would consider it in poor taste to invite both new couples to the same soirée, even when they have established perfectly friendly relations and might be delighted to accept.

A woman who has had to consider the problems posed by other people's marital difficulties can more easily understand the feelings of her friends if she herself should one day be in the process of a divorce. Her principal concern should be to avoid giving the impression of forcing them to take sides. In these conditions, there is no reason why she should not continue to entertain as usual, although a series of small dinners or intimate cocktail parties for a few close friends would be more appropriate during this period than more pretentious forms of entertaining.

If she remarries soon afterward, she will naturally wish to introduce her new husband to her friends, but it seems to me more elegant to resist the temptation of planning a grand party when the ink is scarcely dry on her decree—not to mention her new marriage certificate! A really discreet woman would even prefer to wait until her friends have made the first gesture.

A divorced woman who does not remarry is in the same position as an unmarried woman, as far as entertaining goes, with all of the possibilities but also all of the particular problems that are entailed by the independence she has taken such pains to recover.

(See Single Women)

DRINKS

❡ "Candy is dandy, but liquor is quicker," wrote the witty American poet Ogden Nash—and while I assume that he was thinking of a special kind of entertaining (*see* Romance), it is certainly true that liquor is the quickest means of inducing your guests to relax and of creating a warm and friendly atmosphere. In fact, this is the justification for the predinner cocktail, which cannot be defended on gastronomic grounds.

While wine and brandy are made exclusively from grapes, alcoholic spirits are distilled from a wide variety of raw materials (which are first converted into sugar and then fermented in order to produce alcohol), such as grains, potatoes, molasses, maple syrup, apples, rice, cactus and palm-tree sap, not to mention the countless exotic trees and plants from which even the most primitive tribes procure some form of intoxicating beverage. The distilling process increases the percentage of alcohol or "proof" to forty percent and up (in America the proof figure is twice the actual percentage of alcoholic content), and this is more than some persons like or tolerate. And so, whenever you offer a drink to your guests, it is considerate to provide a choice among a hard liquor, a nonalcoholic beverage, and a drink with a relatively low alcoholic content. These might be for example:

At cocktail time: Whisky (Scotch and bourbon), vodka, fruit juice and one of the fortified apéritif wines such as Dubonnet and dry sherry, or a sparkling wine such as champagne.

In the evening: Whisky, fruit juice or soft drinks, and a drink such as gin and tonic in which the spirits are very much diluted in a non-alcoholic mixer, or a sparkling wine.

Theoretically, it is unwise to mix wine with grain spirits during the course of an evening. For example, when wine is being served throughout a meal, it can be preceded by sherry or an aperitif wine and followed by Cognac and brandy and soda, or champagne, with no ill effects; whereas to start with Scotch whisky and to continue with wine and brandy and then more whisky would be not only less gastronomic but also far more potent. However, this theory is seldom respected in modern entertaining, perhaps because many people prefer to dissipate the tensions of modern life as quickly as possible by means of the strongest available spirits.

In any case, these considerations do not really concern a hostess, for her role is to offer her guests complete freedom in the matter, neither insisting that they drink, nor letting them suffer from thirst.

There is such a wide range of drinks to choose from, not to mention the countless cocktail combinations invented by resourceful bartenders, that it is only possible to consider the most familiar ones here. Leaving aside for the moment wines, brandy and liqueurs, the principal alcoholic beverages served at contemporary social receptions are:

Scotch Whisky. The mainstay of every modern liquor cabinet. Scotch is made from malt and grain and the best quality is aged for eight or ten years in old sherry casks. It does not continue to mature in the bottle. Most Scotch is blended to make it lighter in body and smoother in flavor than straight whisky. Quality is most important, since the fashion is to drink whisky drier and drier: "on the rocks" (simply poured over ice cubes in an Old Fashioned glass); "in a mist" (poured over chipped ice which tends to dilute it a little faster); and seldom more than half and half with soda or plain water (from a pitcher, or bottled water). There is no substitute for imported Scotch whisky. The British prefer it with plain water and no ice, the Americans, on the rocks, and the French, with ice and soda water.

Bourbon Whisky. Many Americans prefer this native product made from malt or barley and corn to Scotch whisky. Only the very finest should be used in a Mint Julep. Bourbon is also an essential bar item, especially if you like Old Fashioned and Manhattan cocktails. The best is never blended.

Canadian Whisky. Might be described as halfway between Scotch and bourbon.

Rye Whiskey. Strictly speaking, "whisky" means Scotch, and "whiskey" means Irish rye. But excellent rye whiskies are also made in America, from rye or barley. A man's drink. Indispensable in an Irish coffee, which is an original treat and a marvelous way to end a meal.

Gin. Made from alcohol flavored with plant extracts (principally juniper or "ginevra" berries, hence the name), gin is so popular that it has reduced the role of French vermouth, its partner in a Dry Martini, to a mere whiff. London gin is very dry, whereas sloe gin is sweetened. Gin and Tonic and Gin Fizz are refreshing long drinks, especially in the summer.

Rum. Made from sugarcane, rum was consumed principally by sailors and planters until the beginning of the twentieth century. Now it is very popular all over the world, but particularly in the warm climates where it is made. Jamaican rum is the darkest and most highly flavored, best with Coca-Cola and in a Rum Punch. Puerto Rican rum is exceptionally light and is preferred for mixed cocktails, such as the delicious Daiquiri. Cuban rum is usually white, while most of the others are colored with caramel. Rum improves by aging in the cask for as long as twenty years. Hot rum drinks are good for colds—and a slight sniffle is an excellent pretext for taking a nip.

Beer. Low in alcoholic content, beer is most refreshing after a hard set of tennis on a hot summer day, and the ideal accompaniment to barbecue meals as well as to Scandinavian cuisine when it is reinforced with aquavit. Only British palates can stand it otherwise than ice cold. Draft beer, from a barrel, is tastier and lower in alcohol than beer from a bottle or a can, and it is also much more picturesque for a patio party. Among the imported beers, Pilsener is pale and light and highly fermented; Munchner is darker with a rather pronounced flavor of malt; Lager is between the two; Danish, Swedish, and Dutch beers are highly appreciated; English beer is of the Pilsener type, and British pale ale is very bitter and should be served less chilled than beer. Bock beer appears at Eastertime and is darker and higher in alcoholic content than the others. Beer should be poured into a wet glass, held slightly tilted. The slightest bit of grease in a glass, even a trace of soapy water, will prevent the beer from foaming. Connoisseurs usually like one-fourth foam to three-fourths beer. As a party beverage, beer is suitable only for informal, preferably outdoor, occasions.

Vodka. This distilled spirit has no color, no flavor, but a great deal of kick. It is reputed never to leave a hangover.

Aquavit and Schnapps. The first is Swedish, the second Danish, and both of them are very strong, colorless, vodka-type spirits, pleasantly flavored with caraway seeds. High in alcoholic content, they seem as harmless as water when you drink them, but the delayed reaction can be devastating. The Scandinavian custom is to serve a tiny glass of iced aquavit (sometimes the entire bottle is frozen in a giant cube of ice) at the same time as a tall glass of cold beer with their famous *smörgåsbord.*

Vermouth. A wine rather than a spirit. However, since it is at home in a bar but unsuitable as a table wine, it might be mentioned here. French vermouth is dry and white, Italian, sweet and red, and that is why only the French should be used in a Dry Martini and only the Italian in a Manhattan. You can also drink it straight, like sherry.

A complete list of nonalcoholic drinks would be practically endless, but to mention a few of the most familiar in modern receptions, there is

Fruit Juice. Canned and frozen fruit juices are very practical and are always ready to serve if you keep a supply in the refrigerator. But it is elegant to add at least a portion of fresh fruit juice whenever possible. A combination of different fruit juices is also refreshing for a change: orange and grapefruit with a little apricot nectar, pineapple and orange, etc. Always serve fruit juice from a pitcher, never from the can. The arrival of the fruit-juice pitcher at eleven o'clock after a boring Paris dinner party is a welcome sight, for it means that the guests are free to leave. (It would be very rude to go home before the fruit juice has appeared.)

Vegetable Juice. Tomato juice, either alone or combined with celery and carrot juice in a vitamin cocktail, is suitable as a nonalcoholic apéritif, but at no other time. Tomato juice and vodka with a dash of Worcestershire make a Bloody Mary.

Cola Drinks. For adults, a sweetish mixer for long drinks, especially with rum. For the teen-agers, a suitable substitute for whisky. But try to wean your children away from the habit of drinking it at mealtimes, and on no account order it as a mealtime beverage when you are in Paris, unless you do not mind being regarded as an object of scorn by all the waiters.

Ginger Ale. Reminds me of cricket, since I always used to think of it as a typically British drink. Useful as a mixer and a refreshing soft drink.

Tonic Water. At the moment, this is the most fashionable non-alcoholic beverage in Paris.

Soda Water (Club Soda). Essential in your bar in case one of your guests still prefers his whisky with soda instead of on the rocks.

Iced Tea and Coffee. Both of them delicious on a hot summer afternoon. But even better than American iced coffee in my opinion is the Italian *granita di cafe*, which is a glass filled with very finely crushed ice, very strong sweetened coffee, and drunk through a straw.

Milk. Might be classified as a food as well as a beverage. Because American milk is the most delicious in the world, Americans drink a lot of it. But in Europe milk is consumed only by unweaned babies.

Fruit Soda. Many of the prepared bottled varieties are excessively sweet and synthetic in flavor. But it might be a good idea to revive the old-fashioned fruit-syrup-and-soda-water drink of our grandmothers, if you are able to procure a bottle of natural fruit syrup or to prepare it yourself. Raspberry is the most delicious.

Root Beer. Popular twenty years ago, it has gone out of fashion to be replaced by Cola drinks.

Ice Water. Unhealthy as a mealtime beverage, and in no way a substitute for a nice little wine, American water must be the best in the world for doing heavy laundry, so strong is the taste of chlorine.

It is always nice to pass a plate of snacks with alcoholic or non-alcoholic beverages. Before dinner, the most appropriate and simplest tidbits are olives, cheese crackers, cashews, pecans, macadamia nuts, or salted almonds, none of which requires any preparation at all. For the end of the evening: an assortment of cookies, or a platter of cheese and crackers.

(See Cocktail Parties, Coffee, Liqueurs and Brandy, Wine, etc.)

DUTCH TREATS

❰ It has become so customary among teen-agers to plan a restaurant dinner or an evening at the movies on a Dutch-treat basis, with each person paying his share, that I suppose the boy who pays for his girl friend too would be considered so infatuated as to have completely lost his head! It is understandable for young people on a limited budget to thus pool their resources for a party they otherwise could not afford, and the same is true for colleagues in an office, a youthful group of tourists, and young married couples. Nowadays, even adults, if they are very close friends, may decide to share the expenses of a gourmet meal, a theater party, or an evening on the town. In the case of restaurants and nightclubs, it is more elegant (and easier for the waiter) to have one member of the group act as treasurer, and to settle up afterward with him, rather than to ask for separate checks.

None of these occasions can really be considered entertaining, since each person is actually his own host or hostess. There are consequently no social obligations involved, and no invitation to be returned, even though one person may have had the idea and made all of the arrangements.

In other words, the Dutch treat is a very practical modern invention, but it is not, strictly speaking, a form of entertaining. It is fine for teen-agers and students, and for very good friends and colleagues. But in adult society—even for young married couples at the end of the month—it seems to me that to invite a few friends to a simple spaghetti dinner or to an afterdinner card party with beer and sandwiches served in the middle of the evening would be far more elegant and not very much more expensive.

(See Economy)

ECONOMY

❲ The most elegant parties are not necessarily the most expensive, even in the case of formal dinners. Of course, a hostess with a very limited budget should restrict herself to less pretentious forms of entertaining, but most of all she should realize that certain economies will not affect the quality of her hospitality in any way while others would demolish it.

The best general rule is always to offer the finest quality of a certain category of food and drink, and if this is beyond your means, to select the best of a more modest category. It is always inelegant to be parsimonious in quantity or quality. For example, if you cannot afford an excellent champagne, then serve an excellent white wine; and if this is beyond your budget, a choice cider or an excellent beer, adapting your menu accordingly. There are even certain party dishes to which cider and beer are the ideal accompaniments, such as sauerkraut and spareribs in the first case, and *sole à la Normande* or duck with calvados and sautéed apples in the second. A millionaire would be able to offer nothing more appropriate than a *sangria* to go with an authentic Spanish paella, and this delicious punch is best when it is prepared with a good ordinary wine.

The most onerous item in a party budget is often liquor, and this is unfortunately one of the things that cannot tolerate mediocrity, for reasons of health as well as gastronomy. If you cannot afford an excellent whisky for cocktails, then serve a delicious rum punch, or a fine dry sherry. Do not imagine for a moment that your guests will be fooled if you simply pour a bottle of cheap whisky into a beautiful decanter! The liquor bill will also be lower if you do not linger too long over cocktails, but arrange to serve your dinner promptly.

By applying this simple rule to every item on your entertaining budget, you will easily see where you can cut corners in perfect safety, and where to do so would place in danger your reputation as a hostess. There is, for example:

Table Linen. Even bargain-basement tablecloths are chic if they are of a bright color and the entire table decoration is gay and unpretentious. But if a white tablecloth is not very fine, it will simply look cheap.

Meat. Another big item in the food budget. Never buy an inferior grade of beef, lamb or veal for a roast; but remember that there are many delicious recipes requiring less expensive cuts, such as *pot au feu* and *blanquette de veau.* A superior quality of stewing beef in a delectable *boeuf Bourgignon* is far more reasonable and even more elegant than a stringy steak.

Fish. In many parts of the country fish and seafood are considerably cheaper than meat, and there is a wealth of wonderful fish recipes suitable for the most refined dinner menus. Also, many fish dishes lend themselves to a particularly appetizing presentation, garnished with a few shrimp or shellfish claws when they are served hot, for example, or with lemon slices, stuffed eggs, cucumbers, tiny tomatoes or baby green asparagus when they are served cold. An inexpensive and impressive party dish is made by simply poaching an assortment of fish and shellfish such as shrimp, mussels, crab, etc., and serving it in a sauce made from the fish broth, cream and Italian vermouth, highly seasoned with pepper, either in a rice ring or in a pie crust.

Another advantage of fish dishes is that it is correct to accompany fish with white wines such as Riesling, Traminer, etc., which are among the most successful products of the California vintners. Chilean Riesling and Portuguese Rosé are also inexpensive wines that are excellent with fish.

Fruit. Fruit served whole should be choice and perfect, but the fruit cut up in a fruit cup, puréed in a Bavarian cream, or baked in a fruit pie, can be just as tasty even though it may have been less presentable (and therefore very much less expensive) in its original state. It is also possible to combine fresh fruit with canned or frozen varieties when the fresh is out of season and sells at luxury prices.

It is particularly chic to serve as a luncheon dessert a fresh homemade compote of fruit, such as strawberries, pitted cherries, red or yellow plums, pears, apricots, peaches, etc.—whatever is in season. The trick is to cook them without a drop of water. Just sugar them and let them stand for half an hour, which will cause the juice to run, and then stew them for five or ten minutes only in a tightly covered pan, until the skins burst. Serve the compote either hot or cold, with little cookies.

Another fantastically simple and refined fruit dessert for a luncheon is simply dried prunes that have soaked overnight in ordinary white wine with a stick of vanilla in it. There is no cooking at all, and the result is delicious!

Flowers. Charming table centerpieces can be composed of only a few blooms from the florist shop if you create a Japanese style arrangement, or mix the flowers with fruits, vegetables or greens. For a floral arrangement in the living room, you can make beautiful composition with flowered or leafy branches that you have gathered yourself. Many ordinary roadside weeds are highly decorative. If you entertain a great deal, a few well-made artificial flowers may be a good investment. Only the finest quality are really lovely, and these are quite expensive, but they can be used over and over again.

Desserts. Pastries and cakes are very expensive to buy from a first-class bakery, and they are complicated to make at home unless you are really a very good cook. But an economical way to provide sumptuous baked desserts at a bargain price is to buy a simple but excellent ready-made foundation, such as a sponge cake or a meringue shell, and to complete the dessert by garnishing it in your own kitchen. Remember too that a heavenly (and most economical) chocolate mousse is far less costly than the same quality in a bakery cake or pie.

Personally, I have often received extravagant compliments for an ice cream dessert that consists simply of an ordinary store-bought vanilla ice cream, surrounded by Bing cherries in Kirsch, and served flambéed. Vanilla ice cream is also delicious served with a sauce of raisins that have soaked overnight in rum. I noted a charming idea at the superb restaurant in the famous Dallas store, Neiman Marcus, where a simple dish of ice cream was given a party air by being served in a miniature flower pot, with three fresh roses planted in it.

If you are a good cook, you might whip up a most economical sweet dessert omelette, filled with strawberry preserves and covered with powdered sugar. Or you might try my mother's recipe for *omelette soufflée*, which couldn't be simpler to make: For four people, separate the whites of six eggs and beat them very stiff. To the six yolks, add a quarter of a pound of sugar and mix it well. Then lightly blend the whites and yolks together and pour the mixture into a buttered baking dish. The omelette should cook for ten minutes in a very hot oven. Sprinkle with sugar and serve at once. Sometimes my mother varied this basic recipe by flavoring the omelette mixture with a little rum, Kirsch, or Kümmel.

It is evident that the cost of labor is more onerous then the cost of materials in many catering bills, and that one of the greatest economies of all is to provide the labor yourself. But what is economical in money is usually extravagant in time, and you must dispose of the necessary leisure hours. Therefore, it seems to me that for busy women the ideal formula is fifty-fifty . . . that is, half your own time and efforts, and half those of a professional baker or chef.

(See Marketing)

EMERGENCIES

❲ The best-laid plans of the best-organized hostess are bound to go awry from time to time through no fault of her own, but fortunately there is usually a satisfactory solution to every unforeseen emergency in entertaining. The least elegant course of action when something goes wrong is to become panicky, go to bed with a migraine, and call the party off. On the contrary, you must make an effort to remain calm, to preserve your sense of humor and to exercise your common sense and ingenuity in order to parry whatever disaster seems to menace the success of your reception.

Here are some of the minor crises I have faced during a lifetime of entertaining, along with the emergency solutions, which may not have been ideal, but which at least permit me now to recall these particular occasions if not always with a smile, at least with a clear conscience and without breaking out into a rash. There was, for example:

— The evening of an important dinner party when my darling dog sneaked into the kitchen and devoured half of the roast leg of lamb before I could rescue it from him.

(After laughingly exhibiting the mangled remains to my guests—to prove that I had really prepared something special in their honor—I quickly heated up some prepared canned delicacies that I always keep on hand for use in an emergency.)

— The night the hired waiter became obviously and progressively tipsy, and his service at table began to resemble a juggler's performance rather than that of a stylish maître d'hôtel.

(I discreetly sent my husband to the kitchen to pay his wages and send him home, explained the situation to my guests—who found it all hilariously funny—and proceeded to take charge of the service myself as best I could.)

— The time the cook suddenly walked out on the very morning of a party.

(I was luckily able to find a caterer who was willing to take complete charge of the dinner on such short notice. If my temperamental cook had left in the afternoon, or just before the guests were to arrive, the situation would have been more awkward. I suppose that, depending on the menu, I would have either finished cooking the dinner myself, or prepared just the main dish and substituted a beautiful canned foie gras for the first course, or else sent my husband out to make some emergency purchases at an all-night delicatessen. As a last resort, I would have served cocktails and then taken everybody out to dine in a restaurant.)

— The night of a dinner party when the stove suddenly broke down and blew out all the electricity in the house.

(I was exceedingly grateful to be on good terms with my next-door neighbors, who kindly loaned me the use of their kitchen, while the neighborhood baker agreed to cook the roast. This is, by the way, a perfectly normal service in France. We spent the entire evening in candlelight, and it turned out to be a lovely party.)

Many entertaining crises have nothing to do with the preparation or service of the meal, and these are perhaps the most delicate of all. For example:

— What should you do if a member of your family, or perhaps your husband, becomes ill just as your guests are supposed to arrive for a dinner party?

(If the illness seems serious and the invalid requires your complete attention, you might enlist the aid of one of the guests—the one you know most intimately. Give him the money to take all of the others out to dinner in a restaurant. If it is just a simple headache or a cold, put the invalid to bed and receive your guests alone.)

— But what if it is one of the guests who suddenly is taken ill?

(Put him to bed in your room or, if he can be safely moved, take him home at once. In both cases, call the doctor immediately.)

— What should you do if you have planned a formal dinner for fourteen people and one of the guests drops out at the last minute leaving thirteen at table?

(Bow to popular superstition. If you cannot find a last-minute fourteenth among your close friends or in the family, do not hesitate to split your table in two by placing the four least important guests together at a separate bridge table.)

— Finally, what if you have proudly planned a sumptuous dinner in honor of an important celebrity—and at the last minute your guest of honor is unable to attend?

(This situation is not uncommon in diplomatic and government circles, where it is an accepted fact of life that a Congressional vote or a major debate takes precedence over social engagements. Even if you feel that it was the occasion of your lifetime to receive such an important guest in your home, and even if you have talked and thought of nothing else during the preceding weeks, you must swallow your disappointment along with your pride, make your excuses to the guests who are present, and remove the extra place setting from the table.)

No social crisis in the world will degenerate into a drama if you face it with a smile. On the contrary, if you show proof of your poise, presence of mind, and good humor, your guests will admire you all the more.

ENGAGEMENTS

❲ Most modern, independent young girls know very well what they are seeking in a husband, and they usually recognize the lucky man as soon as they have the good fortune to encounter him. Most modern women also possess sufficient charm, intelligence, and feminine wile to maneuver the young man on whom their cap is set into proposing marriage, and once their private vows have been exchanged, they are usually impatient for the wedding to take place as soon as possible. As a result, long engagements, which were originally conceived to afford a period of acquaintance to two young people whose betrothal was arranged between the parents, no longer make much sense, and today engagement formalities have been reduced to a minimum.

Nevertheless, it is still expected of the parents of the bride-to-be to invite the fiancé and his parents to an engagement dinner. This should be an intimate, personal occasion, restricted to members of the family and a few very close family friends. Since it may be the first time that the respective parents will have met each other, the hostess will naturally wish to make the best possible impression on her daughter's future mother-in-law, and so she should plan the party and arrange her home for the occasion with the greatest of care.

The most elegant form of entertaining on this occasion would be an unpretentious but extremely refined and perfectly served sit-down dinner for eight, ten, or twelve persons. If the families are very large and there are more than twelve guests, it would be better to have two separate tables with identical decorations. The fiancée's mother would preside at one of them, and her father at the other. Even when there are no more than eight guests, a professional waiter or waitress should be hired for the evening as well as a professional cook, if necessary, so that the hostess can devote all of her attention to her guests. She should also make a special effort with her appearance, and she is far more likely to appear well groomed, well dressed, relaxed, and smiling in the evening if she has spent the afternoon at the hairdresser, than if she had passed the entire day in the kitchen over a hot stove.

There is no reason to splurge on caviar and foie gras for the occasion, but the menu should be rather festive, the service expert, and the decoration and appointments of the table simple but in perfect taste. Since this is one time you want everything to be just right, it might be a good idea to repeat your most successful, most dependable party recipes. The menu should be refined without being ostentatious, for example:

(In the fall and winter)
Smoked Salmon
Roast Pheasant
Salad
Cheese Tray
Chocolate-Chestnut Gateau

(In the spring and summer)
Jellied Trout
Roast Filet of Beef
Asparagus
Cheese Tray
Ice Cream with Cherries Flambée

The most appropriate beverage is, of course, champagne. You may not care to serve it throughout the entire meal, but it is an indispensable accompaniment to the dessert, for it is at this moment that the father of the fiancée is expected to rise and to propose a toast in honor of the engaged couple.

This, then, is the traditional family engagement party. It is an obligatory formality when the parents of the fiancés live in the same city, or at least within dinner-party distance of each other. But it often happens nowadays that a girl from New York or Massachusetts decides to marry a boy from California or Nebraska, or even a glamorous lad from some distant foreign land, and in these cases a family engagement dinner is, of course, out of the question and must be replaced by a friendly exchange of letters.

If your daughter wishes to make the greatest possible fuss over this happy period of her life, you may also give a second, larger engagement party to which you invite her fiancé and his family, as well as a host of friends. You should ask your daughter and her fiancé to help make out the guest list, for it should include their young contemporaries as well as friends from your generation.

The party may be as large or as small, as formal or as informal as you wish. A buffet dinner or a dinner dance would seem to me to be most suitable, and they should be planned exactly like any other buffet dinner or dinner dance, except that at one point during the evening your husband will propose a champagne toast to the engaged couple. If the fiancée's mother is widowed or divorced, she should ask an older brother, an uncle, or a man who is a close friend of the family to fill this role.

EPICURE

❦ An epicure is the most fastidious kind of gourmet who has made a study of all the finer points of gastronomy. To prepare a satisfying meal for an epicure is indeed a challenge, for it is not enough simply to feed him well. Quality interests him far more than quantity, and he is never taken in by the culinary shortcuts and subterfuges to which every busy modern housewife is obliged to resort. It is more important than ever to buy only prime quality ingredients, even of a modest category. True epicures are never snobbish in their taste. In fact, they often appreciate the simplest dishes which less sophisticated palates are apt to scorn. But just to show you how fussy these sybarites can be, here is a miscellany of opinions and tips that I have gleaned from some epicurean Parisians:

— The supreme champagnes (and the most expensive, alas) are Dom Perignon and Comtes de Champagne.

— Foie gras prepared in the Périgord and Landes regions of France is preferred by many gastronomes to the Strasbourg variety, which is pinker in appearance and is prepared by a different process, quite often using imported goose livers from Hungary and Israel. In cooked dishes such as hot fresh foie gras with grapes, duck liver is more refined than goose liver—and a few specialists prefer foie gras made from duck liver too.

— Game hens are more tender and delicate in flavor than cocks when they are consumed roasted and rather fresh. But the male has a stronger, gamier flavor when it is permitted to become a bit "high," and it is therefore preferred for preparations requiring a marinade, for pâtés, salmis, etc. (Incidentally, a favorite trick of French chefs when cooking game birds such as partridge and pheasant that are either very fresh or rather tough is to place a square or two of cream cheese in the cavity of the bird before roasting. It is amazing how tender and unctuous the meat will be, and there does not remain the slightest trace of the cheese.)

—The only veal and lamb fit for a gourmet is cut from milk-fed animals too young for grazing. The pale pink flesh of veal should be milky white when it is cooked.

—It is preferable to use veal kidneys when kidneys are served as a main dish; but, when they are served as an entrée, lamb kidneys are preferred (they are smaller, but just as tasty). Lamb brains are also equal in flavor to calves' brains. The liver from male calves is superior to that from females.

—Trout that has been fished from brooks or mountain streams is infinitely superior to the commercially bred kind, and the choicest morsels are the tiny "cheeks."

—The finest portions of many fish are the two upper filets at the top of the back. With a very large fish such as tuna, salmon, swordfish, etc., which are usually served in slices, the best part is the middle third (or, to be even more precise, the portion that would more or less correspond to the "shoulders"); the head section is generally inferior to the tail part, except in the case of smoked salmon, when the tail end is likely to be saltier than the rest.

—Epicures prefer fish that have been caught at the end of a line to fish that have been caught in a net.

—Oysters and clams should be living when you eat them, and you can verify this by watching for the edges to curl up when you sprinkle them with lemon juice or nudge them with a fork. Removing oysters from the shell and washing them before serving takes away all of the zest of the sea and is a shocking practice, gastronomically speaking.

—The best salad dressing and the simplest as well is made with two-thirds fine olive oil, one-third lemon juice, salt, freshly ground gray pepper, and a spoonful of mustard—but never a hint of sugar or vinegar. With a plain salad, the height of epicureanism is a vinaigrette dressing made with wine vinegar and walnut oil.

—Fresh homemade mayonnaise is so superior to the prepared kind that it is well worth the trouble to learn how to make it.

—Tomatoes should never be served unless they have first been peeled, seeded, and drained; the seeds must always be removed from cucumbers as well, and the liquid eliminated by sprinkling them with coarse salt and letting them stand for several hours (or even overnight) before squeezing out the moisture in a towel. (If you then add a little wine vinegar, freshly ground pepper, fresh chervil, and a tablespoon of sour cream, you are in for a real treat!)

— Only the red part of carrots should be used when the core is pale and fibrous, as is often the case with winter carrots. (In order to remove the hard center, you must cut the vegetable into stick-shaped pieces.)

— The choicest part of a Roquefort cheese is in the center, and the more internal mold the better.

— A perfect Camembert or Brie cheese should not have the slightest trace of white at the center. Many gourmets like to eat the crust of Camembert and Brie, but only after the outer white film has been scraped away, and only when it is not overripe.

— When you share a piece of fruit such as an apple or pear, you should cut it with a silver knife, and it is elegant to offer the half with the stem in it, keeping the stemless portion yourself. The stem half of melons is also considered choicer than the other half.

— When grapes are added to a fruit cup, they should be peeled and seeded.

— Iranian caviar is generally considered to be superior to Russian caviar. As a matter of fact, the finest caviar in the world is almost white, processed in Iran, and entirely reserved for the personal table of the Shah of Iran. Next in quality is the gray caviar from Russia. The larger and paler the grains, the finer and more costly the caviar. Beluga is choicer than the Sevruga variety, although some specialists prefer the extra large grains of Sevruga to all the others.

I do not for a moment suggest that you try to satisfy all of these exigencies—unless, of course, you are an ultrafastidious epicure yourself. In that case, you probably understand better than I do the gastronomic subtleties perceptible only to a highly educated palate. Why, I even know one gourmet who, when ordering a broiled half-chicken in a restaurant, always insists that it be the *left* half, which he claims is tenderer than the right!

EPIGRAMS

⟨ Probably the most famous gourmet of all time was a Frenchman called Anthelme Brillat-Savarin, who was born in 1755 and died in 1826, after having spent three years of exile in the United States during the French Revolution. Although his career was politics, his passion was gastronomy, and he wrote a book called *The Physiology of Taste*, which is the bible of gastronomes throughout the world. His words of advice are just as apt today as when they were written over one hundred and fifty years ago, and I cannot resist repeating here his famous epigrams on gastronomy:

"(1.) The destiny of nations depends on the manner in which they are nourished.

(2.) The Creator obliged man to eat in order to live, inviting him to do so by giving him an appetite, and rewarding him with pleasure.

(3.) The pleasure of gastronomy belongs to all ages, all social conditions, all countries, and all times; it may be associated with all of the different kinds of pleasures, and it remains to the very end to console us for the loss of the others.

(4.) The discovery of a new food adds more to human happiness than the discovery of a new star.

(5.) People who cause themselves indigestion or who get drunk know neither how to eat nor how to drink.

(6.) The order of dishes on a menu should start with the more substantial and proceed to the lightest.

(7.) A meal without cheese is like a beautiful woman with only one eye.

(8.) The most indispensable quality in a cook is promptness. The same is true of a guest.

(9.) Waiting too long for a tardy guest shows a lack of consideration for those who arrived on time.

(10.) A person who entertains friends without giving any personal attention to the meal that is prepared for them is unworthy of friendship.

(11.) The hostess should always make sure that the coffee is excellent; and the host should see that the liqueurs are of the finest quality.

(12.) To offer a person hospitality means to be responsible for his happiness during all the time that he is in your home."

ETIQUETTE

⟨ Almost as soon as living creatures form a group society, they develop rules of etiquette. Even animals living in a pack or kennel observe a certain protocol. Have you ever witnessed the standard ritual with which a strange dog is greeted by members of the pack? And haven't you noticed that there is always one male animal in a household of pets who has supremacy over the others, and one female—usually the oldest—who is accorded precedence over all of them (just as in China), even when it concerns such simple acts as passing through the kitchen door? As a matter of fact, the behavior of savage tribes is far more ceremonial than that of civilized peoples, who are gradually adopting an increasingly simplified etiquette.

Etiquette should never be an end in itself, but merely a means of facilitating agreeable social relations, especially between peoples of different cultures and civilizations, by adhering to a standard form of behavior. The rules of protocol are strictly observed today mainly in government and diplomatic circles and during certain traditional ceremonies such as weddings. Every home should therefore possess an authoritative modern book of etiquette that can be referred to on these occasions. But in ordinary daily life, the intentions of one's behavior are far more important than its form. Eleanor Roosevelt was forever breaking the rigid rules of etiquette, but her intent was always to make her guests feel perfectly at ease, and nobody can deny that she was a very courteous and gracious lady.

While an elegant hostess must be familiar with conventional etiquette, she should also have the courage and presence of mind to throw away the rules when following them might embarrass or humiliate her guests. And if you ever find yourself placing greater importance on the details of etiquette than on the spirit of hospitality, you might remember that one of the creatures that slavishly performs the most complicated rites of protocol of all is . . . the goose. I have heard that there even exists (miraculously, as you will see) a species of goose whose courtship rites are so long and complicated that half of the time the male is too exhausted afterward to perform the actual act of mating!

EXTRAS

❦ An "extra" in colloquial French invariably means the supplementary free-lance waiter who is hired for a party. The most accomplished extras are in very great demand, for there are relatively few of them to cater to the needs of all the hostesses in Paris. At some of the large receptions I have attended, I have found more familiar faces among the waiters than among the guests!

When you hire extra help for a party, it is a great advantage to obtain the services of a highly experienced member of the profession, even though he may charge more than a debutant. He will understand perfectly the vaguest instructions, and he will need no supervision at all. Sometimes he is better acquainted than you are with the tastes and habits of your guests, because he has served them so often in so many other homes—including perhaps their own. There is also an advantage in hiring as an "extra" a person who already knows his way around your house and has learned where the glasses or knives are kept, how to work your kitchen equipment, and that the right front burner, for example, boils water faster than the back ones. So if you find a party waiter whose service satisfies you in every way, it is wise to remain faithful to him in the hope that he will place you on his list of preferred clients.

Nowadays the demand for experienced extras is far greater than the supply and they can pick and choose their jobs, so it is in your interest to make a good impression, too. But do not overdo it by reversing the roles or by giving a ridiculously lavish tip. You may only earn their scorn, for they are a notoriously snobbish breed. On the other hand, you will win esteem and perhaps fidelity as well if you provide them with adequate equipment to do their job correctly, if you treat them with the same pleasant courtesy you accord to any other professional specialist, and most of all, if you retain your calm and composure in all circumstances and are always most explicit in your instructions.

In the English language, the word "extra" can also be applied to a number of different elements in entertaining, such as:

Extra men: Confirmed bachelors are more useful in this role than husbands whose wives are temporarily out of town or sick in bed. Every hostess should try to attach to herself one permanent extra man, who can render her invaluable services during her entertaining career.

Extra women: When you have invited more women than men to a dinner party and must seat two women side by side, it is more thoughtful to juxtapose two married women and to place the single woman between two men in order to avoid her feeling overly conscious of being the "extra" one.

While a dinner table is always more elegant to the eye when there is an equal number of men and women, the conversation is not necessarily any brighter. In fact, many women I know are more brilliant and interesting than many men. At a dinner dance or ball, on the other hand, it is indispensable to invite more men than women, in order to assure every woman guest of a change of dancing partners.

A hostess should always arrange for the transportation of single women guests to the party and home again afterward, either by asking one of the other guests to escort her, or by lending her own husband as an escort-chauffeur.

Extra liquor: It is always a good idea to order more than you think you will really need, with the understanding that you can return unopened bottles after the party is over.

Extra ice: You will always need to order extra ice cubes for a cocktail party, and it may be wise to do so for a large dinner party as well, unless you have the foresight to make an extra batch of ice cubes in your own refrigerator and to store it in your freezer. Most liquor stores also sell ice cubes and crushed ice in plastic bags. If you do not own a freezer for storing them until needed, and if the outdoor temperature is torrid, the ice can still be kept for several hours if you wrap the bags in several layers of damp newspapers and place them either in the refrigerator or in the coolest corner you can find.

Extra food: A well-stocked emergency shelf in the kitchen can come to your rescue when your cocktail canapés have been devoured during the first hour of a party, or when you are obliged to receive unexpected extra guests for dinner. It is best to sample cans of prepared dishes as well as frozen specialties at a family meal before offering them to company, because they vary widely in quality.

You should as a matter of course order more food for a party than you will really need, and you should calculate your quantities more generously than you do for an ordinary family meal. If you adopt this system, you will always be prepared to take care of an extra dinner guest, and maybe even two. Platters that are passed around the table twice should be well filled enough for every guest to serve himself a second helping if he wishes, although it is perfectly proper to cut the second round of a main dish in half-portions, and the second serving of a cake or pie into smaller pieces.

Extra room: Too many people crowded into a small room may not be an ideal formula for a party, but it is generally more successful than too few people feeling lost in an enormous salon.

In the case of extra room at the dining table (which is not a very ordinary occurrence), it would be better to place the guests at one end of the table rather than to space them so far apart that conversation is impossible. But it would be even better to set up a smaller table in another room.

When there are only two people at a very large table, it is more pleasant for the hostess to sit at the end with her guest at her right, rather than sitting face-to-face across a vase expanse of polished mahogany.

Extra special: Sometimes a single detail can raise an ordinary party to the level of a gala occasion, particularly if the detail is
Caviar
Champagne
Dancing
A distinguished, famous, or fascinating Guest of Honor
A really beautiful table with silver, candles, lovely flowers, and a fine embroidered tablecloth
Long evening dresses

ADS

❨ There are fads in entertaining just as there are fads in fashion, and it is not always possible to tell in advance which of them will last. Some fads are forgotten in a few months, others survive for several years or even an entire generation and a very few are permanently accepted by society to become eventually a part of national or local folklore.

Fads in entertaining are just as limited geographically as are most fashion fads, with the majority never spreading beyond the confines of a college campus, and only a few of them sweeping the smart spots of New York, London and Rome within a single season. For example, whisky drinking was practically unheard of in Europe before World War II. But after the Liberation, whisky was imported by the British and American troops; what started as a fad among the International Set in Paris has since become an accepted custom throughout the Continent, and today Scotch (but not yet bourbon) is sold in every French supermarket.

I suppose that there will always be new fads in drinks, such as the Moscow Mule of the war years, then the Bloody Mary, and currently the vogue for Vodka, Gin and Tonic, and a cocktail made from Campari called an Americano. There are also fads in restaurants (picturesque foreign spots with atmospheric décor everywhere, and in Paris at the moment, Provençal herb-seasoned-steak houses); in food (there have been periods of curries, Oriental cuisine, Italian pasta, and I suppose the current mode is barbecued steak); in games (Monopoly was once the rage, then gin rummy, canasta, and TV-style quizzes); in dances (I cannot even begin to keep up with the new ones!); and in entire parties (treasure hunts, costume balls, and barn dances have all had their moment of glory). Teen-agers are particularly ingenious in creating and then demolishing fads as fast as they can be described. But the most durable ones are usually launched by some resourceful society leader who wishes to be different, and who is then imitated by everybody else.

It is, of course, amusing to be among the first to introduce a fad that is destined to last, but there is not much point in being among the last to adopt a fad that is already on its way out. So, unless you have a special flair for sensing the longevity of a new rage, and unless you are endowed with a certain amount of social authority, my advice is to play safe and to remain true to the classic forms of entertaining, at least as a framework. Within this framework you can always serve your guests the latest cocktail or demonstrate the newest dance or introduce an amusing game, in order to add topicality and originality to your parties . . . just as it might be more elegant for an average woman to wear an ultrafashionable new hat with a three-year-old classic suit than to buy the entire outfit that appears on the latest cover of *Vogue*.

FAREWELL

❪ Plane travelers often complain that on a short flight between two important cities they spend more time in driving to the airport than they spend in the air—but this is nothing compared to certain guests who take more time getting from one side of your front doorstep to the other than they do in driving all the way home. Lengthy doorway conversations after a party are a very bad habit in which you should never indulge as a guest nor encourage as a hostess.

Unfortunately, this is sometimes easier said than done, because at a very large party a hostess is often so busy looking after all of her guests throughout the evening that the only moment she can find for a private conversation is when she escorts a departing guest to the door. But it is better not to overdo it. This is not the moment, for example, to launch into a detailed review of the evening, nor to describe the complicated recipe for some succulent dish you served. Instead, promise to telephone in the morning. And in response to your guests' inevitable compliments, simply thank them for coming and say that you were happy to have them, but do not make lengthy excuses for real or imaginary short-comings in your hospitality.

Strangely enough, it often seems that the more boring a dinner party has been, the longer the guests take to say good-by. They are no doubt so glad to see the evening come to an end at last that it is as if they were trying to rescue a bad play by staging a brilliant curtain scene. As for the poor hostess, she hasn't the right to be the first to get up from her chair, nor even to appear relieved when at last someone finally makes a move to go home.

There is also a category of guests who only come to life on the landing. After remaining silent all evening, they wait until they have their coats and hats on and then suddenly think of an irresistibly funny story they simply must tell you. This is another bad habit that a hostess should neither practice nor condone. Even if you must be rather curt, you can very well say, "Remind me to ask you to tell it to me the next time we see each other—but at the moment I have a feeling that Henry [or Joan, his long-suffering wife, who has already heard the same story twenty times] is longing to get home and go to bed."

During my trip to the United States, the vice-president of a depart-ment store in a Middle-Western city told me of the difficulties he had experienced with one of my compatriots, a charming and talented hat designer who is also a very gifted photographer. One evening they had been invited to dine together at the home of a prominent local dignitary. At eleven-thirty, everybody had their coats on, the door was open, and the thank-you's duly recited, when the designer spied a rose in a vase and was transported into ecstasy. Seized with inspiration, he sprinkled drops of water on the petals, took out an array of lenses and films and began to arrange the lighting. During an hour and a half he im-mortalized the flower by photographing it from every angle, while the sleepy host and hostess wished that they had never plucked the cursed bloom from the garden. I could see that after this painful experience the vice-president was not in a frame of mind to organize another "French Week" in his store, nor the host to be as generous with his hospitality to visiting foreigners! But if only somebody had simply taken the rose out of the vase and handed it to my charming compatriot, telling him to take it with him and to photograph it at his leisure in the morning, everybody would have gone to bed in a good mood.

It is a mark of respect for a hostess personally to accompany her guests to the door when they are ready to leave, and she should make a point of doing so with all elderly and distinguished persons as well as with her guests of honor (who should be the first to leave a dinner party). She should also personally escort individual visitors to the front door as a matter of course. At a cocktail party or a very large reception, accompanying each guest is, of course, impossible. On these occasions it is the duty of the guests to seek out the hostess in order to express their thanks and adieux, and all the hostess is expected to do is to station herself not far from the entrance or in some prominent spot where she will be easy to find.

A very attentive hostess sees that all of her guests are provided with transportation home after a dinner party, but after a cocktail party they are more often expected to fend for themselves. As the guests leave after a children's party, it is important to make sure that nobody has forgotten anything—unless you consider sorting out a mass of odd mittens, scarves and party prizes an amusing pastime for the next morning.

Farewell scenes of weekend guests are not often so prolonged, perhaps because of the preoccupation of packing bags, catching a train, and avoiding city-bound traffic jams, which impress upon all concerned the advisability of eliminating needless delays. If your weekend guests leave by the Sunday-evening train, you will learn from experience the proper timing that enables you to get them to the station neither too early nor too late. It is courteous to remain with them until the train arrives, to see that they are safely aboard, and to wave good-by as the train pulls away. If you simply deposit them at the station entrance and then drive off in a cloud of dust, your guests might have the uncomfortable feeling that you could not wait to get rid of them.

FAUX PAS

⟨ Everybody makes them—some people with astonishing regularity. And yet a faux pas is by definition involuntary, and is usually sincerely regretted afterward. Many faux pas can be avoided simply by thinking twice before you speak (especially when you are about to say something derogatory). But once the unfortunate word is uttered or the inopportune act performed, there is nothing to be gained by making a tragedy out of the matter. If you can correct your blunder right away, so much the better. But if you can't, try to forget it, because your attempts to rescue yourself will only get you into deeper trouble most of the time. The late Lady Mendl had a favorite motto: "Never complain, never explain." And it is quite true that lengthy explanations often aggravate an already delicate situation.

The two most frequent kinds of faux pas in entertaining are the breach of etiquette and the thoughtless phrase that unwittingly wounds somebody present. The first is of comparatively minor importance except in diplomatic life, where a detail such as the order of precedence is often symbolic of infinitely more important policies. But some minor slips such as using the wrong fork or pouring the sauce over a dish for which it was not intended, cause no harm to anyone, although they may cause smiles at your expense. The unkind word is far more regrettable, because once it has been uttered nothing can erase it. The only thing to do is to learn a lesson from the experience. In other words, resolve henceforth to express yourself with greater tact (even if this means suppressing a brilliantly witty remark), and accept the consequences of your blunder with philosophy—and above all with a sense of humor.

Finally, when you see one of your guests approaching dangerous territory—figuratively as well as literally—you should come to his rescue at once and pull him onto safer ground before the faux pas is ever committed.

FAVORS

(Except in the case of wedding festivities, and of parties given for children or by millionaires, party favors have practically disappeared from modern entertaining. However, it is a charming gesture to place an attractively wrapped package at the place of each guest at a Christmas feast, and even at an Easter dinner in countries where it is the custom to exchange gifts on that occasion too. Children adore presents, and you will never fail to delight them if you provide some small trinket in a pretty package for each guest at every children's party. But in order to avoid scenes of jealousy, it is best to give everybody more or less the same thing—for example, a miniature car for the boys and a coloring book for the girls.

The Aly Khan used to present each of the guests at his annual party after the final day of racing at Longchamps with some costly bauble from Cartier, such as a solid gold compact, and I understand that the young Aga Khan intends to continue this princely tradition. But how many living deities are there in the world? I must confess that the only party favors I have received in years are the little bottles of perfume that are distributed at charity affairs by perfume manufacturers who wish to introduce a new scent or to obtain a fashionable kind of publicity in return for their contribution to a worthy cause.

I suppose there still exists the custom of placing an impressive jeweler's velvet box on the plate of a pretty woman who has been invited to a romantic dinner for two. But in this case, I am not sure whether it is the host or the guest who is supposed to be dispensing favors—and anyway, that is the subject for a separate section . . . or perhaps, for a separate book!

FINGER BOWLS

❡ Far from being a superfluous table accessory, finger bowls are an essential element of a formal dinner service as well as an indispensable accompaniment to any dish that can cause sticky fingers, such as unshelled shrimp, lobster, clams and oysters on the half shell, artichokes, and fresh fruit. They should be provided whenever you serve a food that is taken in the fingers, even at family meals, and at a formal dinner no matter what the menu.

At a formal dinner, finger bowls are placed on a doily on the dessert plates, with the dessert fork and spoon and the fruit knife on either side. They should be half filled with warm water and garnished with a floating flower petal or a thin slice of lemon or a leaf of fresh mint or geranium. (Lemon and mint are preferable when shellfish has been served because they help remove the fishy odor from one's fingers.) They are served by the waiter, and each guest places the finger bowl and its doily to the upper left of the dessert plate. In other cases, the finger bowls are passed right after a dish that is eaten with the fingers. If the dish in question is the very first course, the finger bowls may already be set in place at the upper left of each plate before the guests are seated.

Crystal finger bowls are the prettiest, but they may also be of silver,

There is no reason to have a complex about finger bowls merely because they may be unfamiliar to you. They are a highly practical accessory, and not an affectation.

FIRST COMMUNION

⟪ In certain religious sects, and particularly in the Roman Catholic Church, the First Communion of a young boy or girl between the ages of eight and ten is the occasion for a traditional family luncheon party after the church ceremony is over. This may be as simple and intimate or as important as you wish. But it should never be really lavish or elaborate, which would be considered poor taste. The luncheon guests all attend the ceremony beforehand, and each one is expected to bring the child a little gift—not necessarily a religious token, but something useful and slightly serious, such as a book, a globe of the world, or a pen.

If it is impossible to organize a nice luncheon party for ten or twelve guests, including the members of the family, the honored child's godparents, and perhaps a few intimate friends, you should at least prepare a meal that is more elegant than an ordinary family repast, and arrange a pretty table decoration. Not only will your extra attentions please and honor the child, who has been preparing for this occasion during so many months, but it will also help to mark the event in his memory for the rest of his life.

Since the First Communion is generally scheduled for the late springtime, it would be a good idea to build your meal around the seasonal foods that are particularly delicious at this time of the year. Here, for example, is an idea for a menu that is simple and yet sufficiently festive for a First Communion luncheon:

Fresh Salmon with Tartar Sauce
Duckling with Oranges
Salad
Cheese Tray
A Pretty Strawberry Dessert

It occasionally happens that a first communicant is an adult who has been converted late in life to the Catholic Church. In this case, discretion is *de rigueur,* and the luncheon should be a very simple one, rigorously confined to members of the immediate family.

The Bar Mitzvah of the Jewish faith is a rather similar occasion, except that it concerns only thirteen-year-old boys and takes place at about the time of the individual child's actual birthday. He is permitted to play a role in the regular Saturday-morning worship by mounting the altar for the first time and reading the day's text from the Old Testament. It is therefore usually a Saturday luncheon party that is given in celebration of a boy's Bar Mitzvah.

Sometimes it takes place in the reception rooms of the synagogue, and sometimes at home. It may be limited to family and close friends, or there may be hundreds of guests, in which case it is not unusual to rent the salons of a fashionable hotel. Usually it is a rather large party, including as many members of the family as can be assembled, friends of the parents, as well as friends of the celebrant and these children's parents.

Tradition should be strictly observed on this kind of an occasion, and the hostess should therefore seek the advice of an experienced friend or relative if she is the least bit unsure of herself in making her plans. Since the party celebrates the child's birthday as well as his Bar Mitzvah, the climax of the meal is always the appearance of the birthday cake. The lighting of the thirteen candles is the occasion for a traditional ceremony, each one being lit by a different friend, the next to last by the boy's parents, and the very last one by the child himself.

The corresponding Jewish rite for young girls is called a Bas Mitzvah. The religious rites are slightly different, but there are the same gifts, the same throng of invited guests, and a similar luncheon party following the ceremony.

FLOWERS

❨ Fresh flowers bring color, warmth and refinement to a room at any time, and they are one of the first items on a shopping list for an important party, since this is one time when every woman wishes her home to look its best.

Whenever you give a formal dinner, you will probably want to order special flowers for the dining table, either to compose a lovely low centerpiece, or (less extravagantly) two or more small bouquets, or (if it is the end of the month) to dress up a pair of candlesticks or decorate a still-life centerpiece with just a few pretty blossoms and greens.

It is lovely to have fresh flowers in the entrance hall and living room all of the time, and especially when you are receiving guests. However, it is not elegant to fill every vase in the house with florist's bouquets simply because you are giving a dinner party. The most effective floral arrangements in a living room form a part of the permanent decorative scheme, and it is much smarter to arrange fresh flowers in the usual places rather than to set a vase of red roses on every available side table.

One rather important, well-composed arrangement is always more attractive than several skimpy ones, just as an artistically arranged spray of mixed flowers, even very common varieties, is more chic (and far less costly) than a dozen long-stemmed American Beauties carelessly stuck in a vase. Long-stemmed flowers, incidentally, should never be placed on the coffee table for the same reason that you avoid massive floral centerpieces on the dining table. Remember that the coffee table in front of the living room sofa usually forms the principal center of conversation before and after dinner, and you do not want to isolate your guests on either side behind an imposing barrier of gladioli or chrysanthemums.

If a guest has sent you flowers before a party, they must be prominently displayed—even though it may mean transferring the ones you bought yourself to the entrance hall or bedroom. If a guest brings flowers to the party with him (a very informal gesture, suitable only at an intimate luncheon), you should arrange them in a vase at once and set them in a place of honor in the living room—even though they may not harmonize perfectly with your color scheme. Elegance of behavior takes precedence over elegance of décor! And at least these experiences will prove to you that flower arrangements on which you have lavished thought and care can be more beautiful than those which have simply cost a lot of money.

When planning a floral arrangement for a party, or at any other time for that matter, it is important to select containers whose form, color, and material harmonize with the flowers they will hold. For example, an exquisite vase of opaline or alabaster requires rather precious flowers. A rustic pottery pitcher, on the other hand, would be inappropriate for delicate roses or lily of the valley, but ideal for an assortment of field flowers or of autumn leaves. Multicolored bouquets look prettiest in vases of a solid color, while ornately decorated containers should be filled with the simplest arrangements, preferably of a single shade. Pewter and silver bowls and urns particularly enhance delicate pastel blossoms, and well-polished copper is stunning with all of the yellow and orange tones, as well as bright green and certain shades of light blue. As a matter of fact, it is a good idea to select your vase before you buy your flowers so that you will know exactly what to look for. Teapots, soup tureens, pitchers, brandy snifters and wine decanters can all be used as flower holders. A slight stem effect always sets off a small bouquet. Remember, too, that a waterproof receptacle such as a cake tin can transform all sorts of objects into unusual flower containers, for example, an inlaid mahogany cigar box or a jewelry coffer, an antique tea caddy, or a rustic woven straw basket. A stunning and unusual flower holder for a table centerpiece is a green Savoy cabbage with curly leaves, into which roses or other blossoms are stuck, after cutting the stems quite short.

The most effective floral arrangements usually echo the colors or form of another object in the same room: a painting, perhaps, or the color scheme of a chintz upholstery fabric or a rug. Flowers are almost always enhanced when they are set against a plain background, and for this reason you should try to keep them away from walls that are papered in a striking pattern as well as from vividly printed curtains.

Color in flowers produces the same psychological reactions as color in fashion and interior decoration, in that the cool shades, such as blue, green, violet, gray, and white, are restful and create an effect of serenity, coolness, and formality; whereas the warm shades, such as red, orange, and yellow, are stimulating and create an atmosphere of warmth and gaiety. The latter are therefore generally the best choice for a functional modern decor, which tends to seem rather cold and impersonal.

There are two simple and dependable kinds of color schemes for flower arrangements: monochrome (using two different shades of the same basic color, such as pale and bright blue, yellow and orange, or pink and burgundy); and contrast (based on two complementary shades, such as blue and orange, green and red, or purple and yellow). By following one of these elementary schemes it is hard to go wrong.

Here, for example, are several examples of effective flower combinations. They are particularly chic when one of the varieties has round blossoms and the others are pointed or elongated.

— Yellow asters and orange chrysanthemums in a copper container.

— The same copper container with a combination of pale blue and deep copper-colored flowers.

— At Christmastime, holly and red carnations in a silver bowl.

— A mixture of pink roses and tea roses in a silver or pewter goblet.

— A crystal vase filled with bright red roses or tulips in a room whose basic color is pale gray or beige.

— Blue iris and deep red roses in a crystal vase.

— Blue iris combined with yellow jonquils or bright yellow tulips for a cheerful springtime bouquet.

— Red carnations and golden dried wheat sheaves in a sunburst arrangement.

The most difficult bouquets to arrange successfully are those that combine many different colors and a wide variety of forms, as in the flower paintings of the Dutch and Flemish schools—but these are also the most sumptuously decorative. Strangely enough, it can be very difficult to compose an all-white bouquet, especially if the blossoms are small. Shiny green leaves will help add character to white flowers, as will an unusual container, a colored vase, or a bright background. On the other hand, I always like to punctuate a red or yellow arrangement with a few white flowers.

During the winter months when cut flowers are most expensive, Japanese-style floral arrangements are very practical because they create a maximum effect with a minimum of material. It is always economical to fill a vase with a variety of foliage, leaves and ivy, accentuated by just a few large blooms. During this season you might also experiment with dried flowers, which appear in the florist shops and department stores at the same time as the first autumn frost. With an assortment of autumn leaves, pussy willow, mistletoe, Japanese lanterns, wheat sheaves, dried sunflowers, artichokes, ears of corn, bullrushes, and thistles, you can compose extremely decorative floral arrangements that will last for months. Even though their colors are necessarily rather pale and faded, dried flowers are more chic in their natural state than when they have been painted or gilded. A container of shiny copper or of highly polished wood will add life to what might otherwise seem to be a rather insipid bouquet.

Some clever women succeed in creating marvelous floral decorations composed of a mixture of fresh and artificial flowers, but this delicate art should be reserved for experts because there is no happy medium with true-and-false bouquets. They are either perfectly gorgeous or perfectly dreadful. And they may even seem rather vulgar if they have not been selected and arranged with impeccable taste and flair.

Remember when you are composing your bouquets that it is easier to form a balanced composition with an odd number of flowers than with an even number. When I am fortunate enough to receive a gift of a dozen roses, I often arrange eleven of them in a vase and place the twelfth in a tiny bud vase on my dressing table. The effect is prettier, incidentally, if the stalks are trimmed to slightly different lengths, and the highest flower of the arrangement should be one and a half times as high as the height of the container. (This, at least, is the general rule, although it really depends upon the individual container, and the rule does not apply at all to low vases, in which, generally speaking, you should try to place the longest flowers in the center or at the back, the heaviest blossoms in the center near the top of the vase, and a few leaves or flowers bent down over the rim.) It is a good idea to fill your vases in the spots where you intend to place them, rather than in the kitchen, so that you can compose your arrangements in view of the setting and of the angles from which they will be seen.

Flowers on the dining table should never be too high, too massive, nor too strongly perfumed. Personally, I prefer a mixed centerpiece of fruit and flowers or vegetables and flowers in a low container to one of flowers alone. It is amusing to exercise one's ingenuity in scattering a few appropriate objects around the centerpiece, such as pine cones, walnuts and chestnuts, sea shells, Christmas tree ornaments, porcelain or silver figurines, etc.—the possibilities are endless. Of course, this kind of table decoration requires a lot of time, imagination, and taste, but it also requires less financial outlay than a centerpiece ordered from the florist, and many of the elements may be used over and over again.

Having devoted a considerable amount of time and thought to your flower arrangements, you naturally wish them to last as long as possible. Many florists deliver with every order a packet of powder or special pastilles to be dissolved in the vase water, and these scientific compounds are probably more efficacious than the lump of sugar, aspirin tablet, or ice cubes that are also supposed to prolong the life of cut flowers. However, none of these methods will succeed if you fail to consider the fact that flowers crave light and air, but they have a deathly fear of sunshine, drafts, tobacco smoke, and heat waves from a nearby fireplace or radiator.

Among the many more or less effective tricks for preserving the life of cut flowers, these are the ones that work the best for me:

— When you cut flowers from your own garden or buy them at a market, always soak them up to the necks overnight in cool water before arranging them. (This is usually unnecessary with florist's flowers, because the florist has done it for you.)

— Arrange cut flowers in a vase containing a lot of water, and then disturb them as little as possible, merely adding fresh water every day to replace what has evaporated. There is an exception in the case of very narrow-necked vases, however, for the water in these should be renewed every day in order to replace the oxygen. There are also a few varieties of flowers, including sweet peas, that require very little water.

— All cut flowers will last longer if you strip the leaves and thorns from the part of the stems that will be in the water.

— Woody stems, such as lilac and forsythia, should be crushed with a hammer in order to facilitate the absorption of water.

— Gladioli will last a very long time if you cut the stems a few inches shorter every day and regularly remove the faded blossoms. (For that matter, these rather unfashionable flowers are only chic, in my opinion, when they are cut very short.)

Unfortunately, I have not yet discovered a way to prevent the stems of certain flowers such as zinnias, asters, and chrysanthemums, from becoming gummy and clouding the water, producing at the same time a most unpleasant odor. It helps a little to remove the leaves from the underwater portion of the stems, but the best practice is to change the water at least every day, rinsing off the stems at the same time, and always to place these kinds of flowers in opaque or colored vases in which the stems will not be visible.

When you have finished arranging the flowers for the dining table and in the living room, you might use any leftover blossoms to fill a small vase for the entrance hall table. A tiny bouquet, even a single flower, is always pretty on the dressing table of a powder room, if you have one. If you don't, a few flowers in your own bathroom, which has been cleared of your personal toilet articles, will help transform it for the evening into a guest bathroom. And whenever you entertain houseguests, remember to place a spray of fresh flowers in the guest room. There is no more charming way of saying "Welcome!"

Flowers are such a joyful luxury that it is a pity to waste them. And so, whenever you entertain in a club or restaurant and have ordered flowers for the table or the salons, there is no reason to abandon them when you could enjoy the pleasure of their beauty for days if you simply remember to take them home with you after the party is over. (But please, never pinned to your coat as a corsage!)

(See Tables)

FOREIGNERS

(Many well-intentioned persons seem to think that when they are entertaining foreigners they ought to serve them foreign cuisine. And yet imagine your disappointment if, during a trip to Paris, all of your dinner menus were composed of steak and Idaho potatoes!

It must be admitted that French cuisine has become so international that it is almost impossible to suppress it completely from your menus. You can therefore perfectly well prepare for French visitors a rather Continental meal. Except at a very few restaurants, such as La Grenouille and the Pavillon in New York, it is bound to be more or less Americanized anyway. But you should never, never attempt to serve sauerkraut to German visitors, spaghetti to Italians, paella to Spaniards, curry to Indians, or chili con carne to Mexicans. Even though you may be convinced that you prepare these dishes in the most authentic and delicious manner, the fact is that they probably bear only the faintest resemblance to the original recipe with its native ingredients, and the foreigner's experienced palate will notice the difference at once.

One of the greatest pleasures of travel comes from immersing oneself in an entirely different environment, and from sharing the customs and habits of the local inhabitants. It is therefore kinder not to deprive the traveler of all of these new tastes and sensations, but, on the contrary, to offer him an opportunity to appreciate your own national specialties. Remember, too, that foreigners also adore to visit "typical" American homes, particularly the rooms they seldom have a chance to see, such as the kitchen, bedroom, bathroom, and the children's nursery.

There is no reason to feel shy about serving California wine to Europeans. It is always most amusing for us to taste it when we are visiting the United States, for we would otherwise never have an opportunity to find out what it is really like. It also gives us something to talk about when we get home. The only time you might serve a French wine to French guests is when you possess a perfectly extraordinary bottle that they alone, among all of your friends, would be capable of appreciating.

These are the specialties of American cuisine that I prefer. All of them are vastly superior in quality to the Continental equivalents:

— Clam Chowder
— Vichyssoise
— Avocados
— Soft-Shelled Crabs
— Red Snappers
— Steaks and Prime Roast of Beef
— Baked Idaho Potatoes with sour cream and chives
— Apple Pie
— All of the countless varieties of Ice Cream and Sundaes (which, in fifty days, added six pounds to my weight and inches to my waistline!)

The problem of entertaining foreigners is not at all the same when the foreigners in question have been living in the United States for a very long time. They are then no longer adventurous tourists, but nostalgic exiles, whose eyes become moist as soon as they glimpse a photo of the Eiffel Tower, the Colosseum or Trafalgar Square. And so, do not hesitate to evoke for them their native land, which they may have been very happy to leave behind, but which, when viewed from a distance, seems to them to be endowed with every charm and grace.

If you haven't the time or do not know how to prepare one of their national dishes, an imported bottle of wine, a cheese, a pot of mustard, in fact any kind of food or condiment or even a decorative object on the table that comes from their homeland will touch them deeply.

In the opinion of most foreigners, the weakest points of American cuisine are certain beautiful but tasteless fruits, and your tea and coffee. Even if you personally prefer these beverages in their American version, do not forget that an Englishman or an Irishman will be horrified by the sight of a tea bag dunked in a cup of hot water, and if you ever entertain such connoisseurs, you should be sure to buy a very good blend of tea and a real teapot. Rinse the pot with boiling water, place in it one spoonful of tea per person plus one for the pot, and very gently pour boiling water on top of it. Place additional boiling water in a separate pitcher, and complete the tea tray with a small pitcher of cold milk, a bowl of lump sugar and a plate of lemon slices. In general, Ceylon tea is served in the morning, and China in the afternoon. It has been said that the social standing of an Englishman can be measured by the color of his tea, which becomes paler and paler as he rises on the social ladder, and I always make a point of excusing myself for my strange Continental predilection for very strong tea with lemon.

As for American coffee (which is so weak that it is like a premature baby, even to the point of spending its life warming on the stove as if it were in an incubator)—it has only the name in common with the strong and flavorful coffee that is brewed abroad, especially in Italy. As a matter of fact, I am astonished that so many Italian-Americans have been able to accustom themselves to this particular horror. I do not believe that its insipidity is due to the coffee itself (although the beans are not roasted in exactly the same way as in other countries), but I do believe that it is indispensable to buy one of the many espresso-type coffee makers if you ever wish to entertain European guests in your home.

FORMALITY

❮ The decorum with which you entertain denotes the degree of respect you wish to show your guests. It is a rather delicate matter to measure out formality and warmth in the ideal proportions for every circumstance, but this is what often determines the success of a reception.

You would not expect the same kind of pleasure from a Governor's Ball as from a picnic with an old school friend. You would even be a little disappointed, in the first case, if you were not slightly bored in an atmosphere of pomp and dignity. In fact, I wonder if President

Johnson's barbecues are not finally the most revolutionary innovation of the century.

The age of stiff collars and starched shirts has definitely disappeared, and the very grand balls on the order of those given by Carlos de Beistegui in his Venetian palace are more of a historical reconstitution in nostalgia for times gone by than an example of contemporary taste.

It seems that when women threw away their corsets, they also discarded the rigid rules of old-fashioned etiquette. Traditional protocol was based principally on class distinctions, but these have become increasingly imperceptible until nowadays they are most often reduced to an address, an accent, and a few subtle details of speech and behavior that only the initiated are able to recognize. Today everybody mingles with everybody else, and there are no longer any public places frequented exclusively by one small privileged segment of society. The formalities of former times have therefore become practically extinct, and there is no code of etiquette to govern one's behavior toward one's peers.

While a relaxed and informal atmosphere is most agreeable, it is still important for a guest to feel that he is surrounded by attention. For example, it is a good idea to tell your guests at the beginning of a weekend, "Please make yourselves at home"—but it is not a good idea to disappear and leave them to look after themselves. It is a good idea to build a dinner around one simple main dish—but it is not a good idea to serve it on an ordinary plastic tablecloth. It is a good idea to play a record of soft background music—but it is not a good idea to force everybody to listen in silence to the entire recording of "Tristan und Isolde," even if you were all in Bayreuth together the summer before.

In short, while elegance in dress can be defined as a perfect knowledge of oneself, hospitality might be defined as a total disregard for oneself. If you think only of giving pleasure to your guests, you will be certain to succeed in entertaining successfully no matter how small or great your means.

FRIENDS

❲ One of the privileges of friendship is the absence of ceremony. As a matter of fact, I wonder if the various social formalities were not invented in order to maintain peaceful relations between people who might otherwise antagonize each other. In any case, between close friends there are few secrets and little ceremony. You receive them in your home almost as if they were members of the family, and you express your mutual tastes and opinions to each other without the slightest reticence. Since you know what they like and even whom they like, it is a very simple matter to plan a party that is certain to please a friend. It is always thoughtful to include a favorite dish or drink or diversion as a special treat.

Remember that friendship is offered and earned; it is not a birthright. Do not allow yourself to take your friends for granted, no matter how intimate you may be. You may invite them to dinner in the kitchen, you may ask them to serve themselves at the bar, you can even accept an offer to help clear the table or do the dishes. But your very best friends should still have the feeling whenever they are in your house that they are being received as guests.

FUNERALS

❨ Because relatives and close friends may come from far away to attend a funeral, it is customary for the bereaved family to prepare a meal following the ceremony in order to fortify those who have a long journey home. The meal, which is most often a luncheon or a sort of "high tea," can take place in the private room of a restaurant or hotel (in which case the bereaved person does not even make an appearance), or, as is far preferable, at the home of a close member of the family, a cousin, for example, or even at the home of a close family friend.

A simple but hearty cold buffet seems to me the best formula. For example: Cold baked ham, roast chicken or turkey, or simply a plate of cold cuts and cheese along with assorted breads for making sandwiches; fruit and a cake or pie; and plenty of hot coffee.

The menu should be comforting rather than gastronomic, which, under the circumstances, would be in very poor taste. In England, all that is customarily offered is a glass of whisky or a cup of tea. Since wine, which always accompanies meals in France, invariably injects a certain amount of warmth and cheer into the atmosphere, we consider it unseemly for the widow and the closest members of the bereaved family to be present at the reception, and the role of hostess is therefore assumed by a more distant relative, while the widow or widower is served separately in a private upstairs room in the company of a very few close relatives.

Because of the simplicity of the menu and the sobriety of the occasion, it should not be necessary to call on the services of a professional caterer, even when there is a rather large number of guests.

AMBLING

As I have never been very lucky at cards, and since I hate to lose money, I have never personally experienced the thrill of gambling— and this, I must admit, is not very Latin of me. I am therefore not very well qualified to discuss it, and if I dare to venture for a moment into this hazardous terrain, it is simply because gambling can pose some knotty problems to a hostess.

Exchanging money is not an elegant gesture. When you are entertaining at an evening of bridge or canasta, the better your luck at cards the worse it is for you as a hostess, for it is very embarrassing to take money away from a guest in your home. It is, of course, less awkward when you are among a few close friends with whom you are accustomed to play at a regular weekly game. But even in this case it seems to me that the best idea is to place each evening's losses in a pool, and when the pool has assumed rather lavish proportions, to blow it all on an extravagant evening on the town. Thus everyone will profit, and you will have avoided the painful scene of money being exchanged among invited guests under your roof.

In other instances, it seems to me preferable to offer a prize to the winners of a card tournament, and if your guests absolutely insist, to play only for stakes that are so low that they cannot possibly cause distress even to the poorest player present. The proper place for high-stake games is a casino or a private club, not in a private home.

With card games such as poker in which the gambling element is essential, this is inapplicable advice, I know. In fact, it is for this reason that I have never cared to assume the responsibility of permitting poker to be played in my home. Gambling is a very risky business in more ways than one, and the odds against acquiring an enviable reputation as a hostess by permitting gambling at your parties are even greater than the odds against your being dealt four aces twice in succession.

(See Bridge, Cards)

GAMES

❲ Within the space of less than a generation, party games have gone out of fashion. It is still useful for a hostess to have a supply of games on hand for entertaining houseguests on a rainy Sunday afternoon, for keeping visiting children reasonably quiet, or for spending a peaceful evening at home with very close friends who happen to enjoy this form of pastime. But to organize parlor games during a dinner party is elegant only in rather special circumstances and with rather special guests.

For example, certain intellectual parlor games, even such ancient ones as Charades, Twenty Questions, and The Game, can be extremely amusing if all of your guests are brilliant and witty. But the danger of intellectual games is that your intelligent guests will shine while the dull ones suffer, and this is hardly the formula for a successful party.

(See Bridge, Cards, Children)

GASTRONOMY

❲ "Animals feed; human beings eat; only the wise man knows how to dine."

(Brillat-Savarin)

Gastronomy is like a religion. It has its rites, its ceremonies and its dogmas. It has its heroes and its saints. It even has its martyrs such as Vatel. It has its prophets in Rabelais and Brillat-Savarin, its painters in such Dutch and Flemish masters as Rembrandt, Teniers, and Jordaens, who glorified the splendor of good food and the pleasure of feasting, and in the French school led by Chardin, Watteau, Lancret, and Boilly, who depicted the charms of intimate romantic dining and of eating out of doors in a bucolic setting.

Gastronomy symbolizes, you might say, the union of spirit and matter. But it is most of all a universal bond among men. The table around which a spirit of harmony and good fellowship prevails is much more often covered with a white damask tablecloth than with the traditional green felt of diplomatic conferences. Sharp differences of opinion may exist among the diners at the beginning of a meal, but if the food is good, they will be magically ironed out by the time the coffee is served. Brillat-Savarin was quite right when he said that the fate of peoples is often decided at a banquet table. The table can unite those gathered round it by their mutual taste for good food; and by creating a climate of optimism and the bliss of good digestion, it can strengthen the bonds of courtesy, amiability, and comprehension that enable men to know each other better.

The happiest hours of our lives have often shared the more or less obvious common denominator of some gastronomic souvenir. Is it a childhood romance? Immediately there comes to mind the memory of a certain picnic in the woods. The tender declaration of love by a distant cousin is inseparable from the memory of Grandmother's jam cupboard. I suppose that the remembrance of a passionate infatuation for a charming coquette must awaken in the mind of an elderly gentleman the vision of a midnight supper shared many years before. Or, if he swells with pride at the memory of some triumph or honor he once obtained, it is again the table—this time a banquet table—that he envisions. If you think of a wedding, there is the wedding dinner; and a christening, the luncheon table with its pretty pastel dragées. Gastronomy thus brings joy to every circumstance and to all ages, and it affects all of the senses at once. It is the sum of many kinds of poetry: the poetry of tone and color, the poetry of taste and smell, and the supreme poetry of feeling.

True gastronomy is not, as it was for Gargantua, the ability to swallow a whole steer, nor, as it was for Heliogabalus, a taste for coxcombs and nightingale's eyelids. Neither gluttony nor eccentricity have anything to do with gastronomy, which, on the contrary, requires above all moderation and simplicity and is based on good, healthy, agreeable cuisine.

As a final word, here are two apt quotations. First, a rather cynical one from George Bernard Shaw:

"There is no love more sincere than the love of food."

The other, more optimistic, from Anatole France:

"French cuisine is the finest in the world. This glory will shine above all others when humanity, having become wiser, ranks the spit above the sword. For remember that man has only two major preoccupations in life: hunger and love."

(See Epicure)

GIFTS

❡ Offering a gift to one's hostess is such a time-honored tradition that even kings and presidents never set forth on a voyage without an appropriate selection of gifts for all the hosts and hostesses who will entertain them during the course of their itinerary.

The conventional gift for a hostess at a dinner party, and still the best, is flowers. It is more thoughtful to have them delivered on the morning of the party rather than the next day so that she can take them into account when planning her floral decorations. If you are not familiar with the interior decoration of her home, it is always safe to order white or yellow flowers, or dark red roses, for these are most likely to harmonize with any color scheme. The hostess should telephone her thanks as soon as the flowers have been received so that the donor will know they have been delivered properly, and she should arrange the flowers of her guest in a most prominent spot in the living room.

A weekend hostess has the right to expect a gift from each guest. These are delivered in person upon arrival and the hostess should open the packages at once and express her delight and thanks on the spot. If the gift is candy, she should pass it around and share it with the others present. If you wish her expressions of delight to be absolutely genuine, I would suggest offering as a hostess gift something practical and attractive for the home or kitchen, something connected with one of her interests or hobbies or something that will contribute to everybody's pleasure during the weekend: an amusing simple game such as darts or deck tennis, some rare delicacy, for instance, a whole canned foie gras or a magnum of champagne or a beautiful or entertaining book.

The same type of gift is suitable when a houseguest arrives to be entertained for a longer period of a week or two or even more. But in this case, the guest should also send a somewhat more important present after returning home. In France, the guest would also probably send a lovely plant or a marvelous bouquet of flowers to the hostess on the following Christmas.

GLASSES

❡ Glasses have been designed in special shapes and sizes for every imaginable beverage, but no more than three different kinds can enable a modern hostess to meet all of her normal entertaining requirements with perfect elegance:

(1.) A tall tumbler for highballs, water, fruit juice, milk, beer, soft drinks, iced tea and coffee, etc.

(2.) A medium-sized tulip-shaped goblet, for all kinds of wine and cocktails. (Even in France, it has become fashionable to serve champagne in an ordinary wine goblet instead of in the traditional hollow-stemmed "flute.")

(3.) A smaller version of the same tulip-shaped goblet, for port or sherry and other aperitifs (filled almost to the top), as well as for brandy and liqueurs (only about one-third filled).

Fine crystal is expensive, but you buy it once in a lifetime, like your silverware. Some names in American crystal are known all over the world, as are the products of Sweden, Bohemia, Finland, Venice, and France (particularly the Baccarat line). There is also a quality described as "demicrystal," which combines the economy of plain glass with some of the brilliance of pure crystal, and this might be a sensible choice if you have a very limited budget. But even more important than its quality is its thickness. Fine glasses are by far the most pleasing to drink from, and they also enhance the color and limpidity of the liquids they contain. As a matter of fact, connoisseurs of wine maintain that it really matters very little whether or not you serve each different kind of wine in a different kind of glass, but they insist that all wine glasses should be fine, plain and colorless—even in the case of Rhine wine goblets, in which the stem may be of colored glass, but the bowls should be colorless.

Long-stemmed goblets are certainly the most elegant to the eye and the most refined for the palate, since they prevent chilled wines from becoming warmed by contact with one's hand, and at the same time permit you to "cradle" a glass of Burgundy in your palm in order to release all of the fragrant bouquet. There is just one objection to long-stemmed glasses, but it is unfortunately a major one: they are extremely fragile. The best compromise is probably to select goblets of the same tulip shape but set on a shorter, sturdy stem. Furthermore, it is always advisable to select glassware that is well balanced, with the center of gravity in the base.

Some precious modern or antique crystal is so gracefully designed and so beautifully ornamented with cutting, etching, or engraving, that they are veritable works of art. But how difficult it is to keep these treasures gleaming clean, and how easy it is to chip or crack them! In our servantless, dishwasher age, it is, alas, impractical to use them except on rare special occasions, and it is advisable to select a simple, sturdy style for everyday use. Besides, a conservative contemporary design is more apt to harmonize attractively with almost any style of dishes, silverware, and dining room.

While beautiful modern or antique cut crystal is supremely elegant, I am less enthusiastic about colored crystal as well as hand-painted gold decorations. The first are, as we have seen, justly condemned by epicures; and the second, no matter how costly and rare they may be, usually seem to me to be either fussy or *folklorique*. A goblet of elaborately decorated Bohemian colored crystal, for example, would be enchanting for holding a simple bouquet of flowers, but much less so for holding wine.

Even if you habitually entertain only a few guests at a time, it would be overly optimistic to order less than a dozen glasses of each essential type, for a certain amount of breakage is inevitable in any household. It is therefore wise to select a model that is permanently carried in stock, so that you can replace any broken items a few at a time without having to buy an entire new set. Moreover, when you entertain at a large cocktail party or buffet dinner, it is best to rent all of the necessary glassware from a caterer or a party rental firm, and to reserve your personal treasures for more intimate entertaining, when there is much less risk of breakage.

It is amusing to treat yourself to a present from time to time of a particularly pretty set of orangeade glasses, for example, with a matching pitcher, or to some gaily decorated oversize highball tumblers for the patio, or to a set of balloon-shaped brandy snifters, if your husband is fond of fine Cognac. But the first addition to your basic minimum supply of glassware should probably be a set of Old Fashioned glasses for serving what seems to have become the chic cocktail-hour drink of the day: whisky, gin, or vodka "on the rocks."

(See Wine)

GOLF

❰ A membership in a golf club is an advantageous resource for a hostess, especially when entertaining weekend guests from out of town, since golf enthusiasts seem to enjoy nothing more than pitting their skill against the challenge of a strange new course. I once ran into an entire chartered planeload of American travelers in Europe who were spending two months flying from one golf course to another, without a single glance at a museum or a monument, and I must admit that I have seldom seen such a joyous and enthusiastic group.

Even a nearby driving range can provide a pleasant afternoon or evening distraction for a houseguest who is mad about the sport. And this diversion has the added attraction of permitting the hostess to stay at home in peace in order to prepare the lunch or dinner.

In Europe, golf is the most fashionable sport at the moment, perhaps because the relatively few golf clubs that exist are very expensive and all of them have lengthy waiting lists for membership. They are far more generous in extending guest privileges to foreign visitors than they are in admitting new members. In fact, I wonder if they will not lose much of their aura of elegance the day the sport becomes as democratic on the Continent as it is in America.

(See Clubs)

GUEST ROOMS

("Did you sleep well?" is the conventional morning greeting of a hostess to her overnight guest, to which the conventional reply is, "Very well, thank you"—even if the guest has really spent a frightful night tossing on a lumpy mattress, battling with a pillow that was too hard or too soft and shivering under insufficient bedding. Instead of accepting at face value her guest's polite assurances, a conscientious hostess ought to arrange to spend at least one night in her own guest room. It is the only way to make sure there are no hidden discomforts that experience alone reveals.

An ideal guest room is private (never adjacent to the master bedroom), and has its own adjoining or nearby bathroom. A real bathroom with a tub is by far the best, but a shower will do; a small room with just a washstand and toilet is adequate, and a washstand installed in a corner cupboard or concealed behind a screen is still better than no sanitary facilities at all. The guest room should be supplied with all the furnishings and accessories that are essential for sleeping, washing, and getting dressed. While it isn't necessary to prepare it to withstand a ten-day siege, it should at least be provided with every normal requirement of a weekend guest.

Twin beds are preferable to a single large one, but if your home is vast enough for two guest rooms, one of them might be furnished with twin beds and the other with a double bed. The sheets should be freshly changed, of course, and the bedding suitable to the season, with an extra blanket for each bed in a drawer or cupboard for particularly chilly nights. It is also a good idea to keep an extra pillow for each bed in the cupboard. The point is to spare your guests the embarrassment of having to ask for anything.

A guest room affords a marvelous opportunity to exercise your talents as an interior decorator, and to indulge in such refinements as matching wallpaper and curtains, printed sheets that harmonize with the decor, and a pretty dressing table (which is very practical when you wish to use the room as a ladies' coatroom and powder room for a large party). But beware of creating an overfeminine decor. The dainty frills that would delight an elderly aunt would seem less enchanting to the teen-age schoolboy your son invites home for the holidays. It is best to create an attractive, comfortable, but rather neutral setting, based on colors such as blue, soft green, and yellow, which have neither feminine nor masculine connotations. Above all, you should avoid letting the guest room become a sort of catchall for cast-off furniture, ugly wedding gifts, broken bric-a-brac, and out-of-season clothing.

The windows should be furnished with lightproof curtains that can really be drawn shut, unless there are Venetian blinds or shutters. One of the inviolable rights of every weekend guest is to sleep late on Sunday morning. Be sure to add screens in the summer, if there are mosquitoes or flies where you live, and as an added precaution, provide an aerosol bomb of DDT.

Aside from the bed, you will need to furnish the guest room with a bed table and a good reading lamp, a chest of drawers (or its equivalent in built-in storage space), a clothes closet with an assortment of hangers for suits, dresses, trousers and skirts, a piece of furniture (perhaps no more than a flat table) to serve as either a dressing table or a desk, a straight chair, and a wastebasket. It is also very nice to provide a comfortable boudoir chair for resting and reading. Unless the entire room is carpeted, a rug should be placed next to the bed.

The basic bathroom equipment consists of a shower curtain if necessary, a bath mat, towels and washcloths, all of them impeccably laundered, one or two clean drinking glasses, a mirror with an excellent light and a socket for electric razors, a shelf over the washstand, a small wastebasket, a medicine cabinet and if possible a cupboard for extra linen. And when you're checking supplies, be sure there's fresh soap and plenty of toilet tissue—an extra roll of the latter can give a guest a pleasant feeling of security, whereas a dwindling supply . . .

These are the bare essentials, to be supplemented according to the means and space at your disposal. But there are also a number of superfluous articles that give a houseguest a sensation of pampered luxury and denote an exceptionally thoughtful hostess:

On the writing table: An ashtray, an assortment of picture postcards of the region, a supply of writing paper and envelopes, a box of stamps. In the drawer: a pair of scissors, a few pencils and ball-point pens. A box of matches (and also a candlestick on the table, if you live in a country area where electricity breakdowns are frequent).

On the dresser: A pretty hand mirror, brush, and comb (scrupulously clean, needless to say). A vase of fresh flowers. All of the drawers should be lined with clean paper, and you might place in the top drawer: a miniature sewing kit for emergency repairs, a packet of safety pins, a clothes brush, and a shoeshine kit. In the bottom drawer: a pair of freshly laundered nylon pajamas and a nylon nightdress (a size twelve in a chemise style would fit almost everybody) for the use of unexpected overnight guests. If you live near the seashore or own a swimming pool, you might also store in the guest room dresser several nylon bathing suits, swimming trunks, and bathing caps, to be loaned to friends who have forgotten to bring their own.

On the bed table: A small alarm clock (wound up and set at the correct time); a carafe for drinking water and its matching glass; a selection of light reading such as a detective novel, a best seller, an anthology, and a few current magazines. In the drawer: an extra electric light bulb for the bed lamp.

In the clothes closet: In addition to an ample supply of assorted hangers, a folding luggage rack. An umbrella.

In the bathroom: A capacious Turkish toweling peignoir for each houseguest. In a cupboard, those extra rolls of toilet tissue, soap, a small box of soap flakes for personal laundry, extra towels and facecloths. In the medicine cabinet or cupboard: a few essential toilet articles in miniature dime-store sizes—toothpaste, shaving cream, a safety razor and razor blades, a couple of new toothbrushes in their cellophane wrappers, a tube of cold cream, cotton, cleansing tissues, nail-polish remover, talcum powder, eau de cologne, aspirin, sanitary supplies, adhesive plasters, Mercurochrome, etc.

In other words, the perfectly equipped guest room combines all the comforts of a first-class hotel with the personal touches that only a considerate hostess can provide. But these are merely suggestions, and if a hostess actually provided all of them she would probably have trouble persuading her guests to leave at the end of the weekend! Just a few of them, however, or simply the bouquet of flowers, would be a warm expression of hospitality.

It is sometimes possible to accommodate an overnight guest even when you do not have a separate guest room, provided that your home includes a playroom, library, or den that is independent from the rest of the rooms, as well as a second bathroom. If so, a studio couch or a convertible sofa may be used as an emergency guest bed, but only for a night or two. Otherwise, it is better not to attempt to house your week-end guests in your own home, but to reserve for them a room at (in order of preference) your country club, a luxury motel, a comfortable local inn, or a hotel.

(See Beds, Houseguests)

ELP

¶ It is one of the minor ironies of life that today, when more people than ever before have the means, the time, and the urge to entertain, it has become practically impossible to find household help to cope with the extra work that entertaining inevitably entails.

The competent all-round maid is as extinct as the dodo, and a first-class cook is as hard to find as uranium and practically as expensive. American women, who have had to struggle along with this problem for some years now, may take consolation in the fact that the dearth of household help has spread to Europe, where it is becoming more desperate every day. At first, the more prosperous nations were able to import personnel from their less fortunate neighbors, luring prospective butlers and cooks with what seemed to them to be fantastically high pay. But as soon as the Spanish girls had earned enough to constitute a dowry (with soaring wages, this did not take very long), and as soon as the Sicilian butlers or chauffeurs had put aside enough money to buy the village grocery store or gasoline station, home they went.

At the moment, a few indomitable friends of mine are prospecting the labor market in Yugoslavia, and even in Turkey, but in the meantime more and more of us are getting by as best we can with part-time cleaning help, and even the relatively undomesticated French husbands are beginning to lend a hand. For once, housewives and economists are unanimous in their vision of the future: the situation is bound to get even worse.

I shall be eternally grateful to the ingenious American manufacturers who have invented a fantastic range of machines and gadgets to lighten our household chores. For the woman who loves to entertain, I cannot recommend strongly enough an investment in all of the labor-saving kitchen devices that she can afford. The time and effort spared by an automatic dishwasher (my dream), an electric can opener, an automatic vegetable peeler, a blender, mixer, infrared grill, timer, toaster, and ice-cream maker, down to the tiniest garlic press and egg slicer, can change a woman's life—even though they can never replace a real live maid. Still, with the aid of these miraculous kitchen helpers, two hands can do the work of four.

Alas, no genius has yet invented a robot to wait on table. And until that great achievement occurs, the principal problem of a hostess is not so much the preparation of a meal, as its service.

Personally, if I could only find or afford a single professional helper to aid me with a dinner or luncheon party, I would not hesitate an instant. I would do all of the cooking myself and hire a person to wait on table, even if it meant doing the dishes myself the morning after.

In most cities there are caterers and employment agencies that provide butlers, cooks, waiters, waitresses, and bartenders for luncheon, cocktail, and dinner parties. Unfortunately, the demand being far greater than the supply, the rates are high. In New York City, for example, the average fee is twelve to fifteen dollars for a waitress, and twenty dollars for a cook, plus carfare and the agency commission. In smaller towns where this service may not exist, it is occasionally possible to find somebody, if only a high school student, whom you could train to help you out from time to time when you have company. For a very informal party, it may even be possible to have your own children play the role of waiters. If you ask this service of them only very infrequently and if they are in the subteen age group, they may even consider it a treat, and they will often handle the job more conscientiously than trained professionals. In this circumstance, the hostess should always announce to her guests beforehand that "Johnny and Linda simply begged me to let them wait on table tonight" . . . and then pay no more attention to them than one would to professional domestic help.

Much more common, alas, is the case of the hostess who can find nobody, but nobody, to help her with a dinner, and who must look after everything, including the service, all by herself. Her very first rule should be to invite no more guests than she can handle with ease. Six people, including the host and hostess, is generally a maximum. Secondly, she should politely but firmly refuse the help that her women guests are bound to offer. Even with the best-planned organization, the hostess will be obliged to leave the table a few times during the course of the meal, and if there is more than one empty chair at the table the atmosphere is sure to suffer and the conversation to limp. Besides, as every woman must have experienced in one role or the other, the well-meaning friend who attempts to lend a hand is usually more of a hindrance than a help. She probably hasn't the same way of doing things as you, she is afraid of making a mistake, and so she is forever asking questions: "In which drawer are the knives? . . . Where shall I put this?" etc., etc. The very most you should permit your guests to do is to pass the plates and serving dishes around the table.

One of the most efficient hostesses I have seen solves the servant-less problem by placing two rolling tea carts at either side of her place at table, one of them holding all the plates and silverware, with the used sets placed on the bottom tray and the fresh on top; the other is loaded with the entire meal: the cold dishes on the bottom tray, and the hot dishes kept steaming over an electric hot plate on top. Everything is in place when she announces that dinner is served, and she thus only has to leave the table once, while the dessert is being passed around, when she whisks the two carts out of sight into the kitchen, prepares the coffee tray in the living room, and removes the cocktail remains. An important point is that she always plans her menu carefully, avoiding any dishes that require last-minute preparation in the kitchen as well as those that leave such debris on the plates that it is afterward impossible to stack them neatly (whole artichokes, oysters, unboned fowl and fish, etc.). Sometimes she serves as a main dish an enormous casserole kept warm on the electric hot plate, and for dessert crêpes suzette or flambéed peaches, which she prepares herself at table in a pretty copper chafing dish. After the meal, the dessert plates are abandoned on the table, the dining room door is shut, and coffee is served on a tray in the living room. Her system works very smoothly— although it would be dishonest to pretend that it is as elegant as a properly served dinner with a maid or waiter.

Experience and observation will suggest other helpful hints for help-less hostesses. For example:

— Limit the menu to three courses at the most.

— Limit the number of serving dishes to one per course by arranging meat and vegetables on the same platter, creamed seafood in a rice ring, or baked ham surrounded by individual mounds of creamed spinach; by serving the cheese course on a long rectangular tray with a space for butter at one end and crackers at the other; by pouring a sauce or whipped cream over your dessert just before it is served, instead of passing the sauce separately, etc.

— Used dishes and platters that are placed on the lower shelves of a buffet or tea cart will be practically unnoticed, whereas dirty dishes placed higher than the surface of the table will attract all eyes and create an impression of disorder.

— Never let your guests catch sight of you with an apron tied around your waist or a kitchen towel in your hand. You will look like a drudge and fill them with guilt and pity.

— Instead of sitting at one end of the table, try placing yourself at the center of one long side, with your husband opposite. In this position, it is much easier to control the service without making it too apparent, for you can pass dishes to both ends as well as across the table. This is one situation where actions do *not* speak louder than words—on the contrary, your gestures will be far less noticeable than your desperate pleas such as "Do pass the spinach down to this end of the table," or "Mary, you haven't any roast yet!" etc., etc.

— Avoid leaving the table during a lull in the conversation; instead, disappear when the discussion is liveliest and your absence is least apt to be noticed.

— You may have to take advantage of all the culinary shortcuts, but be sure to destroy the evidence and to add a personal finishing touch, so that your guests will not be able to guess that the lobster bisque came out of a can, and that the steaming coffee in the silver pot was surreptitiously prepared in the kitchen with a jar of Nescafé.

Let's face it. There is no really ideal technique for serving a servantless dinner, but the women guests who are all in the same predicament, are usually very understanding. As for the men, if you take great pains over your menu, so that every course is not only delicious but also out of the ordinary, they will be so absorbed by their gastronomic pleasure that they will scarcely notice you have prepared and served your dinner without the slightest bit of help.

(See Dinners—and for the lucky women who have actually managed to find one—See Servants)

HOLIDAYS

❦ Entertaining on a holiday has its advantages and its drawbacks. The principal advantage is, of course, that you can be certain nobody has to go to work or school on that particular day, and they can stay up later with a clear conscience the night before. Holiday entertaining also greatly simplifies the problem of finding ideas for the menu and decorations, and even for the entertainment in the case of such occasions as Halloween (bobbing for apples, costumes, ghost stories, barn dancing) or New Year's Eve (the twelve strokes of midnight, paper hats, confetti, dancing, and champagne toasts). The best policy, in my opinion, is either to adhere to tradition in a refined and rather lavish way, or else to be completely original, perhaps by borrowing the less banal traditions of some foreign lands.

You might even borrow the holiday of another country, or celebrate a less hackneyed American red-letter day, for example:

January 6 — The Feast of the Three Kings (Epiphany). In Spain, it is on the eve of this day that the kings arrive to present the children with gifts.

February 2 — Candlemas Day (the *Chandeleur,* in France—where the custom is to flip a pancake in a frying pan while holding a coin in the left hand. If you succeed, you will be prosperous throughout the year. Needless to add, this leads to an enormous consumption of pancakes of all kinds.)

February 14 — Valentine's Day (the fete of lovers and romance)

February 22 — George Washington's birthday (flags and miniature artificial cherry trees)

March 17 — St. Patrick's Day, the patron saint of Ireland

April 1 — April Fool's Day (jokes and pranks)

May 1 — May Day (a spring festival, also the Worker's Day)

May 24 — Empire Day in Great Britain

June 2 — The national patriotic holiday of Italy (commemorating the proclamation of the republic in 1946)

June 21 — The longest day of the year

June 23 — Midsummer Night's Eve

July 14 — Bastille Day in France, similar to your Fourth of July

August 1 — The national patriotic holiday of Switzerland (commemorating the founding of the Confederation in 1291)

September 15 — Battle of Britain Day in England

October 12 — Columbus Day

October 24 — United Nations Day

November 25 — Saint Catherine's feast day, which is widely celebrated in the Paris *haute couture* houses in honor of the young women who have reached the age of twenty-five and are still unmarried. They wear fanciful hats and are toasted with champagne, and all of the fashion business is suspended for the day.

If you decide to give a party on an American national holiday, there is a debit side to the ledger. All of the shops are likely to be closed that day, and possibly the afternoon before as well, so careful preparation well in advance is absolutely essential. If you plan to hire a catering service, you must make your reservations a month ahead of time. And if you intend to hire extra help from other sources, you may find that all of the available waiters are either already engaged or else expect to enjoy the holiday themselves by taking the day off. Finally, you should consider that since this is one of the few days when all the members of the family are able to be at home at the same time, a holiday is generally a family occasion. It therefore seems to me most suitable for holiday parties to maintain a family character. For example, you might invite several entire families to a Fourth of July picnic or barbecue, or give a New Year's eggnog party for friends of every generation, from your parents to the school vacation set, even if you do not have school-age children of your own.

Certain hostesses have established a tradition of giving a party on the same date every year, such as an annual Twelfth Night dinner dance, a Labor Day picnic, or a buffet supper after the Army-Navy football game. I know one woman who gives such a beautiful annual party between Christmas and New Year's that she is invited out to dinner throughout the year on the strength of that alone. There is, however, a definite risk in adopting the tradition of an annual reception: it becomes very difficult to control your guest list. Everybody who has been invited once will expect to be invited next year, too, and as you meet new people and make new friends, your list will grow and grow. Moreover, a number of your friends may be entertaining houseguests over the holiday weekend, and you must naturally invite them too. Short of a major feud or serious illness, none of the regulars can be eliminated tactfully, and within a few years the number of guests you are obliged to invite will have become so huge that the only way to handle the crowd is to transform your reception into a mammoth cocktail party—and this, as you may have gathered by now, seems to me to have become the least enjoyable as well as the least elegant form of entertaining.

Finally, there's no rule against making much of your own sentimental, family "holidays"—the birthdays, anniversaries, special commemorations that may become your own tradition, and you're equally free (until you encounter protests that suggest you've established your own anticipated, welcome rituals) to vary the details as you will. What can be nicer than personal, private "holidays"?

HOSPITALITY

⟨ Whenever you offer hospitality to a guest, you implicitly guarantee to take charge of his comfort, welfare, entertainment, and perhaps nourishment and even lodging for a certain period of time. And in accepting your invitations, your guests give proof of their confidence in you, for their fate is, temporarily at least, entirely in your hands. A hostess should never fail to be aware of this trust, which she hasn't the right to betray. Which means that:

— The choicest morsels of food, the most comfortable chairs, the best seats at the theater or concert, the softest sheets, the first places in the lifeboat should be given to your guests.

— Every guest has the right to know what to expect when he accepts one of your invitations (a large formal dinner? an evening of bridge?

an outdoor barbecue?), just as he has the right to know who is present and what is going on after he has arrived. The tactful hostess therefore always manages to give newcomers to a discussion a resumé of the theme in question, and she avoids conversations devoted to reminiscences that leave one of her guests out in the cold.

— Your guests should be confident every time they accept one of your invitations that they will not encounter people whom they might not care to see, nor the very same people every time; that they will not be fed food or liquor that might make them sick, nor be asked to play games that might make them look ridiculous, nor be embarrassed in any way.

— A hostess should always direct the conversation toward subjects that will interest and flatter her guests, even though these topics may bore her to tears (which she hasn't the right to shed in front of her guests!).

— Every guest, no matter how inopportune, has a right to expect a warm and enthusiastic welcome.

In other words, the perfect hostess always, as a matter of course and principle, places the interests of her guests before her own.

And what has the hostess a right to expect in exchange for all of these privileges and attentions? Simply the satisfaction of knowing that her guests have enjoyed themselves.

You must admit that hospitality is a beautiful virtue.

HOTELS

❲ The elegance of a reception given in a hotel depends almost entirely on the elegance of the hotel. The private salons of the best hotel in town are therefore in such great demand that it is necessary to make your reservations well in advance, especially during the height of the social season. Once you have selected the menu or refreshments with the maître d'hôtel, arranged for appropriate floral decorations, and prepared to deduct a substantial amount from your bank account, you can relax until the day of the party. You should then arrive well in advance of your guests, whom you will receive just as if you were entertaining them in your own home—with one slight difference in the manner of dress: the hostess does not remove her hat when giving a daytime reception in a hotel, whereas she would of course never wear one if she were receiving in her own home.

Entertaining in a hotel is much more expensive than entertaining at home, and it is also much easier on the hostess. But even in a luxury hotel, it is never quite as elegant. On many occasions, however, such as a large wedding reception, you have no choice. When you are obliged to invite a great number of guests, there is the problem of space as well as catering to be considered, and a hotel may offer the only possible solution.

Generally speaking, a reception in a club is more chic than in a hotel, but only if the club is of comparative social standing and equally well equipped to organize the party. In other words, a first-class hotel is naturally preferable to a second-class club, but between a smart hotel and a smart club, my first choice would be the club without hesitation.

(See Restaurants)

HOUSEGUESTS

❪ There is unfortunately seldom sufficient space in a city apartment to accommodate a houseguest, and I do not advise attempting it unless you possess a separate guest room with an independent bathroom, or at least a shower. Moreover, while it is highly agreeable to entertain houseguests in the country, it can be awkward in the city to assume the responsibility of looking after a guest in addition to one's daily commitments, and especially if you have a regular job.

Although it is possible to put up a friend overnight on the living room sofa when there is a terrible storm or when he has missed the last train home, you should absolutely never invite a guest to stay with you for a longer time unless you are able to offer him the same degree of comfort and independence that he would find in a hotel.

The dream would be, I suppose, to own either an apartment near the corner of Fifth Avenue with an entirely separate floor for guests, as does Madame de Miraval of Henry à la Pensée, or a separate guest-house—or even four of them, as Jacqueline Cochran has at her fabulous home near Palm Springs. Each of these little houses is completely furnished and includes a kitchen in which the refrigerator is filled with everything you could desire, plus, of course, a bathroom and a sitting room, where even writing paper and playing cards have been supplied. There is sufficient personnel to take care of all these houses, and the housekeeper, Mrs. Stonebreaker, would be able to outfit an entire Hilton Hotel from her ample stock of sheets, towels, and hand soap. Needless to say, very few people even in the United States are able to receive houseguests in such a royal manner, and there is no reason to deprive yourself of the pleasure as long as your accommodations are adequate, although on a less sumptuous scale.

Even when you are equipped to give a houseguest a private bedroom and bath, it is unwise to invite a person with whom you are only slightly acquainted, for there is the risk of a disagreeable surprise that could ruin the atmosphere of good humor that it is the first duty of the hostess, as well as the guest, to create and maintain. Your guest should know you well enough to feel not the slightest reluctance about asking for whatever he may need, if by chance you have forgotten some essential article for the guest room—even after reading the section devoted to this subject! It is much more embarrassing for a hostess to learn that her guest has been uncomfortable because of something she has overlooked than it is to have him ask her for it. One of my friends can sleep only in a pitch-black room, and even the noise of a clock keeps her awake. But if she hadn't explained this to me, I never could have guessed. Neither can a hostess be expected to know without being told that one person drinks an entire pitcher of water during the night, while another likes to sip a glass of grapefruit juice before retiring; or that one person can only sleep flat on his back, and another when he is propped up on a mountain of pillows.

Be sure to ask your guest what she (or he) likes to eat for breakfast, and whether she would prefer it in her room or in the dining room with you. In the latter case, you should urge your guest to come to breakfast in her dressing gown. If you have a job and no maid and must leave home at an early hour, you can stock up on fruit juices, coffee or tea, bread or melba toast, cereals, eggs, bacon, or whatever it is that your guest habitually eats for breakfast, and arrange everything in the kitchen for her before you leave for work. You should also find out if your guest has any particular likes or dislikes in food, as well as any dietary restrictions, so that you can take them into account when planning the menus of your at-home meals.

Receiving a houseguest means looking after her entertainment as well as her food and lodging. But remember that your guest's stay in your home should be rather like a vacation for her (if not for you!). You should, for example, urge her to sleep as late in the morning as she wishes and provide her with plenty of light reading. Above all, you should refrain from planning so extensive a program that she will need a rest cure afterward.

To start everything off in the happiest mood, it is important for you to be home to greet her the moment she arrives. Meeting her at the railroad station or airport would be an even more hospitable gesture. But as soon as your guest is in your home, it is thoughtful to leave her alone long enough to get settled in her room, to take a bath, to unpack, etc. Then you can share a drink or a cup of tea and discuss the plans you have made for her visit.

When you have invited a houseguest for three or four days only, it is quite possible to shower her with attention during this short time. (But still leave her a little quiet and peace every day as well.) You should take her with you everywhere you go, and if you work during the daytime you should suggest interesting daytime activities to her and plan some kind of diversion for every evening: theater, movies, bridge, or dinner at the home of friends to which you arrange to have your guest invited. As a matter of fact, if you have no household help, it is generally more practical to take your houseguest to a dinner party at the home of friends who are intimate enough for you to ask this service of them. But if your household is well organized for entertaining, it would be preferable to give a small informal dinner or a cocktail party in honor of your guest in your own home—not on the first evening, because of the possible fatigue of her journey; but the second night would be ideal.

When you have invited a guest to stay with you for a week or ten days, it is useful as well as hospitable to give a party in her honor the second or third evening of her visit. A small buffet dinner or an intimate cocktail party would be most suitable. You should invite those of your friends whom she is most likely to find interesting, and even more important, whom she will interest, in the hope of receiving invitations to fill up some of the other evenings during her stay with you. A hostess is expected to include her houseguests in all of her social activities, but the houseguest, on the other hand, can perfectly well accept luncheon and dinner invitations on her own without the presence of her hosts.

When you have invited a houseguest to stay with you for several weeks or even for a month, the problem is somewhat different. It would be unreasonable to expect you to disrupt your personal life during such a long time, and while you should still organize several interesting social activities for your guest each week, she should also be expected to be more self-reliant and to look after herself a large part of the time or simply to share your daily life and activities. At the beginning of her visit, you should explain to her in general what is the daily routine of your household, and what events she can look forward to. Every morning, or every evening, whichever is more convenient, you should check your daily program with your guest to make sure that her time is being pleasantly occupied. But after the first few days she will already begin to integrate herself into your household, and by the end of a week she will probably feel perfectly at home.

The ideal hostess and the ideal houseguest are each careful to respect the other's privacy. You should not overwhelm your guest with obligations and attentions—but do not abandon her completely to her own devices either. Discretion is obligatory in regard to your guest's mail, telephone calls, personal engagements, etc. But at the same time you should behave in a natural, relaxed, and friendly manner where your own private affairs are concerned. She should always have the feeling that she is a welcome guest and not an intruder.

Harmonious cohabitation between unrelated persons is an art that is especially difficult with older persons who have become rather set in their ways. In fact, I know of very few lengthy house visits that have been equally successful from the point of view of the host and in the opinion of the guest. It is therefore wise to be very cautious about extending invitations of this kind to people you know only slightly, for you may be in for an unpleasant surprise.

If your guest should decide to leave sooner than you originally planned, do not feel offended, for it is not necessarily a criticism of your hospitality. She may simply be embarrassed by the trouble she is causing you. Very few homes are organized in such a way as to permit the completely happy integration of another person who is neither a member of the family nor such a long-standing, intimate friend that it practically amounts to the same thing. If, on the other hand, your guest decides to prolong her visit, the situation may be more awkward. When her presence is a pleasure for all concerned, you have only to urge her to remain. But if you inwardly groan at the prospect, the best thing to do is to tell her that, as much as you would love to have her stay on, you have arranged to make a trip yourself the day after her visit was supposed to come to an end. All invitations to houseguests should include a definite starting date and a definite closing, and your hospitality will not be lessened in any way if you insist on adhering to them.

When you invite a friend of one of your children to stay with you for the school holidays or even all summer long, you will face none of these delicate adult problems. Questions of dates, diets, clothing, activities, as well as any special instructions, should all be settled by letter between the children's parents well ahead of time. Instead of your being obliged to adjust your family habits in the slightest way in order to accommodate the new arrival, it is the young guest who will consider it great fun to fit into your life, and the more different it is from his own, the more he will enjoy it. Children are far more adaptable in their ways than grownups are.

A special problem may arise, however, if your visitor is more strictly brought up than are your own children as far as bedtime hours, or daytime study periods are concerned. In this case, you must respect the parents' wishes and, if necessary, oblige your own children to alter their program accordingly. It is impossible to enforce a double standard of child behavior in a single household, for it will always seem terribly unfair to one child or the other. This is the principal point of possible friction, but it is one that you should carefully consider before you ever extend a holiday invitation to your son's or daughter's schoolmates— and which the schoolmate's parents should consider even more carefully before accepting.

When there is no particular discrepancy in the children's upbringing, you will simply have the surprisingly pleasant impression that your family has miraculously expanded overnight. You may also be amazed by the improved manners and the considerate behavior of your own children when they assume the role of hosts to a houseguest of their own.

(See Breakfast, Guest Rooms)

HOUSES

❰ Fashion and entertaining have many points in common, as we have seen, and another one of them is this: just as a becoming outfit is selected in view of a woman's individual figure, a successful party must be adapted to the house in which it takes place. You can never expect to give a sumptuous formal dinner in a tiny, modest dwelling any more than you would think it chic to wear a cocktail gown to a football game, and there is no point in attempting it, when your cozy home is the perfect setting for a gay, informal gathering. On the other hand, it would be just as inappropriate to attempt a zany informal party in a house that is conceived and equipped for formal entertaining.

The experienced hostess is always aware of the fact that her entertaining program is limited and governed to a considerable degree by the kind of house she happens to inhabit, as well as by her own personality and way of life. Fortunately, there are so many different forms and manners of entertaining with elegance that every woman, with a little thought and experience, can discover the ones that are most perfectly adapted to her particular set of circumstances.

HOUSEWARMING

❰ In certain areas, finding a dream house or apartment is almost as great an achievement as decorating it, and I suppose that is why housewarmings, which used to take place only when a new dwelling was completely finished down to the last ashtray and bibelot, are now just as often held in homes that are at best half furnished.

In general, families who have already inaugurated other homes prefer to wait until their latest interior is as perfect as possible before unveiling it to their friends. For them the greatest thrill comes from showing off the modernity and ingenuity of the practical installations, and the elegance of the decor, rather than in having at last a home of their own or simply a roof over their heads! For this kind of a housewarming, you would prepare a rather refined, conventional dinner party for as many friends as you can comfortably receive.

Young married couples, on the other hand, are usually more impatient. They cannot wait to celebrate the acquisition of a home of their own. Their housewarmings are probably the most fun, and certainly the most informal. As soon as the kitchen is in working condition, the paint and plaster dry, and the electricity, heat, and water turned on, they want to show off their treasure to all of their friends. Even though the rooms may not yet be fully furnished, it is possible to improvise an attractive buffet table by placing a long board over a pair of trestles, covered by a floor-length paper or cotton tablecloth; and a bar can be set up in the same way. Cushions may substitute for extra chairs, and paper cups and plates and paper coffee mugs may be used if the wedding-present china and silver are still in their packing cases. The bareness of the setting can be completely camouflaged by means of party decorations arranged with taste and imagination.

The party may be either a cocktail party or a dinner, and I would much prefer the latter. In France, we call a housewarming party a *pendaison de crémaillère*—hanging of the pothook (in the kitchen fireplace)—and in fact, this is the ideal occasion for a dinner built around one great succulent casserole dish, such as *pot au feu, boeuf Bourgignon,* Irish stew, or chicken and kidney pie. Since everything should be easy to prepare ahead of time and simple to serve, the casserole can be completed with hot buttered rolls, a mixed salad, a cheese tray, and a dessert of cake or pie. As for liquid refreshments: whisky or a cocktail mixed ahead of time to start things off, an inexpensive light red or rosé wine to accompany the meal, hot coffee to terminate it, and throughout the rest of the evening the usual long drinks and fruit juice or, if the budget is already in a sorry state, a tasty wine or rum punch.

Since this is a rather personal celebration, only good friends of your own age should be invited. It is better to wait until everything is completely finished before attempting to entertain older people. It is also advisable to resist the temptation of inviting everyone you know. Instead, try to limit your guest list to a reasonable number that can be served without too much confusion and seated in comparative comfort. The very first party you give in your very first home is the most disheartening time and place to face the tragedy of a spilled drink on a brand-new beige carpet or a cigarette burn in a sofa that you haven't even paid for yet.

HUSBANDS

⟨ While it is generally recognized that women exert an enormous influence on their husbands' professional success, it is also undeniable that the role of the host at a party is just as important as that of the hostess, even though it is not mentioned very often.

For example, the merits of the French ambassadress in Washington have been widely vaunted, but who has ever thought of singing the praises of her charming husband Hervé Alphand in his social role? He is a man who knows how to look with appreciation at a woman, a well-set table, a well-chosen cigar, and a fine bottle of wine. He takes his time, he is a charmer and a marvelous conversationalist, warm, friendly, and witty. He also works very hard and succeeds in solving problems that are probably just as difficult and important as those that face the president of General Motors at the end of the month, but he doesn't let his worries show. He is not like the businessman who thinks only of business. He knows how to relax and even to appear to be happy to see you. He is a perfect host.

If ever you have the feeling that you really shouldn't be taking up the time of such an important man as your hostess's husband, one thing is sure: he may be a literary genius or an electronics wizard, a royal prince or a political VIP, a magnate of automobiles, ready-to-wear, or what-have-you—but he is not a good host.

The Ten Commandments for a husband as a host are:

(1.) He should help his wife to make out the guest list in order to avoid social blunders or regrettable oversights.

(2.) He should personally assume the responsibility for the quality and quantity of wine and liquor to be served at a party.

(3.) He should not come home from the office just fifteen minutes before the guests are supposed to arrive.

(4.) He should never roar at his wife on the pretext that his clothes have not been put away in the proper place, that his suit is badly pressed or his shirt badly laundered, or that he cannot find his shorts, his socks, or the cuff links Mother gave him.

(5.) He should take the time to unstick the zipper on his wife's dress, and he should look at her in admiration and compliment her on her pretty gown and hairstyle.

(6.) He should take time to glance at the table and the flower arrangements and tell her that everything is perfectly beautiful—even if he discreetly corrects an error in the table setting when she isn't looking.

(7.) He should help his wife with the introductions, and he should pay outrageous compliments to the women guests—and especially to the least attractive.

(8.) He should never, never utter a derogatory remark about the food or service—even if the guest of honor has a sauceboat overturned in his lap or chips a tooth on a pit in the pie.

(9.) He should make it his business to see that the men do not cluster together in one corner of the living room before or after dinner like a football team in a huddle. He should dance, laugh, and make conversation, and he should urge his guests to stay as long as they like —even if he has to be at the office at eight o'clock the following morning.

(10.) After the guests have left, he should take his wife in his arms and tell her that it was a marvelous party—and that the woman to whom he was so charming was "not really looking very well tonight." Finally, he should help to tidy up without giving the impression that he is a poor slave forced to work overtime, but on the contrary, with the conquering smile of a perfect host and husband.

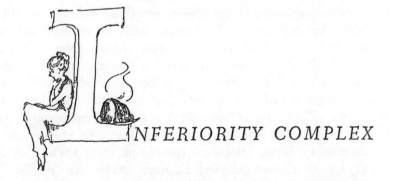

INFERIORITY COMPLEX

❡ I have a friend who only started to give out her address the day she was able to move into the 16th Arrondissement (one of the fashionable residential districts in Paris), and I know several people who practically ruined themselves in restaurants because they did not want anybody to visit their rather modest homes. How foolish it is to develop such ridiculous inferiority complexes, when the fact is that as long as your hospitality is sincere, the setting hasn't the slightest importance. It is only the person who entertains principally in order to impress people who would do better to keep his caviar for himself.

When you have done your utmost to receive your friends to the best of your ability, you should also know how to relax and to accept the inevitable snags and minor tragedies with a smile.

I once knew a woman who was exceedingly meticulous, but also completely lacking in self-confidence, and she worked herself into such a state whenever she entertained that although everything was always perfect, her guests shared her anxiety along with her champagne. She was incapable of following a conversation, for her eyes never left the terror-stricken maid who waited on table, and she would greet each new platter with such an expression of distrust that you finally wondered if all the food was not poisoned.

On the other hand, at the very beginning of my marriage, I had to entertain many highly accomplished hostesses, and in particular one of my husband's aunts who had earned herself a reputation in the family as an authority on etiquette and entertaining. She rather resembled Queen Victoria, and indulgence was not her outstanding virtue. The mere idea of receiving this formidable personage was enough to intimidate the most intrepid young bride. My mother-in-law and another aunt could not conceal their anxiety, and my husband helped me plan the menu a week in advance.

At the beginning of the dinner, everything went off beautifully, but when the time came for the dessert, which was intended to be a mountainous chestnut purée concoction with whipped cream that was called a "Himalaya," but that had turned out to look more like the Dead Sea, an anguished silence gripped the entire table, until I burst out laughing and said, "Well, that's that! I was sure something was going to misfire!" The uncles (who didn't care for desserts anyway) concluded that they had a new niece who kept her sense of proportion about household mishaps instead of considering them national catastrophes the way their wives did. And the aunts decided that "the little girl has a very good disposition," and "for a beginner, she really manages things amazingly well."

INFORMALITY

❨ The superficial signs of informality in entertaining are business suits and cocktail dresses instead of the black ties and evening gowns of formal dinner parties, a less pretentious menu probably containing fewer courses, a simpler table setting and service (perhaps even a buffet with no waiter or waitress at all), and a guest list that is more apt to be composed of friends who already know each other well plus one or two new couples, rather than a larger, less intimate gathering. For the hostess, there is usually less work in preparing her house and her cuisine than for a formal party, and less expense as well. Because of the relaxed familiarity of the atmosphere, she probably will not need to rely so much on her own efforts to keep the conversation going, the guests circulating, and everybody amused.

Informal entertaining is very fashionable. It is also, strange as it may seem, more difficult to carry off successfully than is entertaining within the comforting bounds of conventional formality. A perfect informal dinner party is, in my opinion, the most enriching and pleasurable form of social intercourse. But in order to succeed, the evening must be conceived and carried out with just as much intelligence and care as you would devote to an important formal reception. Your welcome should be just as cordial, the composition of the menu and guest list just as careful, and your solicitude for the comfort and pleasure of your guests just as constant. For example, on a sweltering August evening a hostess should think of telephoning her guests in advance to ask the men to wear their coolest sports clothes, if she wishes to avoid the untidy spectacle of a roomful of women in party frocks and men in rolled-up shirt-sleeves. In the country, she doesn't even need to telephone, since her guests should feel free to wear sport shirts to an informal summer dinner party anyway.

In other words, informality should never be confused with negligence.

INSECTS

⟨ Thanks to the invention of DDT and other modern insecticides, it is no longer complicated and unaesthetic to keep one's home free from bugs. You should take particular pains to spray the guest room thoroughly before receiving weekend guests in the country in the summertime, so that uninvited guests do not disturb the pleasure of your invited ones. It is also a good idea always to leave an aerosol can of insecticide in the guest room.

In some parts of the country there are commercial enterprises that will de-bug a garden or a lawn before an outdoor evening party, when the lighting is bound to attract insects from far away. But it is wise to ask for an estimate before you place your order, because I suspect that this useful service must be very costly. It might, however, be a worthwhile investment before a once-in-a-lifetime outdoor ball, when décolleté evening gowns will offer irresistible temptations to roving mosquitoes.

One woman I know who owns a lovely house on the very edge of the Mediterranean with a charming dining terrace jutting out into the sea, became so discouraged by the apparently insoluble problem of summer mosquitoes that she had a dozen sacks made out of fine mosquito netting, with a drawstring at the top. During August when the bugs are most voracious, every guest slips into one of these bags when dinner is announced, ties the drawstring at the waist, and shuffles to the elegant outdoor table on the terrace. For some odd reason, the Mediterranean mosquitoes, who adore ankles under a table, seem to scorn the bare shoulders above. Anyway, my friend is thoroughly satisfied with her system.

While I hope that such radical steps are not necessary in your home, the point is that some people are terrified by insects and others are allergic to their venom, and if your area is plagued by these tiny monsters, you should call upon science and, if necessary, upon your own ingenuity in order to protect your guests from them if they cannot be eliminated entirely.

INSURANCE

❦ Security is an essential element of hospitality, and to offer hospitality has always implied offering safety as well. In many civilizations, it is considered a greater offense to a man's honor to harm a guest in his home than to cause him personal injury. Today, a guest is unlikely to run the risk of attack or abduction, but there is always the danger of slipping on an icy doorstep or being bitten by the family dog or stumbling over a child's toy and breaking an arm or an ankle. Such minor accidents, which you would accept philosophically if you were yourself the victim, are far more distressing when they happen to an invited guest. Twentieth-century problems require twentieth-century solutions, and I suppose that the modern counterpart of such ancient protective devices as moats, drawbridges, and Swiss mercenaries is simply a good insurance policy.

Americans are very fortunate in having relatively low insurance rates as well as the possibility of insuring themselves and their property against almost every imaginable kind of risk. It is therefore not a luxury but an indispensable precaution to have a reliable insurance broker establish a policy covering injuries and accidents to visitors in your home. While insurance may not prevent accidents from occurring, it will at least alleviate the consequences. If you own pets, a swimming pool, or a tennis court, you should be sure to point this out to the insurance broker in order to avoid the unpleasant surprise of discovering too late that you are unprotected at your most vulnerable point, or in circumstances where there is the greatest risk of accident.

If it is possible for you to insure your home against the theft of property belonging to a guest—if only on the day of an important party —I would highly recommend it. I am thinking of a certain magnificent mink cape belonging to one of the guests at a birthday party I gave with a friend, whose birth date is the same as mine, at her lovely house on the outskirts of Paris. It was an unusually warm June night, perfect for dancing in the garden under the stars, and the women's wraps were soon discarded. At the end of the evening it was discovered to our horror that this valuable mink cape was missing. A minute search was made, the personnel was questioned, all to no avail. And the worst of it was that the fur was uninsured. After twenty-four hours of sleepless anxiety, a friend advised us to spread the word that the cape was, on the contrary, heavily insured and there was no cause for tears since it would certainly be replaced. We followed this advice, not really expecting anything to result from our innocent deception. You can imagine our surprise and relief when, a day or two later, the mink was returned just as mysteriously as it had disappeared. It seems that insurance-company detectives are so renowned for their efficiency in recovering stolen goods that the mere supposition of being insured already offers a certain amount of protection!

At least I learned a valuable lesson from this painful experience. It is always extremely disagreeable for the slightest accident or misfortune to affect a guest in one's home, and peace of mind is well worth the premium cost of a very comprehensive insurance policy.

INTRODUCTIONS

⟮ The manner in which a hostess introduces her guests to one another at the beginning of a party can set the tone for the entire evening. She should try to add to the simple exchange of names a few phrases that will make each person feel very important and seem well worthwhile knowing to the others, as well as a clue that will start them off on a mutually interesting topic of conversation. Some women are very gifted at this sort of thing, and they often possess in addition an amazing intuition for sensing which of their friends are apt to get along together particularly well. This is undoubtedly an inborn talent, but making skillful introductions is simply a technique that anybody can acquire.

The formalities have been very much simplified in recent years. The basic principle is always to present the less important person to the more important, the man to the woman, the younger generation to the older, and members of the family to strangers, unless there is a notable difference in age or standing. In actual practice, the most frequent phrases are:

"Mrs. Jones, may I present Mr. Smith?"
"Mrs. Jones, I don't believe you have met Mr. Smith."
"Mrs. Jones, this is Mr. Smith."

All of these are correct. But the most common form of introduction today is simply a casual, "Bill Jones—John Smith," without any indication as to who is being presented to whom.

Men are often introduced by their first names as well as their family names, but women should be introduced to strangers as Mrs. or Miss— except when a husband is introducing his wife, in which case he says, "May I introduce my wife," or "I'd like you to meet my wife," but never "Mrs.——" or even her name. But then, speaking to his wife, he may say, "Nora, this is Bob Smith." It is considered rather vulgar to introduce or to refer to one's own husband or wife to a social acquaintance as "Mr." or "Mrs."

In more complicated cases, where there is a question of protocol involved, or a long foreign title that is hard for you to handle, or a celebrity who has a married name as well as a professional one, you can, in the first case, consult beforehand an authoritative etiquette book or an experienced person; and when you find yourself faced with the other kinds of situations, there is no reason to feel shy about asking the person in question to tell you exactly how he wishes to be introduced.

Finally, there is the awkward moment when your mind suddenly goes blank and you cannot for the life of you remember the name of the person you wish to present. This has happened to everybody at one time or another, most often toward the end of a large cocktail party or a long evening, when your feet ache, your head spins, and you cannot even hear yourself think. Unless your guest is quite dull-witted, he will immediately recognize your predicament by your blush of embarrassment and your incoherent mumbling, and he will probably come to your rescue by pronouncing his name himself. If he doesn't, you should rush right on into the identifying phrase I so heartily recommend, for example:

"Mr. Smith, I'd like you to meet Mr.——(swallow or cough and then very clearly), who has just returned from the most fascinating trip to India. How long did you stay there in all?" You can then leave them in rapt conversation, which Mr. Smith can always interrupt to say, "By the way, I didn't quite catch your name . . ."

INVITATIONS

◖ It may seem unnecessary to suggest that an invitation should obligatorily include specific information as to the date, time, and place of the reception in question, but it is surprising how often one of these essential details is omitted. I once received an invitation to the vernissage of an art exhibit, at the bottom of which was written, "Do try to come!" followed by a perfectly illegible signature, so that I did not even know *who* had invited me!

There are numerous ways of issuing invitations to a party, but all of them should include the answers to the questions, "Who?" "Where?" "When?" "What?" . . . and sometimes "Why?"

Only an invitation for a formal event such as a wedding or a ball must be engraved. On other occasions, the invitation may be made in person, over the telephone, in the form of a letter or a note or a few lines written by hand on a visiting card or on a folded "informal." It is always advisable to confirm a verbal invitation with a written one, except for the most casual occasions and for parties that are inspired at the very last minute when there is not enough time for mail to be delivered several days in advance. It is always considerate to include as much additional information as possible, so that your guests will know what they are expected to wear ("black tie"—meaning dinner jackets and dressy gowns; "informal"—meaning business suits and cocktail dresses; "white tie"—meaning tails and long evening gowns), and what they are expected to bring ("swimming and tennis," or "to celebrate Mary Smith's birthday").

The more formal the occasion and the more elaborate the preparations, the more in advance the invitations should be sent. For example, you can arrange an informal dinner party with a few very close friends by a telephone call the day before, but you should send out engraved invitations to a wedding or a ball at least three or four weeks ahead of time. Whenever you invite somebody at the very last minute to substitute for an ailing guest, you should make a point of reinviting the same person to another dinner, this time far in advance.

Informal invitations may consist of a few handwritten lines on a calling card, or a short friendly note. But formal invitations should be composed according to conventional formulas, and if in doubt you should consult one of the authoritative etiquette books, which devote entire chapters to the subject. There is, however, one basic principle that holds true for all written invitations: the paper or card should be of good quality, plain and unadorned; the printing should be black, the ink of handwritten invitations blue or black, and all novelty decorations and gimmicks should be avoided—except in the case of children's parties.

There are in addition a number of nuances concerning invitations that are perhaps more a question of snobbishness than of etiquette. It is more chic to write out the date without abbreviations as, for example, "Friday, January seventeenth" than "Friday, January 17th" and never to include the year, just as it is more fashionable to write "Eight o'clock" than "8 P.M."

It is not considered elegant in France to write "RSVP" in the lower left-hand corner of an invitation, but in America and England this has become a well-established custom. The letters stand for, as you know, *Répondez s'il vous plaît*—in other words, "Please reply." But how many people do? Less and less, it seems, especially when it concerns a large reception or cocktail party when it is, nevertheless, vital for the hostess to know approximately how many guests she must be prepared to receive. The situation has reached the point where no response to a cocktail-party invitation is most often equivalent to an acceptance, for practically the only people who send a reply are those who regret being unable to attend. As a matter of fact, it is becoming increasingly customary in America to write in the lower left-hand corner of an invitation to a very large reception a telephone number and the words, "Regrets Only," so that the hostess will not be bothered by fifty or a hundred phone calls just when she is exceptionally occupied preparing for the party.

The RSVP formula should not really be necessary at all in a civilized society, because every invitation merits a prompt reply. We have been obliged to add RSVP simply because so many otherwise well-bred people have adopted the inconsiderate habit of not answering formal invitations. And now that even this method has begun to lose its effectiveness, some hostesses prefer to telegraph their invitations. It seems that a telegram, while infinitely less elegant than a written invitation and less personal than a telephone call, comports a sense of urgency that brings a high percentage of immediate replies.

Personally, I prefer the telephoned invitation, followed by a written reminder, for all but the most formal social events. I have found that most people have the courage to accept or refuse right away, even if it means they run the risk of having to turn down a more tempting invitation for the same evening a few days later.

ET SET

❨ A person who has never had the occasion to frequent very elegant society always tends to imagine that life in these glamorous circles is a round of extraordinary pleasures and feasts. The newspapers describe the activities of the Jet Set with adjectives worthy of the splendors of Byzantium. But the truth is that the difference between their parties and yours lies more in the quality of the guests than in the quality of the cuisine. It is naturally far more amusing to circulate among a group of famous faces and to chat with celebrities than it is to spend an evening with your country cousin, or Uncle John's office manager.

Even when your own social set is much less brilliant, you should always try to attract interesting people to your home. If they are certain of spending an entertaining evening and of meeting other stimulating persons, they will be delighted to continue to accept your invitations. In order to build up an interesting group of friends, do not hesitate to invite foreign visitors to your parties, and always prefer a poet, even if he is very badly dressed, to an important tradesman who can talk about nothing but balance sheets.

If you ever have the occasion to entertain an authentic member of the Jet Set and if all of your personal friends, as charming as they are and as fond as you may be of them, would seem rather dull and provincial by comparison, it would be highly preferable to abandon any thought of a large dinner party. Instead, plan a very simple, almost frugal, luncheon for just the two of you, in which every detail is absolutely perfect: A grilled mutton chop with a salad, or a delicious omelette, if you can procure really fresh eggs from the country (even better if they are from your own hen!). The simplest homemade menu will surely give greater pleasure to a rather spoiled person who is bored to death with caviar, than will the most expensive specialties ordered from a caterer.

At the same time, devote a special effort to the decoration of the luncheon table, which should be sumptuous without appearing to be so. You should therefore take out your most beautiful silverware and your finest plates—but *not* your lace tablecloth. If you buy flowers for the table, do not arrange them in elaborate garlands, but simply place a few lovely blossoms in a crystal goblet or a small silver bowl. It is much better to invest in the services of an impeccable waitress (rather than a waiter, who would seem too gala), instead of squandering your money on champagne and foie gras.

Even if you are desperately anxious to make a good impression with your little luncheon, you should behave as though you were used to receiving important people every day. Never forget that an atmosphere of relaxation is the most elegant thing that one can offer to a guest.

JOB

❡ It is very difficult to entertain with elegance if you are a career woman who has a job but no household help. The most practical solution in this case is to entertain only on Saturday or Sunday evening. But if you simply must invite your friends to dinner during the working week, you will have to establish a very careful plan.

On the morning of the day before, or even earlier, you should order all of the ingredients of the meal, which should only include a single hot dish. If you cannot have everything delivered, it is indispensable to make out a detailed written shopping list before you set out for the supermarket, including all of the food, drinks, and equipment for the entire evening, starting with cocktails and ending with the afterdinner refreshments.

On the evening preceding the party, or early in the morning (depending on whether you prefer to go to bed later or to wake up earlier than usual), you should undertake a thorough housecleaning and set the table. Everything on the table can be covered afterward with a cloth in order to keep it free from dust until the end of the day.

The most efficient procedure is to review in your mind the entire scenario of the party hour by hour, and to imagine each different circumstance. For example: "They arrive. Where do I put the wraps? In the guest closet? On my bed? In my own clothes closet? If so, I'll have to push my own things out of the way. I serve cocktails. Let's see— Harry only likes Martinis—I must check to see that there is plenty of gin, vermouth, and lemon peel. Helen only likes Whisky Sours and Harriet a Bloody Mary. Do I have enough bourbon, lemon, and ice? I must fill the sugar bowl at once and add to the shopping list a can of tomato juice and a bottle of vodka, because I'm all out. Now let's see. They ought to have something to nibble on. I'd better order a jar of macadamia nuts and some cocktail snacks." (Incidentally, it is best to buy nuts and cocktail crackers in small quantities, because they are tasty only when they are very fresh.) Thus you continue to visualize the entire evening—without forgetting the flowers and cigarettes.

If you have decided to serve hors d'oeuvres in the living room with the cocktails rather than a first course at table (which is a very practical system), all you have to do is to prepare them in advance and place them in the refrigerator on a covered plate. This is, in my opinion, the best plan where there is no waiter or waitress, because it is much easier for a hostess to disappear for a few minutes in the kitchen in order to put the final touches on a hot cooked dish, than it is for her to have to leave the table during the course of the meal.

This hot main dish should be either a baked casserole type, which only needs to be removed from the casserole to a serving dish (and can often be brought right to the table in the dish in which it was cooked), or a preparation that can be cooked in advance and then reheated and gratinéed in the oven at the last minute. One of the simplest casserole recipes I know, and one of the most delicious, is *veau provençal*, which can be prepared the night before:

Have your butcher cut an excellent quality of veal (preferably from the chest portions) into medium-sized chunks, half the size of your hand. In a large casserole, brown one large chopped onion or three small ones in olive oil that has been generously seasoned with bay leaves, cloves, thyme, rosemary, and a tiny pinch of cayenne pepper. Roll the pieces of veal in flour, salt them, and brown them in the oil over a hot fire. When they are golden in color, pour in half a bottle of dry white wine and half a can of tomato paste; mix well, cover, and lower the heat. It should simmer for one hour. You can thus complete the cooking the next day just before the dish is to be served. In case the sauce should become too reduced, you should keep a little beef bouillon on hand in order to add it as necessary. Accompany the casserole dish with boiled potatoes or rice, both of which can also be reheated at the last minute. (And if you have any of this dish left over, the next day you can reheat it again and serve it as a sauce over freshly cooked noodles. It may not be attractive to look at, but it is delicious to eat!) You may also add to the casserole pitted green olives (in this case, reduce the salt) and mushrooms. Chicken or rabbit can be prepared in exactly the same way.

If you own a grill, particularly of the infrared type, you can serve steaks or chops as a main dish and grill them right in front of your guests.

Do not forget to leave the necessary time in your schedule on the day of the party for you to get dressed, made up, and to do your hair. (The best plan is to make an appointment with the hairdresser during your lunch hour.) Your technical preparations for the dinner should therefore be completed at least forty-five minutes or an hour before your guests are to arrive. If you have taken the trouble to organize everything three days in advance, on the evening of the party you will be a relaxed and smiling hostess—which is one of the principal ingredients of a successful evening.

(See Cocktail Parties, Dinners, Menus, One Room, etc.)

JOURNALISM

❬ Newspaper publicity is essential to the success of parties whose purpose, avowed or unavowed, is to launch a new product or a new personality or to win support for some political, charitable, or commercial cause. In these cases, it is indispensable to hire a clever professional press agent in order to ensure the maximum possible newspaper and magazine coverage. But the situation is not at all the same when it concerns the private parties a hostess gives for personal friends. As a matter of fact, publicity on the society pages has been so abused in recent years that the most elegant hostesses no longer care to reveal the names of their private dinner party guests to the press, even to a reporter from the New York *Times*.

However, certain social events aside from official and diplomatic affairs are legitimately newsworthy, such as weddings, coming-out parties, and any very large reception or gala ball. In these cases, the hostess (or the social secretary she has engaged to handle the invitations for the reception) should contact the society editors of the local papers by phone or written note ahead of time, and she may even invite a society reporter to attend the event, accompanied by a photographer if it is to be a very grand affair.

Nowadays most of the leading hotels, restaurants, and nightclubs have on their staffs professional press agents who are always on the alert to spot a well-known face in the room or a newsworthy name on the reservation list. And so, unless you specifically request an absence of publicity when you entertain in one of these public places, you may find the photograph of your dinner table or a list of your guests in the columns of the society pages the next day. (And you will probably receive complaints not from the guests whose names appeared, but from those whose names were omitted!)

The publicists of resort hotels and airlines make a practice of sending a news release and photograph whenever possible to the hometown papers of their clients. The success of these methods is certainly due to the fact that more people seem to seek newspaper publicity than to avoid it. But since we are talking about elegant entertaining, I am obliged to say that the elegant thing to do is to cooperate fully with the press when the occasion really warrants, and to remain very reserved about your private social life.

You should be particularly discreet whenever you entertain a celebrity, unless your guest is a stage or screen star, an author, a designer, etc., whose career owes much to publicity and who will welcome any form of it as long as his name is spelled correctly. But many famous figures from the worlds of diplomacy, industry, and government prefer their private lives to remain private, and you might seriously offend them by giving to the local newspaper a detailed account of your dinner party in their honor. In other words, to seek publicity when it is justifiable for professional reasons is perfectly acceptable, but seeking publicity merely in order to build up one's personal ego is not and never has been chic.

I realize that a number of ambitious women have hired expensive specialized press agents, and assiduously paid court to society editors and columnists, in an attempt to achieve fame as figures of society. They might be compared to the women who campaign for a place on the best-dressed list. If they are willing to work at the job twenty-four hours a day, if they have had the foresight to marry a wealthy and co-operative husband, and if they spend a great deal of time, money, and effort, they may eventually experience the thrill of seeing themselves identified in a newspaper column as a society Hostess with a capital H. I have known a number of women who have competed in this mink-clad rat-race, and I must admit that they seem to have gained a certain amount of satisfaction from it, as well as a fleeting but brilliant moment of celebrity. And so I do not for a minute condemn this harmless sport. It is, of course, one of the favorites of the nouveaux riches, but it has also brightened the lives of countless millions of tabloid newspaper readers. I must point out, however, that it is not a very elegant game. Truly elegant entertaining is devoid of ulterior motives—or, to be per-fectly accurate, when there is an ulterior motive, it should be to the profit of one's guests and not to the profit of the hostess.

If you count among your friends newspaper editors, reporters, and photographers, you should not of course be expected to strike them from your guest lists simply because of their professions. On the con-trary, the newspaper world is populated by some of the most brilliant, witty, and intelligent people alive. However, when you invite a famous guest of honor to an unofficial dinner party, I would consider it risky to invite at the same time a member of the press, unless the distin-guished guest has no objection.

While it is good politics to remain on excellent terms with the press and to extend to its reporters and photographers your full cooperation, you should beware of overdoing it. I have attended some supposedly private balls where the photographers and reporters must have out-numbered the guests, and the effect on the atmosphere and elegance of the evening was disastrous. The socially ambitious hostess does not always realize that an excess of publicity will close as many doors as it will open—and the ones that close are often those through which she most passionately aspires to pass.

Finally, remember that publicity alone has never sufficed to sell a product or to create a reputation. The most highly publicized hostesses of recent years, such as Cobina Wright, the Duchess of Windsor, and the Princesse d'Arenberg, owe their reputations not so much to the worldwide publicity they receive, but to the fact that they give spec-tacularly good parties.

KETTLES

◖ A humming kettle is symbolic of hospitality. My own, a lovely red English kettle I bought in Gibraltar, whistles rather than hums, and every morning when it signals that the water is ready for my tea, I am cheered by its familiar music. If I lost my kettle, I would feel as though I had lost a dear old friend. And I suppose that if ever the house burned down, I would attempt to escape the flames with my dog in one arm and my red kettle on the other.

Nevertheless, we must not take too literally the pleasant image of a permanently steaming teakettle, because the fact is that you can make a really good pot of tea or coffee only if you use water that has just barely come to the boil for the first time. And nothing is more horrible than warmed-over tea or coffee.

There are two schools of thought concerning the unpalatable, chemically treated, highly calcareous water of most modern cities. One recommends boiling it in an aluminum kettle, in which a crust of mineral deposits will gradually form at the bottom; and the other advises using an enameled receptacle in which the same deposits will float about in a state of suspension (and eventually end up in your cup of tea). The best course of all would be to use only pure bottled water for coffee and tea, but since a bottle of water is as costly as a bottle of wine in certain regions, this is not always a very practical solution. Still, for the true connoisseur of these beverages, no expense or trouble is too great. When the Duff Coopers reigned over the British Embassy in Paris, it was rumored that the secret of the delicious tea they served was that they had it made from authentic London tap water, which was sent over by the barrel every week along with the diplomatic dispatches!

KIN

⟨ A woman acts as hostess to her family every time she offers them a meal, which may be twice or even three times a day. It would obviously be unreasonable to expect her to serve nothing but party menus, or for her husband and children to practice their "party manners" and to wear their party clothes (although the British tradition of changing for dinner every evening has much to recommend it). She should, however, make an effort to prepare varied, simple, wholesome meals and to present them in an appetizing way. It is possible to set a most attractive table with a plastic tablecloth, ordinary dishes, and paper napkins, if everything is shining clean, if the room is tidy, and if she has taken the trouble to respect a definite color scheme.

Manners should not be completely neglected either, and your own good example is worth a thousand etiquette books. The best way for children to learn correct table manners is to practice them during family meals until they have become so automatic that there isn't the slightest risk of forgetting them during the excitement of a party dinner at someone else's home. Family meals are also the ideal occasion for experimenting with new recipes, because it is always dangerous to try a new dish for the first time when you have invited guests.

During the course of the year, there are always a number of occasions when you must entertain more distant relatives at a larger family dinner. I really should have said "may" instead of "must," because the first rule for ensuring the success of a family dinner is to think of it as a pleasure rather than as a tiresome obligation.

It is a mistake to believe that a family dinner should be planned and prepared any less carefully than a dinner party for friends. The principal difference is in the menu. For members of your family, whose gastronomic tastes and prejudices are well known to you, it is a very simple matter to build your meal around the dishes they particularly enjoy. As a matter of fact, the gastronomic interest of the meal is even more important than at a normal dinner party, because your guests all know each other so well that the only possible note of novelty and surprise must be provided by the food.

You can organize the service in a simple and informal manner, and unless all of the guests are very elderly, you can usually get by very well without any professional help. Family-style service generally means that the serving dishes are passed around the table by the guests. If the main dish is to be a roast (which is often the most practical choice), the host may carve it from his place at the head of the table and pass each filled plate on to the person for whom it is intended. He probably knows that Aunt Martha only likes white meat and little Johnny the drumstick, and if he doesn't, nobody on this occasion will have the slightest reticence about reminding him.

Likewise, the hostess need not feel shy about asking one of the children to help pass the platters and clear the table.

As always, it is simpler and more elegant to serve the coffee and liqueurs from a tray in the living room rather than at table. And this is one of the rare occasions when it is perfectly permissible to stage a showing of home movies after dinner. You will probably find that the very oldest films are even more amusing to this particular audience than those you took during your recent trip to Europe.

If, however, the adult members of the family have family business matters to discuss, it is best to send the children into another room—perhaps your son's or daughter's bedroom, or even the dining room, if you do not have a playroom. If you have thought of equipping it with a record player, television set, and a supply of games, this should keep them occupied and entertained until it is time to go home.

In any case, the party should not be permitted to drag on too long, especially when there are young children or elderly grandparents present.

Aside from the various ceremonies that are essentially family events, such as weddings, christenings, engagements, and funerals, there are also a number of red-letter days during the year that call for family celebrations, such as Easter, Thanksgiving, Christmas and New Year's Day, as well as birthdays and anniversaries. Most families gradually develop their own traditional ways of celebrating these occasions, and continuing the traditions is half of the fun. It is therefore not a very good idea, if you are a new member of the family, to attempt to introduce a revolutionary innovation to the menu or the program. You should instead concentrate your efforts on the refinement of your preparation of the customary things, and limit your original touches to a few minor details.

Family holiday celebrations usually follow a joyous cycle. At first, the Christmas trees and Easter egg hunts are organized for the pleasure of the youngest children; as the children grow into sophisticated teen-agers, the same traditions are continued in honor of the grandparents, who in the meantime have become increasingly sentimental. Soon there is a new generation of young children to be initiated to the wondrous rites, and finally perhaps you and your husband will be the grandparents whom all the other members of the family attempt to please. At this stage, I would be very surprised if the traditions that you may have considered long ago to be foolish or tiresome do not seem to you now to be a symbol of family strength and solidarity.

Family parties are not the only occasions for receiving relatives as guests. When many members of a family inhabit the same town, you are not, of course, expected to invite them to every dinner party you give. But whenever you entertain at a large cocktail party, ball, or reception, it is courteous to include all of the available members of your family in your guest list, even very elderly parents.

KISSING

❲ One of the details of American social behavior that rather surprised me during my last trip to the United States was the increased practice of kissing on the cheek as a friendly greeting. In Europe, a woman kisses her best friend and her relatives on both cheeks, while Ameri-cans apparently feel that one cheek is enough. But to make up for it, they seem to kiss twice as much. I have seen American women kissing on the sidewalk in front of restaurants, and I have seen them cause traffic jams in the front halls of elegant homes after a dinner party, as they pecked one cheek after another. And so perhaps it is time for a few words of advice.

Friendly kisses, just like the less platonic kind, should be reserved for the intimacy of one's own home or family and to very limited com-pany. For example, I would kiss my best friends when they arrive at my home for a dinner with just the four of us, and again as they leave at the end of the evening. But if they were to return the next night for a large party or a cocktail affair where there were many guests, we would merely shake hands. You might say that kissing is a sign of favoritism, and it is discourteous toward those with whom you are less intimate to flaunt this mark of privilege in their presence. I would, however, kiss my parents, aunts and uncles, brothers and sisters, etc. (if I were fortunate enough to have such) on both cheeks every time we met and parted no matter who was present, unless we were in a public place.

Once you have established a kissing relationship with a close friend, it continues for the rest of your life, like the familiar form of address "tu" in France and Italy and "du" in Germany, which starts among school comrades and would be resumed by former classmates half a century later even though they had completely lost contact with each other during the intervening years. Likewise, friendly greeting kisses are generally exchanged mainly between members of the same generation, with the exception, of course, of relatives. A younger person should always permit an older one to make the first gesture whenever there is any notable disparity of age, and a man should let a woman be the first to honor him with this gesture of platonic affection.

With these restrictions, and a final recommendation for discretion, I am all in favor of our Latin ways of exteriorizing our sentiments, and I am delighted if they are gaining ground in the American way of life. Who knows, perhaps Americans will one day reach the point where, as in France, fathers and sons will embrace unashamedly, and families will stage extravagantly emotional scenes in railroad stations.

Hand kissing, on the other hand, always seems to us somewhat affected when it is practiced by an American. But since there appears to be a periodic vogue for this courtly custom in certain arty circles of New York and Hollywood, it might not be amiss to describe its proper usage. In the first place, the kiss itself should be merely a rather vague gesture with no actual contact and above all no sound effects! A man may kiss the hand of a married woman, but never that of an unmarried girl, and never on the street or in a public place. He never kisses a gloved hand. A gentleman of the old school would kiss the hand of his dinner-party hostess at the end of a party, but he would not circle around the salon to kiss the hands of all the other women present, even if they were much prettier.

KITCHENS

(American women's kitchens, like their bathrooms, are the most beautiful and practical ever created, and they are the envy of all the other women in the world. Having achieved perfection in these fields, it would be a pity if you were now to spoil everything, due to your famous American penchant for change and novelty. And so my only suggestion as far as kitchens are concerned is to beware of overdecorating them. It is a charming idea to furnish a kitchen with the same care and taste that you apply to the rest of your home, but the decor of a kitchen should never interfere with its working functions, and it should never be overly frilly or fussy.

As a general rule, when you are lucky enough to have a professional kitchen staff or a full-time maid, the best kind of a kitchen is the streamlined modern type, lined with fitted elements all in Formica and stainless steel, with little visible clutter, and with your decorative effects confined to a tasteful choice of colors. One of the prettiest professional-type kitchens I have seen was based on the simplest possible color scheme: white and pale gray, underlined with black, with a mass of red geraniums in the window boxes. The effect was cool and spacious, workmanlike but elegant.

In a home without servants, on the other hand, where it is most practical to serve family meals in the kitchen, the room should be decorated in a much more warm and comfortable style, with a particularly attractive dining corner slightly separated from the working part of the kitchen. The old-fashioned rustic style is perhaps the most in vogue at the moment, but there are countless possibilities to consider. You might, for example, build your decorative scheme around Colonial pinewood cabinets, painted French Provincial elements, blue and white Delft-patterned tiles, or a lovely patterned washable wallpaper. You might include a number of luxurious details, such as a built-in bar and bookshelves with a concealed television screen, extremely pretty lighting fixtures, perhaps a brass chandelier hanging rather low over the dinette table, or—my dream—an open fireplace. You can create charming effects with plants and flowers and pictures on the wall. Women's magazines are filled with kitchen illustrations, and they are a mine of bright ideas.

It is a pleasure to dine in an attractive kitchen, and there is no reason why you should not invite good friends to have lunch or dinner with you there. As a matter of fact, on many occasions when there are only three or four of you, it would perhaps be more cheerful as well as more practical to serve your meal in the kitchen rather than the dining room, where the atmosphere is naturally more staid and formal.

However, when there are to be more than four at the table, when the preparation of the meal is apt to cause considerable disorder or strong cooking odors, when you are not on very intimate terms with your guests, or when you have the slightest suspicion that they are not the eating-in-the-kitchen type, it would be preferable to serve your meal in the dining room in the conventional way.

*L*ATECOMERS

❲ Customs vary so widely from one country to another and even from one city to another, that it is difficult to set down hard and fast rules concerning punctuality. In the Scandinavian countries, punctuality is a point of honor, and before an elegant dinner party it is not unusual to see all of the guests gathered in front of the host's door, prepared to ring the bell just as the clock strikes the exact hour for which they were invited! In Anglo-Saxon countries, on the other hand, guests are generally expected to arrive fifteen minutes or half an hour late to a dinner party, and ten or fifteen minutes late to a luncheon. A few fashionable snobs take pride in practically doubling these delays, so that the modern hostess only begins to worry when a guest is at least three-quarters of an hour late.

If the delay stretches to one hour, she should, in my opinion, telephone the nonarrivals and if there is no answer she can quite well start to dine without them. When the latecomers finally arrive (and I hope they are armed with a convincing alibi or I would never invite them again to my house), they still have the right to a full meal, even if the dessert is on the table. The previous courses should have been kept warm for them and they should be served as rapidly as possible until they have caught up with the other diners.

Because tardiness is habitual in some cases, and is considered fashionable in others, a hostess no longer dares to include in the menu of a large dinner party dishes that cannot wait a half an hour or even an hour without becoming spoiled; and I pity the popular people who are invited out to dinner every single evening and never get a taste of a soufflé, which is one of the most delicious foods of all!

While it is true that a few quiet minutes between the hour of the invitation and the arrival of the first guest are often a welcome respite to a hostess, since this gives her an opportunity to make a final checkup of her party preparations, an exaggerated delay can ruin her nerves and perhaps the dinner, too.

The only way I know of encouraging one's guests to arrive before the roast is overdone is to telephone them each a few days beforehand to say, "Do try to come at seven-thirty, dinner is at eight"—or whatever the hours may be. They are thus forewarned that they will have time for just one hasty Martini if they arrive at seven fifty-five. At least this method brings better results and is also more courteous than writing or saying "eight o'clock *sharp*." Besides, no matter how precise the latter formula may seem to the hostess, her guests are bound to interpret it in an amazing variety of ways.

Most hostesses have learned to be indulgent with latercomers, especially since parking problems and traffic congestion, unreliable baby-sitters and late commuters' trains, not to mention a hundred other complications of modern life, all conspire against punctuality. Nevertheless, there are two occasions when lateness is inexcusable: At a formal or official dinner for an eminent guest of honor, when protocol requires that all of the guests be present before he makes his entrance; and at the theater, the opera, or a concert, where latecomers not only distract the performers, but also disturb the rest of the audience, which has taken the trouble to arrive on time in order to enjoy the performance in its entirety.

LIGHTING

❲ The most frequent error where lighting is concerned is to provide too little of it rather than too much. It is true that candlelight is elegant, flattering, and romantic, but only when there is a sufficient amount of candlepower in operation. The flickering flames from one or two little candlesticks on a long dining table will make the women present look ghoulish rather than seductive. Moreover, color plays a very important role in taste, and if you serve a meal in light so dim that the color of each food cannot be clearly identified, your most delicious recipes will immediately lose much of their flavor. The modern mania for dim lighting in a dining room can even lead to more serious inconveniences, if you require your guests to cope with the tiny bones of a whole trout or game bird when they cannot even clearly distinguish the tip of their forks. It is therefore unwise to attempt to light a dinner party entirely by candlelight unless you can provide a sufficiently generous quantity of candelabra.

The best system in many dining rooms is to combine the electric lighting from a pair or two of wall fixtures with candlesticks on the table. If your dining room is normally lit by a bright suspended lighting fixture above the table, you might replace the bulbs with less brilliant ones on the evening of a dinner party in order to obtain a soft general lighting in addition to the light shed by the candles on the table. Whatever you do, do not permit yourself to be influenced by the underlit interiors of certain restaurants and nightclubs, and even less to imagine that it is elegant to dine in the dark. On the contrary, it is important for every detail of a gastronomic meal and a tastefully decorated table to be clearly visible, and the colors undistorted.

The modern trend in decoration is to light a living room entirely by table and floor lamps. The most important elementary principle is that the actual source of light (in this case the electric light bulbs) should be invisible, which means that every lamp must be provided with either an inner reflector globe or a well-made, opaque lampshade. Fluorescent lighting of any kind is horribly unflattering, while indirect lighting concealed in a trough around the ceiling or in a pair of plaster urns is rather passé (and in any case suitable only for modern interiors).

On the other hand, it is extremely chic to highlight a vitrine of artistic objects, a bookcase of fine bindings, a piece of sculpture, or a painting. Many different lighting techniques have been perfected in recent years, from concealed spot lighting to the classic fixtures attached to picture frames (the latter, incidentally, should be used only for oil paintings, never for a picture under glass). It is well worthwhile devoting a great deal of care to the lighting of your living room in order to achieve the most pleasing effect. Once you have discovered the ideal lighting scheme, all you have to do is to preserve it—which means that you must dust the light bulbs and lampshades regularly and replace the bulbs when their light begins to dim and not only when they blow out.

The most elegant lighting arrangement for an outdoor patio or garden consists of concealed spotlights in the trees and shrubbery, combined with hurricane lamps on the patio tables. Installing an excellent outdoor lighting system is a rather delicate project and a costly one. But it is well worth the expense of engaging the most competent specialist you can find. For a hostess, a beautifully lit garden or patio is an invaluable asset that can immensely increase the entertaining capacity of her home.

(See Candles, Dining Rooms)

LIQUEURS AND BRANDY

⟨[While I am not as convinced as are many of my compatriots of the miraculous digestive properties of these highly concentrated alcoholic brews, it is certainly very elegant to serve your dinner guests a brandy or liqueur from a tray in the living room after the coffee has been passed. It is customary to offer the choice of an excellent brandy (Cognac or Armagnac) and one or two bottles keyed to feminine taste, such as a fruit liqueur (framboise, Kirsch, cherry heering, Grand Marnier, etc.) or perhaps a herbal type (Chartreuse, Benedictine, etc.—as Helen Hokinson's irresistible clubwoman says, "the kind those nice monks make"), or a crème de menthe.

Since none of these liquors leave a deposit at the bottom of the bottle, it is an affectation to serve them from a decanter. Brandy should be drunk from a balloon glass or "snifter," but there is no advantage in the exaggerated giant size. Other afterdinner alcohols may be served in liqueur glasses. A small tulip shape, about one-third filled, captures and concentrates more of the delicious perfume than do the tiny straight types that are filled to the brim.

The brandy snifter is usually warmed by turning it in the hand in order to release the full aroma of its contents. Liqueurs may be savored in small sips. If you wish to imitate the rather complicated procedure of connoisseurs in the case of fine fruit liqueurs, you can first chill the liqueur glass by swirling an ice cube around in it, then empty the glass and pour in a small quantity (about one-third full) of liqueur—a true raspberry (framboise) is one of the most delicious. Then you take a small sip, which you retain for a moment in the cup of your tongue, as you slowly exhale through the mouth to evaporate the alcohol. When you then swallow the remains, the fruit flavor should be very pronounced and perfectly exquisite. Unfortunately, however, it requires tons of fresh ripe fruit or berries to make a natural fruit liqueur, and most of the modern products have been fortified (if not completely flavored) by synthetic ingredients. If you are ever traveling abroad through the Black Forest region and come across an authentic bottle of framboise (you will recognize it by its astronomical price), taste it at least once. It will be a memorable experience.

In any case, I would advise you to stick to the classic liqueurs distributed by well-established, reputable distillers, because there exist many fantasy concoctions that owe their taste and color to the chemist's tube rather than to any natural distilling process. Among the best-known fruit brandies, there are:

Kirsch (cherry flavored)
Mirabelle (yellow plum brandy)
Framboise (raspberry)
Abricot (apricot)
Poire Williams (pear)
Cherry Heering (a specialty from Denmark)
Crème de Cassis (black currant) and
Grand Marnier (a fine Cognac base with orange flavor)

A rather strong brandy of high alcoholic content is also distilled from apples. The Normandy version is called calvados, but in America it is more widely known as applejack.

Other liqueurs are made from grape brandy that is sweetened and flavored with aromatic herbs, such as Benedictine, Chartreuse (the green kind is more expensive and slightly higher in alcoholic content than the yellow), Drambuie (made in Scotland from whisky, honey, and herbs), kümmel (flavored with caraway), anisette (licorice-flavored), Cointreau (very sweet)—and many others, including a number of more or less recommendable trademarked blends.

In France there is a distinction between brandy that is distilled from grape wine and is called *eau-de-vie-de-vin*, and brandy that is distilled from the residue left in the wine presses after the wine has been poured off, which is called *marc*. Marc de Bourgogne is the most esteemed. It requires a very long aging period in order to attain its full flavor and body.

The finest *eaux-de-vie-de-vin* in the world are Cognac and Armagnac, the first of which is made in the Charente region of France, where, as an example of divine justice perhaps, the areas producing the poorest wines distill the finest brandy; and the second is made a little further south in the Gers department. The best brandy of all comes from the Grande Champagne region of Cognac, and then the Petite Champagne, which is the surrounding area. Armagnac is rich and less refined than Cognac, with a less lingering flavor. The best is made in the Bas-Armagnac district, and it matures somewhat faster than Cognac.

The standard of quality for Cognac is its age, that is, the number of years it has been allowed to ripen and mellow in wooden casks. The type of wood has an important bearing on its color and aroma, and for this reason old sherry casks are used. There is no longer any improvement once the brandy has been bottled. The label on a bottle of Cognac therefore indicates the age of the liquor at the time it was bottled:

* representing three years
** four years
*** five years, and
**** eight years.

VO—which stands for "very old," indicates that the brandy is ten years old;

VVO or VSO—means fifteen years; and

VSOP—"very superior old product," twenty years.

I have never personally seen a bottle of brandy bearing the letters VVSOP (Very Very Superior Old, etc.), which means that it is forty years old, and I suppose that I never *will* see a bottle labeled Extra Old, meaning seventy years of age! As a matter of fact, all very old Cognacs are necessarily blends rather than vintage products, because after a certain number of years, the contents of the barrel need to be infused periodically with younger brandy in order to maintain the balance and body. The term "Napoleon Brandy" is rather deceptive, for it has nothing at all to do with age, but is more of a trade name. The quality of brandy is not controlled in the same meticulous way as that of fine wines, and so you must often trust your own palate rather than the label.

Finally, remember that brandy and liqueurs can be used in cooking in various ways. The better the quality of the liquor, the better the final results will be. Fruit liqueurs can add a subtle gourmet note to cakes, puddings, crêpes, soufflés, and fruit cups, while some of the simplest main dishes, such as sautéed scallops, and sautéed sliced veal kidneys and mushrooms, will be transformed into spectacular company fare if you *flambez* them with a few tablespoons of brandy just before you bring them to the table.

(See Drinks, Wine)

LOCOMOTIVES

❪ A locomotive is the name given to super snobs who, as the term implies, tow in their wake all the other snobs. A really powerful locomotive can lead his followers to the most unlikely destinations! And in this regard, I must express my respect and admiration for the Parisian locomotive who was sufficiently self-assured and audacious as to persuade Princess Grace and Prince Rainier of Monaco to ride the subway, along with two thousand formally dressed international socialites, to the film première of "Cleopatra."

There are probably no more than two or three genuine locomotives in each capital city, and it is highly improbable that they can find time in their busy social schedules to exercise any profession other than public relations. Besides, locomotives seldom possess relations other than public ones, for they haven't the time to develop true friendships. They must get to know all of the talented newcomers in every field before they have become famous. One locomotive may specialize in launching debutantes (at the risk of having to buy a dozen wedding gifts at the end of a particularly brilliant season); another may let it be known that she possesses a fantastic flair for spotting fashion talent, and make it her mission to meet all of the young designers in order to be able to say afterward that it was she who discovered the latest fashion genius (and also in order to replenish her wardrobe with free dresses from the poor struggling designer, who is thrilled to have been singled out for this honor by such a celebrated and influential person).

For every authentic locomotive, how many imitations there are! Most often, they are obscure publicity agents who hope to persuade some naïve newcomer that, thanks to their sponsorship, he will be introduced to the highest inner circles of the particular world to which he aspires. Nothing is easier than to persuade these imitation locomotives to come to your dinners and cocktail parties, even if you aren't the least bit famous, because, after all, they have to eat regularly too. So there is no reason to take undue pride in their presence at your receptions. The success of a true social snob is measured not by the number of parties he attends but by the number of places where he no longer feels obliged to make an appearance.

LUNCHEONS

⟨[With the exception of business luncheons and romantic rendezvous, which invariably take place in restaurants, the luncheon party has become a strictly feminine affair. Because most modern women's daily program is generally very busy even when they do not have to struggle with a professional career, luncheon parties are no longer the all-afternoon receptions that they used to be. In fact, it seems to me that the essential requirements of a successful luncheon party today are (1.) to be brief; and (2.) to be nonfattening.

Neither the menu nor the occasion lends itself very well to buffet-style service, except in the case of a very large official reception or a wedding lunch, and I would therefore recommend inviting only one or two close friends whom you can quite well serve yourself at table, or else no more than six or eight guests to be served by a professional waitress.

Even when you only invite a single friend, it is cozy to serve a cocktail before lunch, and this may just as well be a glass of tomato juice or sherry as a more potent mixture. Accompanying canapés are not essential, but it would be a thoughtful gesture to prepare a bowl of salted almonds or, in the Spanish style, green olives stuffed with anchovies, for nibbling by your fortunate friends who can eat as much as they like without ever gaining an ounce.

Do not think that I am recommending a luncheon-party menu copied word for word from Gaylord Hauser! Nevertheless, it seems to me that since the vast majority of women are obliged to watch their waistlines, and since many of us manage to keep our figures under control only by cutting down on our midday meal, the considerate hostess should take this bitter fact of life into account. The true art of preparing a menu for a ladies' luncheon is to combine the greatest possible gastronomic pleasure with the least possible number of calories.

You can be much more original in selecting recipes for your women guests than you would dare to be if men were present. You can also place a greater accent on vegetables and salads (which my husband, at least, considers fit only for rabbits). It would not be very advisable to deprive your guests of dessert, for most women adore sweet confections. Besides, if the main part of the meal has been quite light, they will feel that they have earned the right to splurge on a rich dessert. Most of the mousses, soufflés, and chiffon pies, which are based on whipped egg whites rather than on cream (like the heavenly Bavarian creams, and all the cream pies) are surprisingly low in calories. But do not carry your campaign for the protection of your girl friends' figures to the point of using synthetic sweeteners and low-calorie ingredients in your cooking, for the results are never as tasty and you should always remember that your principal aim is to offer your guests a delicious meal in an agreeable atmosphere.

You should plan to serve the meal not more than a half an hour after the first guest has arrived. In other words, when you invite your guests for twelve-thirty, your luncheon should be on the table at one o'clock; if you wish to serve at twelve forty-five, you should invite your guests for twelve-fifteen. Promptness is more important than ever at lunchtime, as is the swiftness of the table service. Few people nowadays can devote an entire afternoon to luncheon, and it is very inconsiderate to keep your guests waiting until one-thirty or two because you have miscalculated the time it takes to bake your quiche or to roast the chicken.

Fortunately, many of the dishes that are most suitable for this kind of an occasion are also the quickest to prepare and the simplest to make the night before. The best luncheon menu, in my opinion, consists of a raw vegetable first course, a grilled meat with salad, and a dessert. I realize that this is terribly banal, but you can always add a touch of originality to the details and the presentation of the different dishes.

For the first course, four different hors d'oeuvres are ample. Serve them either in the compartments of an hors d'oeuvre tray, or artistically arranged on a large round plate. Some good combinations are:

— Finely grated carrots with lemon juice, sprinkled with chopped parsley

— Grated celery root in a rémoulade sauce

— Small peeled tomatoes cut in slices not quite all the way through, with a thin slice of hard-boiled egg inserted in each slit, all of it covered with homemade mayonnaise or French dressing and sprinkled with capers or chopped chives

— Thin slices of smoked salmon rolled around hearts of lettuce, or thin slices of smoked ham rolled around wedges of cantaloupe melon

— A cold *provençal ratatouille* (eggplant, onions, tomato, and peppers baked together in olive oil)

— Mushrooms or tiny onions *à la Grecque*

— Red beets with herring and tart apples in a salad, or simply sliced or cubed in a vinaigrette dressing

— Cucumbers in sour cream

— Stuffed celery

— Fresh radishes

— Tiny tomatoes stuffed with crab or shrimp salad

— Cold shrimp with Russian dressing and capers

Other simple and light first courses for a spring or summer luncheon would be

— Cold asparagus vinaigrette

— Chilled melon

— Cold whole artichokes (or, more elaborately, just the large artichoke bottoms filled with a rather highly seasoned shrimp or crab salad)

— Peeled and hollowed tomatoes filled with a salad of tuna fish, onion, egg and mayonnaise

— Avocado halves filled with a highly seasoned seafood salad

In the wintertime, many of these same dishes can be presented in a hot version. For example:

— Hot artichoke bottoms filled with mushroom purée in a Béchamel sauce and gratinéed

— The same artichoke bottoms as a base for a poached egg covered with Hollandaise sauce

— Hot creamed or curried seafood in small shell-shaped ramekins, prepared in advance and gratinéed at the last minute.

The more substantial the first dish has been, the lighter should be the main course. All year round, I cannot think of anything better than small grilled steaks or chops, served in their natural state or with a maître d'hôtel butter (creamed butter, lemon juice and chopped parsley, chilled and cut into butter pats to be placed on the hot meat), garnished with watercress or parsley. Along with it, a simple mixed green salad with an olive oil-lemon juice dressing.

An omelette would be a perfect main dish for a light luncheon for two or three women, but it should be dressed up with a rather gourmet filling, such as diced sautéed chicken livers or mushrooms, tiny green asparagus, or diced cooked shrimp, crab, or lobster. Another very simple egg dish is a *piperade*, which is the Basque equivalent of your Western omelette, made with diced onion, tomato, peppers, and ham, with the cooking completed in the oven and served open-faced rather than folded over.

Quiche Lorraine, or a quiche with crabmeat or lobster, is always highly appreciated, but there is an enormous difference between a perfect quiche and an ordinary one, and the first kind requires a considerable amount of cooking skill as well as an excellent recipe.

For a Lenten or Friday luncheon, or if you live in a region where fresh fish is available, a delicious light main dish can be made from filets of flounder or sole placed in a buttered baking dish, sprinkled with a generous quantity of peeled and seeded white grapes, dotted with butter, seasoned with salt and pepper, and barely covered with a mixture of one-third water to two-thirds dry white wine, in which it should poach gently for twenty minutes in the oven.

If men were present, you would serve at this point a cheese course. Otherwise, you can proceed immediately to the dessert. After a fairly substantial meal a fresh fruit cup, fresh berries in season, or a homemade fruit ice would all be excellent desserts, and all of them should be accompanied by your best homemade cookies—never the packaged kind. But if the luncheon has been light, a beautiful pie or tart would be even better.

Women usually love all kinds of hot breads, but it would be simpler to provide a rather wide selection of small soft rolls—white, whole wheat, raisin, poppy seed, etc.—as well as Ry-Krisp, thin or Melba toast, or a similar dry cracker.

The most elegant beverage would be a very light dry white, rosé, or red wine, depending on the menu. But if the summertime habit of drinking iced tea or coffee with a meal is firmly entrenched in your region, I suppose you could offer one of these instead. I would not, however, go so far as to permit them to drink a cola beverage during the meal, and even less hot coffee! The coffee should come as a finale and be served as usual from a tray in the living room, in demitasse cups.

You should neither expect nor urge your luncheon guests to stay longer than half an hour after the meal is over. Modern life is simply too busy for precious daytime hours to be spent in social chit-chat. If one of your guests seems to have settled down in the most comfortable chair for the rest of the day after the others have gone, you can quite properly excuse yourself by explaining that you have some urgent errands to attend to, or an appointment with the dentist.

As a matter of fact, if all luncheon-party hostesses respected the simple rules of lightness and brevity, perhaps this pleasant form of entertaining would not be menaced, as it is, with extinction.

(See Menus)

ARKETING

❲ Before you can even start to think of being a good cook, you must know how to be a good shopper, for the first step in cooking is to consider the ingredients that will be used.

In recent years there has been a widespread movement to adapt the old traditions of French cuisine to the requirements of contemporary life, and most of the old-fashioned methods have fortunately been modernized. Our grandmothers' recipes, which lightheartedly suggested a pound of butter and twenty eggs in order to make a simple dessert, and required you to boil five pounds of beef in order to obtain a cup of consommé, have at last been discarded in favor of more realistic cookbooks.

Nevertheless, the majority of women still plan their menus in advance, without taking into account the cost of the various ingredients. But an accomplished homemaker—and particularly one on a budget—plans her menus, even her party menus, in view of the current market conditions and prices. After she has seen for herself what is available and suitable in price, she can then build her meal around the most advantageous items.

Generally speaking, it is wise to resist all out-of-season fruits and vegetables. Such items as scallops, asparagus, fresh peas, and strawberries cost twice as much out of season as in. It is also more economical in the long run to buy for a party dinner a large roast, such as a leg of lamb or a whole ham, which you can finish eating the next day, rather than individual beefsteaks. In general, everything that provides an additional meal of leftovers will be a money saver, for it amortizes the cost of the company dinner. For example, a very large fish, which will finish its life mixed with cold rice and mayonnaise in a salad, is a better buy than individual soles or trout. And the dish that provides the most inexhaustible supply of appetizing leftovers of all is undoubtedly *pot au feu*. You can rehabilitate the remains of the party meal in the form of consommé, vegetables, a *purée parmentier* (the leftover meat chopped up with sautéed onions, heated between two layers of mashed potatoes and gratinéed), meatballs, cold meat salad with potatoes or rice, rissoles (the leftover meat chopped and seasoned and used as a filling for pastry triangles, which may be either baked in the oven or deep-fried)—the possibilities are almost endless!

Finally, no matter how limited one's budget may be, it is always preferable to select the best quality ingredients for a very simple dish rather than to try to prepare a pretentious recipe with second-class materials.

(See Economy)

MASQUERADE

❡ Masquerades and costume parties are among the most fabulous forms of entertaining, but they are also the most extravagant in time and money—your guests' as well as your own. This is certainly the reason for their sharp decline since the eighteenth century, when costume balls were one of the favorite pastimes of the Marie Antoinette set.

A masquerade is invariably a ball, starting late and lasting until dawn, with hundreds of guests, a palatial setting, and a sumptuous midnight supper, which is more likely to be served at one or two in the morning than at the stroke of twelve. The only masquerades I have heard of in recent years have taken place in Rome, where the tradition is still observed of having all of the guests wear domino masks, which cover the entire lower part of the face, black tights and tunics enveloped in immense cloaks, and floppy black hats. The guests are thus completely disguised, and often it is not even possible to distinguish the men from the women. I am told that it is all very exciting and sophisticated, and that the unmasking ceremony at midnight is full of surprises. All of the guests must, of course, rent their dominoes and cloaks, and I know of no place outside of Italy where costumers are equipped to furnish a hundred guests or more with these special accoutrements. A classic masquerade is therefore unlikely to figure in the entertaining program of many modern hostesses.

A costume party, on the other hand, may take the form of a lavish ball or of a dinner dance or buffet dinner followed by dancing for a more restricted number of guests.

There are two kinds of costume parties: the sumptuous and the comic. The first (for which the famous ball given by Latin American millionaire Carlos de Beistegui a few years ago in his Venetian palace set a modern standard that is unlikely to be equaled within our time) requires a fabulous and spacious setting, at least two months for planning the decor, costumes, catering, and a guest list studded with international celebrities and members of the Jet Set, for they are the only people left who have the money to invest in extraordinary costumes custom-made by famous couturiers, the time to devote to fittings and preparations for a fabulous headdress and makeup and, most of all, the inclination to devote all of this effort to occupying their leisure hours in a refined and glamorous way. The potential guest list for such a fete is therefore necessarily limited, and I personally know very few people, even among those who can well afford it, who would be willing to invest the necessary thought, time, and money. Moreover, it seems to me that it would almost be a selfish gesture to invite persons of more modest means to this kind of a ball nowadays, since accepting your invitation would oblige them to undertake considerable expense as much for the glory of the host as for their personal pleasure. Finally, most of the men I know would undoubtedly prefer a normal dinner dance anyway.

The comic type of costume party can certainly not be accused of costing the guests a great amount of money, especially when the theme is "Come as you were dressed when you received this invitation," "Come as your favorite movie star," "Hard Times," "Come as you wake up," etc. But as hilarious as some of the costumes may be, the spectacle of your party is hardly likely to be beautiful. Frankly, while this kind of a party may be amusing to teen-agers and college students, it is not in very good taste for adults.

As a matter of fact, the only kind of costume party that seems to me suitable for adults nowadays would be given in the country during the summer holidays, when people are most apt to have the necessary free time in which to plan their costumes. The theme should be either so simple or so vague and general—"The Sea," for example—that your guests can, according to their time and means, just as well come in a witty and imaginative disguise that they have made themselves, or, if they absolutely insist on spending a lot of money, in a beautiful custom-made creation.

In general, however, there simply isn't enough time in modern life to devote to such frivolous pleasures.

Children's costume parties are another matter. Most young children adore to dress up, and their sense of fantasy is so rich that even a few accessories can create for them an entirely different atmosphere and personality. Expense is not a problem in this case, for costumers and toy shops supply charming children's costumes at a very modest price. The hostess might even provide the costumes herself in order to add an element of surprise to the occasion, which is another thing that children love. For example, a feather stuck in a bright headband for the boys, a cheap bead necklace for the girls, plus a few streaks of colored "war paint" and a wigwam in the backyard will immediately transform your little guests into a tribe of Red Indians. In these cases, the party decorations, the games, and even the refreshments should follow the same theme.

(See Children)

MENUS

❡ Every time you invite someone to share a meal, you should realize that the menu you plan for the occasion will be an accurate reflection of the degree to which you wish to honor your guest. Remembering all of their individual likes and dislikes is a mark of thoughtfulness that is just as appreciable as the offering of a small gift or the sending of a thank-you letter.

Should you overfeed your guests, as was once the hallmark of hospitality, or should you on the contrary feed them prudently in order to assure them of a night free from insomnia and indigestion? The second manner is the only elegant one today. Eating well does not mean being stuffed like a fatted calf. It is better to prove by the originality and ingenuity of your parties the consideration your guests inspire in you. Any *nouveau riche* can order a foie gras, a guinea hen, a lobster, and to top it off, a whole ham—but elegant entertaining also means taking charge of your guests' comfort and well-being until the next day by guaranteeing them a good night's sleep and a pleasant awakening the morning after.

There are several rules that govern the planning of a meal, from the simplest to the most elaborate, and the first one is to avoid any similarity between the different courses. In other words, you should not serve during the same meal several dishes in a sauce or in a pastry shell, nor several highly spiced concoctions. Two broiled dishes are more acceptable, but even this tends to give an impression of monotony.

Eye appeal should also be considered, for nothing is more stimulating to the appetite than an attractively arranged platter. Foods of contrasting colors are always more appetizing than a monochrome meal. It may seem amusing to plan an all-pink dinner of borscht, salmon, and strawberry mousse, or an all-black one with caviar, squid in its ink, and devil's-food cake, but such tours de force are more humorous than gastronomic. In actual practice, the only color you have to beware of is white. Try to add a contrasting garnish to creamed dishes, or simply a dusting of paprika, and avoid the insipid effect of more than one white dish in a menu.

Here are a few examples of perfectly balanced menus:

Fish in a sauce. (Soufflé of fish, filets of sole in a cream sauce, curried or creamed seafood in a rice ring, etc.)
Broiled meat. Green vegetables.
Fruit pie.

OR

Broiled fish or raw seafood (oysters, clams, etc.).
Meat in a sauce with rice or potatoes (for example, a lamb or beef stew or a casserole recipe).
Fresh fruit cup.

OR

A cheese soufflé (quiche Lorraine, cheese tart, Welsh rarebit, etc.).
Cold fish with mayonnaise, or a roast (beef, veal or lamb) *or roast chicken.*
Chocolate mousse, caramel custard, Floating Island, etc.

OR

Assorted fancy cold cuts or smoked salmon.
Pepper steak, filet mignon, veal scallops, mutton chops, mixed grill, etc.
Apple, peach, or plum pie, etc.

OR

A wide assortment of raw vegetable hors d'oeuvres (grated carrots, celery, cucumbers, cauliflower, halves of hard-boiled eggs with mayonnaise, cold artichokes vinaigrette, asparagus, etc.).
Chicken and kidney pie, or a similar, rather rich, composed dish.
Ice Cream.

If you serve raw vegetables as an hors d'oeuvre course, there is no point in serving a salad too, and it would be preferable to find a dessert idea that is a bit more original than fresh fruit cup.

It is also necessary to consider the number of burners on the stove and the oven temperature required for the various recipes. For example, in an ordinary oven it is impossible to cook a roast beef at the same time as a cheese soufflé.

If every dish requires last-minute preparation, you will probably face the ordeal of interminable delays between each course, even when there is an efficient professional cook in the kitchen. And just as I dread the two- or three-minute blank during a fashion show when one of the models is late for her turn, prolonged waiting between the courses at the dinner table is one of the agonies I most abhor. If you prepare the meal all by yourself, there is all the more reason to plan your menu so that at least one course out of two can be completely prepared in advance.

Oddly enough, while it is considered quite natural to order hors d'oeuvres in the evening at a restaurant, the classic tradition is to serve them at home only for lunch. Soup, on the contrary, may be served for dinner (already served in the individual plates or cups when the guests take their places), but it is not elegant at luncheon. Luncheon menus are also lighter than dinner menus.

The problem of preparation time should be considered, too. Remember that you have all day long in which to prepare a dinner, while the lunch hour seems to arrive in no time at all when you have an errand or two to do in the morning.

Because choice meat or fowl and garden-fresh vegetables are most savory when they are most simply prepared, an easy way to add gastronomic appeal to a simple menu is to feature a seasonal specialty that is at its delicious best, fresh from your own garden whenever possible, or from a farmer's market. For example:

Springtime:
New garden vegetables
Roast milk-fed lamb
Roast suckling pig
Fresh salmon
Asparagus (served warm as a separate course with a mousseline or Hollandaise sauce)

Summer:
Corn on the cob
Lobster, clams, shrimps, crabs
At the seashore: *fresh fish*
Strawberries, raspberries, blackberries, blueberries, peaches, etc.

Fall:
All kinds of game in season
Mushrooms
Oysters
Squash, eggplant, pumpkin
Apples, pears, grapes

Winter:
Turkey and goose in addition to game
Oysters and clams
Fresh chestnuts in a purée, or as stuffing for fowl and game, or as a sweetened dessert

As you can see, planning a perfect menu is not as simple a matter as it may seem to be at first, and if one of them gives you complete satisfaction, why not repeat it for a different set of guests? Sacha Guitry used to be astonished by the trouble tourists take to write different postcard greetings to friends who do not even know each other; it is the same with party menus. However, it is a wise precaution to keep a record in a special notebook of the date, the menu, the names of the guests, and the decoration of the table, in order to avoid the embarrassment of serving six or twelve months later the very same dishes to the same friends on the same tablecloth, with the same flower arrangement!

MOVIES

⟨ The pride and joy of their amateur producers and the bane of well-bred guests, home movies are of interest nine times out of ten only to those who play a role in them. Family films are entertaining only to members of the family. And while amateur travelogues may amuse friends who have visited the same places, it is generally because of the opportunity they provide to reminisce about their own experiences in the same distant lands, which have most often been quite different from yours. In fact, their comments usually leave you with the deflated feeling that you have missed the very sights and spots that were most extraordinary.

Before they are fit to be shown to even the most indulgent, friendly viewers, home movies should be properly cut and spliced in order to eliminate all of the inevitable repetitions as well as the over- and under-exposed portions. The screen should be prepared so that it can be set up in a jiffy, and the projector should be in perfect working order. Most important of all, the invited audience should be restricted to people who appear in the film.

I know a charming couple of whom I am very fond, who travel every summer to photogenic places, movie camera in hand. In the interest of our long-standing friendship, I have learned never to accept an invitation to spend an evening with them about three weeks after they have returned from a holiday, for this is the fateful moment when they receive the developed film of their latest vacation movie.

(For taking guests to see a movie, *see* Theater)

MUSIC

⟨ Classical music, like classical literature, requires undivided attention. It is therefore very distracting to your guests to put a long-playing record of a symphony or a concerto on your hi-fi under the illusion that you are thus creating atmosphere. The more your guests love music, the more this is likely to annoy them. If the work is one they really wish to hear at this particular moment, they will want to turn the volume up high and to listen to it in its entirety, savoring every phrase in respectful silence. Classical music and conversation are incompatible, and in normal entertaining circumstances it is always better to prefer conversation.

Light music is another matter. A few musical comedy tunes or old Benny Goodman records can indeed create a mood of gaiety and warmth when, for example, you are awaiting the arrival of the first guests at a cocktail party. But as soon as there are three or four people present, the sound of their conversation and laughter will create a more friendly atmosphere than the brightest songs from "My Fair Lady."

Background music in the dining room is suitable only for resort hotels and ocean liners.

Today's popular music, it must be admitted, is more often noisy than harmonious, and the melodious airs of twenty years ago will immediately label you, at least in the eyes of the younger generation, as a "historic monument," or whatever the current term may be.

If you and your friends enjoy dancing after dinner, which is a pleasant way to pass an evening and an infallible means of enlivening a lagging party, you should keep on hand an up-to-date selection of popular records, including the newest novelty dances as well as an ample supply of fox-trots, tangos, and waltzes.

Dance music is an essential element of teen-age parties, for dancing is undoubtedly the favorite party activity of this age group. If you live in a city apartment, you should warn your neighbors that your children will be entertaining until a certain hour, and you must firmly stick to the closing time you have set. The end of the music is bound to break up the party, and this is your most powerful control over the proceedings.

In Paris, every household enjoys the unofficial right to give one late party (later than 10 P.M.) once a month (just as Paris dogs have the right to bark for no more than fifteen minutes every night), and this seems to me to be a reasonable maximum. But even if there are no established rules in your neighborhood, it is only courteous to consider the neighbors when you are planning an evening of dancing. No matter how low the volume is set, the accentuated rhythms of most modern dance records will resound through the thin walls of an entire modern apartment building.

At an adult dinner dance, a small live orchestra is more elegant than recorded music, particularly if it is a special occasion and the guests are asked to come in evening clothes. You must reserve the orchestra well in advance during the busy holiday season and advise the leader of your preference and the preference of your friends in dance rhythms. The ideal arrangement is to have the orchestra play in a room that has been cleared for dancing adjoining the dinner room, as was the case of the party given by the French consul in Philadelphia, which I described in "Dinners." If your living room is very large, practically of ballroom size, you may prefer to place the orchestra at one end. In this case, the tables can be set up around the dance floor and a separate room should be prepared for those of your guests who may prefer conversation to dancing.

The pride of many modern melomanes is their highly perfected hi-fi installations, with loudspeakers in practically every room as well as in the garden. When you are alone, I would be the last to begrudge you the right to have music wherever you go. But when you entertain, it would be better to resist the temptation of filling your entire home with background music. Personally, I find the current mania for music in elevators, airplanes, washrooms, taxicabs, and even circulating under the drier at the hairdresser, terribly fatiguing.

The ideal party atmosphere is relaxed, cheerful, and conducive to conversation. Music may sometimes contribute to creating this mood, but more often it will distract attention from conversation and get on people's nerves rather than relax them. So, no matter how much you yourself may enjoy it, you should always consider the possibility when you entertain that your guests may not necessarily share your penchant for a permanent musical *ambiance*.

(See Performers)

NAPKINS

(The napkins on a well-dressed table should always match the table-cloth, except:

— on a rustic country table, where bright-colored napkins that harmonize or contrast with a printed or colored tablecloth create a cheerful, informal effect;

— with a tablecloth of lace or organdy, when it is most attractive to use plain white damask or fine linen napkins, or colored ones that match the undercloth.

Large-sized napkins are used for dinner, slightly smaller ones for lunch, while cocktail and tea napkins may be ridiculously dainty. However, when I entertain men guests at informal luncheons, I always use the large size, since I suspect that they prefer them.

Napkins may be placed to the left of each place setting or, if a cold first course or a soup has not already been served when the guests take their seats, they may be laid across the plate. A warning that may be useful to you one day: in France, a dinner roll is often ingeniously concealed among the folds.

Although the outspread shape of a napkin is square, it is smartest to fold it in thirds in order to form a rectangle, and it should lie flat on the table or plate. It is not a bit elegant to imitate the restaurant fashion of folding napkins in a complicated way to resemble Alpine peaks or bunny rabbits, no matter how much skill and dexterity such handiwork represents.

Generally speaking, when you have decided on the tablecloth you wish to use for a party, there is no problem at all in selecting the napkins, since they match the cloth. As a matter of fact, I can think of only two special restrictions concerning them:

—*Napkin rings* should appear only at everyday family meals, never when there is company (and besides, napkin envelopes are far more hygienic);

—*Paper napkins* should be reserved for cocktails, picnics, family meals, and children's parties. But there is one important exception: the large buffet dinner requiring dozens of napkins, when you wish to decorate your table with a bright colored cloth. Since rental firms usually supply only white table linen whereas paper napkins come in all colors, you can place art before convention and set your buffet with piles of large, thick, bright paper napkins that match your tablecloth.

(See Tables)

NEIGHBORS

⟨[It is always a good policy to remain on friendly terms with the people who live next door, but at the same time to avoid contracting a more intimate relationship—and this principle is just as valid for people living in a small town where "everybody knows everybody else" as it is for city dwellers, who have the reputation of being completely indifferent toward their neighbors.

Once you establish the practice of inviting your neighbors to your parties, you will face the uncomfortable alternative of either offending them whenever you do not invite them, or of being stuck with them as permanent guests for as long as you live . . . or at least, for as long as you live in that particular location. On the other hand, you should never appear to snub or to ignore them. Remember that a good neighbor can render invaluable services during an illness, an absence, and in all kinds of emergencies. It is courteous—I might even say advisable— to invite the next-door neighbors to your large cocktail parties and outdoor receptions and very occasionally to dinner, but preferably alone. Your relations will be far more harmonious if each of you respects the other's privacy, and if you lead rather independent social lives.

Every time you plan a party that is likely to inconvenience your neighbors because of the noise, the traffic or the outdoor lighting, it is thoughtful to warn them several days ahead of time, so that they can, if they wish, arrange to be away from home on that particular evening. You are under no obligation at all to invite them to the party, so above all do not feel that you have to make excuses. In a city apartment house, the party din may disturb the neighbors on the floor above and on the floor below as well as those on either side, and so you should really pay a call or send a friendly note of excuse in advance to all of them. In the country, if you are expecting a great many cars, you should ask your neighbor's permission before you direct your guests to use his driveway for turning around. Needless to add, all of these little services are rigorously reciprocal. In fact, it is a good idea never to refuse a neighbor's reasonable request, if only because you may wish to ask the same service of him one day.

We choose our friends, but our neighbors are imposed upon us by circumstance. To tell the truth, it is seldom satisfactory for close friends to inhabit the same apartment house or adjoining houses. For every case where life has been a joy in these conditions, there are probably ten where friendship has been unable to endure the strain of permanent proximity.

Finally, if one of your guests should cause the slightest damage to your neighbor's property, by accidentally knocking down his fence post, for example, or by driving over his lawn, you should immediately offer to repair the damage before he has had time to work himself into a rage.

NEW YEAR

❨ The end of the old year and the beginning of the new is undoubtedly the busiest period of the social calendar. In addition to the dinners and parties that are planned weeks in advance, one's leisure hours are filled with innumerable visits and cocktails in order to exchange gifts or simply the season's greetings. Coming toward the end of this festive time, New Year's Eve is usually the climax of the holiday celebrations. But remember, it is not the final point, and if you plan a New Year's

Eve party, it should leave you and your guests in good enough condition to continue the holiday rounds, instead of obliging you to retire for a two-day period of recuperation.

The truth is that large New Year's Eve receptions have fallen into ill repute among the elegant social set in America as well as Europe, due to past abuses. Nothing is more vulgar than the supposedly "typical" New Year's Eve, when a heterogeneous mob is invited to drink too much, to wear ludicrous paper hats, to make ear-splitting noises, to throw discretion and good manners to the winds, to stay up far too late—and to profoundly regret the whole thing the morning after.

The most agreeable as well as the most elegant form of entertaining on New Year's Eve is a black-tie buffet dinner dance for twenty to fifty guests, or a more intimate gathering of twelve to twenty close friends.

In both cases, the meal should be served rather late in the evening, at nine-thirty or ten o'clock, so that there is not too long an interval of dancing and conversation before the first stroke of midnight, which will be the climax of the party.

Planning the menu should not present any particular problem, since this is the time of year that is richest in traditional dishes. The buffet table should be beautiful to see, and the platters arranged with even greater care than usual in order to create a festive mood. This is the perfect occasion for my favorite combination of a bright red, floor-length tablecloth, adorned with white and red flowers or a mixture of flowers and fruits in a pyramid form, set with gleaming polished silver and lit by your most sumptuous candelabra. Since your home will still be decked with Christmas adornments, you can devote all of your decorating efforts to the buffet table.

Although there has been a flurry of popularity in recent years for unusual holiday menus, such as a Hawaiian or a Mexican New Year, I am personally a traditionalist in this particular instance, for I am convinced that the traditional dishes are more likely to bring greater pleasure to the majority of your guests, and particularly to the men. I would therefore recommend building the menu around such dishes as:

For the first dish: A gorgeous, cold seafood platter, with lobster, shrimp, and cracked crab
A cold foie gras in aspic decorated with truffle slices
A beautiful chicken liver pâté or mousse
Cold jellied trout (one per person)

Smoked salmon or sturgeon, finely sliced

A hot seafood Newburg, or individual lobster Newburg (one half a lobster per person, or one whole small lobster)

A whole cold salmon

For the meat dish nothing can top a whole roast turkey on this occasion, but you should remember that your guests will probably have been eating nothing else for the past six days, and you should vary its preparation and presentation, for example, by serving it with a prune stuffing, or a stuffing of sweet potatoes, apples, and walnuts. The same recommendation applies when the principal meat dish is a whole baked ham.

If you wish to be more original without becoming too exotic, you might also consider serving:

Duck with peaches (just as delicious when it is cold in aspic as when it is hot)

Roast game birds (particularly pheasant and guinea hen) accompanied by wild rice and mushrooms

Goose with apples (rather heavy for a late meal)

Chaud froid of chicken (made from chicken breasts only, for an ultrarefined dish)

Poached chicken with oyster dressing and garnish

You might prepare a hot vegetable dish as well as a green salad, but it should be one that can safely be kept warm over a flame or hot plate, such as gratinéed creamed French string beans, broccoli, or asparagus.

It is quite permissible to oblige your guests to wait for ten minutes or so before you bring in the dessert. In fact, I would even recommend it, since this final dish should be spectacular and its arrival should attract all eyes and a chorus of admiring "Ah's." All of the flambée recipes would be most appropriate; vanilla ice cream with flambéed peaches or flambéed black cherries is among the best.

Another dessert that is bound to cause a stir is an omelette soufflée, or you might prefer a Baked Alaska or a magnificent mousse, charlotte, Bavarian cream, or my favorite, chocolate-chestnut gateau. Pineapple is always an excellent ending to a rather rich meal, and one of the most exquisite pineapple desserts I know is made by dicing the pulp from the necessary number of fruits and stirring it into either sweetened whipped cream or slightly softened vanilla ice cream, filling the pineapple shells with the mixture, and chilling thoroughly until serving time when you will add a final garnish of strawberries.

If you haven't the time or skill to prepare a really sensational dessert, you can always serve a delicious ice cream with hot chocolate sauce, and accompany it with a plate of assorted petit fours.

Needless to add, such a gala menu will take a great deal of time, and you must start your preparations days in advance. But the results will surely be worth the trouble and the mere fact of making such a special effort will already lend to the occasion a festive air.

After the dessert has been served, you can place the coffee tray at one end of the buffet table, along with a decaffeinated brew.

The most appropriate beverage for New Year's Eve is, of course, champagne. But since it would be very expensive to keep your guests' glasses filled all evening long with a fine imported champagne, and unpardonable to offer them an inferior cut-rate kind, the best solution as well as the most gala is to mix in a huge crystal or silver bowl imbedded in ice a champagne punch. Do not make it too weak, but do not make it too strong either, for your guests will drink a lot of it.

At about five or ten minutes before midnight, the host can open a magnum, or the necessary number of bottles, of champagne in order to toast the arrival of the New Year in the most elegant, traditional way.

The midnight ceremony on New Year's Eve varies a great deal from one country to another, and even from one part of the country to another. One recent year I happened to be in Madrid on this date, and I found their custom enchanting. A little before midnight, every guest was given a bag containing twelve grapes, and as the clock struck twelve (as a matter of fact, since the clock was the silent kind it was the host who struck the twelve blows on a gong) we ate a grape while making a wish at each of the twelve strokes.

In France, as in many other lands, it is customary to distribute paper streamers and bags of confetti to be thrown at midnight. In America there is in addition general kissing and the singing of "Auld Lang Syne." Whatever ceremony you prefer, do plan some little rite for midnight. This is the moment everyone has been waiting for all evening, and it would be sadly anticlimactic to have prepared nothing at all. At the same time, you should avoid like the plague maudlin speeches, riotous screaming, and the vulgarity of an adult dressed in diapers to represent the New Year, etc. It is the host and hostess who are responsible for setting the tone of the evening, and an atmosphere of friendliness and warmth is a thousand times more elegant than one of hilarity, which can so easily degenerate into rowdiness—and more easily on New Year's Eve than on any other night of the year.

(See Buffets, Dinners, Holidays, Punch)

The mood of New Year's Day is just as joyous but more intimate and cozy. It is the day for telephoning "Happy New Year" wishes to distant members of the family, for making New Year's visits, and for starting out the New Year auspiciously by spreading about as much goodwill and cheer as possible. In this atmosphere of euphoria, it is also a very pleasant custom to be "At Home" on the afternoon of New Year's Day in order to offer greetings and a drink to all one's friends.

Needless to say, if everybody within the same social set were to decide to stay at home on New Year's Day, there would be nobody left to act as guest, so a certain amount of coordination is advisable. In any case, it is a good idea to send out your invitations at least ten days or two weeks in advance. These may follow exactly the same formula as an invitation to a cocktail party, for there is really little difference between an "Open House" of this kind and an informal cocktail party. There may, for example, be a more limited choice of refreshments, and for once you can be conservative in estimating the necessary quantity of snacks and canapés, since most of the guests will arrive with a hearty New Year's Day dinner under their belts. Moreover, instead of the word "Cocktails" in your invitations, you might write "At Home," or "Open House," or even "Egg Nog," which is the traditional New Year's Day drink in many parts of the country. However, if you decide to make it an Egg Nog party, you should plan to provide an alternate choice of drinks as well, for not everybody appreciates this rich and fattening American specialty. And do not neglect to order a supply of nonalcoholic beverages for teen-agers and teetotalers.

In France, the first of January is the one day of the year when the entire family goes visiting en masse, and the usually deserted streets of the fashionable residential districts in Paris are highly picturesque, with all of the *papas, mamans,* and *enfants* dutifully trotting from one visit to another, their arms laden with flowers and boxes of chocolate. In America, these visits are far less ritualistic in character, but it would still be a charming gesture to include the entire family in your invitations, should you decide to be "At Home" on New Year's Day.

(See Cocktail Parties, Drinks)

NIGHTCLUBS

❨ When you are entertaining friends who adore to dance and who enjoy bright nightlife, you can, as a special treat after dining at home or in a restaurant, take them to a nightclub. This kind of an evening should, however, be planned in advance, not only because of the necessity of making reservations but also so that your friends will be properly dressed and groomed for the occasion.

Nightclubs are so expensive nowadays that such an evening seems to me most suitable for entertaining friends or clients from abroad or out of town, for splurging on a gala evening with a couple of close friends with whom you have built up a princely pool of funds at bridge, for example, or for celebrating a special occasion.

In order for nightclub entertaining to be elegant, there are a few important points to be observed:

— The nightclub must be the most fashionable in town—and in this regard, remember that the mode changes very quickly and that last year's number-one club may be considered déclassé today.

— Your party must consist of two couples, or of three at the very most. A large table in a nightclub or a restaurant is never chic.

— In your party there should never be more women than men. Two couples is probably ideal, but an extra man is not a bad formula either.

— The host should be very generous in estimating the cost of the evening (which often surpasses the wildest sum one can imagine) in order to avoid embarrassment to his guests or to himself. And even if he plans to pay for everything with a credit card, he should stuff his pockets with plenty of small bills and loose change in order to dispense the innumerable required tips as quickly and unobtrusively as possible.

BLIGATIONS

❨ In modern life it is inevitable for a hostess to incur a number of social obligations that are a burden to continue carrying and a bore to discharge. The only really poor solution is to allow them to accumulate and then to eliminate all of them at once by inviting everybody you have found dull, pretentious, and unpleasant to the same dinner party. If the evening is a disaster and a waste—as it is sure to be—you will have only yourself to blame. A far better strategy is to invite each of these couples or individuals separately when you are giving a rather large reception, and thus to drown them in a crowd. Most important of all, you should politely but firmly refuse all of their subsequent invitations so that you do not plunge right back into the same uncomfortable predicament.

Theoretically, the obligation incurred by a dinner party can only be repaid in full by an invitation to another dinner party, or at least a luncheon. A cocktail party would not count, nor would a dozen roses. Some very cunning women have mastered the art of inviting people they do not care to see to two or three different dinner parties, always, somehow, on an evening when the unwanted guests are already engaged. In this case, the hostess can consider herself freed from the tiresome obligation, because she has ostensibly made several honest efforts to repay it. But this is a rather risky business, for it often happens that the people whom you least care to see are the very ones who are so anxious to be received by you that they will not hesitate to invent an excuse for breaking their previous engagement in order to accept your perfidious invitation.

(See Business, Kin)

ODORS

❲ Because I spend most of my daytime hours in the Nina Ricci salons, which are continually sprayed with the latest Ricci perfume, it has never occurred to me to perfume my own living room before a party. Besides, the scent you use in your home is bound to alter or drown out the perfume of your women guests, while men do not often appreciate highly perfumed atmospheres and some of them are actually allergic to certain essences.

The atmosphere of your living room should, of course, smell fresh and clean, and usually it is quite sufficient to air the room thoroughly an hour or two before your guests arrive. If necessary, you can spray the room with a deodorant aerosol bomb, particularly among the folds of heavy curtains where a faint odor of stale smoke is apt to concentrate. The scent of aromatic wood burning in a fireplace, of fresh roses or lilacs in a vase, or of a perfumed candle is always delicious. But you should not give your arriving guests a preview of the menu by means of the aromas wafting from the kitchen (which all too often is situated right next to the entrance hall in modern homes and apartments). There are all sorts of "old wives'" tricks for suppressing the cooking odors of certain pungent dishes such as cabbage, cauliflower, and fish. But I have found that a product such as Air-Wick plus a few sprays of a deodorizing bomb are sufficient to eliminate most undesirable culinary scents.

Because of their persistent odor, fish dishes as well as strongly scented cheeses should always be brought to the table only when they are about to be served, and they should be removed immediately afterward. This is a point to remember if you are entertaining without help in a studio apartment, or at a buffet dinner, when it may be advisable to avoid highly odorous dishes entirely.

Fresh scents such as pine and cypress, lemon, geranium, and rose are the most likely to please everybody, if you insist upon perfuming your entrance hall or living room. But tuberose, much as I love it, is apt to give some people a headache, as are my other favorites, lily of the valley and mimosa.

ONE ROOM

⟨[It would be a pity to feel obliged to refrain from entertaining simply because you happen to live in a one-room studio apartment. The fact is that some forms of entertaining, such as small cocktail parties and cold suppers after the theater, are just as easy to give in a one-room apartment as in a twenty-room duplex, and perhaps even easier because your one room already possesses the intimate atmosphere that is desirable on these occasions.

Of course, you should not attempt to receive a greater number of guests than can be comfortably accommodated in your single room, which usually means four or six people for a meal and perhaps as many as twenty for cocktails. In the case of dinners and luncheons, it seems to me that the size of the kitchen is even more important than the size of the studio. With a normal kitchen, equipped with a real stove, sink, and icebox, and large enough for one or two people to work and move around in, it is even possible to hire a cook and butler for an evening and to give a beautifully prepared and served dinner party in the most refined conventional manner.

Most often, however, the kitchen of a studio apartment is merely a kitchenette, sometimes simply a cupboard concealing a miniature sink and an electric burner, and sometimes it is no more than an electric hot plate tucked in a corner of the bathroom. In these cases, entertaining at meals is indeed difficult, but not impossible. It simply requires a little more planning. The most delicate questions are cooking odors, last-minute culinary responsibilities that must be performed in full sight of your guests, and the problem of stacking and concealing dirty plates and cooking dishes. All of these difficulties can be solved by planning your menus within certain restrictions. In general, it is best to:

— Serve only cold meals, or just one hot dish at the most—either an epicurean soup (such as turtle, lobster bisque, etc.) that can keep warm on the stove in a covered pot until dinner is to be served; or a hot main dish that can be cooked in advance and reheated in a covered casserole on top of the stove, or in the oven if you have one.

— Prepare everything in advance, limiting yourself to a maximum of three different courses, and ordering at least one of these from a restaurant or caterer.

— If you have a job, set the table in the morning before you go to work and protect it with a dust sheet.

— Reduce the number of dishes, glasses, and silverware on the table to the strictest minimum. Select main dishes that can be presented in the casseroles in which they were cooked. You can eliminate salad plates and bread and butter plates by serving the salad on the same plate as the meat course and by buttering in advance slices of crusty French bread or rolls (even better if they are warmed in the oven or in a double boiler). You can serve a single wine, and substitute for a first course an appetizing assortment of canapés and raw vegetables that are passed with the cocktails and eaten with the fingers.

— Even if you do the cooking in the morning, avoid highly pungent dishes such as fish, cabbage, cauliflower, and fried foods, for it is very difficult to eliminate cooking odors from a small room.

— Build your dinners around one hearty casserole dish, such as a curry, *pot au feu*, steak and kidney pie, etc. All you need to do is to add a tray of hors d'oeuvres beforehand, a green salad served at the same time, and a dessert afterward, which might be simply fruit and cheese (Cheddar, Cheshire, and Edam go well with apples and nuts), or a fruit pie from an excellent bakery. If you serve a single light red or rosé wine during the meal and a perfect cup of coffee afterward, your guests will be highly satisfied and you will only have had to change the plates once.

— Realize that removing dirty plates in a servantless household is a difficult problem to which there is no ideal solution. Nothing is more repulsive than to scrape and stack dirty plates in front of your guests, so you should at least avoid this unattractive scene by removing the dishes to the kitchen two by two, even though this takes much longer.

— After the party, clean up the debris before you go to bed. It will be much too depressing a sight in the morning.

Whatever the size of the kitchen, all studio apartments have this in common: they must combine in one room the functions of a bedroom, dressing room, dining room, living room (and sometimes a kitchen) all at once. Of all these, it is most important to camouflage its dressing room-bedroom personality, at least until bedtime. In other words, the studio should present the aspect of a normal living room, the studio couch should look like a living room sofa and not a bed, the dresser should look like a salon commode, and the desk like a desk, even if you also use it as a dressing table. Most important of all, your personal clothing and toilet articles should be carefully concealed.

It is a very simple matter to find attractive double-duty furniture nowadays, such as a flat-topped desk with plenty of drawers, half of them to hold your papers and writing materials and the other half silverware and table linen; a bookcase composed half of open shelves for books and bibelots and half of closed cupboards for dishes; a commode that can serve as a bar or a sideboard and can contain clothing as well as bed and table linen; a folding "half-moon" table that can act as a console when it is not in service as a dining table; or, if you prefer, a drop-leaf writing table that can serve as either a desk or as a lamp table placed behind the sofa in the English fashion until it is required for dining. If all of your furniture is thus adapted to play several different roles, you will not really need many different pieces. I have even seen a low coffee table with telescopic legs that can be transformed into a bridge table. And speaking of bridge tables, nothing is more practical for dining in a studio apartment. It can be stored at the back of a coat closet, and can be enlarged with a folding round fitted top in order to provide table room for as many as six or eight guests—and it is unlikely that you will wish to undertake feeding more than that number in a one-room apartment!

The greatest space savers of all are built-in closets and cupboards, and if they are cleverly outfitted with special compartments for shoes, hats, handbags, etc., they will do more than anything else to eliminate embarrassing clutter. An original way of providing extra storage space for bulky articles such as suitcases and sporting equipment is to install a false lowered ceiling in the entrance hall, if there is sufficient height, accessible by means of a trap door. Small odd spaces around the windows and radiators can often be turned into storage nooks. And do not forget the enlarging effect of mirrors, but only when they are placed with careful attention to what they will reflect.

It is simple to coordinate the style and scale of your furniture if you are buying everything new and all at once. But most often a studio apartment has to be furnished with gifts and loans and junk-shop bargains. In this case, the only way to avoid an impression of utter confusion is to establish a very strict color scheme in order to pull everything together. You might select an attractive printed chintz for the curtains and sofa (scrupulously avoid an overly dainty bedroom style), paint the walls in the background color of the print, and cover everything else in one of the colors that appears in the fabric, with perhaps a few brighter accents in another of the print colors. You may prefer solid-colored curtains, in which case you can borrow your color scheme from a picture, or from a Chinese vase. With a little care and thought, good taste, and a sense of humor, a studio apartment can be charming and even elegant if you do not attempt to create a luxurious, formal setting, which is impossible, but instead establish a mood of unpretentious warmth and gaiety. Besides, haven't you noticed that many people who live in spacious homes prefer to receive their guests in the smallest, coziest room?

It is seldom a good idea to attempt to entertain at a really formal sit-down dinner in a one-room apartment. Aside from the practical problems involved, it would even seem rather pretentious, unless your one room is of imposing dimensions and magnificent decor. But forsaking ceremonious dinners should cause no grief to the modern hostess, because the fact is that nowadays, except for official functions, casual entertaining is far more chic than is rigid formality.

(See Job)

ORIGINALITY

⟨[In entertaining as in fashion, there are two kinds of originality: the first might be better described as bizarre than original, for it originates in a desire to surprise and astonish, to be different from everybody else at any cost, preferably by running exactly counter to the current mode. This kind of originality is seldom elegant.

The second originates in a desire to please; it is a reflection of individual taste and imagination, and "personality" might be a better word for it. In its most elegant form, this kind of originality is applied to a few refined details in a conventional framework; for example, one unusual dish in a dinner menu, a particularly delicious hot punch on a cold winter afternoon, or an especially refined presentation of a classic dish.

Your women friends are much more apt to appreciate your efforts to be original than are the men, who, as every married women knows, are inclined to become very much attached to their well-established habits as time goes by, and generally eye all innovations in food and drink with an air of suspicion.

The principal exception to this general rule is found in certain arty, intellectual circles, where conformity is considered practically a sin. When you entertain authentic "eggheads," you can give free rein to your imagination and dig up the most exotic recipes and mix the most extraordinary drinks, reconstitute a menu described by Flaubert, or serve a sukiyaki Japanese-style with all of the guests sitting cross-legged on the floor. But you must be very sure of yourself and carefully check the authenticity of each detail, if you wish your experiment to be perfectly successful.

Many of the occasions that present a pretext for entertaining are so traditional in nature (weddings, Thanksgiving, Christmas, etc.) that it would be poor taste as well as pretentious to attempt to place your own ideas, however worthy, above the time-honored customs that have been practiced for generations. As a matter of fact, much of the fun of these events comes from observing the traditions. So before you try to introduce any startling innovations on such occasions as Easter and Christmas, you should know your guests well enough to be absolutely certain that their reaction will be surprised delight rather than disappointment.

PARKING

❴ While almost every hostess considers the parking problems of her guests when she is planning a very large party (*see* Police), the six or eight guests invited to a dinner party are more often expected to fend for themselves. And yet it is not always a simple matter to find a place for three or four extra automobiles in certain built-up residential areas, and the very considerate hostess should think of providing a place for her friends to leave their cars just as she provides a place for them to leave their coats.

There is no problem at all when the builder of one's house has already considered the likely possibility that its eventual occupants may wish to accommodate three or four cars in the driveway, and a few builders are even realistic enough to provide a means for cars to turn around without destroying lawns and flower beds. In other cases, a hostess can at least attempt to facilitate matters for her motorized guests by, for example: (1.) putting the family cars in the garage before her guests arrive; (2.) clearing the driveway of toys and bicycles; (3.) tying up the family dog—even if he is very friendly; and (4.) sending her husband to the rescue of a departing woman guest who has parked her car in a practically inextricable position!

PERFORMERS

⟨ When Artur Rubinstein and Maria Callas can give a private recital in one's own living room thanks to hi-fi, stereo, and TV, it is not surprising that amateur entertainment is less and less appreciated. Virtually the only remaining enthusiasts are the proud parents of precocious children who, to make things worse, generally violate the basic rule that such entertainment should be voluntary in the true sense of the word, with neither the amateur being forced to perform against his will nor the audience forced to listen.

In actual practice, most guests take care to insist no more than common courtesy requires, so that most budding child prodigies are called upon to exercise their talents only before members of the family and perhaps a few intimate friends. And isn't it generally kinder to provide them with this most indulgent of audiences?

All too often, the slighter a person's proficiency, the more willing he is to display it, for the truth is that really accomplished amateurs, like professionals, enjoy performing only with persons of comparable ability or before an audience they have invited themselves.

While some amateurs are so intoxicated by the presence of a captive audience that it requires infinite tact on the part of the hostess to restrain them from performing, it is not at all the same with professional artists, whose talent is, after all, their livelihood, and not a social grace to be gratuitously dispensed. Few laymen realize that a concert performance requires a special atmosphere in order for the artist to be at his creative best, and this particular mood is generally produced by a period of concentration and solitude beforehand—which is quite the opposite of a relaxed and sociable party atmosphere. And so, when you invite a professional artist or entertainer to one of your parties, you should no more dream of asking him to perform after dinner than you would consider asking a guest who is a doctor to give you a free medical examination after the coffee has been served, or an architect to design a new house for you while waiting for the dessert.

If the temptation is great, you might remember the experience of Mrs. Cornelius Vanderbilt, who once invited a renowned concert pianist to a large dinner party and afterward led him to the piano and insisted that he give an impromptu recital for her guests. The virtuoso graciously acceded to her request, but the next day he sent her an enormous bill, which, he explained, was double his normal concert fee because in addition to performing he had been required to mingle with the audience.

(See Music)

PETS

⟨ Pets should be considered the same as young children when you are entertaining, with one important exception: when you receive other young children in your home, you would permit them to play with yours, but in the case of pets you should, on the contrary, keep them separated by confining the animals to a separate room or to their pens, as much in the interest of the pets as out of concern for the children's safety. You should also try to discourage your guests from bringing their own pets to your home.

In other circumstances, you can introduce your pets to your invited guests with exactly the same restrictions that you apply to your children. For example, you can let your guests admire a litter of young puppies in their pen, just as you would permit a guest to tiptoe into the nursery to admire a new baby. You can present your dog, cat, parrot, mongoose, or what have you, to your guests at the beginning of an informal evening, but only for a very few minutes, after which you should immediately return the animal to its own private quarters. Very well-behaved adult pets, like well-behaved older children, can be permitted to spend an entire evening with a few intimate friends, but it would undoubtedly be a strain and a bore for all concerned to allow them to be present at a large formal party, and there is nothing to be gained by attempting it.

A pet with the slightest symptom of malady, fatigue, or bad temper, should be kept separated from your guests in all circumstances.

I have already insisted on the importance of a comprehensive liability insurance policy for every home, but if you are a pet owner, you should make certain that you have a policy protecting you fully from accident or damage that may be caused by the family cat or dog.

In short, when you have company, your pets, like your children, should be seen very little and heard even less. Much as it pains me to see my dog trailing after me with an accusing, tragic look in his eyes while I am preparing for a party, and much as I hate to shut him up in a room far away from the festivities, experience has proven to me that this is the only safe and satisfactory policy. Besides, he is very quick to forgive and forget the snub once the party is over.

PHOTOGRAPHY

⟨[The presence of a professional photographer is virtually indispensable at an important social event such as a wedding reception, a christening, a coming-out party, or a large ball. The happy occasion can be relived with the greatest of pleasure over and over again if it has been recorded on film. Not only are photographs desirable, I would say that there should be as many of them as possible, including a few essential posed pictures, and dozens and dozens of candid snapshots of the guests, the hosts, the setting, the tables, the buffet, the dancing, the ceremony if any—in short, the most complete possible record of your party. When you receive the proofs, you should immediately destroy any that are un- flattering or indiscreet, and order a sufficient number of the others so that you can provide one complete set for yourself, and send each of your guests a copy of the photographs in which he or she appears. The better the pictures, the more delighted your guests will be, and it is therefore worthwhile to reserve the services of the best available photographer well in advance of the event. If you ever give a costume party, it would be particularly thoughtful to provide your guests with a generous number of photographic souvenirs, considering all the ex- pense and trouble they have taken to prepare their costumes.

On the other hand, it is not at all chic to keep a record of every dinner party you give by taking out your camera and flashbulbs and photographing your guests around the table, as if your private party were an official banquet. Taking snapshots out of doors, during a vaca- tion, a trip or cruise, or within a group of close friends or relatives can be most amusing and would offend no one. But while some people are flattered by the presence of photographers, others simply loathe to have their pictures taken, and to photograph your guests during an ordinary social evening would be abusing the privileges of a host.

(See Journalism)

PICNICS

❨ The charm of picnicking on a grassy plain near a babbling stream can be found more easily in romantic literature than in real life. You have only to compare the relaxed and elegant picnickers of a hundred years ago, as immortalized in the paintings of Renoir and his fellow Impressionists, with the picnic scenes along our modern highways in order to see how times have changed. When, on a Sunday afternoon about twenty miles from Paris, I see the roadside studded with picnickers who have brought along a folding table and chairs, a tablecloth, silverware, and the usual Sunday roast, and, after hours of nerve-racking traffic jams at the city gates, have finally reached the "country" only to discover that the sole picnic spot available is along the roadside, a foot or two away from the onrushing traffic, with the sound of trucks and cars in place of chirping birds and babbling streams, and the fumes of Diesel engines and exhaust pipes in place of fresh balmy breezes, I am filled with pity and struck by the futility of it all.

Due to the disappearance of pastoral sites where picnickers are welcome, as well as to the appalling conditions of modern weekend traffic, the traditional Sunday picnic has been replaced by cold buffet luncheons on one's own patio.

Aside from the picnic carried in a knapsack by a Boy Scout setting forth on an all-day hike, or by a hunter or fisherman devoting a day to his favorite sport (in which cases the picnic lunch should simply provide the greatest number of calories in the smallest possible volume), it seems to me that today there are only two kinds of picnics that are practical, and possibly elegant.

(1.) The romantic picnic for two. I suppose that nowadays this is practiced mostly by sentimental young lovers, and the picnic will be prepared by the young woman, while the man provides the transportation—more likely a souped-up sports car than a bicycle built for two.

Nevertheless, the meal can be romantic and rather refined, particularly since it is prepared for just two people.

In a hamper you would pack an assortment of gourmet sandwiches: smoked salmon, the white meat of chicken, turkey or smoked turkey, sliced very fine and placed between thin slices of white bread, which has been buttered and from which the crusts have been removed, along with a leaf of lettuce and a bit of mayonnaise; thin slices of boiled ham or tongue and Swiss cheese with lettuce on thinly sliced rye bread; whole-wheat or wheat-germ bread with a filling of vegetable salad (grated carrots, chopped radishes, green peppers, celery, shredded lettuce, tomatoes, etc., bound together with homemade mayonnaise and covered with thin slices of hard-boiled egg); the same dark bread filled with a cream cheese spread that has been seasoned with chopped radishes, chives, cucumber, celery, and herbs; or white bread filled with a smooth paste made by mashing a can of tuna fish with mayonnaise, finely chopped egg, and onion, garnished with crisp lettuce and perhaps a tomato slice that has been peeled and seeded. In other words, you should prepare the most refined sandwiches you can invent—without making them actually dainty. The ideal beverage would be champagne, chilled in a thermos bucket of ice that you have brought along for just this purpose; and the ideal dessert would be delicious home-baked cookies, brownies, date bars, etc., and two perfect peaches, apples, or pears. Finally, a thermos of hot coffee.

After sharing this exquisite repast in a romantic spot far from the main highways and preferably in some lovely natural setting, you will stroll through a wood or field, hand in hand, and talk about your future plans. This is, in fact, one of the few ways a young engaged couple can find to escape by themselves during the busy weeks preceding their wedding.

If the twosome is younger and has simpler tastes, they would perhaps enjoy more a very rustic picnic. In the same hamper you would pack a bottle of red wine, a whole sausage, crusty bread, a few slabs of cheese (Edam, Gruyère), a terrine of pâté, a couple of raw washed tomatoes (or a plastic bag filled with carrot, celery, and cucumber sticks), an assortment of fresh fruit that is not very fragile, such as apples, oranges, and tangerines, and a thermos of hot coffee.

The first kind of a picnic for two requires careful preparation at least the day before; but the second can be assembled at the very last minute. As a matter of fact, it is the favorite lunch of many British tourists on the Continent who wish to avoid our expensive country restaurants during their holiday walking and cycling tours. You might very well follow their example and combine this simple picnic with a touristic excursion by visiting some historic site or monument within a comfortable distance of your starting point.

(2.) The other type of picnic still extant is more inspired by necessity than by choice. When you are planning to travel some distance from your home to attend a dog show, a horse show, a tennis match, a football game, etc., where the luncheon facilities are generally limited to a hot-dog stand of dubious quality and perhaps a rather expensive club luncheon restricted to members or exhibitors, it is often more practical as well as much more pleasant to bring your own refreshments with you. This is even a particularly friendly and thoughtful way of entertaining friends who share your enthusiasm for the activity in question. The number of guests will be limited by the capacity of your car—in other words, an absolute maximum of six, but four would be better.

Most often, this kind of a picnic will have to be served in or near your car, especially at an outdoor dog show or horse show. It is therefore a good idea to bring along a few folding chairs if your car is not a convertible model, for the interior of a closed sedan will be very stuffy; nor is it very pleasant to sit on a blanket on the grass (more often dirt) surrounding a horse-show ring or a parking lot.

If you have attended the sporting event since early in the morning, you will probably be ravenous when the lunch hour arrives, so you should plan a rather hearty menu that is simple to eat and easy to keep fresh. For example: In the winter and fall, to start with, a thermos full of hot soup drunk from plastic coffee mugs with handles. Simple but hearty soups are best, such as cream of tomato, Potage St. Germain, potato and leek, creamed spinach, cream of celery, and all of the delicious purées that can be made so easily nowadays in an electric blender, not forgetting the appeal of a rich beef bouillon. In the summer, you can start with a thermos of cold tomato juice cocktail, or you can simply eliminate this course entirely. Then come the sandwiches, preferably also of a rather hearty type but very carefully prepared. Be sure to season them well and to butter both slices of bread, for this will not only help the sandwich to stick together but will also prevent the bread from becoming soggy with the mayonnaise or whatever other dressing you have used. A choice of turkey and roast beef, or chicken salad and ham and cheese, or roast chicken and tuna fish-egg salad would all be good combinations, and you can include as relishes a jar of stuffed olives (with toothpicks for handling them) and one of dill pickles or sweet gherkins. Two or three large-sized sandwiches per person is not too much, and if there are any left over they may come in handy as a snack later on in the afternoon. As beverage, an ordinary red wine or beer would be the simplest choice. If there is a refreshment stand at the show, you can buy your cold beer there. You might also bring along in a cooler an assortment of soft drinks, milk, or whatever you prefer. For dessert: a beautiful homemade pie, the kind you make the best (and so much the better if it is apple, apricot, or pecan). But avoid creamy fillings and chiffon pies that not only require chilling to prevent spoilage but are also too fragile to transport in safety. The pie should be served on paper plates but with your normal knives and forks. If you prefer, your dessert may consist of cookies or brownies and fresh fruit, or even ice cream, if you buy individual cups and keep them frozen by placing them in a cooler with dry ice. Finally, hot coffee with the sugar and cream in separate hermetic containers.

If you must leave home very early in the morning, you should prepare your picnic the night before—unless you do not mind getting up at the crack of dawn. The sandwiches will keep very well overnight in the icebox if you wrap them first in waxed or aluminum paper or plastic bags, and then in a damp towel. You must in any case prepare the dessert the day before, but if you prefer to do the rest early in the morning it is a very good idea to make out a complete list of everything you must assemble so that you do not, in your half-awake state, forget some vital detail—like the can or bottle opener, the forks, or the paper napkins.

Packing a picnic is no problem nowadays, thanks to the invention of aluminum foil, plastic bags of all shapes and sizes, and hermetic containers guaranteed to retain the heat or cold for a certain number of hours. You should take advantage of all these possibilities, wrapping everything individually and labeling each package if the contents are not immediately recognizable. Always try to avoid messy foods, fragile foods, and foods that are apt to spoil. Your friends will never criticize you for serving a banal picnic menu, but it would be unpardonable to give them ptomaine poisoning.

(See Barbecues, Beach, Yachting)

PLACE CARDS

⟨ Never necessary at a small party, place cards are very practical when there are more than six or eight guests for dinner, and they are indispensable at a very large reception. The hostess should, however, still attempt to seat personally as many guests as possible, and always the guests of honor. At a large party it is also useful to display a plan of the table or tables near the entrance to the dining room where the guests can consult it before seeking their places.

The most elegant place cards are also the simplest: a plain, stiff, white rectangular card. People who entertain a great deal order them engraved with their monogram in one corner. Perfectly plain ones are no less chic, but fancy shapes and cute designs should be avoided.

Personally, I have never been in favor of place-card holders, even when they are made of solid gold, and I prefer to place the cards in the conventional way, flat on the table above each place setting or on top of the wine glass. It is, of course, no more than elementary courtesy to spell the names of your guests correctly. At formal dinners they should be written by hand, as always, and also in full, preceded by Mr., Mrs., or Miss, as the case may be. At an informal dinner party where everybody is on a first-name basis, you can write only the first names on the cards. But you should never mix the two, with some of the place cards bearing first names and others written out in full. First-name place cards are, however, customary at children's parties as well as at large family gatherings, where full names would be rather ridiculous.

When you are entertaining a limited number of good friends, let's say no more than twenty, you might write a witty descriptive phrase in place of the name on each card, for example: "The Dior of Tomorrow," which was once attributed with outrageous flattery to me. As a matter of fact, the phrases should always be absolutely eulogistic and not too difficult to assign to the different guests. They will be pleased as well as amused, and an atmosphere of gaiety will be established at once.

I am rather hesitant about recommending the other popular place-card game, in which the hostess pairs off her guests by having the men and women draw from separate baskets little folded slips of paper on which is written the name of half of a famous pair, such as Romeo and Juliet, Elizabeth and Essex, etc.—the point being, of course, to find one's dinner partner by seeking the holder of the complementary slip. This is rather risky, in my opinion, for it is always preferable to place one's guests at table according to their interests and affinities. And I wonder if the hostesses who have played this game with apparent success realize how many furtive exchanges of place cards have been transacted behind their backs.

(See Dinners, Seating)

PLACE MATS

⟨[Less dressy, and more informal than a tablecloth, place mats can be used to compose a perfectly charming table, especially when there is a matching runner for the center. They are, however, of more limited use in entertaining than tablecloths, which immediately set an elegant party mood.

Pretty place mats are made in all sorts of materials, from cork, plastic, and straw, to the finest linen and lace. The plastic kind should be reserved for family meals, and the fabric ones should always be placed over a pad cut to the same size. An oval or oblong shape is undoubtedly the most practical, and they should be large enough to hold the glasses as well as the plates and silverware for each setting, since the effect of separate coasters or doilies is neither as attractive nor as chic.

Where elegant entertaining is concerned, such as at dinner parties, I personally prefer a tablecloth. But individual mats with matching or contrasting napkins are lovely for a luncheon party, perfect on the breakfast or brunch table, and indispensable on a breakfast tray.

(See Dinners, Tables, Tablecloths)

POLICE

❡ It may seem quite irrelevant to devote a chapter to policemen in a book on elegant entertaining. But modern life being what it is, and the law of cause and effect being as inexorable in entertaining as in other activities, if you start with a big party, you will have a lot of guests, which means a large number of cars, which may result in a traffic jam and parking problems, and consequently in minor violations of the traffic or parking laws, which finally may bring upon the scene the corner cop. It is therefore advisable to notify your neighborhood police station the day before you intend to hold a very large reception in your home. In some towns, the officer in charge will even assign one or two auxiliary policemen to supervise the traffic and parking problems and to keep an eye on the empty cars. If so, you should not fail to invite the policemen into the kitchen after the party is over or when they are about to go off duty and offer them some party refreshments, along with the standard fee, which is generally ten dollars, plus a tip if you wish. It is also thoughtful to have them served a mug of hot coffee in the winter and a cold drink if the weather is very warm.

In a large city, the relationship between the police force and the taxpayers is, of course, less friendly than in a small country town. But it still might be worthwhile to notify the local precinct when you are giving a very large party, especially if your guest list includes any diplomatic or government dignitaries. You may find that the local authorities are willing to relax the parking restrictions on your street for the occasion—at least, it might be worth trying.

In France, if there is a cabinet minister among your invited guests, you are entitled (for a fee) to bring out the Garde Republicaine, with its colorful uniforms, shiny plumed helmets, and prancing steeds. Needless to add, in order to merit the mobilization of even a tiny fraction of the police force or the Republican Guard, your party should be very big, very important, very lavish, and the company very distinguished. I hasten to add that on normal entertaining occasions, the presence of a uniformed policeman in front of your house is far more likely to disquiet your guests than to reassure them!

POT LUCK

❲ I cannot think of a single instance in which it would be really un-reasonable to ask a hostess to accept an unexpected guest for dinner or a supplementary guest at a party. Moreover, it seems to me that it is one of the responsibilities of a wife to organize her household, and particularly her kitchen, in such a way that her husband can feel free to bring home an unexpected dinner guest whenever he wishes.

Perhaps my feelings are somewhat influenced by the fact that I hap-pen to adore eating party leftovers at luncheon the next day, and so I always estimate the quantities of my dinner party shopping list very generously. If there are to be four of us, I prepare enough for six (but in this case there is seldom anything left over!); if the dinner is for eight, I prepare enough for ten or twelve. (And when you organize a large buffet for fifty people or more, it is safest to order one and a half times the normal quantities of food—*see* Buffets.)

Every woman is aware of the invaluable services that can be ren-dered by a well-stocked emergency shelf. Each time I discover some new product that is particularly quick and easy (quick-cooking rice, for example) or a canned food that is really good (but unfortunately there are not very many truly delicious canned or frozen preparations), I buy an extra supply for my emergency shelf. There are certain basic ingredients that should always be kept on hand in ample quantities: milk, eggs, cheese (the hard types such as Gruyère and Edam keep the longest, and when grated they can be used to transform any ordinary vegetable into a tasty gratiné dish), potatoes, rice, pasta, carrots, onions, oranges, canned fruit compotes (peaches, pears), canned vegeta-bles and macédoine, chocolate, etc. Almonds and walnuts are surpris-ingly useful in various ways, as are canned tuna fish, sardines, crab-meat, anchovies, olives, canned lobster or shrimp bisque (as a base for sauces), bouillon cubes, tomatoes and tomato paste, chutney, and vari-ous sweet and tart condiments. It is an excellent insurance to have in the pantry some luxurious treat as well, such as a whole canned foie gras, a whole canned ham, or canned wild rice.

Since you should always plan your dinner parties so generously that you can easily take care of an extra guest or even two without having to make the slightest adjustment in your menu, the only kind of unexpected company that is likely to cause a problem is the guest your husband brings home unexpectedly from the office, the surprise visitor who happens to be passing through your town, or the close friends who have come for a drink and whom you spontaneously invite to stay for dinner and to share with you, as we say, *la fortune du pot*—pot luck.

There are two principal methods of transforming a simple family meal into a company dinner: to devise an entirely different menu, or to expand the menu you had originally planned to serve.

If it was to be an extremely simple, frugal meal, it would perhaps be better to scrap everything and to start again from scratch, relying on the resources of your freezer and your emergency shelf—and also on the goodwill of your husband, whom you can ask to stop at the liquor store and drugstore on his way home to pick up some wine and ice cream, and perhaps at the bakery and delicatessen for a cake and an assortment of cold meats.

A number of the sections in this book are filled with appropriate menus and recipes for pot-luck entertaining. An omelette, for example, is always an excellent entrée for a very informal dinner, even one that has been planned days in advance. With a can of crabmeat, a jar of capers, mayonnaise, and tomato ketchup, plus a few lettuce leaves and tomatoes if you have any, you can prepare a very tasty cold seafood salad for a first course. Then there are all the canned soups, hot and cold, which are simple to dress up with a dash of sherry or an attractive garnish. With a few hard-boiled eggs and some tins from the emergency shelf, you can always compose an appetizing tray of hors d'oeuvres.

The main course is, I must admit, more difficult, when you have nothing fresh to use as a base. Meat, fowl, and delicate fish seldom take well to modern processes of conservation, with the exception of cooked ham. If you have on hand a whole canned ham, you can serve it in any number of ways, hot or cold. First of all, you can follow the directions on the can for heating it in the oven after coating it with a brown sugar and mustard paste and studding it with cloves; and if you place around the ham peach halves, prunes, or pineapple slices dotted with butter and baste it all from time to time with the fruit juice, you will have prepared quite a gala main dish. Cold sliced ham is always an acceptable main course for a light meal, accompanied by a mixed green salad or a Russian salad made from frozen or canned mixed vegetables seasoned with mayonnaise. Finally, an excellent way of disguising your canned cooked ham is to cut it in rather thick slices, which you sauté in butter; then add a glass or two of port, Madeira, or sherry wine, cover and let the ham absorb part of the wine as it heats; the rest will blend with the butter and ham juices to form a delicious sauce. If you serve this with frozen chopped spinach, plain or creamed, you will have created in no time at all an amazingly good imitation of one of the specialties of Fouquet's restaurant in Paris.

Most of the time, however, you will not need to rely entirely on your emergency supplies to prepare your pot-luck dinners, because your original menu can usually be expanded to fulfill the requirements of a company meal.

Here again, there are two basic methods: you can either retain your present dishes but simply serve them in smaller portions, and add an extra course or two; or you can enrich and expand each different dish.

For example, if the main dish was to be a roast of meat or fowl, you can serve the same roast in smaller portions and add an entrée course (omelette, hors d'oeuvres *variés*), a cheese course, if possible, or a rich dessert. You might transform a plain lettuce and tomato salad into a delicious *salade Niçoise* and serve it as a refreshing first course instead of as an accompaniment to the meat. To do this, you simply line a large salad bowl with the lettuce, place in the middle the contents of a drained, chilled can of French string beans, and in the middle of that chunks from a large can of tuna fish; surround it with tomato wedges (and cucumbers and radishes, too, if you happen to have them), and quarters of hard-boiled egg; decorate with olives, green or black, and with anchovy filets. Just before serving, you pour over everything a well-seasoned vinaigrette dressing, and mix well.

If your main dish was to be individual steaks, you might expand them into a mixed grill by adding bacon, broiled tomatoes and mushrooms, and sausages. Or, if you have bought veal scallops, you can pound them thin, cut them in two, roll them around a stuffing and prepare a dish of veal birds, which will serve twice as many people. Another idea is to cut the scallops in half and pound them thin, cover with a thin slice of ham and one of Swiss cheese, top with the other half of the scallop, dip in egg and fine bread crumbs, and sauté; serve them with buttered spaghetti and a green salad, and you will have a very filling Italian-style main dish.

You can "stretch" a small roast chicken by serving it with a hot (canned), unsweetened chestnut purée, whipped like mashed potatoes with butter and cream.

Small roasts of meat can always be enriched by presenting them with a surrounding vegetable garnish: *jardinière,* for example, which means little mounds of assorted vegetables, such as carrots, parsnips, tiny onions, peas, and string beans; or surrounded by little cups of heated canned artichoke bottoms filled with heated canned peas. If the meat is obviously insufficient in quantity to be served as a roast, there is always the possibility of cutting it into small pieces and combining it with buttered noodles or curried rice, vegetables if you wish, a sauce and herbs to make a genuine "pot-luck" casserole creation.

As you see, there are infinite possibilities for transforming a simple family meal into company fare, and it can be most amusing to exercise your ingenuity in this way. So, if your husband should telephone you from the office as you are setting the table for dinner to announce that he is bringing home a guest or even two, you should consider it a delightful surprise. Review your menu quickly and coolly, and instruct your husband as to what he is to pick up on his way home. Prepare some excellent Martinis in the living room and set out a few bowls of cocktail snacks to keep your guests occupied while you are busy with your kitchen sorcery. Treat the occasion as a lark and not as a tiresome chore. I would be very much surprised if you do not spend a most agreeable evening, and if you do not enjoy immensely the admiration of your unexpected company and of your proud husband—and last but not least, the warm appreciation he expresses to you after the guests have gone.

(See Quick Tricks)

PUNCH

❲ Punch drinks have gone out of fashion in recent years everywhere except in the Tropics, probably because of the current penchant for straight, unmixed alcoholic beverages. Perhaps they also came into disfavor because they were too often made with inferior materials, in the hope that the taste of a cheap rum, for example, would be drowned out by the taste of the lemon juice, grenadine, or other flavoring ingredients.

And yet a delicious punch invariably adds an original note to an informal cocktail party, as well as a great deal of *ambiance*. For a very large reception on a budget, an excellent cold champagne punch made with imported wine is far preferable to a cheap imitation champagne served from the familiar bottle. A wine punch, such as the Spanish *sangria*, is a very pleasant accompaniment to a buffet menu, especially in the summertime. And finally, there are the hot punches, such as hot buttered rum and hot mulled wine, all of them festive holiday drinks that are particularly appropriate at Christmastime.

The first rule for making a successful punch is to use only first-class ingredients. You would not use a vintage wine, of course, which would be heresy. But you should select a good ordinary table wine; the cognac, rum, or liqueurs should be of excellent quality; and the fruit and fruit juice should be fresh rather than canned or frozen.

A cocktail punch, usually with a rum base, should be stronger than a wine punch that is served in accompaniment to a meal or that is destined to be drunk throughout an entire evening (in which case it is often diluted with fruit juice or Seltzer water). In order to avoid diluting the cocktail mixture too much with melted ice, it is best to chill the punch in a pitcher in the refrigerator for at least an hour before serving. As a matter of fact, all punch recipes should be mixed at least an hour ahead of time in order to permit the various ingredients to blend. To prevent overdilution of wine punches served in a large punch bowl (which can be rented), you should also chill the mixture ahead of time, use only very large blocks of ice inside the bowl and, whenever possible, imbed the bowl in a block of ice or in a container filled with cracked ice.

Cold punches are usually garnished with fresh fruit. Sliced lemons and oranges are generally essential ingredients, but you should not let yourself be carried away by the appealing image of strawberries, cherries, and pineapple rings afloat in a frosty punch bowl. Most fruit becomes soggy very quickly and the bowl soon looks like a mess. It is therefore better to place the nonessential fruit garnish around the edges of the bowl rather than inside it.

Here are a few recipes for punch that I have managed to gather from among my friends in Paris. Most of them, I must admit, said that they never serve punch themselves, but they remembered a recipe that their great-uncle had brought back from a voyage to Martinique, or that their grandmother used to serve. As I said, punch is not very fashionable at the moment! But, who knows? A good recipe for punch, which is rather hard to come by, may one day again become a useful element in the recipe collection of an elegant hostess.

Hot Mulled Wine

As for all wine punches, use a wine of good ordinary table quality that you would be perfectly willing to drink in its natural state. Since the addition of spices will make the wine cloudy, you can, if you like, strain it when pouring it into the mugs or glasses. The principal problem is to keep the wine very hot without ever boiling.

To serve six people, dissolve 1 cup of sugar in ½ cup of water in a saucepan. Add and heat 2 bottles of red wine, and 1 cup of lemon juice. Then add the rind of an orange and the rind of a lemon, each cut into a long spiral, 24 cloves, 3 sticks of cinnamon and 2 jiggers of brandy. (The rinds may be replaced by 2 whole tangerines into which the cloves are stuck.) Heat without boiling and serve very hot, sprinkling each serving with a little powdered or grated nutmeg.

Trinidad Rum Punch

Mix in a pitcher 1 part cane-sugar syrup to 2 parts rum, or 1 part sugar syrup, 1 part rum and 1 part fresh lemon juice. Add a little grated lemon rind (only the outer yellow part), and a few slices of fresh pineapple. Chill for one hour. Fill a tumbler with cracked ice and pour the punch mixture into it through a strainer. Serve with straws.

White Wine Cup

The recommended proportions are 1 bottle of dry white wine (Muscadet, Moselle, etc.) to 1 bottle of club soda or Seltzer water, but the soda can be reduced to ½ or even ¼ of a bottle if a stronger punch is desired. In a bowl, place a generous quantity of cut fresh fruit: peaches, pineapple, strawberries, apricots—either a single variety or a combination. Sprinkle over the fruit 1 cup of powdered sugar. Let stand for one hour. Stir, pour over a block of ice in a large punch bowl. Add the wine, soda water, and a liqueur glass of brandy for every 2 bottles of wine.

Hot Mulled Cider

Pour into a large saucepan 1 quart of hard cider. Add the rind from 1 lemon (only the yellow part), 3 tablespoons of honey, ½ teaspoon of powdered cinnamon, and a pinch of nutmeg. Heat gently, stirring occasionally. When the mixture is very hot but not boiling, add 6 slices of unpeeled orange, with a clove stuck in each slice. (Six servings.)

Peach Cup

For four people, cut 2 large peaches into small pieces with a silver knife and place them along with the peach juice in a large glass pitcher. Add 2 tablespoons of granulated sugar and about 8 ice cubes. Pour over everything 1 bottle of chilled Rhine wine and ¼ cup of Grand Marnier liqueur. Stir thoroughly, cover, and place in the refrigerator until serving time.

QUANTITY

❴ Preparing refreshments or an entire meal for a very large number of guests is a specialized branch of the culinary art, requiring special recipes, special techniques, and special equipment. It is therefore advisable whenever possible to hire an experienced caterer to handle mass receptions when, for example, you must feed more than forty or fifty guests.

When you are preparing a meal for over twenty persons or so in your own kitchen, you should know that doubling a normal recipe will give satisfactory results in most cases, but if you attempt to triple or quadruple it, you may be in for an unpleasant surprise. Furthermore, certain dishes such as omelettes, soufflés, and custards will succeed perfectly only when they are made in moderate quantities. And the larger a roast, fowl, or piece of game, the older and less tender it is likely to be. There is also a maximum size for many kinds of fish, beyond which the taste and texture deteriorate noticeably in quality. It is always safer to prepare two batches of a normal recipe, two medium-sized roasts, two turkeys, etc. Besides, when there are two serving platters passed simultaneously around the table at a sit-down dinner or placed at opposite ends of a buffet table, the service will be smoother and twice as fast. As a general rule, if there are more than twelve dinner guests, it is advantageous to prepare duplicate serving dishes.

Even if you are able to manage all of the cooking for a large party in your own kitchen and with your own equipment, it will probably be necessary to rent or borrow a large-sized coffee percolator in order to serve all of your guests with freshly brewed coffee at the same time.

Remember, too, that a great quantity of string beans, carrots, or fresh peas can take a very long time to prepare. You must, for that matter, leave more preparation time for everything, even for setting the table. It is only logical that laying twenty-four place settings will take twice as long as laying twelve—perhaps as long as two full hours. But many hostesses never think of this. Finally, don't forget to take into account the size of your oven and the number of burners on top of your stove.

It is always wise to select simple, familiar recipes for quantity cooking, such as *pot au feu,* spaghetti and meatballs, boeuf stroganoff with rice or noodles, chop suey or sukiyaki, Hungarian goulash with dumplings, etc. The simplest plan of all would be to have this main dish prepared by a local Italian, Chinese, or Hungarian restaurant, as the case may be, and to concentrate your own efforts on a delicious original salad and a marvelous homemade pie or cake for dessert. (You will probably have to make several of them.)

But the most important point is never to underestimate the longer time required for quantity cooking. And do not underestimate the appetite of your guests either! The more copious the quantity of food in view on a platter or a buffet, the more generously your guests are apt to serve themselves.

To help guide you in your marketing, here are the quantities of various foods that you may use as a basis for your calculations. These portions are generous rather than skimpy, but you should realize that certain fatty meats and fowl reduce a great deal during the cooking process and therefore require a large amount per serving.

Fish & Seafood

Whole fish	½ to 1 pound per person
Boneless fish, such as swordfish, halibut, haddock, cod	⅓ pound per person
Fish steaks, such as tuna and salmon	½ pound per person
Small or medium soles and trout	1 fish per person

Filets of sole	2 filets per person as an entrée, 4 as a main dish
Oysters on the half shell	6 large or 9 medium per person
Mussels and steamed clams	1 quart per person
Broiled lobster	1 1¼ pound live lobster per person, or ½ lobster on a mixed seafood plate
Shrimp and scallops	⅓ pound per person
Cherrystone clams	6 or 9 per person
Caviar	2 ounces per person

Meat, Poultry & Game

Beef steaks	⅓ to ½ pound per person
Roast beef	⅓ to ½ pound per person
Lamb roast with bone	½ pound per person
Lamb chops	2 large or 3 small per person
Bacon	3–4 slices per person
Egg dishes	2 eggs per person or 3 if they are very small
Spareribs	1 pound per person
Hamburger	¼ pound per serving
Sweetbreads	½ pair per person
Kidneys	1 veal kidney, 3 lamb kidneys per person
Tongue	⅓ pound per person
Rabbit	1 rabbit yields 6–8 portions
Roast chicken	⅓ pound per person, or 1 chicken for four persons
Broiled chicken	½ broiler per person
Fried or sautéed chicken	2 pieces per person
Roast turkey	1 pound per person
Partridge	½ a large bird per person, 1 whole young partridge at the beginning of the season
Duck and goose	1–1½ pound per person
Squab, quail	1 small bird per person
Pheasant and guinea hen	1 bird serves 3–4
Woodcock	2 per person

Vegetables & Miscellaneous

Potatoes—1 pound of raw, unpeeled potatoes yields 2 cups of mashed
  potatoes
Macaroni and spaghetti—1 cup uncooked yields 2–2½ cups cooked
Rice—2½ cups uncooked yields 8 cups cooked

Fresh vegetables	½ pound unprepared per person
Dried vegetables (lentils, split peas, etc.)	¼ pound per person
Rice, pasta, macaroni, etc.	¼ pound per person (raw)
Cookies (accompanying an ice cream dessert)	4 per person
Canapés:	
At a cocktail party	6–8 per person
As a first course	8–10 per person

Soup—one quart yields 6 servings

Wine & Beverages

1 pound of coffee	makes about 40 cups
1 pound of tea	makes about 250–300 cups
1 bottle of wine (⅘ of a quart)	6–8 wine glasses
1 bottle of Champagne	6 champagne glasses
1 bottle of aperitif	12–16 cocktail glasses
1 bottle of whisky (⅘ of a quart)	20 jiggers

1 magnum of wine contains twice as much as a normal bottle
1 jeroboam contains the equivalent of 6 normal bottles of wine

QUARRELS

⟨ Even if you have been screaming invective at your husband, or if
he has been treating you with the most abominable mental cruelty
before your guests arrive, it is your absolute duty as a hostess to bury

the hatchet, to dry your tears, to mask with a smile your expression of outraged anger, and to adopt the air of serenity and sweetness that is suitable to a happily married couple—at least as long as your guests are present.

In no case should you relax your self-control by murmuring snide insinuations concerning your husband, or, at the other extreme, by assuming an attitude of stubborn silence, punctuated only by painful sighs, or by doing anything that might in any way cause the slightest embarrassment to your guests.

I will never forget a certain weekend my husband and I spent with friends in the country. The intensity of their passion for each other was only equaled by the violence of their quarrels. We arrived right after one of these terrible scenes (which, I suppose, they actually enjoy very much since their marriage has thrived on this particular regime for over twenty-five years.) A terrified cook met us on the doorstep, in a state of helpless despair because she had received no orders for dinner since Madame was sobbing in her bedroom and Monsieur had left for Paris in a rage.

The next day, everything was patched up and the household returned to normal. But nobody has the right to impose this kind of a family drama on even the most intimate of friends, and oddly enough, we have never happened to be free when this stormy couple invited us again.

Moreover, it is a well-known fact that the protagonists of such untimely family scenes are even less likely to forgive and forget than are the innocent witnesses. In this particular case, we did not see each other for at least ten years afterward, while previously never a week went by without our getting together.

QUICK TRICKS

— To make canned soup appear homemade, add a fresh garnish such as diced, peeled, and seeded fresh tomatoes to canned tomato soup; a handful of cooked leftover peas to pea soup; finely chopped raw celery to cream of celery soup; chopped chives, cream, butter, or Parmesan cheese to all sorts of cream soups.

—Canned artichoke bottoms can be sautéed in butter and filled with heated canned peas to make an excellent accompaniment to grilled steak or chops. You might also fill them with sautéed or creamed canned mushrooms.

—A box of pancake mix is a mine of quick dishes. You can make them very thin and roll them around a filling of creamed leftover meat, chicken, or seafood, or even creamed spinach for a vegetarian entrée. You can serve them (salted) with salmon caviar, or (sugared) with jam. Different fillings can turn them into an entrée, main dish, or dessert.

—Drugstore ice cream can be transformed into sumptuous sundaes if you always keep in the pantry jars of chocolate fudge and butter-scotch sauce and tins of almonds, walnuts, and pecans.

—To prepare an ultrarapid three-course meal, plan on having one cold dish, one egg dish, and one broiled.

—An individual omelette takes two minutes to cook and no more than five to prepare. Depending on the filling, it can be served as an entrée, main dish, or dessert.

—To make creamy scrambled eggs in five minutes, stir them constantly in a frying pan, removing the pan from the burner whenever they seem to be cooking too fast, and briskly stir in a generous tablespoonful of fresh butter the moment they start to set.

—To make a vinaigrette dressing in two minutes: place all of the ingredients in a screw-top jar and shake hard.

—To prepare tomatoes quickly, dip them for one minute in boiling water and the skins will come off in one piece. Cut them in half and squeeze to remove the seeds.

—Hard-boiled eggs can be shelled in no time at all if they are plunged in cold water as soon as they are removed from the fire.

—You can heat your dinner rolls at the same time you cook your vegetable, if you place them, covered, in the top part of a double boiler, while the vegetables cook in a very little water in the bottom part.

—If you are often called upon to prepare last-minute meals, you might cook your potatoes and rice in double quantities in order to use the leftovers cold in a salad or reheated in any number of quick casserole main dishes.

—At the back of your personal recipe book, make a special list of quick dishes, emergency shortcuts, and complete menus. With a little practice and a well-stocked emergency shelf, you will be surprised at the number of appetizing meals you can prepare in less than twenty minutes.

(See Pot Luck)

AIN

❨ Unless you live in a region where not a drop of rain has fallen during a certain period for the past two hundred years (and even so, the best established meteorological patterns seem to me to have changed since the advent of the atomic bomb, no matter what the experts say), a hostess should always pose herself the question when she is planning an outdoor party: "What will we do in case of a sudden shower?"

The organizers of outdoor summer concerts and theatrical productions generally select a second date to which the event will be postponed in case of rain, and they are even eligible to subscribe to rain insurance. But postponing a private party is impossible, for you cannot ask your guests to reserve two evenings. Moreover, such events as wedding receptions, birthday parties, Fourth of July celebrations, etc., must be held on a definite date, rain or shine.

Since no effective preventive measures have yet been invented where rainy weather is concerned, the only thing to do is to take as many precautions as you can but still prepare yourself for the worst. If possible, you should select the date for a very large outdoor affair only after taking into account the official weather forecast, the Farmer's Almanac predictions, or—best of all—the opinions of local farmers and sailors.

It is always risky to invite more guests to an outdoor party than you could possibly handle if you were suddenly obliged to transfer the festivities into the house. If your indoor reception rooms are small, and your backyard immense, you can of course have a tent put up for the occasion. This always creates a festive atmosphere, in addition to being good insurance, but a tent is expensive to rent and to install and is therefore suitable only for a very grand party. If you should decide to erect one, you might rent from the same firm a sufficient amount of long canvas carpeting to make runways leading from your house to the tent, for if it rains the ground will become muddy, too. This passageway should really be covered with tenting as well.

In the case of an outdoor barbecue, it is generally possible in the event of a downpour to transfer everything onto a covered patio and to cook your steaks under cover on a portable barbecue grill. You can rent or borrow one if you do not possess one of your own. Otherwise, you must simply transform the barbecue into an informal buffet dinner, doing the cooking in the kitchen and setting the buffet table in the dining room.

If you can entertain twelve people comfortably inside your home, you should be able to receive eighteen in an emergency—in other words, one-third to one-half again as many, although I would not pretend that you will be able to offer this increased number the same degree of comfort and elegance. It is, however, excessively optimistic to imagine that you can handle twice the normal guest capacity of your home if you really had to—unless your house happens to be designed by a Japanese architect and you can roll back all of the inner partitions to make one large room!

Where rain is concerned, we can all take a lesson from the British, who are plagued by one of the wettest climates in the world. This does not stop them from holding garden parties and outdoor receptions, from wearing silk dresses and flower-trimmed organdy hats to the opening of Ascot, and from gaily smiling and chatting even when they have to balance a champagne glass in one hand and an umbrella in the other.

(See Umbrellas)

RENDEZVOUS

⁋ Every time you issue an invitation, you are arranging a rendezvous, and the two vital elements of the rendezvous—the time and place— should always be clearly specified. It is unwise to assume that your best friends know quite well that you always dine at seven-thirty, for they may just as well imagine that since you dine at seven-thirty when you dine alone, you must plan your dinners for eight o'clock when you have company.

Engraved invitations to formal affairs should always bear the address where the party is to be held, and if you are entertaining in a club or a hotel you must be sure to make it clear that it will not take place at your own home. If you live in the country, it is a very good idea to provide your guests from out of town with a hand-drawn printed map of postcard size that clearly shows the way to get to your house from the center of the village, or the parkway turnoff, or some other prominent landmark.

It is never elegant to make a rendezvous on a street corner or in front of a restaurant or hotel. Instead, the hostess should take the trouble to arrive at least ten minutes before the appointed hour and occupy her place at table or in a private salon, as the case may be, after instructing the maître d'hôtel or the hotel reception clerk to direct her guests to her. In a private club, it is often more pleasant to make your rendezvous in the bar, where you can offer your guests a cocktail before dinner and where the headwaiter will announce to you that your dining room table is ready.

In other words, whenever possible you should avoid arranging a rendezvous in a crowded public place. The principal situation in which this is unavoidable is when you have invited friends to the theater, a concert, or the movies. Either you will have dined together beforehand (which is the simplest plan) and you will therefore all arrive at the theater together; or else you will plan to meet at the theater and go on to supper at home or in a restaurant after the program is over. In the latter case, you should try to avoid inflicting on your guests the crush of the line at the box office, and for this reason you should manage to be at the theater well ahead of time and await your guests, tickets in hand, near the entrance. If your guests are late, I do not see why you should be obliged to miss the opening curtain too. You can quite well leave their tickets at the box office in their name and let them grope down the darkened aisle alone to join you.

While absolute promptness is never expected at a dinner party or a luncheon, it is most inconsiderate to make a person wait for you at a rendezvous in a public place. How long should a woman wait in this case? I would say:

For her mother, sister, or her best friend — a half an hour.
For her beau — fifteen minutes.
For her husband — forever!

RESTAURANTS

❡ Modern life is so tiring and household help so rare that very often the simplest solution to entertaining is to take your guests to dinner in a restaurant. At the beginning of the century, married women never dreamed of accompanying their husbands to restaurants, which were frequented only by men and by demimondaines, but today many entire families dine out regularly at least once or twice a week, and I have been told that Americans spend one dollar in restaurants for every three and a half dollars that they spend on home-cooked meals. For foreigners and guests from out of town, this formula is even particularly attractive, although it is less complimentary than inviting them to your own home. Furthermore, a very discriminating hostess would avoid inviting to a restaurant guests whose professional or social position is superior to her own, whereas you can receive the Queen of England in your own house, no matter how modest it may be.

In a restaurant as at home, there are various more or less elegant ways of entertaining. In my opinion, the most pleasant is to invite just one other couple, or two at the very most, and to let them select their own menu. Certain very chic restaurants have special menus on which the prices do not appear, supposedly in order not to embarrass one's guests. But I personally find it much more embarrassing to wonder whether I am ordering the most expensive or the cheapest item and thereby running the risk of either bankrupting my host or of offending him! While it is always tactful for a guest to order dishes in the average price range, the host and hostess should make a point of selecting something rather expensive (even if they secretly long for spaghetti) in order to put their guests at ease.

Normally, you should choose a restaurant well within your means, where you have already dined at least once—and preferably quite recently, if you wish to avoid unpleasant gastronomic or financial surprises. If your budget is very limited indeed and your friends enjoy foreign food, it is useful to know that Chinese and Italian restaurants are generally less expensive than French or American, while in Russian bistros there is always the ruinous temptation of caviar and smoked sturgeon, and in seafood restaurants of smoked salmon and lobster, which can double or triple the bill.

If you are entertaining people whom you do not know very well, it is safe to choose either the most classic, renowned restaurant in town, or the one that serves a cuisine typical of your region. With close friends, on the other hand, it is often amusing to be more adventurous and to try the newest restaurant, or one in a neighboring town or a different part of the city that they would not ordinarily frequent.

Seating your guests at a restaurant table is exactly the same as in your dining room: the honored guests at the right of the host and hostess. But in addition, you should think of placing the women where they will be able to see the rest of the room and especially to be seen themselves! For this reason, places on the banquette are always reserved for the ladies, with the men opposite. But a round table is by far the most agreeable.

It is preferable to reserve your table in advance, and with more than six persons this becomes indispensable. With eight or ten, it is also wise to order the menu twenty-four hours in advance at least, and to decide with the maître d'hôtel exactly which table you wish to reserve. If there is an orchestra, as in many hotel restaurants, it is better not to be too close to the drums and trumpets. If the restaurant you have selected is a very chic one, the guests will be delighted to be seen by everybody else; but if it is merely a bistro where the service is simple and the clientele attracted more by the joys of gastronomy than of elegance, it is preferable to reserve a private dining room whenever possible, or at least to have your table placed in the most secluded corner. If you happen to be celebrating a special occasion such as a birthday or a promotion and you intend to make speeches or toasts, you should by all means reserve a private dining room—unless your guests are so numerous and your means so great that you can reserve the entire restaurant! A private dining room is the formula that most resembles entertaining in your own home, and you can perfectly well invite more important guests.

It is so customary for the man to pay a restaurant check that it is always a rather delicate matter for a single woman to entertain men guests in a restaurant. The most elegant way for her to pay the bill is either to select a restaurant where she is well known or a club to which she belongs and which will mail her the bill afterward; she can also slip away from the table at the end of the meal on some pretext or other and have the bill delivered to her out of sight in the hall or even in the powder room; or she can avoid all of these maneuvers by simply handing her credit card to the waiter and signing the bill, having taken the precaution of selecting a restaurant that honors her particular card.

Unless she herself is hostess, a very courteous woman never gives her order directly to the waiter, but lets her escort do it for her (even if her masculine companion happens to be her own seventeen-year-old son).

It is the custom in most fashionable and pretentious restaurants to write the menu by hand and in French, and it may be comforting to know that the most experienced Parisian gourmets do not hesitate to ask the waiter what some of these mysteriously christened specialties actually consist of, particularly if it is a creation of the chef or any especially recherché recipe. However, there are certain menu terms that every sophisticated woman should understand, some of the most common being:

à l'Anglaise — boiled
Argenteuil — asparagus garnish
à la Basquaise — with pimentos, mushrooms, onions, tomato
en Beignets — fritters
à la Bolognaise — with spaghetti in a meat sauce
Bonne Femme — a rich white wine sauce with mushrooms
à la Bordelaise — with shallots, red wine, beef marrow
à la Bourguignonne — with tiny onions, bacon, spices, mushrooms, red Burgundy wine
en Brochette — broiled on skewers
Chantilly — with whipped cream
Chasseur — tomatoes, onions, mushrooms
Clamart — garnished with green peas
Colbert — usually deep-fried
à l'Espagnole — with tomatoes, olives, onions
Farci — stuffed
Financière — a sort of chicken à la king
Fines Herbes — mixed fresh herbs
à la Florentine — with spinach
au Four — baked or roasted

au Gratin or Gratiné — covered with bread crumbs and butter (and sometimes with cheese) and browned under the broiler, to form a crust

à la Grecque — with a sauce of lemon, olive oil, spices, peppercorns

à l'Indienne — with rice and a curry sauce

Jardinière — an assortment of diced vegetables

Lyonnaise — with onions

Maître d'Hôtel — parsley lemon butter served with grilled meat

Meunière — fried in butter

Milanaise — spaghetti and a tomato sauce

Mornay — in a cream sauce with cheese

Mousseline — mashed potatoes, or a light purée or sauce

Nantua — a rich cream sauce with pieces of shrimp or lobster

Niçoise — with tomatoes, capers, black olives, anchovies

Normande — cream sauce with mushrooms and mussels

à l'Orientale — with rice and a highly spiced sauce of onions, eggplant, tomatoes

Parmentier — with potatoes

Périgueux or Périgourdine — with truffles in a rich sauce

Princesse — with asparagus tips

à la Provençale — tomatoes, onions, peppers, olives

Ravigote — a cold sauce with herbs and diced pickle

Rossini — a slice of foie gras and truffles

Suprême — in a velvety cream sauce

Vert Pré — with watercress and shoestring potatoes

Vinaigrette — French dressing

Vol au Vent — creamed seafood or chicken in a pastry shell

It is easy to guess that:

truite is trout
boeuf is beef
mouton is mutton
veau is veal, etc.

But some French words are completely unrelated to their English equivalent, as for example:

marrons — chestnuts
Coquilles St. Jacques — scallops
ris de veau — sweetbreads
cervelle — brains

rognons — kidneys
foie — liver
poulet — chicken

Nowadays an à la carte restaurant meal (with each dish ordered and priced separately) customarily consists of no more than three courses, starting with an appetizer (hors d'oeuvres), or a soup (*potage*), or eggs (*oeufs*), to be followed by a main dish such as a roast or grilled meat (*rôti* or *grillade*) or a special dish prepared by the chef (*plat du jour*), and finally completed with either a dessert (*dessert* or *entremets*) or cheese (*fromage*). A fish dish (*poisson*) or seafood (*crustacées*) may be chosen either as a first course or as the main course. But the table d'hôte formula is increasingly prevalent, with a selection of several dishes in three or more courses at an inclusive price.

Some restaurants list their main dishes as "Entrées" and it may seem strange to you that throughout these pages I use the word to describe the first course of a meal, such as a fish or egg dish. The reason for this apparent confusion is that modern menu terms have been inherited from the eighteenth century, when a menu was composed of twenty or thirty different dishes, and since our menus have been radically simplified and abbreviated, the old terms have simply been attributed to the courses they seem to fit the best. There is no definite rule, but since the entrée was originally the dish preceding the roast, it is the general usage in France today to designate as an entrée the dish that precedes the main course. There is the same confusion concerning the term *Entremets*, which nowadays is attributed solely to desserts, whereas they originally included vegetables as well. And while we are on the subject, the term "hors d'oeuvres," which literally means "detached from the principal subject," originated in the fact that they used to be served between the courses of a meal, as a sort of extra snack to keep the diners occupied while awaiting the following course.

One of the responsibilities of the host is to order the wine. While he should always consult his guests as to their personal preferences, it is usually simplest, when a variety of different dishes has been ordered, to choose a single wine that will go with everything: champagne, rosé, or even a young Beaujolais served slightly chilled. On the other hand, if everybody has ordered the same menu, for example fish or steak, the host can display his knowledge of wine by making a more epicurean selection. If you are inexperienced in this field, it may reassure you to know that many recognized connoisseurs prefer to ask the wine steward for his recommendation.

Incidentally, the wine waiter's tradition of pouring a bit of wine into the host's glass and awaiting his verdict before serving the others is not merely empty ritual. Neither is the purpose (as I have actually heard it claimed) to make sure that any stray bits of cork will be served only to the host! The fact is that improper storage or traveling conditions may cause wine to become vinegary or "corked," which means that it is irremediably spoiled. Normally you can detect the peculiar bitter or sour taste with the very first sip, but it is somewhat more difficult if you have had several cocktails and cigarettes immediately beforehand. If you have had any serious doubts but are unsure of your own competence in the matter, do not hesitate to ask the wine steward discreetly to taste it for you. While nothing is more affected and ridiculous than to stage a lengthy wine-tasting session in order to impress your guests, there is no reason either to oblige them to drink a bad wine.

In elegant restaurants you can dally over your coffee (followed by liqueurs and brandy and cigars, if you feel like Croesus) for as long as you like. Host and guests leave all together, even if the dinner has taken place in a private room, and you bid each other good night at the door where you separate to find your respective transportation. In a restaurant-cabaret, you would naturally stay until the end of the show, when the hostess gives the signal to leave at her discretion.

But in a small bistro, where other clients are perhaps waiting impatiently for your table, it is awkward to linger after the meal has been finished. At the same time, you may not wish to see your party break up prematurely. In these circumstances, the best plan is for the hostess to ask everybody to meet for an afterdinner drink at her home, where she has had the foresight to prepare the necessary refreshments (long drinks, brandy, fruit juice, perhaps champagne and, as a thoughtful gesture, some particularly delicious bonbons).

As a matter of fact, except in the case of a restaurant with dancing or a floor show, it is always more personal if at least a small part of the evening is spent in the home of the host, either for cocktails beforehand or for a drink afterward. The only major complication is the transportation problem, but this exists only when there are more than eight of you altogether, in other words, when you need more than two cars. For a larger party, you can be sure that the meal will take far more time to serve, and if you ask your guests to meet you at the restaurant at, say, eight o'clock, it will probably be at least eleven before the coffee has been cleared away, which is a perfectly respectable time to say good night to all but inveterate night owls.

In short, entertaining in a restaurant is far simpler, less personal, and usually more costly than entertaining at home. The only awkward moment occurs when it is time to pay the check, and the host should always arrange in one way or another to settle his bill out of sight of his guests. Even when I have been invited by a millionaire, the spectacle of a huge sum of money being handed to the waiter has always filled me with embarrassment and a sense of wastefulness—although I must admit that I have never given a thought to the expense my hosts may have gone to when they entertain me in their home!

(See Nightclub, Wine)

ROMANCE

❲ Ever since Eve, clever women have been enticing their masculine prey with gastronomic temptations, and with such a high degree of success that no doubt far more proposals of marriage have been inspired by the aroma of a steaming oyster stew than by the musky scent of exotic perfume.

Romance and entertaining go hand in hand, since the courtship period is often no more than a series of luncheon and dinner dates. In our society at least, the burden of the entertaining is on the suitor. However, it is only natural for the woman to respond occasionally to these attentions by entertaining him in return, the most conventional forms being an invitation to a concert or the theater, a small dinner with several other friends, or a cocktail party. If a woman wishes to show her interest in a man whom she would like to know better, she can ask him to escort her to a cocktail or dinner party given by friends.

Whether or not a woman who lives alone should invite a man to dinner *à deux* in her home or apartment is a more delicate question, which depends upon local etiquette and customs as well as upon the age, character, and intentions of the persons involved. I am not personally very experienced in this field, since I was never even permitted to be alone with my future husband until we were engaged, and come to think of it, the first time we dined alone together was on the evening of our honeymoon. Nevertheless, I am convinced that the more serious a woman's romantic intentions are, the more scrupulously she should avoid any obvious attempts to create a romantic atmosphere. Compromising tactics frighten away many more potential husbands than they attract. It is far more effective strategy for a woman who wishes to encourage a timid suitor to invite him to an informal dinner party with one or two other couples—preferably those who are obviously happily married, for this is not the moment to expose the negative side of married life. And so, paradoxically enough, the entertaining that is most likely to further romance is the least romantic in mood and character—at least until a woman is married.

After that happy day, you can indulge yourself to your heart's content in preparing charming little romantic meals for your husband. You can even amuse him from time to time by dressing in a femme fatale at-home ensemble and setting the table for a change in front of the fireplace with candlelight, champagne, and a choice menu, in the best Hollywood tradition. But don't overdo it, or his initial amusement may turn into anguish as he calculates the percentage of the household budget that has been invested in your seductive scene.

Whatever the mood and the occasion, it is wise to remember, when you plan a meal to please a man, that masculine taste in food is often quite different from a woman's. While each individual has, of course, his particular preferences, there are certain generalities that are usually valid. As a rule, men prefer:

— Straightforward, familiar dishes of excellent quality, perfectly prepared and generously served.

— Food that is easily recognizable for what it is.

— Dishes that are simple to eat and do not necessitate an assortment of special tools.

— Dishes that "Mother used to make," which recall their happy childhood.

— Hearty foods, with the emphasis on meat and fish (particularly beef, game, fresh salmon, and trout).

— Simple garnishing. A few sprigs of parsley or watercress, a fan of lemon wedges, are more appetizing in their eyes than fancy cut-out pastry and elaborate kitchen sculpture.

—Marvelous sweet desserts, especially freshly baked homemade fruit pies served hot from the oven, and anything with chocolate in it.

Unfortunately, as you may have noted, many of the dishes men like the most are also most apt to make them feel drowsy rather than amorous after dinner. If you are determined that your husband's passion for food should not conflict with his other passions, you might consider incorporating in your menu certain ingredients that have acquired throughout the ages a reputation for favoring romance, such as:

—Asparagus and artichokes (The latter were even considered taboo for unmarried young girls at one time, because of the stimulating properties that were attributed to them.)

—Truffles (Napoleon is said to have ordered a steady diet of truffled turkey in order to further his chances of fathering an heir.)

—Celery (Madame de Pompadour, afraid of losing the affections of Louis XV to a younger, more exciting mistress, is supposed to have eaten quantities of raw celery every morning in the belief that this would increase her "temperament.")

—Oysters (Casanova is reported to have swallowed no less than fifty a day.)

—Fresh shrimp, crayfish, and all lean fish, in particular the salt-water varieties

—Anise, cinnamon, curry (an invigorant), nutmeg, freshly ground black pepper, saffron, and especially vanilla

—Fresh eggs

—Caviar and shad roe (The second is less spectacular in effect than the first, but then it is also much less expensive.)

—Calves' brains

—And finally, champagne—but only in moderation!

SEATING

[Aside from diplomatic and official functions where protocol is law, the modern hostess is more often concerned with personal affinities than with rules of precedence when seating her guests around a luncheon or dinner table.

The starting point should always be the places of honor to the right of the host and hostess, which are reserved for the most important and distinguished guests, with the others placed in the order most likely to produce an interesting and animated conversation, alternating the men and women as far as possible, and separating husbands from wives. Among a group of close friends where no one particularly outranks another, the place of honor should go to a foreigner (who is accorded a courtesy precedence over all others), the oldest guest, or one whom you are receiving in your home for the first time. Precedence in family reunions is always according to age. Strangers rank higher than family, married people higher than bachelors, and wives are accorded the importance of their husbands.

It is perfectly simple to seat a group of six, ten, or fourteen guests, but seating a party of eight or twelve or sixteen at a rectangular table is more complicated, because it becomes impossible to avoid placing two men and two women side by side when the hostess sits at one end of the table and the host at the other. The best solution is to have the hostess sit at the middle of one side of the table, opposite the honored woman guest who will be at the right of the host, or to set two places at each end as if the table were square, with the hostess placing the honored man on her right and a woman on her left, while the host, who is diagonally opposite, has the honored woman next to him on his right and a man at his left. The hostess can thus place opposite her in the usual seat of the host the most important woman guest, who will have the most important man on her right and the host on her left. A single woman would seat opposite her the most important man or woman guest, depending on the number of guests, that is, with six, ten, or fourteen, a man, and with eight or twelve, a woman.

There is no seating problem at all with a round table, which is one of the reasons why it is the formula I prefer.

For a large dinner of ten or twelve or more, it is a good idea to place a handwritten plan of the seating arrangement on a table at the entrance to the dining room or on the sideboard. But most of the guests won't bother to consult it (or won't have their reading glasses available), so it is indispensable to have place cards as well and for the hostess to know her plan by heart so that she can indicate their places to bewildered guests.

The superstitious fear of thirteen at table is so widespread that it should be avoided by all means. If you cannot find a last-minute guest, you may ask one of your grown-up children to join you at table. Or you can seat your guests at two separate tables, or even serve the meal buffet-style.

An experienced hostess plans her seating arrangement practically at the same time that she plans the menu. In any case, it should never be left to last-minute inspiration, no matter how informal the party nor how intimate your friends may be. Nothing is more gauche than to have to ask a guest to change his place once he has been seated, or for the hostess to keep everybody standing in awkward anticipation while she frantically improvises a seating plan. Since there is no insoluble problem in this field (unless you are involved in high-level diplomatic entertaining, in which case you can always telephone for advice to the Protocol Office of the State Department, which adores really knotty problems), and since it is usually a matter of no more than a few minutes' reflection, unpreparedness is inexcusable.

(See Place Cards)

SERVANTS

⟨ Haven't you noticed that certain families have the same household personnel all their lives, while in others there is a permanent parade of new help? All of the faults are not always on the side of the employers, but it seldom occurs to the women who are unable to keep the same servants for any length of time that they have perhaps failed to respect the most elementary rules of simple courtesy in dealing with those who serve them.

Gone are the days of "Come here, my good man," as one would say, "Here, Fido!"; and vanished forever the fourteen-hour day with no holidays or Sundays. The relations between employers and servants have changed as much during the past fifty years as have our means of transportation.

In this day and age when there are more employers than servants, you must, if you wish to keep your help:

(1.) Consider them as human beings and interest yourself in their personal problems, without, however, prying or being too familiar.

(2.) Never ask them to do anything that you would not be willing and capable of doing yourself. In the case of cooking, you should at least be able to furnish the correct recipe.

(3.) Give them the same food and the same degree of comfort that you yourself enjoy.

(4.) Never gild the lily when you engage new servants by saying that they will have very little to do, but on the contrary explain in detail everything you expect of them, including the exact daily schedule.

(5.) Pay the normal wages and pay them on time. (I have put this last because nowadays it is the servants who set the rates and not the employers.)

At the same time, you are perfectly within your rights in requiring that:

(1.) They should always be neat and well groomed (hair as well as their clothing).

(2.) They should address you with respect, neither obsequiously nor as if they were members of the family.

(3.) They should be scrupulously honest in their household accounts.

(4.) They should be willing to give you an extra hour or two without quibbling in the case of illness or a big party.

(5.) They should not expect you to support all of their relatives.

(6.) They should never borrow your prettiest sweater to wear to the movies on Saturday night.

(See Help, Service)

SERVICE

❲ The organization of a formal dinner is a rather delicate undertaking, and even very complex if you wish everything to be absolutely perfect. Without considering for the moment the problems involved in planning the menu and preparing the food, there remains the no less important question of serving it.

Have you never been troubled during a dinner party by a well-meaning waiter whose hesitant or brusque gesture collides with your own, leaving visible traces of the accident on the tablecloth or on your sleeve? And have you never experienced the disappointment of seeing a harried waiter whisk away your plate containing the choice morsel you had purposely saved for the end—perhaps that last little piece of cheese that was to accompany the last sip of a fine Burgundy wine, and at the very moment you were vaunting the gastronomic pleasure of this particular combination to your dinner partner? And have you never had to wait for the Hollandaise sauce so long that the filet of turbot as well as your plate had become stone cold? The art of serving at table is no less complicated than the art of cooking, and a meal that is well prepared but badly served is no better than one that is well served but badly prepared. Both preparation and service must be excellent if the final result is to be perfect.

Hot dishes, which should always be served very hot, must be arranged on their serving dishes very rapidly, and consequently in a simple manner. The platter should be just as presentable and appetizing when the last guest is served as when it first arrives from the kitchen, instead of becoming as devastated as a battlefield as soon as two or three guests have served themselves. This is another good reason for avoiding complicated presentations such as towering structures that are certain to collapse the moment a portion is removed.

Elaborate garnishes such as croutons of fried bread piled with mounds of truffles, prawns, fancily cut mushrooms and artistically sculptured lemons are also eliminated from modern cuisine. Such culinary fancies as coxcombs dipped in sauce and congealed in a coating of gelatin are no longer in fashion. It wasn't only aspic that used to be the object of this mania for architectural effects. How many packages of gelatin have been used to reinforce the natural gelatinous properties of meat, fowl, game, and fish, thus sacrificing finesse of taste in the interest of bolstering the presentation so that it would hold up until the end of the meal! Modern gourmets appreciate the delicate flavor and consistency of natural gelatin enough to forgive its tendency to melt in the warm atmosphere of the dining room, and since it cannot resist the warmth for very long, we have fortunately abandoned the custom of placing cold jellied dishes in the center of the table as a decoration. Nowadays these dishes are kept in the refrigerator until the very last minute and are taken out only just before they are to be served, which is a very good thing.

Fish that is served whole and is cooked in a court bouillon should be removed from the hot liquid only five minutes at the most before it leaves the kitchen en route for the dining table. In a flash, it must be boned and skinned and slipped onto the platter, which has been covered with a folded napkin and decorated with a very thin border of parsley. Like all serving dishes, the fish platter should be of ample size, in this case large enough to contain the entire fish without having the head or tail overlap at either end. With a sharp knife, the cook should detach the entire upper part of the fish from the central bone; then, with a few rapid diagonal incisions, it is cut into individual portions while still retaining the appearance of a whole fish. The sauce should be poured hot (and not merely warm) into a heated sauceboat. A cook who is worried that her Hollandaise sauce will turn should understand that this risk is simply due to the fact that it does not contain any water. A sauce that threatens to turn can be easily corrected by adding a few tablespoonfuls of water; even better, this process will permit you to reheat the sauce as high as 160 degrees without the slightest danger, this being a temperature that does not coagulate egg yolks.

If the fish is accompanied by boiled potatoes, as is often the case, they should not be arranged on the same platter but presented separately, like the sauce. The ideal method is to have the potatoes and sauce served by a second waiter. When this is impossible, it is best simply to place the sauce and potatoes on the table and have them passed by the guests.

When accompanying garnishes, such as potatoes and vegetables, are arranged on the same platter as the fish, it is quite awkward for the guests to serve themselves, the original arrangement is inevitably upset at once, and the platter soon looks very unappetizing. As far as possible, you should buy a size of fish that will provide enough portions on the top side to serve every guest the first time around the table. Afterward, the waiter should take the platter back to the kitchen or place it on the sideboard in order to remove the central bone and to cut the second half of the fish into somewhat smaller portions than for the first service. In the meantime, his assistant should have returned to the kitchen to refill the sauceboat and the potato dish with hot sauce and potatoes, which he will serve around the table right on the heels of the waiter serving the fish.

Do not worry, I am not going to go into such detail over every separate course of a formal dinner! But I have so often noticed that it is the fish course that is most frequently ill presented and badly served.

The edges of all the serving platters should always be free from garnish, and it goes without saying that they should also be free from drips of sauce or stray pieces of food and, needless to add, from the cook's fingerprints. It is unnecessary to mention the fingerprints of the waiter, for he should always wear immaculate white cotton gloves.

I have seen some hostesses, in their attempt to simplify the problems of table service, present their guests with plates that have already been filled in the kitchen, like a cafeteria blue-plate special. Personally, I am horrified by this method, which is only slightly less shocking in a restaurant. To see the entire fish or roast, to enjoy its aroma, to be able to choose for oneself the wing or the drumstick (especially if you prefer the latter, because most hostesses automatically serve their guests the choicest pieces of white meat) or the heel of the roast—these are joys that a serious gastronome hates to be deprived of. However, at a large formal dinner it is neither necessary nor chic to present a roast or fowl to be admired in its entirety before it has been carved into portions, as is the custom of many smart restaurants.

While the cook should cooperate with the waiter in arranging the serving platters, she should not make the slightest concession as to their temperature. Many waiters protest as soon as a serving dish is too hot to be carried comfortably—but it is my opinion that they should never be allowed to do so. The best method is to have two platters of the same size, one very hot and the other cool, and to place the former inside the latter. This increases the weight, it is true, but it is the only system that permits you to serve a hot dish as hot as it ought to be.

The platters may be arranged several minutes ahead of time, covered with a lid or another platter turned upside down, and kept hot either in front of the open oven or on an electric hot plate or simply over a large receptacle containing boiling water. Serving dishes are always presented to the left of each guest, just as clean plates are served from the left (but removed from the right). If the edge of a platter is ever spattered by food or sauce, the waiter should wipe the spot away discreetly before presenting the dish to the following person.

Among the dishes that ought to be served boiling hot, soup is certainly the one, next to fish, that is most often served merely lukewarm. Perhaps this is because soup is often thickened with egg yolk, and the cook, afraid that it will turn, keeps it at much too low a temperature. And yet it is so simple to place the beaten egg yolk in readiness in the soup tureen and to pour the hot soup over it just before the waiter is ready to serve it. Soup that comes hot from the kitchen should not be ladled into soup plates that have been placed on the table long before the guests are seated. And so it takes two waiters to serve hot soup correctly: one to put the heated soup plates in place, and the other to serve the soup. This is one time when it is advisable for the waiter to call attention discreetly to his presence at a diner's elbow, for a sudden movement could easily result in a calamity that would dismay everybody but the dry cleaner.

Generally, every course of a formal dinner is accompanied by a wine, and the wine should be served at the same time as the dish it accompanies. But it happens all too often that the wine is poured too late, sometimes after the dish has already been consumed, and this is profoundly regrettable. Following a dish is not at all the same as accompanying it.

Although we eat much less bread today than we used to, the waiter should see to it that no guest is ever lacking bread or rolls. A conscientious waiter is not only constantly on his guard to see that the glasses and plates are empty as seldom as possible, but he also frequently casts a rapid glance around the table to make sure that nobody is trying to catch his eye. The host and hostess should also be on the lookout for all of these tiny details, which may be unimportant in themselves, but which contribute much to the pleasure of a well-served meal. The slightest oversight should be quietly brought to the waiter's attention.

Clearing the table is no less delicate a process than serving a meal. The plates should be removed at just the right moment, neither too soon nor too late. The waiter should not remove a plate before it is completely empty without the tacit accord of the diner. He should also be quick to recognize the discreet nod or gesture requesting that a plate be removed.

The perfect guest tries to facilitate the task of the waiters by being attentive when a dish is presented and by refraining from continuing a conversation while the waiter waits!

Knives and forks for each course are removed along with the plates. Most important of all, the waiter should never pile one dish on top of another in railroad dining-car style. Each plate must be served and removed individually—which is why a single waiter cannot be expected to take care of more than six dinner guests, or eight at the very most, and only when the menu is unusually simple to serve. The plates for hot courses should be really hot, and for cold courses and frozen desserts really cold.

All of these recommendations probably seem quite unnecessary to accomplished hostesses who know how to direct the service of a formal dinner. But, alas, there are so few of them!

SHOWERS

❲ The bridal shower is, as far as I know, a strictly American custom, and a very thoughtful one. Its purpose is to equip the newlyweds at the start of their married life with the myriad miscellaneous articles that are indispensable to a home, but that are not very suitable as wedding gifts, and that can amount to a considerable expense if they must be furnished by the bride. In other words, the offering of useful gifts is the raison d'être of a bridal shower, and the entertainment on this occasion consists of opening the packages.

Showers are usually strictly feminine parties in the form of an afternoon tea, and the guests are invited for four or five o'clock one day during the two or three weeks preceding the wedding date. It is common for a fiancée's school or college friends or her colleagues at the office to plan a collective shower, with everyone contributing to the cost of the party. The hostess may also be one of the fiancée's closest friends, or even the best friend of her mother. She should, however, never be a member of the immediate family of the bride.

There is no limit to the number of showers that may be given for a popular bride-to-be, but the number is usually limited automatically by the necessity of avoiding duplication in the guest lists as well as in the gifts. The most useful and usual kinds of showers are a Kitchen Shower (pots and pans, cookbooks, kitchen gadgets and utensils), a Linen Shower (bath, bed, and table linen), and a Lingerie Shower (slips, nightgowns, handkerchiefs, etc.). For widely feted brides whose kitchen and linen showers have already been reserved by other friends, you might plan a Cocktail Shower (bar equipment, highball glasses, liquor, and prepared snacks), a Pantry Shower (deluxe canned goods), a Bathroom Shower (towels, bath, and toilet accessories), a Party Shower (party and guest room equipment), a Record or Book Shower or simply a Miscellaneous Shower—in fact, anything that your imagination and the bride's particular interests and needs may suggest.

It is indispensable to check your guest list with the bride-to-be or, if you're hoping to surprise her, with the other hostesses, in order to avoid inviting the same guests to several different showers. Because of the obligation to bring a gift, a great number of shower invitations would be considered an exaggerated financial burden rather than a compliment. It is also important to include in the invitation as much helpful information as possible to aid your guests in selecting appropriate presents: the bride's lingerie size and preferred shade for a Lingerie Shower, the color scheme of her kitchen or bathrooms, as the case may be, and perhaps a clue as to whether the decoration of her home is to be modern or traditional. Since the packages are opened in front of everybody, it is only considerate to help your guests select gifts that are certain to be admired by everyone. It may also be a good idea to avoid embarrassing contrasts between modest offerings and more lavish presents by setting a general price ceiling, for example, of five or ten dollars. Whenever possible, it is best to offer only articles that can be exchanged.

There is another sound reason for going over your guest list with the bride, if feasible, before you issue your invitations. Unless the wedding is to be a very intimate one, limited to the members of the family, it would be a faux pas to invite to a bridal shower a person who has not been invited to the wedding.

Between twelve and twenty is a good number of guests, and the procedure is generally the same. Everybody is expected to arrive more or less on time, and a glass of sherry or fruit juice may be served right away. When all the guests have assembled, the bride settles down in a prominent spot—behind the living room coffee table, for example—with all of the packages piled before her, and she proceeds to open each one, reading aloud the name of the donor and expressing her ecstatic delight as she examines each item. The opened gifts are then passed around for all to admire. At the end of this performance, the hostess leads everybody to the dining room where the table has been arranged for tea, buffet-style, with a pot of coffee at one end, tea at the other, platters of sandwiches and petit fours, and perhaps a beautiful homemade cake.

The entire party will seldom last longer than two or three hours, and the bride-to-be should remain with the hostess until all the guests have left. At this point, an extremely thoughtful hostess will provide a huge receptacle such as a large laundry hamper—and perhaps the sturdy arms of her husband, too—in order to enable the happy guest of honor to carry home her shower of gifts.

A baby shower is somewhat simpler in that the gifts all have a common denominator, as it were, and the occasion is not likely to take place more than once, which is preferably a few weeks before the due date. The problem of whether pink (for girls) or blue (for boys) will turn out to be suitable is easily resolved by choosing white, which is always acceptable. The refreshments may be the same as for a wedding shower.

SILVER

❲ Silver is the most lustrous metal known to man, but it is only during the last hundred and fifty years that it has been prized more for its beauty than for its intrinsic value. Before 1800, silverware was possessed only by royalty, the Church, and the aristocracy, who converted it into coin whenever they were short of funds. (But even if it were still permitted by law, this practice would no longer be very profitable, because a silver American dollar contains 90 percent silver and 10 percent copper, whereas sterling silver is composed of 925 parts of pure silver and only 75 parts of copper.)

Today, almost every young bride starts out married life with at least a few silver wedding gifts or heirlooms. As a matter of fact, most women have only two opportunities in their lives to acquire an important amount of silver at one time: at their wedding, and on their silver wedding anniversary twenty-five years later. And so it is advisable to take advantage of the wedding-gift period by equipping yourself with the most essential items of silverware that you will need during the next twenty-five years. Some brides are too young to realize that it is far preferable to ask for a wedding present of silver than for a new car.

Silverware place settings are always bought in a complete set, for all of the different pieces should match, with the exception of dessert forks and spoons, which are more chic if they are different from the rest, particularly if they are antique in style or of vermeil. Tiny demitasse spoons may also be of an entirely different pattern and material.

Young brides-to-be ponder a great deal over the problem of selecting their silver pattern, and it is rather difficult to advise them since the most important point, it seems to me, is for them to choose a pattern they really like, for they are going to have to live with it for the rest of their lives. It is, however, generally best to avoid romantic, rococo patterns, not only because it is terribly difficult to keep them clean but also because they harmonize less well with a wide variety of tableware and dining room decors. Modern patterns, if they are not too futuristic, go with every style, and simple classic patterns may be very successfully combined with either classic or modern dishes and decor. In my opinion, many of the pure and modernistic Scandinavian designs are more practical and effective when they are in stainless steel rather than in solid silver, and these informal services are ideal for a country house and family meals.

Wedding silver is usually engraved with the monogram of the bride, and the best choice of a monogram depends principally on the silverware pattern, but also to a certain extent on the particular letters to be interlaced. Although I cannot imagine why, experience has proved to me that smooth modern silver loses its luster much more quickly than pieces that are covered with engraving. In any case, it is always important to select a pattern that will be continued by a well-established silversmith, so that your silver collection can be augmented as your needs require and your means permit.

Just as a woman can train her eye for fashion by visiting the collections of the leading dress designers, she can acquire a sense of dining table elegance by visiting the displays in the finest shops, even though her means may only permit her to buy her clothes in the budget department and her household furnishings in the basement. It is also worthwhile to study the decorating magazines and those for brides, which devote many pages to the subject of silverware. As with fashion, you will generally find it is best to avoid extremes and fads and to take into account your personal problems and requirements before you buy.

As dinner and luncheon menus have become less elaborate and their service ever more simplified, nobody needs an enormous trousseau of silverware today. A basic minimum for a bride—which would permit her to receive six people for dinner—might be:

    12 dinner forks
    12 luncheon forks
    12 teaspoons
    12 soup spoons
    6 or 12 coffee spoons
    4 serving spoons
    4 serving forks

Later she can add dessert spoons, additional knives and forks for luncheon and dinner, butter knives, salad forks, special knives and forks for fruit and fish, a sauce spoon, a soup ladle, lemon fork, cake knife and server, sugar tongs, tongs for serving asparagus, and any of the many other more specialized articles that may appeal to her, such as ice cream and iced-tea spoons. These pieces are often practical and are always pretty on a table, but they are seldom indispensable. As a matter of fact, many aristocratic Paris hostesses would never consider setting a table with fish knives and forks or even with salad forks, because these fairly recent inventions are not included in precious ancestral silver services.

Nevertheless, certain instruments are essential for coping with certain dishes. For example, do not attempt to serve oysters without proper oyster forks, snails without escargot tongs, or unshelled lobster and crab without the appropriate picks and crackers. Moreover, the only really refined way to eat soft-boiled eggs is with an ivory teaspoon.

While sterling silver is undeniably more elegant than silver plate or stainless steel, the latter materials are very well designed nowadays and these services are perfectly acceptable for all informal and family occasions. The most important consideration is their weight, for it is very disagreeable to eat with featherweight utensils, and you should always try to select knives and forks that feel slightly heavy in the hand. Furthermore, when you set a dinner table with stainless steel, the entire table setting should strike the same informal note. Aside from the question of appropriateness, experience will prove that stainless steel is far more attractive when it is laid on a bright-colored tablecloth, beside simple, rustic dishes, than when it is placed on a fine lace cloth.

Silver serving dishes are not only the most beautiful and luxurious but also the most practical, because silver is an excellent conductor of heat and electricity and keeps hot dishes hot longer. But it is customary to possess serving dishes that match your tableware as well, and to use these for everyday meals. To start with (and here again the best opportunity for acquiring such a sumptuous present is as a wedding gift), you might choose an oval platter, then a round platter; next, a vegetable dish with a cover that can be transformed into two uncovered dishes, and then perhaps a gravy boat, or additional serving platters of a different size.

While nothing is lovelier than silver, certain table accessories are just as elegant and correct, and in a few cases even more so, when they are made of crystal, porcelain, or even earthenware. For example, a crystal finger bowl placed on a doily on a silver dish is more chic than if the bowl were of silver too. Metal bowls on a table, even precious metal, always remind me of a restaurant. On the other hand, silver bread and butter dishes make a prettier table setting than crystal.

Salad serving spoons and forks are most elegant with wooden bowls and very long handles of olive wood, bone, horn, or ivory; and the most appetizing way to present a salad on an informal buffet table is in an olive-wood bowl.

A cheese tray is most attractive when it is made of wood or even of rustic woven straw, covered with vine leaves or equipped with a glass lining. But a single round cheese such as a Camembert is often served on a small silver plate. (The blade of the cheese knife, incidentally, should always be of stainless steel, while fruit knife blades should always be of silver, because of the chemical reactions involved.)

Many fruit desserts and sauces are preferably served in a crystal bowl rather than in a silver one. For that matter, a great number of desserts, such as puddings and mousses, are more appetizing when they are presented in a transparent bowl—but most elegant of all, it is true, when the bowl is placed on a silver dish.

A gravy boat and a sauce bowl for mayonnaise are perhaps richest looking in silver, but just as smart in porcelain or earthenware, if they match your dishes. Crystal is inappropriate, not to say risky, for hot sauces, but acceptable for cold ones.

The prettiest way to serve a molded ice cream dessert is on a doily (to prevent slipping) placed on a round silver platter. But when it is served in a mound of individual scoops, it is often more practical to serve ice cream in a crystal bowl.

Silver wine goblets and liqueur glasses are unpleasant to drink from, and the mere thought of them is enough to scandalize a connoisseur. If you have acquired a set of silver goblets thanks to your prowess at riding, golf, or tennis, it is better to line them up in a display case or even on the mantelpiece rather than on your dining table. But they are most chic of all when used to hold flowers and cigarettes.

Silver salt dishes and shakers, silver ashtrays and cigarette urns, silver candlesticks and candelabra are certainly very elegant table accessories. But crystal is also lovely on a dining table, particularly by candlelight. And with a bright red, blue, or green tablecloth, nothing is more strikingly decorative than a chalk-white earthenware centerpiece and candleholders.

Silver coffee and tea sets on a silver tray are undeniably the most precious and formal. Because these will not usually appear on the dinner table with the rest of your silverware, you can select any style that appeals to you without attempting to match them to what you already own. In actual practice, however, you often have no say in the matter, for the style of your tea set is the one that appealed to your mother or grandmother. And this is just as well, for these traditional articles are often most elegant in traditional designs. At the same time, tea sets and afterdinner coffee services are made of porcelain in charming modern and traditional patterns, and these are most practical for many ordinary occasions. For example, unless your silver tea set is of small proportions, it would be more elegant to offer a cup of tea to your best friend from one of these pretty tête-à-tête sets and to reserve your impressive silver service for large tea parties. Earthenware tea sets are also most attractively designed, and the traditional English patterns are particularly fitting at teatime. But this material does not retain heat as well as either porcelain or silver.

The pleasure of possession often entails a certain amount of responsibility, and a woman who is fortunate enough to own lovely silver should at least be willing to keep it well polished. This is no longer the chore it used to be, thanks to magical modern polishes and tarnish preventives. But if you are unwilling or unable to go to the trouble of always keeping your silver gleaming bright, it is better to store it in flannel bags.

When planning your table decorations for a party, you might consider your silver and try to set it off to its best advantage. Silver is most enhanced by lace, crystal, bright red, pink, pale blue, dark polished wood, fresh roses, and particularly by candlelight, which brings out all the beauty of its soft luster. Silver may sometimes be combined effectively with pewter on a sideboard, but this is not attractive on a table. For that matter, pewter is rustic and most often Colonial or Renaissance in style, and it is generally prettier in the country or in an Early American setting than against the more formal and refined backgrounds of later periods.

No matter how ancient your silver is, it should be in perfect working condition when it is laid on the table. You should never soak the knives with the rest of your silverware, because the handles will eventually separate from the blades. They can be repaired, of course, just as specialists can remove most scratches and dents and resilver worn or damaged pieces. It is also useful to know that certain elements are apt to tarnish silver very quickly: heat, smoke, the sulphur that is in most city air, traces of soap that have been insufficiently rinsed, eggs, tea, and vinegar. You can lacquer such articles as lamps and picture frames with the special products that leave a protective coating (and at the same time slightly diminish the luster), but this is not possible for table silverware.

Nowadays charming copies of antique silver are being made at a fraction of the cost of the authentic antiques from which they are modeled, but most of the modern versions are silver-plated rather than of solid silver. For once, it is easy to tell exactly what you are getting when you are shopping for silver. All solid silver is government-controlled and stamped with official marks. The hallmarks on antique pieces frequently indicate not only the quality of the article but also the date and place of its fabrication, and sometimes the name of the particular silversmith. Sheffield plate is also stamped with a distinctive mark. This, incidentally, is a special process invented in England in which a sheet of silver is fused onto a copper base, whereas ordinary silver-plating is performed by an electroplating process onto a base of copper, nickel, or an alloy. The value of solid silver depends on its weight, workmanship, and sometimes on its rarity, while the value of silver plate depends on the thickness of the plating. So-called "German silver" is not silver at all, but a mixture of nickel, copper, and zinc.

If you are interested in beautifying your home, it might be worthwhile to study one of the many excellent books on antique silver and then to put your learning to the test by seeking out beautiful or unusual silver at auctions, in antique shops and junk shops. When you are in Europe, you may be lucky enough, if you have some knowledge of hallmarks and styles, to find a real bargain in one of the Left Bank antique shops of Paris, at the Flea Market or (and here your chances are best of all at the moment) at the Flea Markets of Barcelona and Madrid. A visit to the Silver Vaults in London is a fabulous experience! In all of these treasure troves, you will find mostly silver of the nineteenth century and later. Fine eighteenth-century silver has become so rare and costly that it is handled largely by the leading antique dealers, while very little seventeenth-century silver has survived, and most of the existing authentic pieces are in museum collections. Fortunately, excellent modern copies are made from the simple, graceful patterns of these early periods.

In short, silver is lovely to own and to admire. But like exquisite table linen, it is not at all indispensable to elegant entertaining. It would be ridiculous to feel that you cannot receive your friends properly simply because you do not own sterling silverware for the table or a silver tea set! Just remember to plan the mood and style of your table decor in view of the kind of tableware you possess. And if you do not own a single silver wedding gift or heirloom, you can console yourself by thinking of the countless number of afternoons that are spent in polishing a collection of silver, while you can simply dump your stainless steel into the dishwasher and go to see a good movie.

SINGLE WOMEN

❰ Bachelor girls, widows, and divorcées sometimes wonder if they can entertain as freely as if they had a husband to act as host, and my answer is yes, a thousand times yes!

There is no difference between the manner of entertaining of a single woman and of a married hostess except at a dinner party, when the former should include among her guests, if possible, a single man in order to balance the seating arrangement at table. It is also in very good taste for the single woman to place opposite her, in the place of the nonexistent host, the most distinguished or oldest man guest, even if he is accompanied by his wife, rather than to have the dinner table presided over by the single gentleman, who might be embarrassed by this flattering promotion.

A single woman often has at her disposal a more limited budget than a married couple, and it is quite natural for her to entertain on a more modest scale. But there is absolutely no reason why she should deprive herself of the pleasure of receiving her friends as often and as elaborately as her means permit.

SMOKING

❲ Even if you are violently allergic to cigar smoke, there is no elegant way of preventing your gentlemen guests from smoking a cigar after dinner if they happen to feel like it. All that a hostess can do is to provide cigars of excellent quality, preferably Havana if available (a good cigar is always less offensive than a cheap one), and then attempt to smile philosophically through the smoke clouds.

The proper moment for passing cigars and cigarettes is after the coffee has been served in the living room along with brandy and liqueurs. Cigars should be presented in a humidor or in their original box, and cigarettes in a good-sized, flat cigarette box. It is chic and amusing to fill a rather large cigarette box with a wide assortment of different cigarettes: plain, filtered, nicotine-free, and one or two of the more exotic varieties, such as the aromatic Turkish blends and the long, slender Russian kind with their gold-paper tips. It is better to keep mentholated cigarettes in a separate box, or their mint flavor will permeate all the others.

Cigarette smoking is still so widespread that it is also customary in many modern homes to place several small cigarette urns on the dining table and to permit your guests to smoke after the main course and before the cheese. You may either set the example by lighting a cigarette yourself, or, if you do not smoke, you may offer a cigarette to your dinner partners. At a formal dinner party it is elegant to have the waiter pass a silver tray holding an opened silver cigarette box and a special small, lighted candle in a silver holder. It would be very ill-mannered for a guest to light a cigarette early in the meal, especially if he does not first ask for the hostess's permission. His request, however, is a mere formality, for the hostess hasn't the right to refuse.

Cigar smokers are not accorded the same degree of indulgence. Moreover, most men who appreciate the savor of a fine cigar also consider it to be the perfect finale to a good dinner, and they scorn the cigarette addicts who dull their palates by smoking during the course of a meal. Many noted gourmets are, like the French ambassador in Washington, Hervé Alphand, great connoisseurs of cigars as well. In fact, the ambassadress once laughingly confided to me that the principal reason why he married her was because she knew how to light his cigar correctly. I must admit that I was rather surprised the day I dined with them in Washington to see the maître d'hôtel present the cigar box to the ambassadress instead of to the ambassador. After selecting a cigar with the greatest care, she skillfully pierced the end, slowly lit it by turning it gently over a candle flame, and handed it to her husband. Incidentally, even a nonsmoking hostess should know that a cigar may be lit from a candle, a gas lighter, or from the fine sheet of cedar wood in which some cigars are wrapped, but it should never touch the flame of an ordinary cigarette lighter or a paper match.

The aroma of an excellent cigar is seldom unpleasant. It is the smoldering stub in the ashtray that emits that dreadful reek. The hostess should therefore keep an eye on the ashtrays and see that they are emptied regularly during the course of the evening. A "silent butler" is a very practical receptacle for emptying ashtrays filled with cigarette butts, but it is best to remove the cigar remains from the room whenever possible. She should think of opening a window if the temperature permits, and of keeping in the room a lighted candle in order to absorb some of the smoke—either an ordinary candle, or the deluxe kind that releases a refreshing fragrance of cypress. You might also try concealing a bottle of Air-Wick somewhere in the room—behind the curtains on a windowsill, for example, or behind a row of books. It will not be as effective as if the bottle were placed right in the middle of the coffee table, but this object is unfortunately far too unaesthetic to be seen in an elegant gathering.

Finally, after the guests have gone home, you should air the room thoroughly—and again the next morning, if necessary. The cigar and cigarette smoke from a single evening is quickly dissipated, but if you allow it to accumulate from one party to the next, your living room will eventually acquire the distinctive scent of a political back-room during a national convention.

(See Ashtrays, Odors)

SNOBS

❲ It has been said that the snob is somebody who doesn't dare admit that he is bored when he is bored, or that he is amused when he is amused.

It is a rather delicate matter to entertain snobs successfully, and even more difficult to win their faithful attachment. Of course, there are really a thousand and one different kinds of snobs, and if you wish to learn to distinguish each variety, all you have to do is to read Pierre Daninos's witty book, *Snobissimo*, or even Thackeray's *Book of Snobs*, which is remarkably timely considering that it was written over a hundred years ago. But those who concern us here are the social snobs, the people who wish to be seen where it is the place to be seen, and who will do anything at all in order to get themselves invited to a chic or exclusive party—and who, at the same time, would rather stay at home nibbling on a raw apple than go to a dinner party, or even less a ball, where among two thousand guests there is, according to their special definition, "nobody who is anybody."

This type of snob possesses remarkable antennae for detecting in advance the theaters, restaurants, and nightclubs where one must be seen, and the charity balls where one simply must make an appearance. In Paris they consist principally of the annual charity ball given by the Baroness de Cabrol, and the evening at the Opera when La Callas is the star and where all the snobs in Paris sit through three hours of Puccini, even if they secretly loathe operatic music. Their reward is to be seen—and, what joy! perhaps even photographed—during the intermission. I sometimes think that the impresario who had the courage to produce only an intermission would score a fabulous success. The snobs could then go directly to supper at Maxim's without having to conceal their yawns during three hours of arias. Until then, they do not dare miss the evening at the Opera, especially if they have the great thrill of being invited by Onassis, and the even greater thrill of reading all about it in the society columns the next morning.

The dream of every ambitious society hostess is to add to her string a few of the leading snobs who then attract the others and thus consecrate a reputation. If one wishes to become a famous hostess with a capital H, this is, it must be admitted, one of the first essential moves to make. But it is the same as trying to win a place on the list of the ten best-dressed women. What work is required, what patience, what humility with the Big Names and what ferocious disdain toward the Nobodies. And most of all—what a bank account!

SOUP

([Soup is seldom served in fashionable Paris homes any more as the first course of a dinner party, for practical as well as gastronomic reasons. Practically speaking, a good homemade soup takes a long time to prepare and is fattening as well; gastronomically, we no longer have the capacity to devour the six- or seven-course menus of our grandparents, and while the soup course can easily be suppressed in favor of a fish or egg entrée before the main dish of a meal, the dinner would lose much of its interest and elegance if the entrée were to be eliminated in favor of the soup. In any case, soup is never served at a formal luncheon, just as hors d'oeuvres are never served in the evening when you are receiving dinner guests.

The only soups that are often seen on elegant dinner tables these days are during the winter—consommé, a seafood bisque, or perhaps canned turtle soup among the snobs (although no canned soups are really suitable for company meals); and during the summer—jellied consommé or madrilène, vichyssoise, gazpacho, or some other cold soup. But this means adding a supplementary course to the entrée, main dish, salad, cheese, and dessert courses, and therefore increases the already considerable problems of preparation and service.

It is very difficult to serve a hot soup correctly in a servantless household, because it should be poured from a steaming pitcher or tureen into heated plates; and in the case of cold soups, the soup plates should be chilled.

Most canned and dehydrated soups, as practical as they are for family meals, for expanding pot-luck dinners, and for a busy woman's light luncheon, cannot compare to homemade soups in quality. A tablespoonful of sherry will add zest to many canned clear soups, two tablespoonfuls of red wine will improve many of the stew-type varieties, such as oxtail, and the same amount of dry white wine is often a good addition to fish soups. But remember that the soup should never be permitted to boil after the wine has been added. The best thickeners for soup, incidentally, are egg yolk, cream, and a handful of rice. Never thicken soup with flour if you can avoid it. This is, in fact, the worst fault (along with excessive saltiness and synthetic flavoring and coloring agents) of many canned and dehydrated soups.

As in the case of desserts, certain soups are considered suitable company fare, while others are preferably reserved for family meals. In the first category there are:

Hot Consommé — garnished with diced vegetables, croutons, julienne strips of ham, tongue, or chicken, poached eggs, etc.

Cream of Mushroom — but it must be homemade

Turtle Soup — almost always canned

Cream of Spinach, Tomato, Celery, Asparagus, Broccoli, Avocado, Artichoke, Watercress (hot or cold) — homemade

Lobster, Crayfish, and Shrimp Bisque — expensive, but exquisite when homemade with a blender

Jellied Consommé and Madrilène — in the summer, before a light entrée and a rather hearty main dish; garnish with lemon, chopped chives or parsley, sour cream, caviar, etc.

Gazpacho — more informal, and filling enough to replace an entrée due to the accompanying croutons, chopped scallions, peppers, and tomatoes

Vichyssoise — serve very cold with chopped chives

Exotic Oriental Soups (usually based on clam broth or consommé) — as a first course of a Chinese or Japanese meal

Onion Soup — In Paris, a sizzling bowl filled with a rich onion soup and toasted croutons heavily sprinkled with grated cheese and gratinéed in the oven (preferably eaten in a brasserie around the central wholesale market) is the traditional finale to a long night on the town.

While soup is losing favor as a dinner course (except, perhaps, in winter in the country), some soups are so hearty that they are virtually an entire dinner in themselves. *Poule au pot,* goulash, *pot au feu, potée, bouillabaisse,* borscht, *moules marinière,* and even a thick clam chowder chock-full of clams and vegetables, are all sufficiently substantial to compose the principal part of a very informal dinner or Sunday-night supper. For a family meal, they can be followed simply by a green salad and fruit, but when you are serving these unpretentious dishes to friends, it would be better to apply more care to the rest of the meal and to offer country bread or home-baked rolls, an excellent mixed salad, a cheese tray, and a hearty, simple dessert.

My mother left me a marvelous collection of recipes for delicious soups. But, alas, I have seldom found the time to try any of them, for most of them require hours and hours of cooking and a market basket full of different ingredients and herbs. If, however, you are willing to devote an entire afternoon to the preparation of a succulent, extremely informal meal for a few close friends, you might try her method for making *La Potée:*

If it is for dinner —

At 2 P.M.

Place in a large pot 2 quarts of water.

Cut in tiny pieces, leeks, carrots, parsnips, potatoes, celery, cabbage.

Add, if you like, a handful of white dried beans and a handful of lentils.

Boil gently. Do not add salt.

At 4 P.M.

Add a piece of smoked ham and a pork butt.

At 5:30 P.M.

Add a small, cooked ham.

At 7:30 P.M.

Add pork sausages. At this point you can also add, if you wish, a handful of well-washed rice.

At 8 P.M.

Serve the soup with all of the mixed vegetables. Keep the meats hot in the casserole, and serve them afterward with a green salad.

SPONGERS

❨ Generally bachelor and male, the sponger is willing to swallow any affront as long as it is garnished with caviar. Nothing causes greater consternation in his soul than to be invited to two different dinner parties on the same evening. What a waste!

He always sincerely regrets having to refuse an invitation: the only time he will decline one of yours is when he has a chance to dine at the table of a richer hostess. So there is no point in being embarrassed about inviting him at the very last minute. The only thing that really matters to him is the free meal. But if he arrives uninvited at about seven o'clock in the evening, or if he shows no sign of leaving at the end of a cocktail party, do not hesitate to let him know that there isn't a thing left to eat in the house.

It is when you decide to go out to dinner in a restaurant with the sponger and a group of friends that you must be most on your guard. Perfectly relaxed until the moment for the bill to be presented, he will suddenly become absorbed in a fascinating conversation that isolates him from the rest of the party, or he will be struck by a terrible headache or the need to slip out and buy a package of cigarettes; and he will only reappear, smiling and relaxed once more, after the painful process of paying the bill has been safely concluded.

The perfect sponger should be handsome, well dressed, charming, adept at flattery, and rather aristocratic in bearing, skilled in all the fashionable sports, and with plenty of free time on his hands. While he will not lower himself so far as to offer to help with the dishes, he is nevertheless always willing to mix a divine little salad—for which he will give you a list of ingredients to buy beforehand, complete with truffles or caviar, for example.

In short, he is what the Latins called "a client," that is to say, a habitué of your house. If you feed him well, he will in return purringly envelop you in a cloud of protective fidelity, so long as you do not experience any serious financial setback. But it cannot be denied that spongers are comforting accessories with which many wealthy persons enjoy surrounding themselves.

SUPPER

❴ An elegant modern woman has supper on only two different occasions:

(1.) On Sunday night, when the servants (if any) have taken the half-day off, the menu (if any) consists of leftovers discovered by raiding the icebox, the guests (if any) are very close friends of the family, and the setting is far more likely to be the kitchen or even in front of the television screen rather than the dining room, since nobody is very hungry anyway after the latest, most hearty midday meal of the week.

(2.) At midnight, or even much later, when she is dressed in her loveliest evening gown and her finest jewelry and has returned home from a theater, concert, or ball, with or without a few friends, and suddenly discovers that the hours of spectacle or dancing have left her starved.

Otherwise, supper does not exist in the smartest circles, because to have supper in the evening implies that one has had dinner at noon and, despite the fact that medical authorities have always advised us to eat our heaviest meal in the middle of the day, nowadays this custom is practiced mainly in farming areas.

There is little point in discussing Sunday-night suppers in a book on entertaining. While you can very well ask a close friend to "stay for supper" on Sunday evening, it is rather rare to invite a guest to "come for supper" on that particular night.

As for the midnight supper, it may be either planned well in advance in the most elegant fashion, like the supper dance described in "Dinners," which is exactly like a dinner dance except that it is held at a later hour and the meal is lighter; or (and this is the more frequent case) it may be a completely spontaneous affair, when you suggest to friends whom you have accompanied to the theater, or to guests with whom you have hit it off particularly well at someone else's party, to come home with you for one last drink and a snack before calling it a night.

The latter occasions are typical pot-luck meals, where, before expressing your impulsive invitation, you should be cool-headed enough to make a mental inventory of the resources of your icebox and your emergency shelf. A cold meal is perfectly appropriate, even an array of leftover roast, turkey, chicken, tinned sardines, cheese, pâté, salads, etc., from which the guests can concoct their own sandwiches or cold plates, right in the kitchen. A delicious dish of creamy scrambled eggs with ham, bacon, or chicken livers is always appreciated at one o'clock in the morning, as are *croques Monsieur* (the French version of grilled ham and cheese sandwiches, sautéed in butter), an epicurean chicken or roast-beef hash—in fact, any of the traditional brunch specialties. Half of the fun of these midnight suppers is that they prolong an already joyous atmosphere. It is seldom possible at this late hour to create an *ambiance* of gaiety and warmth that has been absent all evening, so you should think twice before you permit yourself to be carried away by a hospitable impulse toward the old friends or new acquaintances you have met at a party. Nine times out of ten, when you are all finally assembled in your own home, you will feel much more sleepy than hungry, and your one idea will be to get to bed as quickly as possible.

When you have invited friends to the theater and for supper afterward, the simplest solution is generally to take them to a smart supper club or a late restaurant for your midnight meal. But you can also plan a very elegant little snack in your own home. In this case, everything should be prepared in advance before you leave for the play, with the table set, the food arranged on covered platters (in the refrigerator, because it is simplest to make it an entirely cold meal), along with the wine. Champagne, Rhine wine, or Moselle would be perfect. Because of the lateness of the hour, the menu should be light, easy to serve, and quick to consume and digest. If there are only four of you and you can afford the luxury, the ideal supper menu would start with caviar accompanied by thin white toast and lemon, then an appetizing cold dish such as *chaud-froid* of chicken, cold duck in aspic, jellied *boeuf à la mode* cut in thin slices with the carrots sliced in very fine sticks, cold tongue, etc. All of these are especially well prepared by professional caterers, but you must persuade them to refrain from an overelaborate presentation. To accompany this dish, a green salad, and to conclude the meal either a plate of petit fours or a very light cake—a frozen ice cream cake, angel food, or a meringue type would combine the proper degree of lightness with the right amount of sweetness. A less extravagant version could be built around a cold roast filet of beef, cold tongue or ham (or an assortment of the three) as a main dish, accompanied by a cold macédoine of vegetables with mayonnaise, and, as an appetizer, small grilled cheese canapés, smoked cod-liver canapés, or one of your personal favorite hors d'oeuvre creations.

Always remember when you entertain guests at a midnight supper that it is more elegant to let them go home a little bit hungry and to enjoy a sound night's sleep, than it is to stuff them with heavy sauces, onions, garlic, strong cheese, and any of the other rich foods that are guaranteed to give them nightmares.

SURPRISE PARTY

◖ For every surprise party that has been a genuinely pleasant surprise to the guest of honor, at least twice as many have probably caused greater consternation than delight. And I can think of very few instances in which a successful surprise party would not have been even more successful if the guest of honor had been tipped off in advance. When the person to be surprised is a woman, it is only considerate, it seems to me, to let her know ahead of time that all eyes will be upon her, so that she can take the precaution of wearing her most becoming dress and going to the hairdresser in the afternoon.

Nevertheless, I know a charming young couple whose happy married life seems to be one long series of affectionate practical jokes—and this is the category in which most surprise parties must be listed. The birthday dinner this young woman recently gave in honor of her husband was, I must admit, the only surprise party I have attended in years. I had been asked to pretend to invite them to dinner on that particular evening, and it was arranged for the husband to come straight to my home from his office. When he arrived, he was rather surprised not to find his wife. He was even more astonished when we bundled him into the car and took him to his own house. And there he was utterly enchanted to discover a lovely buffet-party setting and a large gathering of guests all shouting, "Happy Birthday!" I do not know how the wife managed to keep her husband in the dark concerning her party preparations, for it seems to me difficult enough to plan a large buffet dinner dance without the added complication of having to do it all in secret. But this, I suppose, is the part of the game she most enjoyed.

In short, surprise parties for adults are apparently highly amusing to hostesses and guests of honor who like that sort of thing, although they cannot really be considered as either fashionable or chic. As for children's surprise parties—much as young people are known to adore surprises, I have found that they enjoy even more the suspenseful pleasure of looking forward to some promised event.

SWIMMING POOL

❨ When a family decides to install a swimming pool in the backyard, everyone is generally so enthralled by the vision of unlimited swimming and sunbathing that nobody stops to think of the upkeep, and especially of the danger that a swimming pool represents. Before your pool is ever filled with water for the first time, you should draw up a maintenance contract with a reliable firm of specialists who will test and treat the water every week in order to ensure its perfect sanitary condition. You will probably be given a chemical algicide powder to add to the pool water every day. This regular care is extremely important for, as you know, swimming pools are an ideal breeding place for various disease germs and private pools, being smaller, can become polluted even more quickly than public ones.

It is also indispensable to take out a comprehensive insurance policy to protect you in case of injury or accidents occurring in or around your pool. As a matter of fact, you ought to be protected by insurance from the moment the contractor starts to dig a hole in the ground. Reduce the size of the pool, if you must, but never stint on the insurance.

Neither is it an economy in the end to reduce the width of the cement or tile area bordering the pool to that of a narrow footpath. The broader the paved border, the cleaner your water is likely to remain. You will soon learn that even in the most favorable conditions it is difficult to keep the pool free from the dirt and grass cuttings of the surrounding area.

It is practically essential to provide some kind of a bathhouse. Whether it is merely a prefabricated shed behind a clump of trees, or an elegant miniature Roman villa, it should preferably consist of two separate dressing rooms, one for the women and the other for men. You should equip it with a supply of Turkish towels, extra bathing caps, trunks, and suits, and a few toilet articles such as combs and talcum powder. It is also a good idea to install nearby but out of sight a line for drying wet bathing suits and damp towels. It would be luxurious to provide showers as well, but the expense of this may be prohibitive and a shower is not really an indispensable accessory to a freshwater pool.

However, it is necessary to install some kind of lighting around the pool, not only in order to permit midnight dips on sweltering moonless summer nights but also to signal the presence of the pool to guests (as well as to trespassers, for that matter) who may decide to take a stroll in the garden in search of a breath of air—and not a sudden dunking. Even greater precautions must be taken when the pool is empty.

Once your pool has been installed and equipped, you must arm yourself with unflinching courage and a heart of stone to face the invasion of neighborhood children who will beg you for permission to swim in it. It would be inviting disaster to let them have their way, and at the risk of seeming as selfish as Scrooge, you should adopt the only prudent policy: insist that an adult be present before a child is allowed to stick so much as a toe in the pool water. Even your own children should not be made an exception to the rule. Furthermore, if you do not exercise restraint as well as caution in extending pool privileges, your backyard will soon resemble a noisy municipal playground and the pool will be as dirty as a stagnant pond.

A swimming pool and its surrounding area can be a most attractive setting for a party on a hot summer evening, for the mere sight of water is always romantically refreshing. If the pool is adjacent to your house, adjoining a large terrace in the Mediterranean style, for example, or even jutting into the living room as in Raymond Loewy's fabulous Arizona ranch house, it can be an integral part of your party decor. But if, as is more often the case, the pool is at some distance from the house, the serving problem alone should discourage you from poolside entertaining on a grand scale. While there is no better place to drink a gin and tonic on a hot afternoon than beside a pretty pool, it is more practical to hold your dinner parties on the patio or in the dining room and to let your guests admire the pool from a distance.

I once attended a charming poolside dinner party, with floating gardenias in the water, Japanese lanterns strung among the trees, small candlelit tables around the edges of the pool, a swarm of guests in evening dress, and a crew of waiters in white gloves. I also saw the setting the next morning, and it was a depressing sight. The gardenias had become a brown and sticky mess, the pool was polluted with cigarette stubs, dirt, and grass; there was even a dinner napkin soggily floating near the bottom of the deep end, a half-filled whisky glass at the end of the diving board and a shattered champagne glass right next to the swimming ladder. And it had been such an elegant party!

All things considered, it seems to me that the most practical and carefree way to profit from a swimming pool in entertaining is to suggest to your guests that they bring their bathing suits and have a swim before or after a summer luncheon party or a Sunday brunch. You might also plan a poolside picnic for your teen-age children and their young friends once or twice during the summer holidays. In this case, the simplest arrangement is to serve a classic picnic lunch from a hamper, to provide an assortment of water games and toys, and be prepared to supervise the party (assisted, perhaps, by one of the other mothers) from a discreet distance from the time the first child has arrived until the last one has gone home.

One of my friends on the French Riviera has established a pleasant tradition of giving an outdoor buffet luncheon and swimming party every Saturday during the month of August. At the beginning of the month, she issues a standing invitation to her friends for every Saturday from noon until five, requesting simply that they telephone their confirmation the night before. Since her buffet is built around an assortment of cold meats, salads, a cheese tray, fruit, and a cake or pie, she has no difficulty in expanding a feast prepared for ten to satisfy twice as many if necessary by adding a roast chicken, ham, or tongue from the village delicatessen, a large bowl of cole slaw, celery root, or potato salad, and a couple of quarts of ice cream. On the other hand, should a sudden shower reduce her guest list to zero, she simply serves her family a cold luncheon in the dining room and has no trouble at all inventing ways to use up the extra party food in her family menus during the next few days. Moreover, her Saturday open house has won her such a reputation for unbounded hospitality that nobody seems to have noticed that she categorically refuses to let anybody use her swimming pool at any other time.

TABLES

(Whether it is set for a buffet, a dinner party, a luncheon, or a tea, the decoration of your table sets the tone of your entire reception. Since it is seldom possible to redecorate your entire home according to the kind of party you are giving, party decorations are generally concentrated in the flower arrangements and in the table setting.

In the case of a luncheon or dinner party, there are certain conventions that must be observed:

The plates should face each chair, with the water glass behind the plate and slightly to the left, and the wine glasses in decreasing size toward the right, which means that when there are three glasses, the medium-sized one is exactly at the center of the plate.

The silverware is placed on each side of the plate according to the order in which it is to be used: the forks to the left, the knives to the right, so that if the first dish to be served is a fish course, the fish knife and fork would be at the outside, and the meat knife and fork next to the plate, with the cutting side of the knives turned toward the plate. In France, it is the custom to place spoons and forks face down on the table, but Americans have adopted the English manner, with the fork tines and the bowl of the spoon facing upward. The English also usually set the table with a dessert fork and spoon placed horizontally between the plate and the glasses, whereas in France the dessert plates are distributed with the necessary silverware upon them. In America both methods are used, with perhaps a slight preference for the British.

To the left of the plate is placed a small side dish with a butter knife for bread and butter, which may also be served in separate tiny butter dishes. This little bread dish may also be used, in the practical British fashion, for the cheese course. You should think of placing a small ashtray to the right of each place, as well as several silver cups filled with an assortment of cigarettes in the middle of the table on either side of the centerpiece.

It is always best to change the knives and forks with each course, but if your silver chest is insufficiently stocked, you might consider the French method of providing each place setting with a *porte-couteau* (a knife holder), which is no more than a little object, usually rectangular, on which each guest poses his knife and fork between the entrée and the main course. But this is only used on the most informal family occasions. For a formal dinner in France, as elsewhere, the silverware is changed with every course.

Individual silver salt and pepper dishes with their spoons are more chic than shakers, although they are somewhat less practical since the salt will turn the silver black if it is not emptied after every meal (a small ivory saltspoon solves that problem if you can find one!). A wooden pepper mill is unfortunately quite out of place on a formally set table, although it may be used on very informal occasions and in rustic settings.

A separate salad dish (the most fashionable is the crescent-shaped kind) is placed to the left of each plate, but only just before the salad is served.

As a relic from the days when the chef alone planned the menu, certain aristocratic tables are still ornamented with one or two hand-written menus. Personally, however, I find this mode slightly affected and think it should be avoided except for very large formal dinners or if your household is run on a very grand scale. In any case, it would be extremely vulgar to ask all of your guests to sign the menu at the end of the meal. (Don't laugh, I have seen this happen!) Above all, remember that elegance in entertaining, just as elegance in clothing, should appear to be an everyday habit and not your Sunday best. Even if your secret ambition is for this evening to be the one grand dinner of your life, you should still act as though you were used to dining in the same way three or four times a week.

There are two schools of thought concerning the decoration of the table itself: a traditional tablecloth, versus individual place mats. The practical and decorative possibilities of the latter seem to me to be more limited. The fact is that place mats are only elegant when the surface of your table is extraordinarily pretty—and a very pretty table surface is unlikely to remain so for very long if it is unprotected by a tablecloth with a pad underneath! Even if you place waterproof coasters under all of the glasses, and doilies under every dish, your precious table is almost certain to be scratched by a sauceboat or a salad bowl, particularly in servantless households where the platters must be passed around from guest to guest. Furthermore, if you have enlarged your table by adding extra leaves, you will need to use a tablecloth in order to conceal the joints.

There are fashions in table decorations just as in clothing, and the stylists of tableware and linen manufacturers even present "collections" from time to time, just like the Paris couturiers. And so the hostess who wishes to have a well-dressed table should know what is considered at the moment to be

Very Chic:

—Monochrome color schemes or, rather, several shades of the same color, such as pink to burgundy, ciel to dark blue, etc.

—A combination of fruit and flowers, vegetables and flowers, feathers and fruit, etc., in your centerpiece, and even a combination of fresh and artificial flowers, artfully composed.

—An unusual flower container in the center of the table or buffet such as a hunting horn, or a curious porcelain bibelot.

—Unpretentious rustic settings (with menu to match).

—At least one set of plates that is different from the rest of your service, such as separate dessert plates with a floral or fruit decor, or plates with a marine motif for the fish course.

. . . and an elegant hostess should also know what is:

Not Chic at All:

—A huge floral centerpiece that is overwhelming, pretentious, and obviously prepared by a professional florist.

—To make not the slightest attempt to dress up your dinner or luncheon table in party attire.

—A lazy susan in the middle of the table, laden with condiments.

—Mustard, ketchup, etc., in their original bottles, as well as plastic gadgets for pouring honey, ketchup, etc. All of these are very useful, but they belong in the kitchen.

—To have absolutely everything match.

—Napkins folded in an elaborate fashion.

—An array of vitamin pills, health-food supplements, and various medicines on the table or even on the sideboard. All of these belong in the kitchen—or in the bathroom.

Having determined the invariable elements of your table setting, now let us see how we can embellish this basic composition on various special occasions in order to illustrate the special event you wish to celebrate with a few tastefully selected decorative accessories.

To start with, there are the traditional family events:

Christenings: For a christening luncheon, which is essentially a family reunion, the table should be decorated carefully but without excessive luxury, for example, by using an embroidered or white damask tablecloth and your usual dishes, glasses, and silverware. It is a sufficient mark of festivity to place a bouquet of white flowers in the center of the table, with white, blue, or pink satin ribbons running from the centerpiece across the tablecloth in a star pattern. You might also surround the centerpiece in the Continental fashion with little pyramids of pastel, sugar-covered almonds, which we call dragées, and which are always distributed at French christenings. As a matter of fact, any color aside from pastel shades should be avoided on this occasion, even in your menu, for the mood should be one of innocence and ingenuousness.

First Communion or Confirmation: The decor is practically the same, for this is also a luncheon party. The dragées are replaced by little bouquets of flowers: roses, sweet peas, pansies, peonies, daisies —all of them white. On this occasion even pastel shades are inappropriate.

Engagement Party: Because this family event is less innocent and much more romantic than the first two occasions, an entirely different decor is in order. Since it is really a gala dinner party, the table should be dressed in evening attire, for example: a tablecloth of embroidered organdy placed over a pink cloth, pink candles in silver candlesticks, and pink and white flowers, which you might arrange in the shape of a heart. In any case, every bakery and ice cream maker possesses a heart-shaped mold for the dessert. All sorts of romantic decorative touches are appropriate and you can display your ingenuity as well as your good taste. Do not forget that you are receiving the parents of your future son-in-law, perhaps for the first time (because it is the parents of the future bride who are hosts at the engagement dinner), and that your daughter will be grateful to you for making a favorable impression on her future mother-in-law.

Weddings: Contrary to the engagement party, a wedding feast is more often a luncheon than a dinner, since the majority of modern weddings take place in the morning. There are still a few ultraelaborate wedding luncheons, such as the one given for the daughter of the celebrated Milan couturière Biki at the Crespi Palace in Milan a few years ago, where there were several round tables set with glittering golden goblets, plates, and candelabra for the most important guests, and tables set with silver for the others. But these are really exceptional cases.

As a general rule, a wedding luncheon is held nowadays only in the case of an informal wedding with just a few guests, either because there has been a large reception a few days earlier (which is more and more the fashion), or because it is an intimate occasion limited to the family.

In actual practice, this intimacy is often rather relative, for the luncheon guests will include the family, the wedding attendants, and a few very close friends, which usually adds up to a minimum of twenty or thirty people. It is therefore practically impossible to seat all of the guests around your dining room table in the usual way, and so you must rent a long narrow table, if your room is large enough, or else plan to set up one large table for the guests of honor with, say, eighteen places, and in addition two smaller round tables of six places each, where you will seat the children, distant cousins, and the bride's devoted nursemaid.

The main table should be sumptuously decorated in white and pink, with the same flower arrangement repeated in miniature at the center of the smaller tables. The wedding cake can be placed in the middle of the head table with flowers on either side, and you will of course take out of their tarnishproof cases all of your precious silverware and your most handsome crystal. It is unlikely that you possess a sufficiently large tablecloth, but these can be rented (as can everything else, for that matter), and you might adorn it with pink and white satin ribbons. Even the most banal white damask cloth will seem magnificent if it is lavishly decorated with ribbons and flowers.

Golden Wedding Anniversary: If you are fortunate enough to celebrate your golden wedding anniversary, here is another occasion for a gala dinner party with an obvious decorative theme: gold, needless to say, and the traditional wheat sheaf motif.

The height of luxury would be to lay a transparent organdy tablecloth embroidered with golden wheat sheaves over an undercloth of gold lamé. Perhaps you can rent a few gilt table accessories for the dinner, and this is the only occasion when gilded candles are perfectly elegant. Pine cones, wheat, and various fruits and vegetables all painted in gold can be used to compose a stunning centerpiece.

Having passed in review the principal family receptions, now let us consider a few ideas for table decorations that are less tradition-bound and more imaginative.

When you are short of inspiration, or when the dinner in question has no natural built-in theme, you can always place the decorative accent on the season of the year.

Spring: A blue or pink tablecloth and spring flowers: lilies, tulips, lily of the valley, roses, etc.; mounted butterflies (you can buy them at naturalist shops) stuck on the candles; around Eastertime, decorated Easter eggs, little baby chicks or bunnies, or any of the thousand objects that are symbolic of springtime.

Summer: A sunny yellow tablecloth, sheaves of wheat and a straw basket of fruit with field flowers stuck in here and there will evoke the opulence of this time of the year.

Fall: This is perhaps the season that is easiest to illustrate, with the hunting season, autumn leaves, and the fall harvest. You can compose charming table arrangements with an ocher-colored tablecloth as a background, and a decoration of pheasant feathers, which may either be stuck in a bowl of fruit along with branches of colorful autumn leaves, or laid flat on the cloth around the fruit centerpiece in a star pattern.

You can easily find nowadays lovely sets of plates with colorful patterns of hunting scenes or autumn leaves, and these might be a good investment if you entertain a good deal. Your candles should be selected in the same warm tones; the base of the candlesticks can be garlanded with autumn leaves, and chestnuts strewn around the centerpiece.

Winter: Santa Claus and Christmas trees naturally suggest the color scheme of red, green, and white. Evergreen branches sprayed with artificial snow create a marvelous effect on a bright red tablecloth. You can either dye one of your old white damask cloths or buy a large length of washable red material.

In a fruit bowl at the center of the table, you can combine fruits of the season with a few exotic varieties and shiny Christmas tree balls. You might also strew artistically around the table gilt stars, tiny Christmas trees, garlands, or any of the various bright baubles that fill the shops at this time of the year.

If the four seasons do not inspire you, you might find your decorative theme in the fact that your party takes place in the country, at the seaside, on a terrace, or that the date coincides with a national holiday, or that the menu is built around some exotic foreign dish.

In the Country: A red-and-white checked tablecloth, simple rustic dishes, colored glassware, rustic silverware (such as knives and forks with bamboo handles), pewter pitchers, round loaves of peasant bread, whole sausages, etc. Rusticity is very much in fashion and all of the gift shops sell a selection of simple, naïve accessories for the table. But you must be careful not to overdo it, if you do not wish your dining room to resemble a second-rate country inn.

At the Seashore: Pebbles, driftwood, and sea shells you have gathered yourself can be arranged to compose a perfectly charming table decoration that doesn't cost a cent. You can even use small shells as pepper and salt dishes, and larger ones as ashtrays. Articulated silver fish immediately add a more precious note. The tablecloth might be printed or embroidered with marine motifs, and the plates decorated with fish or shell designs. The menu in this case should be built around seafood dishes.

On a Terrace: In the city, an outdoor dining table can be just as elegantly decorated as in the dining room. You only need to replace the usual candelabra with hurricane candleholders that are protected by a glass shield.

National Holidays: Red, white and blue for patriotic occasions of course, or the colors of the country you are honoring. Tiny flags and tricolor ribbons can be found in the large department stores, and national emblems and flags from many nations can be bought from the United Nations Gift Shop. A shiny toy trumpet is another decorative accessory that suggests patriotism, as do drums and drumsticks. The floral arrangement should also be in the national colors.

Folklore: Whether your theme is Chinese, Spanish, Italian, or whatever, merely a few inexpensive objects typical of the country are sufficient to create an atmosphere. Naturally, the menu, too, helps a great deal, especially if you are able to equip yourself with the special dishes and utensils used for certain foods, such as Chinese soup and rice bowls, Spanish paella casseroles, *sangria* pitchers, etc.

Japan and China: Pepper and mustard sauces in tiny porcelain bowls, tea caddies, chopsticks, fans, imitation jade figurines of dragons or dancing girls, an Oriental-style flower arrangement, or a "Japanese garden."

France: A toy Eiffel Tower or Arc de Triomphe, a few packages of Gauloise Bleu cigarettes, champagne bottles, a pair of dolls dressed like French traffic policemen, long loaves of French bread, etc.

Italy: A white tablecloth decorated with red and green ribbons, Chianti bottles, bowls of spaghetti and Italian mortadella sausage, toy mandolins, a floral centerpiece set in a gondolier's hat, background music.

Spain: Yellow, red and black is the color scheme, paella the main dish, and for your beverage, a *sangria* punch in a large glass pitcher. Bowls of olives with miniature bullfight banderillas (really decorated toothpicks) stuck in them, castanets, toy plastic bulls (you can find these and other objects at souvenir counters and toy departments), fans, flamenco music.

Russia: A red tablecloth, lots of brightly polished silver, candlelight, caviar, vodka, shashlik, and dreamy Gypsy violin music in the background.

Mexico: Sarapes, sombreros, marvelous cut-out silver candlesticks, or candlesticks brightly festooned with paper frills in the Mexican style, chili, enchiladas, dried gourds, etc.

I am well aware that all of this is not very original and has been done hundreds of times before. If you are determined to be different, there is nothing to prevent you from giving an African dinner (couscous and tribal masks), or one from Lapland (fur shoes and raw fish)—but on these occasions you should be careful to invite only friends whose digestion and sense of humor can stand the strain.

(See Dining Rooms, Flowers, etc.)

TABLECLOTHS

❲ The choice of a tablecloth, like the entire table setting for a party, depends upon your menu more than any other single factor. You would not, for example, serve a hearty platter of sauerkraut and spareribs or an earthenware pot of Boston baked beans on a table covered with a fine lace cloth, just as it would be obviously lacking in harmony to set a table with rustic place mats of raffia or straw when caviar and pheasant are on the menu. Good taste, remember, is first of all a question of appropriateness.

A well-equipped hostess possesses one or two suitable tablecloths with matching napkins for each of her customary forms of entertaining, because various degrees of formality require different kinds of tablecloths. The principal sorts are:

Lace or Embroidered Organdy. These are the most formal tablecloths of all, and the effect is particularly lovely when they are laid over a colored undercloth.

White Damask. A classic standby for a dining table's dressy wardrobe, lacking in originality perhaps, and not particularly fashionable anymore, but always correct, especially for buffets. In order to be elegant, the quality must be fine.

Solid-colored Linen or Cotton. The finer weaves are chic on any occasion and are very dressy indeed beneath a lace or transparent organdy cloth. The coarser weaves are gay and informal, ideal for country tables. The color is of considerable importance, not only because it should be selected to harmonize with the decor of the room and the pattern of your dishes, but also because of the reflection it casts on the faces of your guests. In this respect, pink is the most becoming shade of all; yellow is cheerful but more flattering by daylight than in the evening; green is very hard on most complexions.

Printed Cotton or Linen is definitely informal and these materials are therefore more suitable for luncheon than for dinner. When you are shopping for a printed tablecloth, remember that motifs that are all concentrated in the center will be hidden by the centerpiece. For this reason, small all-over patterns are usually the most attractive.

Plastic tablecloths are marvelously practical for family meals, and they can now be found in a vast range of lovely colors and textures. Strictly speaking, they are inappropriate for company meals, and this includes the plastic laces, which are an amazing imitation of fabric lace. (Nevertheless, a spotless plastic tablecloth is preferable, in my opinion, even at a company dinner, to a priceless heirloom linen that is discolored, shabby, or soiled.)

Your tablecloth should always be placed over a thick table pad. On a round table you would, of course, use a square or round cloth, the latter being particularly romantic and charming; on a rectangular or oval table a rectangular cloth, and on a square table a square one. The cloth should overhang the edges of the table more or less halfway to the floor, or at least there should be sufficient overhang so that it does not seem skimpy, but not so much as to interfere with the diner's legs. A buffet table, on the other hand, is prettier when the tablecloth hangs right down to the ground, and in this case the corners should be pinned up so that they do not trail on the floor and risk getting caught in somebody's high-heeled shoe with possibly disastrous results.

Whatever its style and material, the tablecloth at a dinner party should be absolutely spotless and perfectly pressed. The best method is to add an extension cord to your electric iron and to press the cloth, which has been laid over a thick table pad, right on the dining room table.

Unfortunately, it is seldom possible to use the same cloth a second time before laundering, and since reliable hand laundries are scarce and expensive, it is a good idea to remove a soiled or spotted tablecloth as soon as your guests have gone home and to put it in a basin to soak overnight. Spots of grease, wine, or coffee are very difficult to remove if they have been permitted to set. It is also indispensable to use only dripless candles on the table, since dripping wax is the cause of some of the most stubborn tablecloth stains.

There are changing fashions in table linen just as there are in dresses, and modern textile designers are becoming increasingly imaginative and audacious. Generally speaking, if your dishes, silverware, and glasses are rather plain, you can indulge in greater fantasy where your table linen is concerned. Let your good taste be your guide, and do not forget that simplicity is always in fashion.

Finally, remember that tablecloths are merely one small detail in the art of entertaining. While it must be delightful to own a magnificent collection of table linen for every imaginable occasion, the lack of such a luxury has never prevented anyone from entertaining—and what is more, from entertaining with elegance.

TEA

❮ As the formal tea party for thirty or forty women has gradually disappeared from the entertaining program of elegant private hostesses (although many women's clubs still feel obliged to schedule at least one of these quaint reunions every season), an increasing number of chic women are rediscovering the charm of serving afternoon tea to two or three close friends.

The traditional formal tea party was often a deadly bore. Restricted to women guests, with the possible exception of the local minister, it used to provide an opportunity for exchanging gossip, circulating rumors, passing judgment on the absent and criticizing in whispers the manners and dress of those who were present. It was the ordeal by fire through which every young bride and every newcomer to a community had to pass in order to qualify for membership in the inner social circles.

At the same time it must be admitted that the traditional tea party also offered quite a gracious spectacle. No woman would have dreamed of not wearing a hat and her most elegant afternoon ensemble. The tea table (which was the dining table dressed up for the occasion) was obligatorily covered with a long lace cloth and laid with gleaming silver: a silver tea set complete with strainer, sugar bowl, creamer filled with cold milk, a plate of thin lemon slices, and a hot-water pot on a silver tray at one end, and a coffee service (which had replaced the Victorians' hot chocolate) on a silver tray with sugar and cream at the other. The rest of the table was artistically adorned with the necessary number of porcelain cups and saucers, silverware and tea plates (really salad or dessert plates), and trays of dainty sandwiches, cookies, petit fours with pastel icing, and a pretty floral centerpiece. Regally enthroned at either end of the table were two distinguished dowagers—for the act of pouring was an honor to be accorded either to the hostess's closest friends or to socially prominent women whom she wished to please.

In places where the formal tea party still survives, these customs have not changed in the slightest. However, while five o'clock has long been the traditional hour for tea (in France it is often referred to as *"le* five o'clock"), nowadays the party may just as well be from three to five, four to six, or five to seven, since the custom varies from one region to another. London tea shops even serve tea as early as three o'clock.

There are many different varieties of tea, and professional tea tasters can recognize the species and origins of a particular blend just as wine tasters can identify the type and vintage of a wine. The best teas are blended from a mixture of different kinds of leaves. China tea (Pekoe and Orange Pekoe are the best) is light and pale and should be drunk with sugar but without milk, especially when it is perfumed with jasmine or rose. Ceylon tea is darker, stronger, and more stimulating, and may be drunk with or without sugar, cold milk, or a slice of lemon. The latter is the favorite of the British, and a Ceylon blend is perhaps the best choice for afternoon tea, although this is a question of personal taste. One pound of tea will go a long way—it can provide as many as three hundred cups—so a hostess has every interest in buying a very choice brand.

I have already described the best way of making tea in "Foreigners," but since there is such an enormous difference between well-made tea and the drugstore tea-bag kind, perhaps it can bear repeating.

Always start with cold fresh water—pure bottled water is highly recommended if your tap water is extremely chlorinated—and bring it to the boil. Never use water that has already boiled and then cooled off, or water that has boiled for a long time, for both of these will make poor tea. Rinse out the teapot with boiling water. Place in the pot one teaspoon of tea for each cup and one for the pot. Add boiling water to cover the leaves and let them steep for two minutes before filling the pot with more hot water. You should reduce the proportions of tea for very large quantities, or the brew will be too strong. Serve at once, with a pot of very hot water for those who like their tea weaker, and for adding to the more concentrated brew at the bottom of the pot. If you need to make more tea, empty, wash, and rinse the pot, and boil some fresh cold water—in other words, start from scratch. Never add fresh tea leaves to tea that has already steeped.

I have never been able to discover the reason why some people insist on pouring the cold milk into a teacup before the tea. Was the original purpose to protect fine china from cracking upon contact with the hot tea? Or did this practice favor the perfect emulsion of the milk and tea before we had invented homogenized milk? In any case, this custom is not considered at all elegant in England.

With the exception of a copious "High Tea," which sometimes replaces the evening meal in the British provinces (and which is not fashionable any more either), the refreshments for a tea party should be light and rather dainty. The simplest method is to prepare the sandwiches in the morning and to keep them fresh in the refrigerator, wrapped in waxed paper and a damp towel, until teatime. Some of the little cakes may be ordered from a fine bakery, and some of them made in your own kitchen, if you are a good pastry cook. You might also buy a plain bakery cake and tiny individual tart shells from the baker and prepare the fillings and icing yourself.

These are some of my favorite tea sandwiches:

— Asparagus tips with a dab of mayonnaise rolled up in slices of thin white bread.

— Egg salad and finely shredded lettuce with mayonnaise on thinly sliced whole-wheat bread.

— Very fine slices of boiled ham and Swiss cheese on very fine white or rye bread.

— Cream cheese with finely chopped radishes, carrots, and chives on thin whole-wheat or wheat-germ bread.

— Cream cheese and chopped walnuts or dates on raisin bread.

— Thinly sliced raw mushrooms with mayonnaise on white bread.

— Crabmeat, shrimp, or chicken salad on white bread.

— Very fine raw cucumber slices with mayonnaise on thin white bread.

— Baby watercress with egg salad on thin whole-wheat bread.

The bread must be one-day old in order to be sliced very thin, and both slices should be buttered in order to prevent the mayonnaise from making them soggy. Try to use a wide assortment of different kinds of bread, and decorate the sandwich trays with watercress, radish roses, parsley, etc.

To vary the sandwiches, you might also fill tiny éclair or tart shells with sweet preserves or salad mixtures.

Cookies and cakes such as brownies and date bars, which can be cut into small portions, are the easiest to serve. If you bake a cake, it is best to make just one square or oblong layer (which you can always split and fill if you wish) and to cut it into rather small squares or fingers. Crystallized ginger, candied orange peel, and thin chocolate-covered mints are also tasty additions to a tea table.

Do not place all of your refreshments on the table at the same time, but retain sufficient in reserve for refilling the platters as they begin to empty. The hostess should discreetly keep an eye on the tea table throughout the reception to make sure that it never acquires an air of devastation, and also to remove any used tea or coffee cups her guests may have placed there. Nothing can so quickly ruin the appetizing aspect of a tea table than a few lipstick-stained teacups scattered among the sandwich trays.

If it is a large, late tea party, and some of the husbands plan to pick up their wives at the end of the day, or in case some of the late guests arrive at an hour more suitable for cocktails than for tea, you might also prepare in the living room a cocktail tray for serving sherry or whisky.

While this kind of a large tea party may still exist in provincial cities, it has practically vanished from cosmopolitan social life. On the other hand, it is increasingly fashionable for nonworking women to invite one, two, or three close friends to tea at four or five o'clock, for a refreshing interlude of chatter and relaxation that marks the end of the day and the beginning of the evening. Personally, I know of nothing more pleasant and cozy than to settle down in front of a warm fireplace on a winter afternoon and to share a pot of steaming tea with one or two dear friends.

In these most informal circumstances, your refreshments can be more limited, but they can be even more refined. In the winter, my favorite teatime snack is hot, thin cinnamon toast, and if you share my taste for this, you do not need to prepare anything else. Otherwise, you might serve any two varieties of the sandwiches already mentioned, plus a small plate of sweet cookies or petit fours. Your tea should be perfectly delicious and very hot. You will not take out your silver tea set for such an intimate occasion, unless it is of small proportions, but preferably use a pretty porcelain ensemble decorated with a flower or fruit motif. Beautiful porcelain tea sets are designed nowadays. But do not make the foolish economy of buying earthenware instead of porcelain, for its heat-retaining qualities are vastly inferior.

The coziest way to serve an intimate tea of this kind is, in the winter, on a tray set on the coffee table in front of a gently blazing fire—and it is useful to have an extra occasional table or (extremely elegant) an English-style tiered "cake table" for holding your plates of sandwiches and cakes; in the summer, the same general arrangement on a patio or terrace. If you possess a tiny apartment balcony or garden, you might arrange the refreshments on an attractively set card table with chairs around it. And if you have a very grand home, nothing is more elegant than to serve afternoon tea to one or two of your best friends in the cozy boudoir end of your own bedroom, especially if there is a fireplace.

TEEN-AGERS

❡ Modern teen-agers are probably the most sociable creatures ever born. They group themselves together in sets, cliques, clans, crowds, classes, teams, troops, clubs, and, on the least privileged level of society, in gangs. They travel in twos, threes, fours, and larger groups, but seldom do you see a teen-ager all alone.

This highly developed sense of sociability naturally leads to a great deal of entertaining, and while it is safe to say that dancing to recorded music is and will undoubtedly remain the principal social activity of the teen-age set, young people are forever inventing new kinds of parties, which may be the rage one year only to be completely abandoned the next. Conformity is often a consequence of gregariousness, and, no matter how loudly some sophisticated teen-agers may protest, the truth is that they usually want to entertain in exactly the same way that their friends do, to serve the same refreshments, and to offer identical entertainment. At the moment, dancing is in but games are out. Every teen set has its preferred kinds of parties, just as each has its own language and behavior code. Since these can vary widely from one community to another, it seems to me that the wisest course for fond parents to follow is to permit their teen-age children to entertain their friends in the current fashionable way, to lend a helping hand in the preparation of the decoration and refreshments, to maintain a very discreet supervision of the proceedings from a distance, but, at the same time, to insist upon controlling the three most delicate potential danger points:

(1.) *Liquor*. The famous teen party in Darien, which ended up in the police courts where the parents of the young host were arraigned for having served alcoholic beverages to minors, was reported in head-lines all over the world and brought into the limelight this particularly knotty question, which seems to be far more critical in the United States than abroad. In France, for example, whisky is always provided at debutante dancing parties, but never for the age group of sixteen or under. Anyway, most of the young people in Europe prefer soft drinks or an innocuous fruit and wine punch to stronger beverages.

It seems to me therefore that teen-age drinking is a community problem rather than a question of individual conviction. If I were an American mother, I would discuss the subject with the parents of my children's friends and decide upon a mutual policy, and then, after explaining it to my children, I would adhere to it very strictly. But the important thing is to face the fact that there is a decision to be made and a policy to be formulated. The least recommendable course would be simply to close your eyes and hope for the best. Moreover, the most practical way of discouraging alcoholic consumption at your teen-age children's parties is to provide plenty of diverting activities, lots of hearty refreshments, an enormous quantity of assorted nonalcoholic drinks, to avoid above all any resemblance to the style of adult cocktail parties, and to set a definite closing hour. Which brings us to the second trouble point:

(2.) *Curfew.* This question should also be settled once and for all, and no exceptions should be either necessary or permitted if the general policy is reasonable. This is also to some extent a community problem, because you naturally do not wish to appear either overly indulgent nor overly strict in comparison with the parents of other teen-agers. In Paris, the general rule is that informal weekday- or Sunday-evening parties must be over by ten o'clock at the latest, because of school the next day. As a matter of fact, the five-to-nine informal supper dance on Sunday afternoon is particularly popular with our younger set. Late dances are scheduled exclusively on Saturday night, with the exception of holidays, and for these one o'clock is the usual curfew hour, and perhaps two o'clock for older teens. The signal for the end of the party is the stopping of the dance music. If absolutely necessary, the parents can make a friendly brief appearance to say good-by to any difficult guests who seem to have settled down for the night. And this brings up the third possible trouble point:

(3.) *Guests.* Parents are perfectly within their rights in wishing to know exactly whom their children intend to receive in their home.

They should go over the guest list together beforehand and, if necessary, exercise a tactful censorship. If your daughter invites a certain number of girl friends, requesting each of them to bring an escort of her choice, the girls should be required to telephone in advance the names of the boys who will accompany them. For very large parties and debutante balls, it is obligatory to send engraved invitation cards, which must be presented by each arriving guest at a control point near the front door. If you are always perfectly reasonable in reviewing the guest list, and—most important of all—if your recommendations are in no way based on snobbishness or personal prejudice, your teen-age children will feel that they are being aided rather than policed.

Do not forget that the purpose of their parties, just as yours, is simply to have fun. Teen-agers do not enjoy an atmosphere of disorderliness any more than you do. They discipline their own society sometimes more strictly than you would do, and in this regard, if there should ever be an unpleasant incident, such as a guest who has had too much to drink, or one who is becoming loud or rowdy, it is preferable to charge one of his young friends with the responsibility of escorting him home or requesting him to leave, and to reserve your parental intervention as a last resort. Needless to add, in order for parental intervention to be a possibility, at least one parent should remain at home throughout the evening, tactfully out of sight (and for your own comfort, out of earshot),—in your bedroom, for example, with an interesting book.

There have been numerous reports in recent months of rowdiness, destruction, and general irresponsibility at certain teen parties. I am sure, however, that these are exceptions rather than the rule—(if they were not unusual, they would not be considered news). Moreover, I suspect that some of these distressing scenes might never have occurred if the young guests had been offered plenty of food, plenty of light beverages, and sufficient activity and entertainment to keep them occupied without having to invent mischief.

In short, where informal small parties are concerned, and in the case of spontaneous teen-age entertaining, it is preferable to permit your children to organize everything themselves according to their own taste and standards, and to request simply that they respect your reasonable restrictions concerning drinking, the selection of guests, and the closing hour that you have decided upon together.

When, however, your teen-age children wish to give a more elaborate kind of dancing party, you will have to offer them greater assistance. Although you will probably end up by doing most of the preparation yourself, you should ask your daughter to help. This is the ideal occasion for her to serve an apprenticeship in entertaining, so that she will have learned how to be an elegant hostess all by herself in a very few years.

If I say daughter rather than son, it is because teen-age dances are far more often given by girls than by boys. Teen-age boys are in such great demand as dancing partners that they seldom have the time or feel the necessity of organizing a party themselves!

The ideal number of guests for an informal dance in an apartment or house of average size is about thirty, with one-fourth to one-third more boys than girls—for example, twelve girls and eighteen boys, or fifteen girls and twenty boys. The guests should be sent written invitations, the hours might be specified as "from 9 P.M. until 2 A.M.," depending on local custom, and the date should be a Saturday night.

The living room should be arranged for dancing, and the dining room for a buffet supper, unless your living room is very spacious or unless you have a vast playroom where the dance floor can be installed at one end and the buffet at the other. You may simply remove the rug if there is one, but in the case of nailed-down, wall-to-wall carpeting you will have to rent a portable dance floor of the required dimensions from a party rental firm. Let your daughter help you to arrange flowers around the room, on the mantelpiece, and in the center of the buffet. The decoration and setting of the table is just the same as for one of your own buffet dinners, including the candles. But you will need to remove everything fragile and all unnecessary bibelots from both rooms, and to distribute an even greater number of large ashtrays than when you entertain your adult friends.

The menu should be simple but hearty. Teen-agers are not yet experienced enough in gastronomy to be either refined or adventurous in their taste. In the spring and summer, for example, you might serve an assortment of substantial sandwiches (turkey, ham and cheese, chicken salad, etc.), platters of cold cuts and cheese, cold fried chicken, bowls of salad and cole slaw, and a rather wide choice of cakes and pies and ice cream for dessert. In the winter, spaghetti and meatballs, a huge pizza pie, hot dogs and hamburgers with potato salad (or a hot potato-onion casserole), cole slaw, and relishes; or a huge steaming chicken and kidney pie or a hot casserole of sauerkraut garnished with boiled and smoked ham, frankfurters and sausages, which may be accompanied simply by cheese and rolls and crackers, a salad, an apple pie (or rather several apple pies), and perhaps beer, in addition to a fruit punch and a very generous amount of assorted soft bottled drinks.

The buffet dinner may be served an hour or so after the guests have assembled, but it is important to provide the buffet with snacks as well as drinks throughout the entire evening, since dancing will develop ravenous appetites. Besides, many teen-agers seem to prefer eating a snack every few hours to one copious meal. With a cold buffet menu, you can simply prepare very large quantities of everything, enough to keep the platters filled until late in the evening; in the case of a hot dish, such as the sauerkraut, you can leave the cheese and pie on the buffet table and prepare a heaping tray of sandwiches to be served at midnight.

You will need a large amount of ice, a great quantity of rented tumblers as well as paper straws for those who prefer drinking straight from the bottle. In any case, you can be sure that the liquid consumption will be enormous, since the present types of athletic ballroom dances develop a terrific thirst. One quart of beverage per person is not an exaggerated estimate.

It is important to arrange the dance records with your daughter beforehand, first of all marking her own so that they do not become inextricably mixed up with the records that her guests are bound to bring. The latter should also be marked, in order to avoid confusion and disputes at the end of the evening, when everyone recovers his own belongings. It is best to begin the dance program with the liveliest, gayest, most rhythmic music in order to create an *ambiance* right away, and to taper off toward the end of the evening to slower, dreamier fox-trots, for even teen-agers will no longer have the energy to twist and rock at one o'clock in the morning. You should vary the different rhythms with, for example, a few rock records, then a few slow fox-trots, a novelty dance, a couple of tangos, a few more rocks, etc. Your daughter can advise you in this field far better than I, but the point is to help her to prepare the pile of records and to start the music before the guests arrive.

You should set aside a separate coatroom for the boys and another for the girls. Generally the best plan is for the boys to use the front-hall closet and the downstairs or hall bathroom, and for the girls to be assigned your daughter's own bedroom and bath. A charming friend whom I consulted for advice on teen-age parties told me to be sure to mention that it is very useful to provide a generous supply of safety pins in the girls' powder room for making emergency repairs to ripped hemlines, and also several packages of extralarge hairpins for repairing upswept hairdos and chignons that begin to tumble down after an hour or two of dancing.

At a party of this kind it is always extremely helpful for the young hostess, who has been aided in the preparations by her mother, to be aided during the actual party by a brother, cousin, or, lacking these, by a boy who is "just like a brother" to her. To this young friend or relative can be given the personal responsibility of looking after wall-flowers and of maintaining order as well. Pretty girls will always take care of themselves, but the plain ones must also dance all night if the party is to be a complete success.

It might be a good idea to prepare with your daughter two or three partner-changing games, such as the concentric circles of boys and girls, in which you dance with the person facing you when the music stops; or the game of simply changing partners each time the music stops; or perhaps the game of assigning partners by having the boys and girls match slips of paper drawn from two different hats, each slip containing one half of a short joke, a riddle and its answer, half of a famous saying or of a celebrated couple. None of these games may finally be necessary, but it is worthwhile preparing them in case the party should strike a dull spot.

The best general policy is for the parents of the young hostess to remain at home all evening but out of sight. You can therefore settle down in your bedroom with your husband and enjoy a long evening of reading or a marathon game of double solitaire. Remember that the purpose of your staying at home is to be available in case of accident or emergency, and not to act as a spy or a policeman. So do not let your curiosity get the better of you. If, however, your daughter should come and beg you to join the party for a moment in order to demonstrate the "letkiss" or the "surf"—I prefer to leave the decision up to you!

(See Buffets, Debutantes, Dinners, Drinks, etc.)

TELEPHONE

⟦ The telephoned invitation is nowadays just as correct as a written one in all informal entertaining. It is quicker, more spontaneous, allows for more detailed explanations as to who will be there and what to wear, and it has the added advantage of letting the hostess know at once which of her guests accept and which ones regret, so that she can immediately revise her guest list if necessary.

When the occasion in question is a cocktail party, no additional reminder is necessary. But for a luncheon or a dinner, it is courteous and practical to send a "reminder card" four or five days ahead of time. This is no more than a calling card or an "informal" with your name engraved, and the date, time, address, and the occasion written by hand in the usual way. In France we always add the words *pour mémoire* in the top corner, but this would probably seem rather affected in other countries even though our RSVP formula has been adopted throughout the world. A reminder card of this kind is also very practical in the case of an engagement made a very long time in advance, even if a written invitation was originally sent.

There are correct and incorrect hours for telephoning just as there are for visits, because the person you speak to over the phone is, in a way, being received in your home, and to accept a telephone call already amounts to offering a certain degree of hospitality. While customs vary in different parts of the world, it is generally discourteous to telephone on other than a very urgent matter before nine o'clock in the morning, after nine or ten o'clock at night, and at mealtimes. As a matter of fact, the three universally valid reasons for a woman's not accepting a telephone call are that she is at table, in her bath, or asleep.

When you are entertaining, it would be very rude indeed to neglect your guests and to devote your attention to a telephoning interloper. You should firmly refuse to become involved in conversation, but offer to call back later or in the morning or, if it is a very urgent matter, you should excuse yourself to your guests and take the call on the kitchen or bedroom extension.

Likewise, a guest who requests permission to use the telephone should be led to the bedroom extension, if there is one, so that he can make his call in private.

(See Invitations)

TELEVISION

❲ Television can provide agreeable entertainment when you are spending a quiet family evening at home, and it can keep you company when you happen to be alone. But it would be a dreadful mistake to invite those heroic cowboys, valiant interns, infallible detectives, or even the lovely girls who sell shampoos and refrigerators, to one of your parties. And do not believe that a television set turned on low provides a good background for conversation. Nothing is more certain to monopolize the entire evening, to prevent any kind of intelligent discussion among your guests, and to ruin the atmosphere you have prepared with so much care.

Even when the television set is turned off, there is a risk that the mere sight of the screen will exercise its irresistible attraction on a guest whose habit of turning the dial at eight o'clock sharp every night has become a veritable conditioned reflex. There are several methods of defense against this particular public enemy: moving your television out of the living room and into the den or kitchen, or, as it seems to be increasingly the fashion, into your bedroom; concealing it so cleverly in the woodwork or a bookcase that nobody will suspect its presence; or, as a last resort, pulling out the plug and pretending that it is out of order.

Although television can spoil an ordinary party, it can provide an easy and casual form of entertainment when the entire evening is built around a particularly worthwhile program. You might, for example, invite a few friends to join you in watching an important boxing or tennis match, an international telecast via satellite, a Spectacular play or musical, or a program in color if you happen to be the only member of your group who possesses a color set.

This kind of an evening should, of course, be restricted to a few intimate friends, for everyone should have a comfortable place to sit and a clear view of the screen. Furthermore, it is wise to specify the program you have chosen when you telephone your invitations, because not everybody shares the same taste in these matters.

It is practically impossible to serve a meal correctly, even a very simple one, when the guests' eyes are all riveted on a television screen, and I certainly do not recommend a frozen TV dinner as company fare. The best method is to plan a normal dinner menu, but a bit earlier than usual if the program is scheduled for nine or nine-thirty, for example, and to time everything so that only the dessert and coffee will be served in front of the television. There should be plenty of ashtrays and little tables near the chairs, perhaps a few thick cushions for floor-sitters (since this is a most informal occasion), and above all a dessert that is simple to handle, such as a magnificent chocolate cake or a mousse. Anything runny, melting, sticky, or requiring skillful manipulation of knives and forks is bound to result in spattered upholstery and spotted neckties.

If, on the other hand, the television show you have in mind starts rather early in the evening, then it should be finished by nine-thirty or ten o'clock, and in this case it would be better to serve a late dinner afterward. You can calm the appetites of your hungry guests by serving along with cocktails (not too strong, because everyone is bound to drink several of them during the course of the program) a generous quantity of hot and cold hors d'oeuvres, hearty enough to substitute for the entrée. It is a good idea to avoid dips and pastes that the guests must spread themselves, and to confine your choice to easy-to-eat snacks, such as cheese balls, tiny, hot, puff pastry shells filled with thick, creamed seafood or chicken, squares of smoked salmon wrapped around tiny hearts of lettuce, squares of smoked ham rolled around bite-sized pieces of cantaloupe melon, or plain ham rolled around green asparagus tips. Plenty of cocktail toothpicks and piles of paper napkins will help to avoid sticky fingerprints on the furniture.

The moment the program is over, you should usher everybody into the dining room—and do not weaken at this point, because it is very risky to let your guests catch a glimpse of the following attraction. One of them is certain to become intrigued by what is to follow, and either you will be unable to tear him away from the screen or, if you do, he will feel strangely ill at ease during all the rest of the evening.

The second formula, with a late meal, is the most enjoyable, because your dinner party is just like a normal one except that the guests are hungrier, they have had more to drink, and, if the program has been an interesting one, you will have no problem at all in starting off an animated table conversation.

Television entertainment need not be restricted to dinner parties. I remember a most enjoyable television party at the Paris apartment of friends who owned one of the first sets on the Continent and who invited us to watch the Coronation of Elizabeth II. Because the ceremony took place at noon and lasted all day long, the party started as a buffet luncheon, gradually turned into a sort of open house and ended up as a cocktail party, with friends wandering in and out, husbands going back to the office to return a few hours later, wives slipping out for half an hour to pick up the children at school. I realized then that it is often more fun to watch this kind of a spectacle in company rather than alone, and it is a friendly formula that might be employed on any number of occasions. For example: to share with a small group of friends the excitement of the Olympic Games, the election results (with the risk that the fate of your social party is apt to be the same as that of your political party), or a royal wedding. The important point is for the telecast in question to be of genuine general interest and of long duration.

The only other occasion I can think of on which a television set is an advantage rather than a disaster in entertaining is at a children's party. Since tiny tots possess a very limited power of concentration, it is always prudent to plan at least twice as many games and diversions as you feel are really necessary. Then, when they have devoured all the refreshments, broken all the toys, become bored with all the games you've planned for them, and their parents haven't yet arrived to take them home, you can bring to the rescue television, which, thanks to its cleverly conceived programs especially for children, can magically transform a horde of wild Indians into a silent choir of little angels.

THEATER

❦ It has always been an elegant form of entertaining to invite a person, a couple, or two couples at the most, to the theater, and to offer them either dinner beforehand or a late supper after the play is over. Today it is also a rather lavish gesture, since theater tickets have become very expensive. Neither is an evening at the theater as simple a project as it may seem, for the tickets to a successful play are sold out long in advance. As a matter of fact, London is the only city I know where you can decide at the last minute to see a play and still be reasonably certain of procuring good seats and of spending an enjoyable evening. In cities where the only available theater-going is provided by a limited run of the touring company of Broadway successes, it can be very difficult to book good seats even at scalpers' prices if you are neither a regular subscriber to the theater nor a friend of the star. Of course, these difficulties add value and glamour to your invitation, but they also complicate the practical organization of this kind of an evening.

If you are mad about the stage, you may very well find just as much of interest in a distinguished flop as in the latest smash hit—perhaps even more. But everybody does not share the same taste, and it is therefore a safe rule to restrict your theater entertaining to two general categories:

(1.) To invite one or two close friends whose taste you know well to see a rather offbeat play, which you are certain they will enjoy;

(2.) To invite one other couple to accompany you to the latest hit production, which, no matter what its intrinsic artistic merits may be, "simply has to be seen." A restaurant-theater invitation of this kind is perhaps the ideal way of entertaining people whom you know only slightly, those who do not fit very well into your circle of friends, people whom you find it very difficult to talk to, or those whom you do not care to invite to your own home for one reason or another.

You may arrange your rendezvous either in the restaurant where you plan to dine together beforehand, or in the theater lobby five or ten minutes before the play is supposed to begin, if you prefer to have supper afterward. Your choice will be determined by your respective time schedules as well as by the curtain time, which may be as early as seven-thirty or as late as nine. During the working week, it is usually more convenient to dine rapidly beforehand in a restaurant not far away from the theater; but on the eve of a nonworking day, it may be more pleasant and certainly more gala to serve just cocktails and sandwiches before the play, and a midnight supper afterward. The second formula is the more chic, requiring dressier clothes, a smarter restaurant (or a rather luxurious cold supper at home)—consequently, a bigger bankroll.

If your afternoons are free, a theater matinée following a light luncheon is an excellent means of entertaining an older, single woman, who may not have the opportunity to see many legitimate plays and who would never dream of going to the theater alone. You need not splurge on the most expensive seats in this case, and you may perfectly well replace the luncheon with a more economical tea after the performance, if you are limited in time or money.

Since I have always adored the theater, I believe that every child should be introduced to it when he is still young enough and imaginative enough to come under the full spell of its magical world of make-believe. And so, whenever possible, it is well worth the effort to organize a children's theater party during the school holidays, and to take your own children, along with as many of their young friends as you are able to transport and supervise, to attend a matinée performance of a suitable play or musical. In this case, luncheon or tea would probably create impossible complications, and besides, the children would undoubtedly prefer a gooey ice cream sundae after the show. Remember, however, that tickets to children's entertainments are in great demand during the holidays, and you must make your reservations far in advance.

Inviting friends to accompany you to the theater is certainly less personal than inviting them to a dinner party in your own home with other guests. But it is undeniably an elegant form of entertainment, which is paradoxically ideal in two completely opposite social situations: when you wish to offer a special treat to very close friends, and when you are obliged to entertain people with whom you have nothing in common.

(See Rendezvous, Restaurants)

TIPS

⟨ It is often possible to judge the character as well as the manners of a person according to his method of tipping: the poor and timid have a tendency to give too much, and the rich and confident not enough.

Tipping practices also vary from one country to another, and it is wise to inform oneself of the customs in a foreign city at the beginning of one's visit. For example, a twenty-percent tip for a taxi ride would be considered generous by a Parisian chauffeur, but it might inspire insults from his colleagues in Brussels! Moreover, Europeans never tip the waiter who brings the breakfast tray in a hotel, and the American habit of writing in a tip when you sign the bill is absolutely unheard of.

In private homes, there is only one occasion when it is obligatory to tip the household personnel, and that is when you have spent a weekend or longer as a guest in the home of friends. In England, the largest tip always goes to the butler, with a smaller sum for the chambermaid and cook. England is also the only country where servants are addressed by their family names rather than by their first names. But very few modern homes, even in England, are equipped with such a large household staff, and if your hostess has only a daily maid, you must either think of giving her a tip before she goes home on the last night of your visit, or else you can leave an envelope for her in the kitchen containing a minimum of two dollars in France and five dollars in the United States.

In the French provinces, it is the custom to leave a tip of about a dollar even if you have only been invited to dinner, and it is best to go to the kitchen and hand it to the cook in person. When you have been invited to dinner at the home of friends very often during the course of the year, it is more elegant to give the cook or maid a little Christmas present, such as a scarf, gloves, stockings, eau de cologne, etc., in addition to a sum of money (ten dollars or so).

In restaurants, even if you pay the bill with a credit card, it is necessary to tip the wine steward and the waiter, and this should be done as discreetly as possible, especially when it is a woman who pays.

If a friend sends a car and chauffeur to pick you up or to take you home after a party, you should give him a tip. In fact, you should discreetly tip other people's servants every time they perform a personal service for you. Even in the case of your own personnel, you should always think of giving them a special gratuity the morning after a big party, because what has been fun for you has meant a lot of extra work for them.

Finally, you should always prepare your tipping money in advance, for nothing is more embarrassing to everyone concerned than an interminable moment of fishing in the troubled waters of an overstuffed handbag.

TOASTS

⟨ Even outside of political life, where candidates are forever raising their glasses to such entities as Liberty, the Republic, the Party, or the Queen, a person may be called upon to propose a toast to an honored guest. This responsibility seldom falls upon a woman, I am happy to say, except perhaps for a few rare occasions, such as the banquet of a women's club or a college reunion. And so this chapter is particularly addressed to men.

It is obviously much more elegant to seem to improvise your speech, even if you have actually rehearsed it for hours in front of a mirror and with a recording machine. But if you haven't the time to memorize your toast, or if you haven't confidence in your talents as an orator, you can always read it from a paper—although this tends to create an atmosphere of solemnity and the audience is likely to be far less indulgent.

The best recipe for a toast, which is generally a paean of praise to an individual on the occasion of a promotion, an anniversary, or the awarding of an honor, is as follows:

(*Note:* the entire recipe should be completed in five or ten minutes at the most.)

Basic ingredients: A chronological review of the most flattering exploits of the person's life, which you should not be afraid of describing in the most grandiloquent terms, at the same time keeping in mind the fact that while some people pride themselves on having started at zero and risen to the top, there are others who do not like to be reminded that they were born on the wrong side of the tracks.

In order to render the dish more digestible, it should be seasoned with one or two witty anecdotes, perhaps describing a mutual prank at the age of ten, or making fun of a personal idiosyncrasy in a kindly, lighthearted way.

Sugar with several eulogistic phrases, and *flamber* with a few eloquent and affectionate words designed to set off a chorus of "Bravos!"

There exist a certain number of people who cannot refrain from proposing a toast on the slightest pretext. This can be most amusing if they are very witty, but it can be terribly vulgar if they are not. In any case, it usually indicates a desire to seek the limelight rather than a genuine affection for the person in whose honor the toast is offered.

TRAVEL

❲ Modern travel is so rapid and the stopovers scheduled in each city are generally so brief (I myself once visited thirty different American cities in fifty days!) that traditional travel etiquette is no longer observed the way it used to be. Moreover, hospitality in America is so much more casual and more generous than in most other lands, that it is easy to understand why so many American tourists accept the hospitality offered to them abroad as a matter of course, almost as if it were a special privilege issued along with their passports. Today, the only travelers who meticulously discharge their social obligations when they are far from home are diplomats and chiefs of state, who never set forth on a voyage without a trunkful of gifts for their foreign hosts, and who invariably terminate their visit to another land by hosting a magnificent reception at their country's embassy or some borrowed palace, to which they invite everybody who has entertained or been presented to them during their stay.

Social obligations incurred during a voyage are not as lightly regarded in Europe as they are in younger nations. It is, of course, very much more difficult to give a party when you are traveling in a foreign country than it is to entertain in your own home. Furthermore, it would be expected of you only if you had spent at least several weeks in the same city and had been widely feted. However, in these conditions, it would certainly be elegant on your part to reserve a small salon in the hotel where you are staying and to invite all the people who have entertained you and the new friends you have made to a cocktail party a day or two before you leave. If you have been the houseguest of friends abroad, you can either adopt the same formula and give your party at the best hotel in town, or you can consult with your hostess about the possibility of holding your cocktail party in her home, at your expense of course. In order to avoid imposing on the goodwill of your hostess, it would be most thoughtful to insist on hiring a caterer for the event, unless your guest list is really very limited or your funds very low.

When only a few people have invited you to dinner and luncheon during your stay in a foreign city, it is preferable to return their invitations individually. Unless you know their city as well as they do, the best idea is to plan the most "touristy" evening you can imagine. The first time I had dinner at the Eiffel Tower was as a guest of English friends, and I owe my delightful memories of a summer-evening cruise along the Seine in a Bateau Mouche to the charming American tourists who invited me to accompany them. In other words, when you wish to entertain foreigners who have offered you hospitality abroad, it would be a mistake to attempt to compete with them in their own specialties on their own home ground. Instead, introduce them to the fascinating aspects of the city that are well known to tourists, but very likely to be a revelation to permanent residents. It is certain to amuse them and at the same time to make them swell with pride in their hometown, which, thanks to you, they are perhaps viewing for the first time through the admiring eyes of a foreign visitor.

(See Foreigners, Voyage)

TRAYS

❡ Every well-equipped household possesses several different kinds of trays, and the way in which they are arranged is often an accurate indication of the degree of refinement of the mistress of the house. Personally, I always judge the class of a hotel according to the manner in which the breakfast tray is presented. In a private home, I prefer the old-fashioned rimmed wooden breakfast trays with a handle at either end, covered with a pretty tray cloth (a plastic material is quite acceptable), to the modern printed plastic trays whose patterns are not always very attractive.

For serving coffee after meals, it is undeniable that a silver tray, without a cloth, is the most elegant of all. If you do not own a rolling tea table, you will also need a perfectly plain, rather large tray for clearing the table.

Finally, in every home there should be a tiny silver tray for presenting a glass of water to a guest, and for the morning mail. As a matter of fact, along with vases and flowerpot holders, a small silver salver is one of the most useful wedding gifts that you can offer to a young couple.

❨ Etiquette books tell you what is the correct way to behave in every circumstance, but few of them describe what is chic or "U" (to use the term witty Nancy Mitford coined to indicate "upper class"), and what is not chic, or "non-U." I suppose that the current American equivalents might be "in" and "out."

It is a fact that while certain manners of speech and action have always been a sign of a lack of social education, such as (in France, at least) constantly shifting one's fork from the left hand to the right or saying "Pleased to meet you" or speaking of one's husband to a social acquaintance as "Mr. Smith," and (in England) of serving High Tea every day in place of dinner, or (in America) of a man's failing to remove his hat in an elevator or failing to rise when a woman enters the room, there are many other attitudes that are more a question of mode than of etiquette. For example, at the present time

— It is U to give small cocktail parties for twenty guests, but non-U to give a cocktail party for two hundred people.

— It is U to give a "Black Tie" buffet dinner; and non-U to give a sit-down dinner for twelve guests dressed in ordinary business suits.

— It is U to arrange flowers in mixed bouquets, non-U to fill a vase with long-stemmed gladioli. (And least U of all when the vase is placed on the rear deck of a yacht.)

— It is more U to decorate your home in an authentic 1900 style than in imitation Louis XV, which is elegant only if every piece of furniture is a signed antique. And it is super-U to combine Louis XIII furniture with ultramodern abstract paintings and sculpture.

— It is U to leave on the living-room coffee table a copy of *The Words* by Jean-Paul Sartre; but non-U to leave the *Reader's Digest*.

— It is more U to inhabit a small apartment in a very fashionable neighborhood than it is to live in an immense one situated in a more ordinary part of town. There is one important exception in Paris, however, where it is more U to live in a historic private house to which you always refer by name ("l'Hôtel des Ambassadeurs de Hollande," for example) near the Place des Vosges in the Marais, a practically miserable district, than it is to buy a brand-new apartment on the Avenue Foch.

— It is U to invite two or three friends to tea and to serve a few choice homemade refreshments, while it is non-U to give a catered tea party for fifty women.

— It is obviously much more U to be able to say that you dined with Marlene Dietrich in the kitchen, than it is to talk about the chamber of commerce banquet you attended, even if it took place at the Waldorf.

UMBRELLAS

❰ If one of the guests you have invited to a party should be drenched by a downpour on his way from his house to yours, it would be a pity but it is not your affair. However, as soon as a guest has crossed your threshold, his welfare is your concern, and it would be unforgivable for you to allow him to be soaked by the rain between your own front doorstep and the shelter of his car. Every household should therefore have a large umbrella in readiness in the front hall for just such emergencies. And for this purpose no umbrella is more practical and smart than the very large, very concave type carried by the doormen of smart hotels and restaurants. Besides, this giant size is least likely to be borrowed or to disappear.

An umbrella stand in the front hall is an essential accessory that is often lacking in an otherwise perfectly equipped home. The most practical and chic are the simple brass stands with a shallow plate at the bottom for collecting dripping rainwater. These are perhaps less decorative and more expensive than the models resembling oversize wastebaskets, but it is much easier to empty the water from them. Moreover, they are preferred by the British, whose example I am always willing to follow whenever rainy weather is concerned.

A perfect hostess should also think of hanging an extra umbrella in the guest room closet for the use of houseguests. I have often been touched by the blind optimism of friends from out of town whom I have invited to stay with me. They are, I suppose, so thrilled by the prospect of spending a few days or a week in Paris, that they expect everything to be divine—including the weather. But, alas, this is seldom the case. And since this may be true of your hometown too, it is a good idea to consider an umbrella as an indispensable item in your guest room inventory. For that matter, you might even have two: one to loan to guests, and the other to borrow yourself when you have forgotten your own in a shop or restaurant.

(See Rain)

UNIFORMS

❡ Even the most aristocratic French families no longer require their household personnel to wear their traditional livery, whose colors and designs were as unchanging as the family crest. From the gatekeeper to the butler, including the valets and the coachman, each member of the staff used to wear a special costume, and the white jacket that has become the present-day uniform of all male domestic personnel was exclusively reserved for bartenders.

In a very few elegant homes, the butler still wears a tailcoat for formal dinner parties, and the only difference between his evening dress and that of the guests is that his revers are plain rather than silk-covered, his vest is black rather than white, and he wears a bow tie. During the day, the same butler would wear a jacket edged in black, striped trousers, a black necktie, and a white shirt with the points of the collar turned up. However, to repeat, this uniform is seldom seen today, and then only in the homes of diplomats or government officials, or where an exceptionally luxurious standard of living is maintained. The valet, whose presence alone implies a high degree of luxury, is dressed in black trousers, a washable white cotton jacket, a plain white shirt, and a black tie, to which he adds white cotton gloves whenever he waits on table. The chauffeur's uniform consists of a navy blue suit, a navy blue gabardine overcoat, and a cap with a shiny visor. The chef wears an enveloping white apron and the traditional towering white starched hat.

As for the feminine personnel, the cook may be dressed all in white or in light blue, with a blue apron for heavy work and a white one for the afternoon. The children's governess wears a blue-and-white striped cotton dress with a white collar, cuffs, and apron, and white shoes. But when she takes the baby for a walk in the park, she dresses in navy blue. The chambermaid's uniform is a black dress with white collar, cuffs, and apron, and sometimes a little white starched headband, worn with plain black shoes.

This, at least, is the theory of domestic uniforms. In actual practice, everything is quite different! Just try to persuade your maid to wear a black nylon dress with white collar, cuffs, and apron, instead of the bright purple sweater of which she seems so fond. Just try to insist that she wear stockings at all times and closed oxfords instead of open-toed sandals. If you finally succeed without her throwing a scene or sulking for days, all that I can say is, "Bravo!"

(See Help, Service)

UNINVITED GUESTS

⟨ Party-crashing is a rare occurrence today, and when it does happen it is more often the result of a misunderstanding than the desire to attend an affair to which one has not been invited. For example, a friend of mine once "crashed" a cocktail party quite unwittingly because she had been directed to the wrong salon of the hotel where two different parties were being held at the same time. And another friend once attended the wrong funeral, realizing her error only when she found herself expressing her condolences to a perfectly strange widow. But these embarrassing incidents are no more than innocent faux pas.

There does however exist a certain amount of party-crashing at large debutante balls, at least so I am told. It seems that a young invited guest who, for one reason or another, does not care to attend a particular ball, considers it an act of friendship to give his invitation card to a friend. If you ask me, it is also an act of service to the hostess, who always attempts to assemble as many dancing partners as possible for the debutantes. Furthermore, the young man in question is only interested in spending an enjoyable evening, and in order to attract as little attention as possible he will probably be on his very best behavior.

The very rare cases of malicious crashing are confined to teen-age parties. But if, whenever your teen-age son or daughter gives a very large reception of this kind, you always follow the normal procedure of sending written invitations and having someone (preferably a husky young man) check the guest list at the door, it is most unlikely that an uninvited guest will ever appear to cause an unpleasant incident.

UNPACKING

❲ Nowadays only the most princely private homes are provided with sufficient personnel to be able to assign to a chambermaid the job of unpacking the baggage of a houseguest. As a matter of fact, modern houseguests are so unaccustomed to this attention that they may find it disconcerting rather than welcome. In most contemporary homes, guests are simply given a good luggage rack, an empty closet with plenty of assorted hangers, and a moment of privacy during which they are expected to unpack their bags themselves.

If there is any help at all in the house, even a part-time maid, it is very thoughtful of the hostess to offer to have her guest's clothing pressed before it is put away, in order to remove the inevitable travel creases. In a servantless home, she might think of setting up an ironing board in the laundry room or kitchen before her guest arrives, so that the guest can do the necessary pressing herself. In the case of a man guest, the hostess can offer her personal valet service. If he is obviously in need but shy about accepting, she can simply brush and press his things at the same time that she looks after her husband's clothes at a moment when both of them are absent. The point is that most modern, plane-traveling guests have carefully planned a minimum wardrobe, and it is essential for every garment to be wearable if they are to honor you by being well dressed on every occasion. Their morale as well as their appearance is therefore bound to be improved if they start off their visit with their clothing in perfect condition.

All of this may seem to be an unnecessary additional chore. But attention to such details is what can make the difference between entertaining well and entertaining with elegance.

VENTILATION

❡ Many a hostess whose heart sinks as she spies one of her guests stifling a yawn in the middle of the evening would do well simply to open a window for a few minutes before resigning herself to the possibly erroneous belief that her party has been a bore. It is amazing the effect a breath of fresh air can have on lagging conversation and drowsy guests! And yet few hostesses ever think of trying this simple remedy.

Perhaps American men are too polite to complain about an atmosphere that is stuffy and overheated, for it is they who suffer most when they are forced to spend an evening in an airless room. It is a notorious fact that restaurants and nightclubs are deliberately overheated out of consideration for women in décolleté evening gowns, without the slightest compassion for the men who swelter beneath several layers of silk and wool. The European railroads have solved once and for all the eternal dispute between passengers who wish the window open and those who want it closed by ruling in favor of the latter. In other words, if only one person in a crowded compartment requests that the window be closed, then closed it must be. However, in my own home I prefer to lend a cashmere cardigan or mohair stole to chilly women guests, rather than to risk suffocating the men. Very often it is sufficient to open a window for only a few minutes out of every hour or so in order to refresh the air. Sometimes the best method is to leave a window open in an adjoining room. For the lucky American women whose homes are air-conditioned (one out of every four, it seems), the problem is very simple indeed: they merely have to adjust the dial to the appropriate temperature. Remember, in this regard, that a large crowd produces a considerable amount of heat, and you should therefore select a lower heat setting for a big cocktail party than for a small dinner.

The proper ventilation of a room is a highly individual matter, depending not only on local climate and personal preference but also on mysterious factors that are peculiar to each different room. It is usually by a process of trial and error that you will find the ideal solution for your own home. Once you have discovered which windows or doors should be opened how far and for how long in order to provide a well-ventilated atmosphere during the course of an evening, all you have to do is to add this particular question to your already lengthy list of preoccupations. It may seem to be a minor detail, but it can mean the difference between a gay and animated group of guests and company that is gradually overcome by somnolence.

(See Odors, Smoking)

VIPs

❮ Whenever you entertain a Very Important Person, remember that the more important he is, the more he is likely to appreciate an evening of simplicity and relaxation, if only because this is what he seldom has an opportunity to enjoy. He is probably surfeited with pomp and ceremony and red carpets, not to mention champagne, caviar, and official banquet fare. And so the hostess who is also a keen psychologist reserves the VIP treatment for her *least* important guests, realizing that nothing is more flattering to simple people than a certain amount of pomp, nor more reassuring to timid, insecure people than a certain amount of ceremony. For VIPs, on the other hand, she prepares a small, select guest list, an atmosphere of warmth and refinement, and a menu built around dishes that are perfectly prepared and appetizingly presented but rather original, or even homespun, in character—such as paella, *pot au feu,* and chicken pie. Even President Johnson has served hamburgers to visiting heads of state.

If your VIP is renowned for his predilection for a certain food, by all means do *not* serve it. Everybody who entertains him will have the same idea. Charlie Chaplin, during a triumphant visit to England at the height of his popularity, once mentioned in a press interview his nostalgia for a certain suet pudding his mother used to make, and as a result thoughtful hostesses proudly presented him with the same pudding for dessert night after night until he could no longer bear the sight of it!

There is, of course, a minimum of protocol to be observed when you entertain a genuine VIP. The first and most important rule is to be absolutely accurate in your pronunciation of his name and titles, if he has any, and in your understanding of his functions. You will naturally accord him the place of honor at table, and the other guests should be tactful enough to permit him to be the last to arrive as well as the first to leave.

You should take even greater care with the guest list than with the menu, for it would be unpardonable to invite the Great Man to dine with his worst enemy, or in a company where he will meet nobody of the slightest interest to him. You should, however, allow him to be the undisputed star of the evening, rather than attempting to impress or flatter him by inviting all of the most important people you know. Rival egos seldom get along well together.

In the case of royalty, a hostess must submit her guest list to be endorsed by the royal equerry before she issues her invitations, and it seems to me only courteous always to inform your illustrious guests of honor as to whom you intend to invite with them, even when this is not obligatory.

VISITS

❮ Among close friends and good neighbors, a visit may be arranged for any hour of the day or evening, but in this day and age most people are simply too busy to be interrupted by an unexpected caller, and I am personally of the opinion that all unannounced visits should be ruthlessly banned.

No matter what the hour or who the caller is, a hostess should always seem enchanted to see her visitor, and she should offer something to eat and drink that is appropriate to the time of day (with the ex-

ception of condolence visits, when refreshments need not be served).
It is therefore a good idea to be prepared for short-notice visits by always keeping on hand a box of chocolates or candied fruit, a large tin
box of cookies, and a few cans of cocktail snacks, in addition to a supply
of tea, chocolate, coffee, and the essential ingredients for various alcoholic and nonalcoholic beverages. It is not chic to offer a visitor the
leftover remains of last night's dessert, no matter how delicious it may
have been.

The normal duration of a daytime social visit is forty-five minutes to
an hour, and no more than half an hour if one is recuperating from
an illness or the occasion is after the birth of a baby. If a visitor shows
no sign of leaving within a reasonable length of time, do not hesitate
to explain that you have an appointment, or an errand to do, or that it
is time for your nap or treatment.

It seems to me that nowadays no woman should feel the slightest obligation to receive a caller who has not announced her visit by telephoning ahead of time. However, when you hear the doorbell ring and
glimpse an unwelcome silhouette on your doorstep, it is undeniably
more elegant to go to the door and make your excuses in person, rather
than to hide behind the curtains and pretend that nobody is at home.

VOYAGE

〔 Traveling has become so simplified and is now such a routine matter
for so many people, that the old-fashioned bon-voyage party is practically obsolete. Even though you may be thrilled beyond description by
the prospect of your very first trip to Europe, as I was by my first visit
to the United States, it is more elegant to take it all in your stride and
not expect your friends to make a big fuss over you.

A traditional bon-voyage party would be considered somewhat provincial today, and certainly unsophisticated. But it is a very good idea
to organize a normal dinner party on the eve of their departure for
friends who are leaving on a long trip to some distant land, because the
last few days are invariably hectic and a woman is much too preoccupied
with questions of baggage and passports to be in a mood to plan tasty
meals at home.

You should invite only very good friends of the guest or guests of honor—in other words, people whom they would really enjoy seeing one last time before they leave. Many hostesses go to great trouble to invite as well persons who have already inhabited or visited the countries that your guests of honor are setting forth to discover. While this is undoubtedly thoughtful and may result in a certain amount of useful advice for the travelers, I would prefer to let them be the undisputed stars of the evening. I assume that they have already gathered all the practical information they require, and I do not like to risk dimming their pleasure or their sense of adventure by confronting them with more experienced globe-trotters who, nine times out of ten, enthusiastically recommend visits to hotels and cities that are not on your guests' itinerary (which it is too late to change), and invariably declare that the country in question was of interest five or ten or twenty years ago, but has since been thoroughly spoiled by foreign tourists (that is to say, by people like themselves). All of this may be true and even helpful, but it is wise to remember that your role on this occasion is to be a hostess and not a travel agent, and your principal aim should be to see that your guests depart, not with an ideal itinerary in their pockets, but with the memory of a very pleasant evening.

The day before a departure is a better time to schedule a large bon-voyage dinner rather than the evening when the plane leaves at midnight. However, very close friends might very well plan an intimate dinner for no more than six or eight before a midnight departure, with some of you accompanying the travelers to the airport, train, or boat—if you have the courage to assume the responsibility of getting them there in time. Remember that even though you may be in the habit of setting forth at the very last minute without ever having missed a train or plane, your friends may be of a more nervous disposition, so be sure to leave plenty of time for the drive to the airport or dock. And if you accompany your friends to a plane or train, do not embarrass them by staging a loud, affectionate, or hilarious farewell scene in the public waiting room.

The only occasion when it is correct to give a bon-voyage party for oneself is when you are traveling by boat. In this case, you can invite as many friends as you wish for a bon-voyage cocktail before sailing time, on board the ship. You can assemble just a few close friends in your stateroom, or you can hold a larger party in one of the ship salons. You merely have to make the arrangements with the purser ahead of time, telling him the number of guests you expect and the kind of refreshments you wish to serve. Everything will be taken care of by the ship's staff, and you will be billed for it by the purser afterward.

A shipboard bon-voyage party is the only occasion when a bon-voyage gift is really welcome, especially if it consists of flowers for the stateroom, a box of candy, a basket of fruit, or an amusing book—in other words, something to be enjoyed and consumed during the course of the voyage. Selecting a bon-voyage gift for plane travelers is, on the other hand, a practically insoluble problem. When the time comes to wish them bon voyage, they have already equipped themselves with everything that is indispensable to their travels, and are probably already worried about their overweight baggage charge. I have never yet discovered a gift item that takes up no space, weighs nothing, and yet contributes in some way to the enjoyment of a trip.

In any case, never, never, under any circumstances offer a bon-voyage corsage. Not only are corsages extremely inelegant fashionwise, but you will do your friends the disservice of making them resemble the unkindest caricatures of "typical" American tourists. Besides, during my own travels I have most appreciated not the going-away gifts, but the welcome-home flowers that have greeted me on my return.

(See Travel)

WEDDINGS

❅ Sometimes I have wondered aloud whether it would not be kinder and more intelligent to make an outright gift to a young newlywed couple of the five or six thousand dollars (minimum) it costs to arrange a large formal wedding, to which my more astute friends reply that this enormous expense is more than compensated for by the shower of wedding gifts. Of course, having reached the age of fifty, I no longer possess the same point of view I used to have when I was twenty—nor do I possess many wedding gifts, for most of them have been broken or lost during the intervening decades—and so I suppose that I would do better to avoid bringing up this question and running the risk of being attacked by all the marriageable young girls who dream of organ music and tons of flowers on their wedding day.

In France, which is a Catholic country, the civil formalities take place two or three days before the religious ceremony, and it is very bad taste to invite to the town hall anybody other than one's close relatives and the witnesses.

On the other hand, at a noon church wedding, it is very elegant to have an enormous crowd of guests stepping on each other's toes and filing through the reception line in the sacristy for three hours or more in order to offer their congratulations. The reception takes place afterward from about five o'clock until eight-thirty. We still practice the barbarous custom of inviting some people to the wedding and not to the reception afterward, the latter honor being symbolized by a little card slipped into the wedding invitation.

The wedding invitation consists of a thick folded sheet of paper engraved on the outside. The family sending the invitation places its own invitation on top of that of the other family. Both of them should be worded as follows:

The four grandparents (what is left of them!)
The parents
have the honor of announcing the marriage of
their granddaughter and daughter
Mademoiselle Laure Durand
to Monsieur Yves Dupont
and beg you to attend the Nuptial Benediction
which will take place at the Madeleine Church,
Place de la Madeleine, Paris ler, on Monday,
February 12, at noon sharp.

Of course, the groom's family employs the same formula for the young man.

The invitation card to the wedding reception is no larger than a visiting card, and is written thus:

Madame Durand (mother of the bride)
Madame Dupont (mother of the groom)
will receive after the religious ceremony

RSVP Hotel Crillon
5 to 8

If you ever receive a wedding invitation from French friends that is not composed in exactly this way, you should know that they may be terribly nice, but they are certainly not *comme il faut*.

In America the customs are somewhat different, and the best course, if you are not absolutely sure of the rules, is to consult an authoritative etiquette book or, where the formula of the wedding invitations is concerned, a leading engraver.

In any event, in both countries the families of the bride and groom greet the guests in a receiving line at the entrance to the salon where the reception is held. To have an orchestra playing at a luncheon reception is not very elegant, but it would be considered indispensable for an afternoon or evening wedding, and in the latter case the reception is exactly comparable to a ball. In all of these instances it is necessary to arrange a rather quiet separate room with an adequate number of chairs for elderly guests, and it is better to have several different buffet tables instead of one large one, in order to disperse the crowd.

In France the expense of the ceremony and reception is shared between the two families, but in America it is the custom for the family of the bride to pay for everything, although it is courteous to consult with the family of the groom when planning the reception, even when it is to take place at the home of the bride.

The most charming weddings of all are those that are given in the country in the summertime, followed by an outdoor reception. Unless you live in the desert where it never rains, you must arrange for one or more tents, beautifully decorated with plants and flowers, to be set up in the garden as a shelter from the rain and sun. This may well be one of the most expensive items in your budget, but it is an indispensable precaution, unless you have an enormous house with vast reception rooms and are able to transfer everything indoors should the need arise.

Because there will probably be a large number of guests from out of town, the best plan is to offer a full-course luncheon. Depending on the number of guests and the available personnel, this can be either a buffet luncheon, with everybody serving himself at a huge buffet table and then taking a seat at a small table wherever he wishes, or it can be a regular sit-down luncheon with small tables, waiters, hot dishes, and place cards. The second manner is more elegant than the first, but also much more expensive. In both cases the newlywed couple should be seated at the head table in the center of the tent, surrounded by their attendants. They should be the first to be served, and then they must make the rounds of all the other tables as the waiters are serving the wedding cake, after the bride has solemnly cut the first piece while making a wish. When the young newlyweds have seen, thanked, and been congratulated by all the guests, and when they have stayed on for about an hour after the luncheon is over, they can at last slip away. And the exhausted parents will certainly be very grateful if the guests do the same.

WEEKENDS

⟪ So you have a house in the country! It is, of course, your pride and joy and you want all of your friends to come and admire it. You also secretly hope to dazzle them with your good taste and your hospitality

—but beware! The forty-eight hours of a weekend conceal at least forty-eight hidden snares.

When you issue your invitations, you should be absolutely precise concerning the program so that your guests will bring their bathing suits, tennis racquets, etc., as well as a dressy ensemble, if you have decided to give a dinner party on Saturday night.

It is wise to avoid inviting "irregular" couples, unless their liaison is so long-standing that it is practically official. Imagine your embarrassment if an irate husband or wife were suddenly to appear and make a scene in your home! The *School for Scandal* is very amusing—but only on the stage. As a matter of fact, it is better not to encourage clandestine romances by your weekend invitations, even when there is no risk of their causing trouble. Neither is it a very good idea to assemble people who do not know each other at all, especially if your house does not contain several separate bathrooms. It is usually necessary for people to have hit it off well around a dinner table before they can enjoy each other's company in dressing gowns.

When your guests arrive, you should be at the door to greet them. But let them have a breathing spell before inflicting upon them an inspection tour of the house and grounds. If they arrive before luncheon on Saturday, as is frequently the case, here is the program they would prefer:

(1.) To be taken to their rooms and to unpack. This is the moment to show them where to find the closets, bathrooms, etc., so they do not have to embark on a treasure hunt. (Count on at least fifteen minutes.)

(2.) Leave them alone and tell them to join you for a drink when they are ready—out of doors in a comfortable garden chair in the summertime, in front of the fireplace in the winter.

(3.) Luncheon.

(4.) A long, leisurely interlude over coffee in the living room.

(5.) A nap.

(6.) And ONLY NOW show off your interior decoration, the view, the chicken house, orchard or stream, and the beautiful countryside.

Afterward, they will perhaps be happy to have a game of golf or tennis, or simply to stretch out in the sun. Do not transform your home into an army barracks, with a rigid time schedule, reveille with or without fanfare, and fatigue duty in the guise of organized games. Try also to restrict the use of the hi-fi and the transistor radio. Silence has become a very great luxury. You should propose amusements rather than impose them, and you should always suggest a nap or rest as an alternative.

It is more pleasant to serve breakfast in their rooms to those that are not very close friends, after having decided on the menu and the hour the night before. As for myself, I adore long breakfast-table chats with very good friends, when we are all in our bathrobes gorging ourselves on hot buttered toast and homemade jam.

It would obviously be in very poor taste to oblige your guests to mow the lawn or paint the barn. On the other hand, if you have a flower garden, you can give the women a pair of garden shears on Sunday afternoon and tell them to gather the flowers they would like to take home with them. I must confess that I am terribly stingy where my flowers are concerned, because I hate to see the young buds cut, and so I prefer to prepare the bouquets myself as well as the fruit or fresh herbs that also give enormous pleasure to city dwellers.

For rainy days and for the evening hours, you should be prepared to provide playing cards, parlor games, dance records, television, and an assortment of light novels. In a pinch, you can even arrange a showing of home movies, if some of your guests appear in them. Always keep on hand a generous supply of tea (China and Ceylon), whisky, fruit juice, bottled soda, etc., some delicious cookies, a cocktail specialty—and a complete first-aid kit.

For one of the three meals, it is a good idea to prepare an amusing, definitely country-style dish, such as a fondue or a *potée,* and to plan more classic menus for the other two principal meals, for example, a roast, steaks, or chicken. Do not forget that new-laid eggs, garden strawberries, and string beans that have just been picked in the garden are the rarest of delicacies to city people. You can reserve the most refined dishes for your Saturday-evening dinner, when you might invite a few neighbors in order to inject a bit of new life into your group of houseguests, who have already spent eight straight hours together. If you have a lot of friends in the neighboring regions, you might even organize a buffet dinner with dancing afterward.

Throughout the weekend, you should try to manage things so that each of your guests shines in his particular specialty: the beautiful but dumb blonde beside the swimming pool; the lawyer or explorer over brandy and cigars; and the woman who has led a rich, full life and shows it, seated in the shade with the light behind her, where she can be clearly heard but seen only in the most flattering conditions. Most of all, try to be perfectly relaxed, happy to share the things you love with people you like. Above all, never give them the impression that you are wearing yourself out in your efforts to receive them well, for you would only succeed in making them feel ill at ease.

(See Guest Rooms, Houseguests, etc.)

WHITE LIES

(Although most upright citizens consider habitual prevarication to be one of the deadliest of sins, it must be admitted that honesty is not always the best policy for a hostess. I would even go so far as to say that in certain circumstances, falsehood is *de rigueur*. For example:

"The maid will do the dishes in the morning" . . . when cheerfully refusing a friendly offer to help clean up after a party. (The maid, needless to say, is a totally fictitious character, and your cheerfulness is also histrionic, for you really dread the prospect of all those hours you are going to have to spend in front of the kitchen sink.)

"Don't give it another thought! Everybody knows that ashes are excellent for carpets—they have a mothproofing effect" . . . as one of your guests apologizes for dropping two inches of cigar ash on your living room rug. (And, of course, you pretend not to notice that the hot ash has burned a hole right through your precious Oriental rug, which cost a fortune.)

"What a wonderful surprise! I'm so happy you could come!" . . . when your husband arrives home in the evening accompanied by a totally unexpected dinner guest. (And you mask with feigned enthusiasm your frantic search for an answer to the problem of how to feed three hungry adults with four little lamb chops.)

"Fido simply adores to play with children" . . . when your visitor's obnoxious children are pulling the tail of your faithful family pet. (Remember that animals are amazingly patient with young children and besides, you must try to avoid at all cost a painful scene between a scolding mother and a child in a tantrum.)

"How careless of me! But there's no harm done because champagne doesn't leave a stain" . . . as you glibly pronounce two lies in one when a dinner guest knocks over the wine glass you have just filled.

"We've loved having you! You must come again soon" . . . as you bid good night to a disagreeable guest to whom you owed a dinner. (And you scrupulously conceal what you are really thinking: "Ouf! At last that's over. Never again!")

WINE

⟨ Although it is produced in considerable quantity in the United States, wine has never been accepted as part of the daily diet of most Americans, but is usually reserved for special occasions. As a result, a great deal of prestige is attached to wine drinking in this country, and a long-stemmed glass of wine—especially champagne—is practically symbolic of a festive event such as an important anniversary, a triumphant theater première, a wedding—in fact, of any occasion when toasts and congratulations are in order.

Because the only way to get to know wine well is to drink a lot of it, it is therefore quite difficult to become a connoisseur of wine in America. Even in Europe, where its production and consumption are far more widespread, this can be very hard on one's budget, not to mention the liver. There is much to be learned from the dozens of erudite books that have been written about wine, describing its ancient and illustrious history and explaining the highly civilized art of wine drinking. But most of these fascinating works are far too specialized for the average hostess, who merely wishes to flatter her guests by serving them wines that taste good and that harmonize with the menus they accompany.

Her best course of action is either to place her wine problems in the hands of a reliable wine dealer and to follow faithfully his advice, or to acquire gradually an elementary education in the matter by trying different types of wine within her family circle (and within the family budget) and to build up an adequate supply of those that most appeal to her. But the most recommended procedure of all is to interest her husband in the question and encourage him to take charge of the family wine cellar. In Europe, the selection and buying of wine has always been considered a masculine prerogative. In a restaurant, for example, your host may ask you if you prefer red, white, or rosé, but he always reserves for himself the responsibility of selecting the particular bottle. Strictly speaking, a woman should not even pour the wine at the table. In a home where a maid waits on table, it is the master of the house who serves the wine; but if there is a butler instead of a maid, the butler may serve it.

Wine is simply the fermented juice of fresh grapes with no added flavoring. The different types result from the different varieties of grapes that enter into their composition, the different conditions of soil and climate, and sometimes from slightly different processes of production. Alcoholic beverages are made from many raw materials other than grapes, including cereals, wood pulp, potatoes, rice, and various fruits, but these are classified as liquors.

The leading wine-producing countries of the world are Italy and France, followed by Spain, Algeria, Argentina, Portugal, and the United States. Germany, which produces some of the most delicious white wines of all, is surprisingly far down on the list, while the Algerian production has suffered a great deal in quantity and quality since Algeria became independent.

There are two general categories of wines: table wines, such as Bordeaux, Burgundy, Chianti, etc., which are meant to be drunk throughout a meal as a beverage; and fortified wines, such as sherry, port, vermouth, Madeira, etc., which are drunk as an aperitif before a meal when they are dry, and as a liqueur after meals when they are sweet; occasionally they may also accompany a sweet dessert. Table wines contain from eight to thirteen or fourteen percent alcohol, while fortified wines possess an alcoholic content of at least eighteen to twenty percent, due to the addition of brandy or some other spirit. Sparkling wines, among which the original and most famous is, of course, champagne, may be drunk as an aperitif, throughout a meal, throughout an entire evening, or in fact at almost any time.

There are three principal colors of wine: red, white, and rosé (pink), in addition to a few varieties produced in certain regions, such as "gray" wines from some parts of France, "green" wine from Portugal, and the "black" ordinary wine of Spain. These color descriptions are not, however, very accurate. White wine is almost always yellow, sometimes a deep golden or amber color, and certain rosé wines are as ruby-toned as some of the lighter reds. The color comes from the skins and pips, with those from black grapes being permitted to remain with the pulp and juice in order to produce red wines. A proportion of black grapes is also used to make many white wines, including champagne, but the skins and pips are first removed.

Most wines take their names either from the type of grapes from which they are made, such as Malaga, Riesling, Sylvaner, etc.; from the region where the wine originates, such as Bordeaux, Burgundy, the Rhine and Moselle valleys, etc.; or from the district, commune, town, or vineyard where they are produced. Sometimes all of this information is on a single label. For example, a famous red Bordeaux wine, Château Lafite, is identified as:

Château Lafite (the vineyard)
Haut-Médoc (the region)
Pauillac (the commune)
1er Cru (the "growth" of grape vines, in this case the first growth, a mark of quality)
1949 (the date of the grape harvest, not of the year in which it was bottled—in this case, a great year)

Many wines, however, are labeled simply according to type, such as "Bordeaux Rouge," or "Bordeaux Supérieur," plus the name of a French wholesaler or of a foreign dealer who has imported the wine in barrels and bottled it himself in New York or London. In this event, the words to look for on the label are *appellation contrôlée,* which is a guarantee that the origin as well as the quality of the wine has been carefully controlled. Some wines that have been imported by the barrel, selected and bottled by a knowing dealer, may be just as agreeable as a table wine as those that have been *mis en bouteille au château,* that is, bottled in the original castle vineyards, which is often pictured on the label along with an impressive coat of arms. But if the words *appellation contrôlée* are absent, you should be very wary.

Despite the efforts of their originators to protect their appellations, the principal types of European wines are imitated in many other countries by wine makers who attempt to reproduce the same wine by using the same varieties of grapes and the same processes of fabrication. But soil and climate cannot be artificially reproduced, and these are also vital factors in determining the flavor and quality of a wine. One vineyard, for example, may produce superb wine grapes, while those from an adjacent plot may be inferior, simply because of a slight difference in the exposure to the sun, or the grade of the slopes. It is therefore not surprising that few of the imitation Bordeaux, Burgundies, champagnes, etc., are comparable to the originals, although some of them are very worthy beverages in their own right.

Thus American vineyards alone produce their own version of more than forty famous European wines, including fortified wines such as sherry, port, and Madeira, as well as table wines such as Chianti, Burgundy, Rhine wine (frequently called "Hock" in Anglo-Saxon countries), and Bordeaux (which may also be called, in the British fashion, "claret").

Bordeaux is a wine from the area surrounding the city of Bordeaux in southwest France, which has produced many of our greatest wines, and in particular fine red wines.

The regions in this area producing the best red wines are Médoc, Graves, Palus, and the Côtes, and the finest of these is Médoc (or, to be even more precise, the Haut-Médoc, whose vineyards are superior to those of the Bas-Médoc and the Petit-Médoc). This is not merely a matter of personal opinion, for all red Bordeaux wines are given an official quality rating ranging from 1er Cru (the finest), to 2eme, 3eme, 4eme, and 5eme Cru. All of these crus indicate superior quality, and there are only four in the first group: Château Lafite, Château Latour, Château Margaux, and Château Haut-Brion—with Château Mouton-Rothschild close behind. With the exception of Haut-Brion, which is produced in the Graves region, all of the wines of the first four crus and most of the fifth are from the Haut-Médoc. Many of these are better known by the name of the particular commune in which the grapes are grown, such as Pauillac (where there are a score of world-famous vineyards), Saint-Estèphe, Saint-Julien, Margaux, Cantenac, and the less important Labarde, Ludon, Saint-Laurent, Macau, Arsac, Soussans, Cussac, and Listrac. These fine wines are matured from five to six years in barrels at the vineyard before being bottled, and they continue to mellow until they reach their peak of quality at the age of twelve or fourteen.

Red wine from the Graves district is generally stronger and richer than the Médocs and can mature in the bottle until the age of twenty or even twenty-five. This is the home of the great Château La Mission-Haut-Brion, as well as many less fine but pleasant table wines from the communes of Pessac and Léognan. Palus wines, from the communes of Ambès, La Bastide, Quinsac, and Saint-Gervais, are similar to Graves, rather heady and rich in color. The Côte production is not of the same superior quality, with the important exception of the Côte Saint-

Emilion, whose outstanding vineyards are the prestigious Château Ausone and Château Cheval Blanc. Pomerol, from the same area, is an ordinary wine of good quality.

Although all of these wines are red Bordeaux wines, each one possesses a distinctive flavor that is instantly recognized by connoisseurs. They harmonize perfectly with most main dishes, with the exception of game and highly spiced foods, for which a red Burgundy is the classic accompaniment.

The Graves region of Bordeaux is, however, most noted for its white wines, which are classified according to quality as *Hors Ligne* (in a class by themselves), 1er and 2eme Crus. There is only one *Hors Ligne*, the famous Château Yquem from the commune of Sauternes. There are also a number of other fine white Bordeaux wines from Sauternes, including the Château Guiraud and the Château d'Arche, as well as from the other communes of Graves: Léognan, Barsac, Bommes, Fargues, Preignac, and Cérons. White Bordeaux wines are mostly rather sweet, and the finest of them all, the Sauternes, are generally too rich and sweet to accompany a fish course. French gourmets most often serve Sauternes with the dessert, or even after a meal, while many connoisseurs consider them to be the ideal companion to foie gras. As a matter of fact, the only well-known white Bordeaux wine that is really dry is Château Haut-Brion.

Burgundy, the ancient eastern province of France, is the other principal wine-growing district in the country. Its red wines are fuller-bodied than Bordeaux, and often headier, and it also produces a relatively small number of white wines. The most important wine-producing regions of Burgundy are the Haute-Bourgogne, Basse-Bourgogne, Mâconnais, and Beaujolais.

The red wines of the Haute-Bourgogne are further subdivided into three regions: the Côte de Nuits, which resemble a rather strong Bordeaux and include famous wines from the vineyards of Chambertin, Clos Vougeot (whose château is the home of the elite wine-tasting fraternity, the "Chevaliers du Tastevin"), Richebourg, Nuits-Saint-Georges, Echézeaux, Malconsorts, Musigny, La Tâche, and the illustrious Romanée-Conti, whose small vineyards constitute the most valuable agricultural property in all of France; the Côte de Beaune, whose heady yet delicate wine is produced in the communes of Aunay, Chassagne, Aloxe, Meursault, Pommard, Santenay, and Savigny; and the

Côte Chalonnaise, which are lighter and drier and are grown mostly in the communes of Mercurey, Volnay, Vosne, and Bourgneuf.

The wines from the Basse-Bourgogne are more varied in flavor and quality, and its vineyards are located in the communes of Auxerre, Tonnerre, Joigny, Epineuil, and Irancy.

From the Mâconnais region of Burgundy, the most famous red wines are produced in the communes of Chénas and Romanèche.

The Beaujolais wines are more ordinary in type and quality than the finest red Burgundies, but they are a most pleasant table wine, neither too heavy nor too light, neither too strong nor too weak. The most refined Beaujolais is from the commune of Fleurie, but the production from other vineyards, such as Chénas, Brouilly, Chiroubles, Juliénas, Romanèche, Morgon, Moulin-à-Vent, Saint-Amour, and Beaujolais—villages—is also much favored in France as an everyday table wine. All of these are also excellent party wines, for they accompany a maximum of different dishes agreeably, they appeal to most palates, and they are not terribly expensive. Since they mature quickly, they are best when they are consumed young.

While few white Burgundies are as celebrated as the Sauternes or the German white wines, a number of them are excellent, full of character, and justly appreciated as an accompaniment to fish and shellfish, the most noteworthy being Chablis, Montrachet (the Montrachet-ainé is rated *Hors Ligne*), Meursault, and Pouilly Fuissé.

Champagne, of all the world's wines, is undeniably the most festive and the most at home in elegant society. True champagne is made only in the Champagne district east of Paris, whose principal towns are Rheims and Epernay, and its production is jealously guarded in the control of a few famous houses including Bollinger, Veuve Cliquot, Heidsieck, Irroy, Krug, Lanson, Moët & Chandon, Mumm, Perrier-Jouet, Pommery & Greno, Louis-Roederer, and Pol-Roger, whose relative ranking in the opinion of gourmets varies from year to year. But the name "champagne" has also been adopted (in spite of vigorous protests) by various sparkling white wines made in other countries, which sometimes employ the same varieties of grapes and the same or similar processes. A considerable amount of this champagne-type wine is produced in Germany, Spain, in New York State, and in Canada. (California "champagne" is made by a slightly different process.) The Italians christen their light, rather sweet, sparkling white wine Asti Spumante. The Russians are said to produce great quantities of Crimean "champagne." But it cannot be denied that none of these compare to the original French champagne from the Champagne region.

Sparkling wines, by the way, start out life exactly like still table wines, but they are permitted to continue their fermentation in the bottle in order to produce the sparkle, which is no more than carbon dioxide. For that matter, any wine can be turned into a sparkling wine. Sparkling Burgundy, red, white and rosé, is practically unknown in France, but a considerable quantity is exported to America, where it is highly esteemed. At one time experiments were made with sparkling Bordeaux, but this novelty failed to capture the fancy of the wine-drinking public. Because of the slight difference in production methods, some purists claim that champagne is not, strictly speaking, wine— and for this reason, it used to be the custom to separate the champagne glasses from the others on a dinner table by setting them slightly behind the row of wine glasses at each place.

Champagne is made in different degrees of sweetness: Doux (sweet), Demi-Sec (slightly sweet), Sec (dry), Extra Sec (very dry) and Brut (very, very dry). Nowadays, connoisseurs unhesitatingly pre-fer the drier types, while the sweeter ones find favor mainly in southerly and Anglo-Saxon countries. The amount of sparkle also varies, so that champagne is further described as Grand Mousseux (the most spar-kling), Mousseux (sparkling), Crémant (delicate and slightly spar-kling), or as Still Champagne, Blanc de Blanc (made exclusively from white grapes), or Champagne Nature (which has no sparkle at all). A festive novelty is pink champagne (champagne rosé), of which only a small quantity is produced. Permitted to color slightly, it is otherwise exactly the same as normal champagne, from which the color has been laboriously removed. Vintage champagne, made from the grapes of a single year, is considerably more costly and rare than nonvintage cham-pagne, which is made by mixing the produce of several different years, as is the case with the vast majority of champagne. Only two or three times in a decade is the wine crop exceptional enough to merit bottling as a vintage champagne.

There are also two superelite champagnes, which are produced in a very limited quantity. Specially treated in the champagne caves for eight years (twice as long as all the others), they are extremely ex-pensive: Dom Perignon, made by Moët & Chandon (the favorite champagne of James Bond), and Comte de Champagne, produced by the Taittinger firm.

There is little point in considering in detail the numerous varieties of wine from other regions of France, such as the *Loire Valley*, with its sparkling white Vouvray and Saumur wines, its light red Bourgueil, Chinon, and Saint Nicolas, its greenish-white Sancerre, dry white Puilly-Fumé and Muscadet (the latter three, all from the Anjou district, are excellent light wines to drink with oysters and shellfish); the *Rhone Valley*, which produces the rather rich, full red Hermitage and Côte Rôtie, the famed Châteauneuf-du-Pape (which is rich and strong, too heavy to drink throughout a meal but marvelous with the cheese course) and a superior rosé called Tavel; *Alsace*, whose vineyards furnish a variety of wines similar to the German in type and flavor, and mostly white. The two most famous names in Alsatian wines are Riquewihr and Ribeauvillé, but like many German wines, most of them take their name from the grapes rather than the locality, and the principal of these are Sylvaner, Riesling, Traminer, and Gewurtztraminer; *Provence*, with its refreshing rosé (a very popular luncheon wine), its greenish cassis, and its unpretentious reds that are the *vin ordinaire* of much of the French population. The list could go on for pages! But each of these varieties is produced in far less quantity than the Bordeaux and Burgundies, comparatively little is exported to the United States, and they are less often honored by being imitated in other wine-producing lands. Consequently, you are more likely to meet them during a holiday trip to Europe than on the shelves of your local liquor store.

In *Italy*, as in France, a vast quantity of wine is produced in every province, but the principal exports are red Chianti and Montepulciano from Tuscany; Valpolicella and Bardolino from Venetia; and two sweet dessert wines: Marsala and muscatel. The most famous white wines are Vito Sano, Soave, and Orvieto, the latter being either dry or sweet, and, of course, the sparkling Asti Spumante, as well as a number of aperitif wines, including vermouth.

Spain exports mostly fortified wines, and in particular sherry. According to whether it is dry or sweet, sherry (or *jerez*, in Spanish, from the name of the city where it is made) is described as Fino (pale, dry, an aperitif wine), Amontillado (less dry and stronger), Oloroso (sweet, dark, a dessert wine), or Amoroso (paler and sweeter than Oloroso). There is also the very dry manzanilla, which is the traditional beverage in Spanish cafés and flamenco nightclubs. The sherry that is produced in great quantities in California is said to resemble Madeira more than Spanish sherry.

Since the British were the first foreigners to discover and appreciate sherry, and since most sherry is exported in barrels to England to be bottled there, many of the best known names in sherry are English, such as Dry Sack, Dry Fly, Harvey's, Sandeman, etc. But there are also a few famous Spanish firms, such as Pedro Domecq and Gonzales Byass, which produces a very fashionable, very dry aperitif sherry under the name of Tio Pepe.

The English and Scandinavians frequently serve sherry at a dinner party to accompany the soup course (with which the French generally serve no wine at all), and in Sweden it is served with ice cream desserts as well. But most often sherry appears slightly chilled and rather dry at cocktail time. It is, in fact, an error to serve anything but dry sherry as an aperitif; Bristol Cream, for example, is strictly a dessert wine. In the kitchen as well as in the bar, a bottle of sherry can render useful service. For example, a few tablespoons of dry sherry will bring a subtle flavor to many kinds of soups, and a dash of sherry in the Russian dressing for a seafood cocktail adds an indefinable tang that is very cordon bleu.

The rather strong and coarse Spanish table wines are reserved mostly for Spanish consumption, and the barrels that are exported are usually destined for other wine-producing countries, which use them to add body and alcoholic content to their own ordinary wines.

Portuguese wines are mostly red or rosé (like the pleasant Matteus), but there is also a light, slightly acid and very refreshing Vinho Verde (Green Wine). Delicious when you drink it in Portugal, the latter seems to lose much of its quality when it travels, as I once learned to my disappointment when I brought a few bottles back to Paris from Estoril in the trunk of my car.

Portugal is, of course, most famous among wine drinkers for its port, a fortified wine of great body, which has the distinction of improving with age for an amazing number of years. A great deal of port-type wine is also produced in California, where modern methods have been developed to hasten artificially the maturing process. Authentic port exists in both vintage and blended varieties. Like vintage champagne, vintage port is only bottled in an excellent year when the promise of developing a deep purple color and a rich mellow flavor is outstanding. Maturing usually takes from seven to ten years, but a bottle of fine port may continue to improve for forty years or more. As a general rule, however, port experts claim that ten years of age is the minimum, and twenty years ideal. Port exists in three varieties: White, ruby, and tawny. The white, which is made from white grapes and is the sweetest, is more or less snubbed by connoisseurs; mellow tawny port is actually ruby port that has been permitted to age for a longer time. Although it was a popular aperitif in Europe before the war, taste has veered to drier drinks before a meal, and now port is served mainly as a dessert or afterdinner wine.

Madeira, which is produced on the Portuguese island colony of that name, is another fortified dessert wine, which is even longer-lasting than port. It has, in fact, never been known to reach a turning point in age, as do all other wines, beyond which they gradually deteriorate in quality.

German white wines are among the finest, if not the very finest in the world. For that matter, Germany produces very little red wine, but her white Rhine wines and Moselles, which are made along the banks of the rivers of the same names, are justifiably renowned. They are deliciously delicate and fragrant, ranging from very dry to rather sweet. Many Moselle wines are slightly sparkling. The majority are a bit sweet, high in alcoholic content and in flavor. Unfortunately, comparatively little is produced and they are considerably more expensive than the Alsatian versions of some of the principal types, such as Sylvaner, Traminer and Riesling. Liebfraumilch, which is made from a blend of various kinds of grapes, is produced only in Germany. This popular wine is generally too sweet to drink with the main part of a meal, but it is lovely with the dessert course and for afterdinner.

The great names in Rhine Wines are Johannisberger, Rudesheimer, and Steinberger, the first of these vineyards belonging to the family of the princes of Metternich, and the last to the state. But there are many other well-known names taken from the villages in which the different vineyards are situated: Diedesheimer, Durckheim, Marcobrünner, Hinterhause, Hockheimer, Rupertsberger, Ungstein, etc. The towns of Nierstein, Oppenheim, Laubenheim, and Bodenheim are all in the southern part of the valley, and their wines are somewhat lighter and milder (some would say less fine) than the others.

Moselle wines are almost all white wines, which vary from acid dry to rather sweet. They should be drunk young, at four or five years, for they do not age well. The most celebrated Moselle wine is Bernkasteler, and Bernkasteler Doktor is considered to be one of the greatest wines in the world, in a class with Château Yquem, Château Haut-Brion, and eight or ten others. A few of the other well-known names in Moselle wine are Piersporter, Aberommel, Braueneberger, Graach, Grunhau, Saarburg, and Schwartzberger.

Another German wine of some reputation is produced in Bavaria and is called Steinwein. It is sold in a special, squat round bottle and resembles a good Chablis.

In addition to their name (which is most often the name of the vineyard preceded by that of the district), German wines may be labeled *spätlese* or *auslese,* meaning that the grapes were gathered late when they are bursting with ripeness and will produce wine that is full of flavor, sugar, and consequently high in alcoholic content, which generally indicates superior quality. (Not because of the alcohol, but because a high alcoholic content is symptomatic of other desirable qualities, including the ability to age and travel well.) When only the best grapes are selected from the vines, the resulting wine is labeled *beerenauslese,* meaning "choice berries"; while the choicest of choice is *Kabinett* wine, meaning, I have been told, that it is worthy of being placed in the owner's personal wine cabinet.

Most of the South American nations, the other countries of Europe including Switzerland, Austria, Luxembourg, Greece, Yugoslavia and the Middle European nations, the Far East, North and South Africa, all produce wine. But it is generally sufficient in quantity and quality only for internal consumption, with a few notable exceptions such as Chile, which exports a Riesling-type white wine that is moderate in price and most agreeable.

United States wine is produced almost entirely in California, which accounts for ninety percent of the total, and along the shores of Lake Erie. The latter region makes a sparkling white wine that is unfortunately quite inferior to the French champagne whose name it borrows. California wines are made in many different types, most of them also bearing the name of the European variety they imitate or most closely resemble. Because scientific American methods differ somewhat from the laborious European wine-making processes, and also because the climatic conditions in California are more stable than on the Continent, these wines are more regular in quality, more standardized in flavor, and they vary little from one year to the next. While the quality is therefore more dependable, and while there is never a "bad year" for California wine, neither is there apt to be an exceptionally fine vintage. But a good California wine is a perfectly acceptable and highly agreeable beverage for informal luncheons and dinners, and even—why not?—for family meals. If a bottle of wine were eventually to succeed in replacing the coffeepot on the American dinner table, what a victory for gastronomy!

Among the leading California wines are:

California Red Wines

Grignolino and Barbera: robust Italian types
Cabernet Sauvignon: California's version of a fine red Bordeaux, and the pride of American vineyards. The best is made in the northern counties.
Gamay: a Beaujolais type
Pinot Noir: a red Burgundy type
Zinfandel: created by a Hungarian-born vintner, this widely produced type varies greatly in quality.

California White Wines

Chardonnay: a Chablis type
Chenin Blanc: a light, inexpensive white wine
Emerald Riesling: a California version
Folle Blanche: a dry Chablis type
Pinot Blanc: a white Burgundy type
Versions of Sylvaner, Traminer, and many other famous European wines are made, as well as a wide range of rosé, some of which are pleasant table wines but others, alas, resembling a rather acid lemonade.

There is often a good deal of unnecessary snobbishness attached to the price of a wine and to the name and picture on the label. Where price is concerned, it is wise to remember that high cost is not necessarily synonymous with high quality, since a good portion of the price of imported wine represents charges for transport and handling, and for tariffs and taxes that are determined by political rather than epicurean considerations. As for the impressive labels, it seems to me inappropriate, and therefore in poor taste, to serve a prestigious wine with a menu that is not also rather extraordinary, on an occasion that is not rather special, and to guests who would not appreciate it. In most entertaining circumstances, I would advise you to select your wines from the standard quality range, as we do abroad. As a matter of fact, today the height of wine snobbishness is to discover a very simple, inexpensive wine that is delicious!

Likewise, an inordinate amount of importance is sometimes attached to the date that is printed on a wine label, undoubtedly because of the widely distributed cards indicating the "good" and "bad" years for different types of wine. The truth is that these generalities are no more accurate than are most sweeping statements. Many a wine from a small vineyard has been particularly excellent in a so-called "bad year," and the contrary is also true. Experienced wine dealers are well aware of this, and some of their most advantageous buys in wine are the result of the layman's blind faith in his printed list, which makes the price of certain wines soar while others, just as worthy, are neglected. Furthermore, many undated wines are delicious.

It must be admitted, however, that the date on a bottle of wine is of considerable importance because it shows how long the wine has aged, and the aging process is indeed one of the most important steps in wine-making. Wine is a living fluid, which, unlike hard liquor, continues to develop after it has been bottled, reaching its full maturity after a certain length of time and then gradually deteriorating. It can become ill, and it can even recover from certain maladies after a period of convalescence. The most desirable age at which a wine should be consumed varies a good deal from one type to another, and even within a single type. Generally speaking, the finer the quality of a wine and the higher the alcoholic content, the longer it will take to "ripen." For example, the widely heralded 1964 Bordeaux vintage is expected to be at its best only in ten or twelve years. But certain other 1964 types, such as Beaujolais, will be enjoyed at the end of 1965.

Fine red Bordeaux wines reach their peak at about the age of ten, while Burgundies usually ripen in half the time. Ordinary red wines change little over the years, and it is most pleasant to drink them when they are young. Very few white wines improve with age, and some of them begin to deteriorate rather quickly. Moselle wine, for example, does not age well. One outstanding exception to the rule is Rhine wine, which retains its fine quality for fifteen years or more. Fortified wines, on the other hand, such as port, sherry, and Madeira, are extremely long-lived. As for champagne, its quality cannot be clearly determined until it has aged in the special champagne caves for about five years. It does not improve with age once it has been bottled, and the prestige of the date it bears is due to the reputation of certain exceptionally fine vintages, such as 1961, 1957, 1955, 1947 (a superb year for almost all European wines), and 1945. Alsatian wines are at their best between the ages of five and eight. Finally, the date of most California wines is of little importance due to the scientific methods employed, which standardize their quality to a remarkable degree. I would be inclined to prefer the more recent vintages simply because it seems to me that California wines are steadily improving.

To tell the truth, this whole subject is so complex that the best course is to consult some of the good books by specialists and to seek the advice of a reliable wine dealer. And this means that you should select a specialized dealer in whom you can have complete confidence, just as with a furrier or a jeweler. Moreover, with wine as with furs and jewels, it is always better to buy the best quality of an unpretentious variety rather than the cheapest quality of a famous one.

Having completed a round-the-world tour of the principal wine-producing regions, and having paid our respects to the world's greatest wines, we can practically dismiss them from our thoughts, because we are unlikely to meet such celebrities as Château Yquem, Dom Perignon, or Bernkasteler Doktor very often in our everyday lives. In normal entertaining there is seldom any reason to serve other than a well-selected standard wine that is tasty without being ruinous—and since the production of the great wines is very limited, they are extremely expensive. (But it is twice as expensive to order them in a restaurant than to buy them from a dealer for one of your home dinner parties, and this is a point to remember!) Another reason for the restricted supply is because the proprietors of these renowned vineyards are so jealous of their reputations and so anxious to protect them, that if a year's grape harvest does not meet their high standards, they will either bottle the wine under a different label or, if it is really a very poor crop, they will sell it to makers of *vin ordinaire,* or to be distilled into ordinary brandy.

If you have persevered throughout this capsule survey of the wines of the world, Bravo! You already know enough about wine to read intelligently the wine list of any elegant restaurant in the world and to appreciate the gesture of a connoisseur friend who opens a choice bottle of wine in your honor. And you certainly know more about wine than the average Frenchman or Italian, who consumes a liter of wine a day at least and cheerfully orders his favorite *ordinaire* without ever attempting to broaden his knowledge and experience. There remains, however, the problem of storing and serving your wine, as well as the important question of selecting the most appropriate wines to accompany your party menus.

Since the ideal conditions for wine storage require a cool room where the temperature is maintained at an even fifty or fifty-five degrees (but abrupt changes of temperature are far more damaging than a temperature that is a little too high or too low), preferably dark, and equipped with racks in which the bottles can be stored lying down so that the cork does not dry out and allow air to enter, it is probably more practical to rely once again on a reputable wine dealer—unless, of course, you possess a cool basement in which a wine cellar can be improvised. If not, you can either buy your wine a few bottles at a time according to your needs, and should you wish to acquire a larger quantity of a type that particularly appeals to you, you can ask the dealer to keep it in storage for you.

Selecting the wines to accompany a menu is not as complicated as it used to be, principally because it has become increasingly fashionable to serve no more than two different wines at a formal dinner, and only one at luncheon. A single wine is also often the best solution for buffet and informal dinner menus that are built around a single main dish. Among the best types for this purpose would be a light red Bordeaux, a rosé, a chilled Moselle, a young Beaujolais served slightly chilled, or, needless to add, champagne. When more than one wine is served, the lighter one should always precede the heavier, the white comes before the red (except for sweet white wines which are served afterward), the dry comes before the sweet, Bordeaux before Burgundy, and a more ordinary wine should be served before a wine of finer quality.

Aside from these basic principles, here are the most important rules to remember:

—Only red wine should be served with cheese (although a dry white wine such as Meursault goes well with Roquefort and fresh cream cheeses).

—Only a dry white wine should accompany oysters and shellfish.

—Only a white wine or a rosé should accompany fish.

—Only red wine should be served with game and red meats, preferably a rather rich red, such as Burgundy or Rhône wines. With lighter meats, such as lamb, veal, and chicken, a light red Bordeaux is best.

— If one of the dishes includes a sauce made with wine, the same type of wine should accompany it.

— The more delicate the flavor of a dish, the more delicate should be the accompanying wine; robust wines should be served with highly spiced dishes.

— Rosé wine is the classic accompaniment to cold luncheon dishes.

— Sweet white wines are best with desserts and foie gras.

It might be worth adding that most of these widely accepted rules concern in particular the fine wines of each type, for it would indeed be a pity and a waste to serve an expensive bottle of choice wine with an inappropriate dish. As a matter of fact, when you intend to serve a very special wine at a dinner party, you really should plan your menu in view of the wine you have selected rather than the other way around. With unpretentious wines, however, you have much greater latitude. After all, the final criterion of food and wine is whether or not they taste good, and the rules have been formulated simply in order to avoid unfortunate combinations that would destroy the flavor of the wine, the cuisine, or both. For example, a very dry white wine served with fruits, sweets, or mild dishes will merely taste sour. On the contrary, a rather coarse red wine served with spicy dishes and strong cheese will taste finer and smoother than it really is. But there are many exceptions to the rules, and if you feel that a certain light red wine, for example, is the perfect complement to a certain fish recipe, there is nothing to prevent you from serving them together—but you must be very sure of yourself.

Here are a few of the classic combinations of wine and food, and by adhering to them you cannot go wrong:

Food	Wine
Oysters, hors d'oeuvres	A light dry white wine such as Muscadet, Sancerre, Chablis, etc.
Eggs	Rosé, a light dry white wine
Lobster and shellfish	A dry white wine, such as Chablis or Riesling

Food	Wine
Fish	A fine dry white Burgundy, such as Pouilly Fuissé, or a Graves, Rhine, or Moselle wine
Red meat and game, duck, goose	Red Burgundy, Saint Emilion, a Rhône wine
Chicken, veal, lamb	A fine red Bordeaux (Médoc)
Spaghetti, macaroni, etc.	Chianti, Valpolicella, Beaujolais
Pork	Rosé wine
Cheese	A rich red wine, such as Burgundy, Châteauneuf-du-Pape, Saint Emilion
Roasts	A fine Médoc, a fine red Burgundy (Mercurey, Nuits, Beaune, etc.)
Desserts and pastry	Champagne (Demi-Sec), Sauternes

The simplest wines as well as the finest should be served in the proper way, and in this regard there are again a few important rules:

—Red wine should be served at the temperature of the room in which it is to be drunk, except for Burgundy, which is served slightly cooler than room temperature. You should warm the wine gradually (never artificially—you may spoil it) by placing the bottles in the room an hour or two beforehand. Some experts also like to "air" young or full-bodied red wines by uncorking them an hour before serving. You may replace the cork with a loose wad of cotton, which will permit air to enter the bottle while keeping out the dust. Red Burgundy, however, should always be uncorked at the last minute.

—White wines are served chilled, and they are never decanted. An ice bucket half filled with ice and water is still the best cooling method, with the bottles first uncorked and then loosely recorked in order to avoid bursting; it takes about twenty minutes to chill a bottle of wine in a cooler, turning the bottle from time to time. Nowadays white wine is most frequently chilled by placing the bottles in the refrigerator (not too near the ice compartment and never in the freezer) for two or three hours. Sweet white wines such as Sauternes, as well as champagne, are served a bit cooler—as the French say, *frappé*. They should be left in the refrigerator a little longer, about four or five hours. Remember that wine can be damaged if it is chilled too long or at too low a temperature.

—Rosé wines are chilled in the same way as white wine.

—Red port is served at room temperature, and white port slightly cooler.

—Sherry, unless it is very dry, is served at room temperature. Dry sherry and manzanilla are slightly chilled. Sherry may be served either from the bottle or in a decanter.

—Very old red wines (and, in fact, any wine that leaves a deposit at the bottom of the bottle) should be filtered into a decanter a few hours before serving, after the bottle has been standing upright for a day or two in order to settle the sediment. Vintage port should be decanted in the same way. It should be poured slowly and gently so that the sediment remains in the original bottle and is not transferred to the decanter. It is safest to leave at least two or three inches of wine in the bottom of the bottle. Out of consideration for those of your guests who are true connoisseurs (as well as those who recognize the quality of a wine more from the label on the bottle than from its flavor and bouquet), you might follow the example of Bordeaux society and place the empty bottles from which the wine has been decanted on the sideboard, with their corks beside them, for all to see and admire.

—Before decanting wine, and before pouring it from the bottle, you should always wipe the inside and outside of the neck with a clean cloth. When pouring, the bottle should be brought to the glass, not the glass to the bottle.

—Wine glasses should only be filled one-half to two-thirds full, in order to permit the bouquet to gather and to remain in the glass. Aperitif wines such as sherry, port, and vermouth are served in cocktail glasses, which are filled almost to the top. Champagne glasses are no more than half filled.

—Whenever you open a new bottle of wine, you should change the wine glasses, even if it is of the same type and vintage as the wine you have been drinking.

—Wine baskets are not chic, and they are useful only for serving a very old red wine in which the sediment has collected at the bottom of the bottle. Since it is far more elegant to filter these fine old wines into a decanter, wine baskets are a superfluous and slightly affected accessory on a dining room table and should be reserved for restaurants that are not equipped to decant wine correctly. Even in a restaurant, it is nonsensical to serve very young red wines, white wines, rosé, or champagne in a wine basket, because none of these deposits a sediment.

— Finally, remember that wine is not a thirst-quencher, but a complement to a meal. It should be savored first, then sipped, but never gulped. Watch how an epicure drinks a glass of wine and a glass of water, and you will see the difference immediately.

When preparing the wine you will need to serve your guests, it is useful to know that the average wine bottle contains about six glasses, in other words, one and a half glasses apiece for four people, which is a bit skimpy for an entire dinner. One-half a bottle per person is perhaps overly generous, but it may be the safest rule of thumb. Besides, you can always use leftover wine in cooking, and an opened bottle that has been recorked or leftover wine in a closed decanter will be perfectly good the next day—but not for very much longer. If there are four or eight of you at the table, you might consider buying your party wine in a magnum. It contains twice as much as a regular bottle, costs no more than two ordinary bottles, and is highly impressive.

When decanters are placed on the table, the nearest male guest should serve those seated around him, the ladies first and himself last. Even though she may have taken charge of the selection and preparation of the wine for her dinner party, an elegant hostess permits the host or one of the men present to perform the noble gesture of pouring it.

(See Dinners, Drinks, Glasses, Liqueurs and Brandy, Menus)

MAS

(To me the synonym of Christmas is tradition. This is the only event that should always be celebrated, year after year, in exactly the same way so that you can relive the joys of childhood if only for a day.

Try to repeat every year the same kind of a Christmas tree, the same decorations (red and green), the same menu, with the same guests. In order to make sure that the guests will always be the same, it is best to limit your Christmas invitations to members of the family and very old friends, and all of them should know for certain that they will be invited to your house for Christmas every year for as long as they live. They will be much happier to find always the same traditional festivities and to know in advance on which branch of the tree their present will be tied, than to have no idea as to what to expect. For you, the hostess, this will be practically a restful time of the year, since you will know months ahead of time whether it is necessary to order a foie gras or a turkey or a big plum pudding, and that you must check the box where the Christmas decorations are stored to make sure they are in good condition. The only things you will need to vary from one year to the next are your clothes and your gifts.

You can be as original as you like on New Year's Eve, but please, not on Christmas!

ACHTING

❡ The call of the sea has apparently lost none of its legendary attraction, judging from the phenomenal development of boating during the past decade. Miraculous modern inventions such as plastic hulls, aluminum masts, synthetic materials for sails and rigging, and continually improved marine motors have placed yachting within the means of an increasing number of amateurs, and today there are more pleasure boats afloat on seas, lakes, oceans and riverways than ever before. Nevertheless, yachting is still a luxury sport. It is as costly to buy and to maintain a medium-sized family yacht as it is to own a racehorse, while such fabulous floating palaces as the yachts of Onassis, Guinness, Henry Ford II, and Lady Docker must represent as great an investment as that of an entire racing stable.

Yachtsmen are a varied breed. There are the born sailors with the sea in their blood, to whom yachting is a sport, an art, a passion. Then there are the rugged individualists, such as our national hero Eric Tabarly, winner of the recent one-man transatlantic race, who find only at sea the simplicity and solitude they crave. The mere suggestion of entertaining on board a boat would fill all of these true sailors with horror. For them, one of the charms of maritime life is that it offers an escape from the frivolities and obligations of society.

Finally, there are the vast majority of modern pleasure-boat owners who consider yachting an agreeable pastime for their leisure hours, an ideal way to spend a holiday, a means of giving pleasure to their family and friends and, last but very often not least, as a status symbol. For these sociable sailors, a motor or sailing yacht can be an appreciable asset in entertaining.

A yacht, even a rather small one, can be the setting for an informal luncheon, dinner, or cocktail party, either at the dockside, anchored off-shore, or moored in a deserted cove. On very hot summer days it is always cooler on the water than ashore, there is usually a pleasant breeze, and there is always the possibility of a refreshing swim. You can also invite friends on an all-day cruise with a picnic lunch and interludes of fishing, swimming, or underwater exploration. You can even invite a carefully selected few to share a longer cruise over a weekend, a week, or an entire summer vacation.

In all of these projects, there are certain indispensable precautions to be taken, for entertaining on a yacht is at the same time simpler and more complicated than entertaining on dry land.

In general, if you wish to play perfectly safe, you will invite as guests aboard your yacht only experienced sailors who know how to swim, and never any very young children or very elderly persons requiring constant supervision. You should never invite more guests than your boat is equipped to accommodate in reasonable comfort.

When your boat is tied up at the dock of a marina or a yacht club, you can enlarge the guest list somewhat, particularly for a cocktail party, since the guests may overflow onto the quay if necessary. In these conditions there is also little risk of seasickness, and if you should run out of ice or whisky, it is a simple matter to replenish your supplies from the yacht-club bar.

Be sure to be explicit in your invitations, especially where dress is concerned. Slacks or shorts are the only really practical attire for a small boat and, most important of all, flat rope- or rubber-soled sandals or sneakers. It is a good idea to keep on board a supply of suitable footwear for forgetful guests whose high heels would ruin your deck in no time. The rubber Hong Kong sandals held on by a double strap between the toes are very practical for this purpose, since an average size will fit almost any foot. You might also warn your landlubber friends that the evening air is always cooler over the water than on dry land, and on a warm night there may be a great deal of condensed humidity, so they should come prepared with a light wrap or sweater.

For a cocktail party, you should order a great quantity of ice, and for once you might even mix your cocktails in advance and store them in a cold thermos or in the refrigerator, if there is one aboard. But beware of mixing drinks too strong, for salt sea air makes many people very thirsty. It also stimulates the appetite, and so you should provide a generous quantity of rather hearty hors d'oeuvres. Fillings based on sea-food are particularly appropriate, such as sandwiches of minced clams and cream cheese, tuna fish and tomato, crabmeat mayonnaise, shrimps, anchovies, or sardines with eggs. All of the various preparations of hard-boiled egg, liverwurst, ham, and cheese are quite filling. During very hot weather you must be extremely wary of food spoilage and either prepare the refreshments at the last minute or, as is more practical, make your sandwiches several hours ahead of time and store them in the refrigerator or in thermos food containers. It is not often a good idea to attempt to serve hot hors d'oeuvres on a small boat, but you can vary your sandwiches with bowls of macadamia nuts, cashews, and various tinned snacks. Do not buy too large-sized cans, however, for once they have been opened the contents will very quickly become soggy in the damp sea air.

Fire is one of the greatest hazards on board a ship, especially when there is butane gas or gasoline aboard, and at a cocktail party there are bound to be many smokers. Sailors, of course, would never dream of tossing a cigarette into the wind, which would simply blow it back on board. But it is best to provide an ample quantity of strategically placed ashtrays and hope that your guests will use them. You can improvise an ashtray that is both stable and capacious by buying a number of children's toy tin sand pails and filling them half full with sand.

It seems that there exists in America a special cocktail party flag which, when hoisted, is an invitation to anyone in sight to come aboard for a drink. But I would not recommend displaying this particular symbol of American hospitality when you are in a foreign port. The quay-side loungers might be intrigued, but the other yachtsmen would more likely be aghast.

For a luncheon or dinner party on board your boat, you will probably have invited your guests to spend the entire day or at least the afternoon with you, in order to enjoy a swim or fishing or a leisurely coastal cruise before the meal.

Even though you leave the harbor for no more than a few hours, you should first take your guests on a guided tour of the boat and explain to them how everything works: the water faucets or pump, the toilets, etc. Show them where the lifesaving apparatus is stowed, and where they can help themselves to cold drinks when they are thirsty. Young children should be made to understand that the captain's word is law and must always be obeyed immediately. If they cannot swim, they should be obliged to wear a lifesaving belt. It is amusing as well as prudent to show the adults how to steer and handle the boat, and most of them will be delighted to be given a few simple tasks and responsibilities. You should also be prepared to treat sunburn and seasickness, and to lend a sun hat, sunglasses, a waterproof garment, or a warm sweater should the need arise.

As far as the meal itself is concerned, organization is more important than ever, because if you have forgotten anything you must simply do without it. The best plan is to prepare everything in advance in your own kitchen at home. Again, you should keep in mind the danger of spoilage during warm weather, and in particular avoid ground meat, stuffed fowl, creamed dishes, salads prepared in mayonnaise and creamy desserts, unless your refrigeration facilities are absolutely trustworthy.

For luncheon on a summer day, an entirely cold meal is easiest to prepare and simplest to serve. It may be either a typical picnic menu, with sandwiches, fried chicken, hard-boiled eggs, tomatoes, salad, and cake, wrapped in individual portions; or, if there are not too many of you, you might serve the meal at table on deck or in the cabin (where it is often cooler than on an open deck when the midday sun is blazing). A light but hearty menu might start with an enormous *salade Niçoise*, then a platter of assorted cold meats (roast veal, beef, ham, chicken, or turkey, etc.) with relishes, a cheese tray (Edam, Gruyère, and goat cheeses are better in this case than the softer varieties), and finish with a cake or pie, or with ice cream if you are able to conserve it properly. The hot coffee may either be freshly brewed in the galley, or prepared at home and kept hot in a thermos container. Plastic or paper plates, goblets, coffee mugs, and paper napkins are perfect for this kind of a picnic meal.

During cooler weather, you might start the meal with a steaming, hearty soup, kept hot in a thermos bottle, such as beef with vegetables, split pea or bean soup with squares of ham or rounds of frankfurters and a splash of sherry, or onion soup with croutons and plenty of grated cheese. When there are more than one or two guests, it seems to me inadvisable to attempt to cook a hot main dish, except perhaps for a stew or casserole that has been prepared in advance and merely needs to be warmed up on top of the stove. The important point to remember, whatever the menu may be, is that each dish should be very copious, easy to serve and eat, and appetizing in appearance.

Cleaning up will present no problems if you have used paper plates, which can be dumped into a covered pail and emptied after you have returned to port. The serving dishes can be carried home dirty and washed in your own kitchen. You should be sure to instruct your guests to throw nothing overboard unless the boat is well at large, which is unlikely to be the case during this short cruise, when you are more interested in finding calm, sheltered waters than in seeking adventure on the open sea.

For a longer cruise, the most difficult problem of a yachting hostess is to find among her friends congenial yachting guests. You might think that the perfect choice would be another sailing couple like yourselves, but this is seldom so. It is vital during a sea voyage for the captain of the craft to enjoy complete and autocratic authority, and since every skipper has his own methods and routine, your expert sailor friend may not always be in agreement, and his disaccord will be aggravated by the fact that he is accustomed to giving shipboard commands rather than to obeying them. A tiny grain of resentment can grow over a period of days or weeks like the pearl in an oyster, and it may even eventually mar a pleasant friendship.

A guest who has never before been to sea represents a different kind of risk, because there is no way of telling how he or she will react to the very special conditions of community life on a small boat. Traits and mannerisms that seemed charming in a drawing room can drive you crazy at sea. The ideal yachting guest should possess good health, a calm, even disposition, simplicity, adaptability, good sportsmanship, and self-discipline—plus a genuine love of the sea. Needless to add, unless you are willing to compromise on some of these qualifications, you will do all of your sailing alone. But do not forget that your choice of a guest or guests is the single most important factor in the success or failure of your cruise. Finally, never make the mistake of inviting too many guests.

Well in advance of the sailing date, you should give your guests detailed information and instructions as to what they should wear and bring, as well as what the itinerary and activities will be. You should warn them against heeled shoes and hard suitcases and advise a minimum washable wardrobe (including a cocktail or dinner outfit if you intend to visit ports where you will dine in chic restaurants or yacht clubs), plus fishing or skin-diving gear, etc.

Your introductory tour of the boat should be very complete, including the galley and its equipment, the electric installations, the toilet and washing facilities. Explain to your guests that they must make an effort to conserve water and electricity, ask them to restock the refrigerator with soft drinks and drinking water every time they remove any, and insist particularly that they put everything they have used back in its proper place. Each guest should be given a private locker, and you should also show them how to make up their beds or bunks and where to store the bedding.

It is always more fun for your guests if they are permitted to share the work by assuming the responsibility of a few simple tasks on deck or in the cabin. And it is a matter of security to explain to them the general handling and steering of the craft, the fire and smoking rules that must be observed, the location and operation of the fire extinguishers and lifesaving equipment.

Before you order your provisions for the cruise, it is thoughtful to find out what foods your guests particularly like, what they are accustomed to eat for breakfast and to drink at mealtimes and between meals. It is always a good idea to prepare a maximum number of dishes at home in advance, and to carry aboard your first supply of salads, tomatoes, fruit, etc., already washed and prepared, as well as a dozen eggs already hard-boiled, a roast beef, veal, or pork, ready to serve, a boiled tongue in aspic, a cake, pie, cookies, etc., all of them carefully wrapped in foil or in hermetic containers and placed at once in the refrigerator. Thus you will have very little cooking to do during the first few busy days. Afterward, you can permit your guests to help you with the meals, but since most galleys are quite tiny, it is generally more practical for the guest to help by peeling vegetables, mixing salad dressing, and especially by marketing, while you reserve the actual culinary chores for yourself. It will greatly facilitate your menu planning if you maintain an up-to-date inventory of all the provisions you possess on board. Considerate guests will certainly insist on taking you out to dinner or lunch when you are in a port.

I would be distressed if all of this advice concerning cooking chores, sunburns and lifesaving gear should make the idea of a cruise seem more of an ordeal than a pleasure. For the truth is that I know of no happier experience, no way of cementing a friendship more firmly, and no better means of enriching one's understanding of man and nature than by going to sea with a few congenial friends.

OO

❡ Because this alphabet of entertaining must end with a Z, why not say a few words about the zoo—that is, the social kind, composed of animals often more dangerous although less picturesque than those found in the jungle and the farmyard, and which you are more likely to see seated in a Louis XVI armchair than behind the bars of a cage.

To start with the most harmless species, what hostess has never received in her home the lowbrowed, silly goose, or the nice hen who fusses and clucks all day long without even stopping to catch her breath? Or the parrot, who tirelessly repeats the same phrase over and over? Or the innocent lamb so tragically fleeced at the bridge table? Or the long-haired monkey with her flashy, tawdry trappings? Alas, they will all probably be gobbled up by the cunning wolf with his pointed nose and calculating eye, by the crocodile who is all teeth, or even by the rat, with its sparse yellowish hair, whose aspect is as shabby as its bite is painful. The gentleman guest who laughs like a hyena (at his own jokes) is perhaps less dangerous, but really not very pleasant, and you should also beware of the little cock, red-faced, short, and stocky, who crows to the point of apoplexy in attempting to reassure himself of his own existence. The lion, who has achieved outstanding success in life or business, actually roars very little as long as you treat him with respect, and he is perhaps one of the social animals I prefer. For once, I do not really like the human replica of the sad-eyed cocker spaniel, who licks your hand when you have stepped on his toes. As for the snake, it is certainly feminine in sex and strikes when one least expects.

If, like a good keeper, a hostess feeds the inmates of her social zoo regularly and well, provides them with appropriate distractions, separates the incompatible species from each other and remains at a safe distance from the dangerous ones, she will be rewarded by the respect of all, the devotion of many, and a few may even be willing to jump through hoops for her.